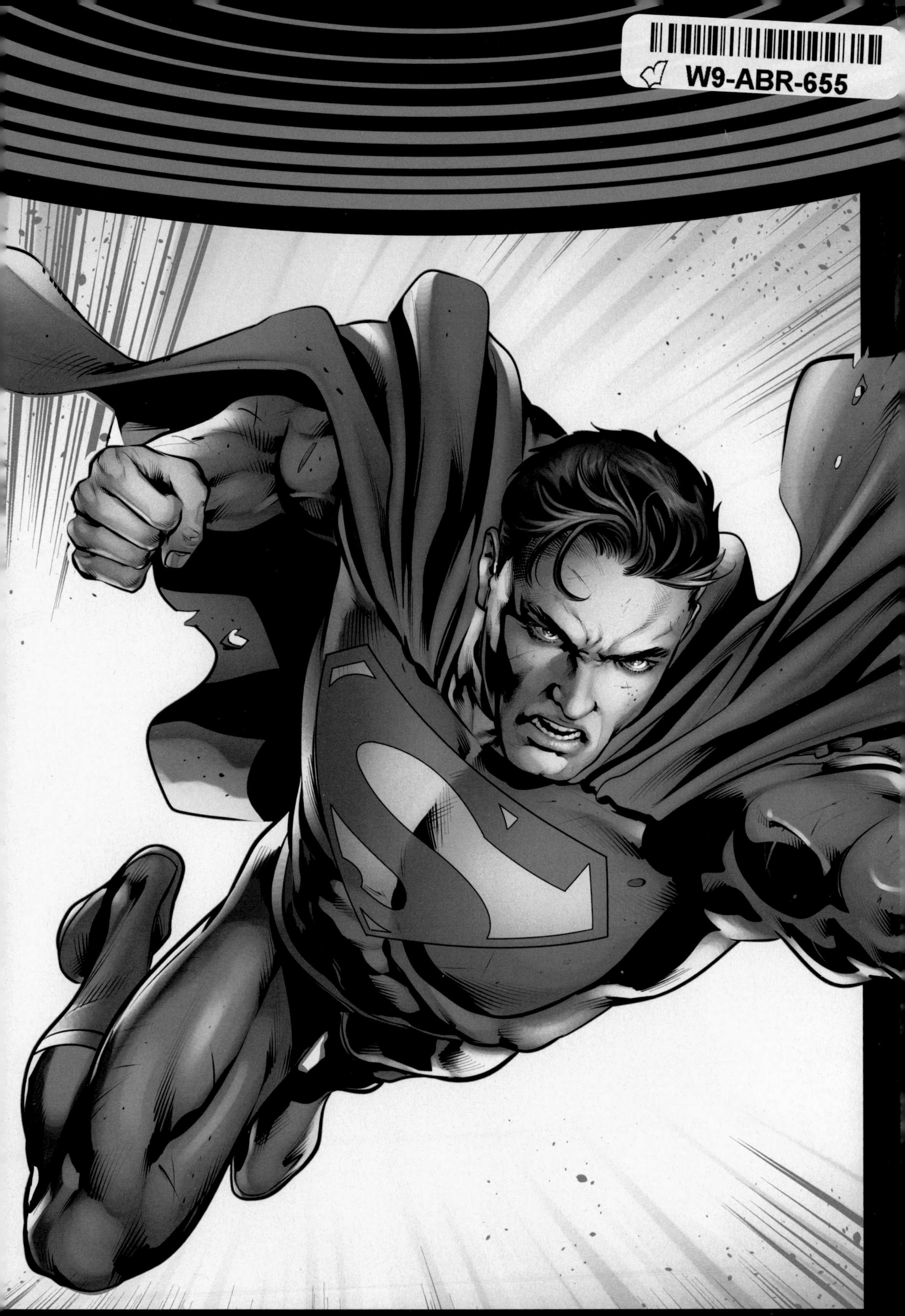

SUPERMAN ACTION COMICS
VOL.5 BOOSTER SHOT

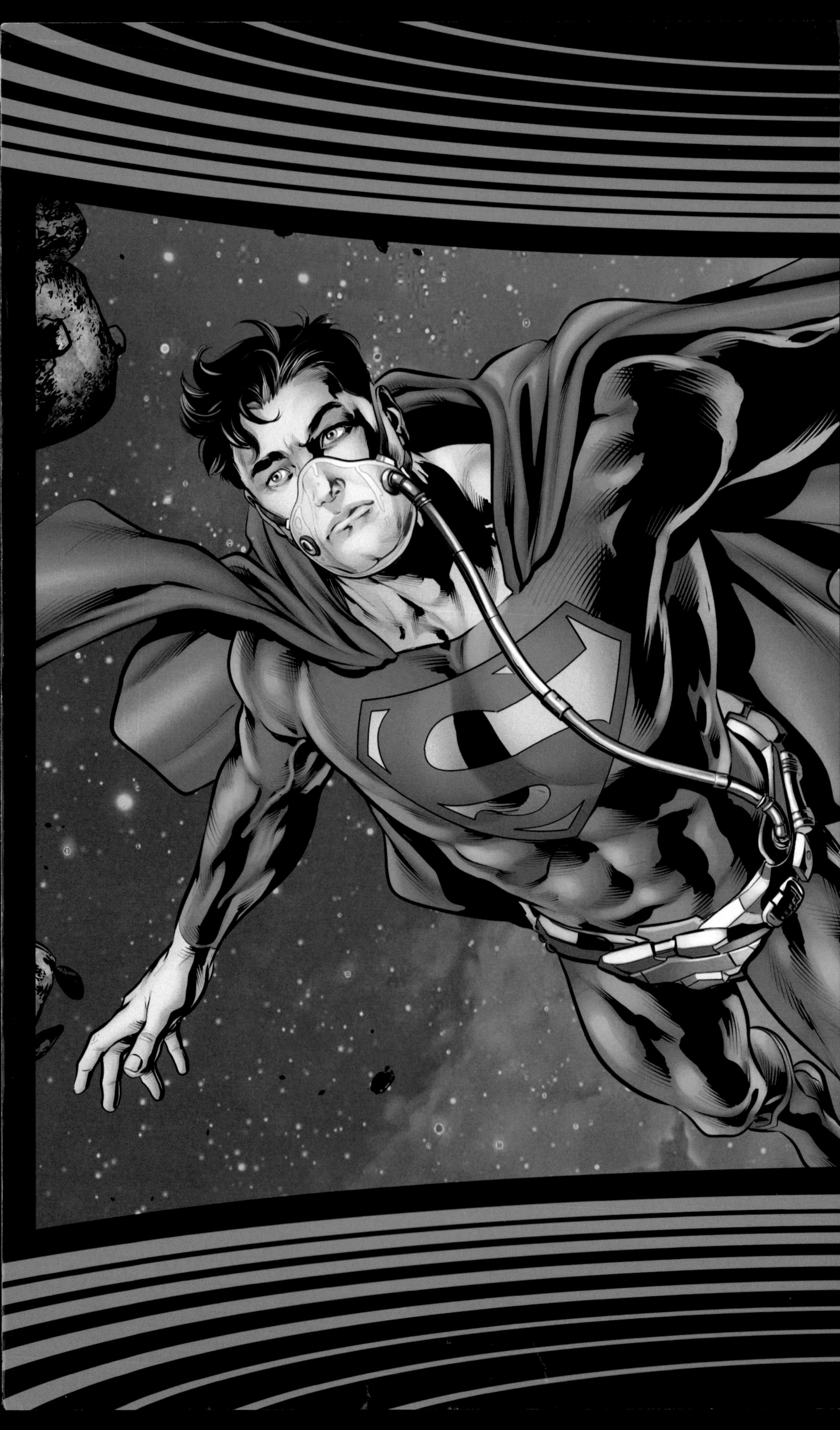

SUPERMAN ACTION COMICS
VOL.5 BOOSTER SHOT

DAN JURGENS
writer

DAN JURGENS * **BRETT BOOTH** * **WILL CONRAD** * **NORM RAPMUND**
pencillers

NORM RAPMUND * **WILL CONRAD** * **JOE PRADO**
CAM SMITH * **ART THIBERT** * **TREVOR SCOTT** * **JOHNNY DESJARDINS**
inkers

HI-FI * **ANDREW DALHOUSE** * **IVAN NUNES** * **WIL QUINTANA**
colorists

ROB LEIGH
letterer

FRANCIS MANAPUL
collection cover artist

SUPERMAN created by **JERRY SIEGEL** and **JOE SHUSTER**
SUPERBOY created by **JERRY SIEGEL** and **JOE SHUSTER**
By special arrangement with the Jerry Siegel family

BOOSTER GOLD created by **DAN JURGENS**

PAUL KAMINSKI Editor - Original Series ✷ **ANDREA SHEA** Assistant Editor - Original Series
JEB WOODARD Group Editor - Collected Editions ✷ **ALEX GALER** Editor - Collected Edition
STEVE COOK Design Director - Books ✷ **SHANNON STEWART** Publication Design

BOB HARRAS Senior VP - Editor-in-Chief, DC Comics
PAT McCALLUM Executive Editor, DC Comics

DIANE NELSON President ✷ **DAN DiDIO** Publisher ✷ **JIM LEE** Publisher ✷ **GEOFF JOHNS** President & Chief Creative Officer
AMIT DESAI Executive VP - Business & Marketing Strategy, Direct to Consumer & Global Franchise Management
SAM ADES Senior VP & General Manager, Digital Services ✷ **BOBBIE CHASE** VP & Executive Editor, Young Reader & Talent Development
MARK CHIARELLO Senior VP - Art, Design & Collected Editions ✷ **JOHN CUNNINGHAM** Senior VP - Sales & Trade Marketing
ANNE DePIES Senior VP - Business Strategy, Finance & Administration ✷ **DON FALLETTI** VP - Manufacturing Operations
LAWRENCE GANEM VP - Editorial Administration & Talent Relations ✷ **ALISON GILL** Senior VP - Manufacturing & Operations
HANK KANALZ Senior VP - Editorial Strategy & Administration ✷ **JAY KOGAN** VP - Legal Affairs ✷ **JACK MAHAN** VP - Business Affairs
NICK J. NAPOLITANO VP - Manufacturing Administration ✷ **EDDIE SCANNELL** VP - Consumer Marketing
COURTNEY SIMMONS Senior VP - Publicity & Communications ✷ **JIM (SKI) SOKOLOWSKI** VP - Comic Book Specialty Sales & Trade Marketing
NANCY SPEARS VP - Mass, Book, Digital Sales & Trade Marketing ✷ **MICHELE R. WELLS** VP - Content Strategy

SUPERMAN: ACTION COMICS VOL. 5: BOOSTER SHOT

Published by DC Comics. Compilation and all new material Copyright © 2018 DC Comics. All Rights Reserved.
Originally published in single magazine form in ACTION COMICS 993-999, ACTION COMICS SPECIAL 1. Copyright © 2017, 2018 DC Comics. All Rights Reserved.
All characters, their distinctive likenesses and related elements featured in this publication are trademarks of DC Comics.
The stories, characters and incidents featured in this publication are entirely fictional.
DC Comics does not read or accept unsolicited submissions of ideas, stories or artwork.

DC Comics, 2900 West Alameda Ave., Burbank, CA 91505
Printed by LSC Communications, Kendallville, IN, USA. 7/20/18. First Printing.
ISBN: 978-1-4012-7528-0

Library of Congress Cataloging-in-Publication Data is available.

PEFC Certified

Printed on paper from
sustainably managed
forests, controlled
sources

PEFC/29-31-337   www.pefc.org

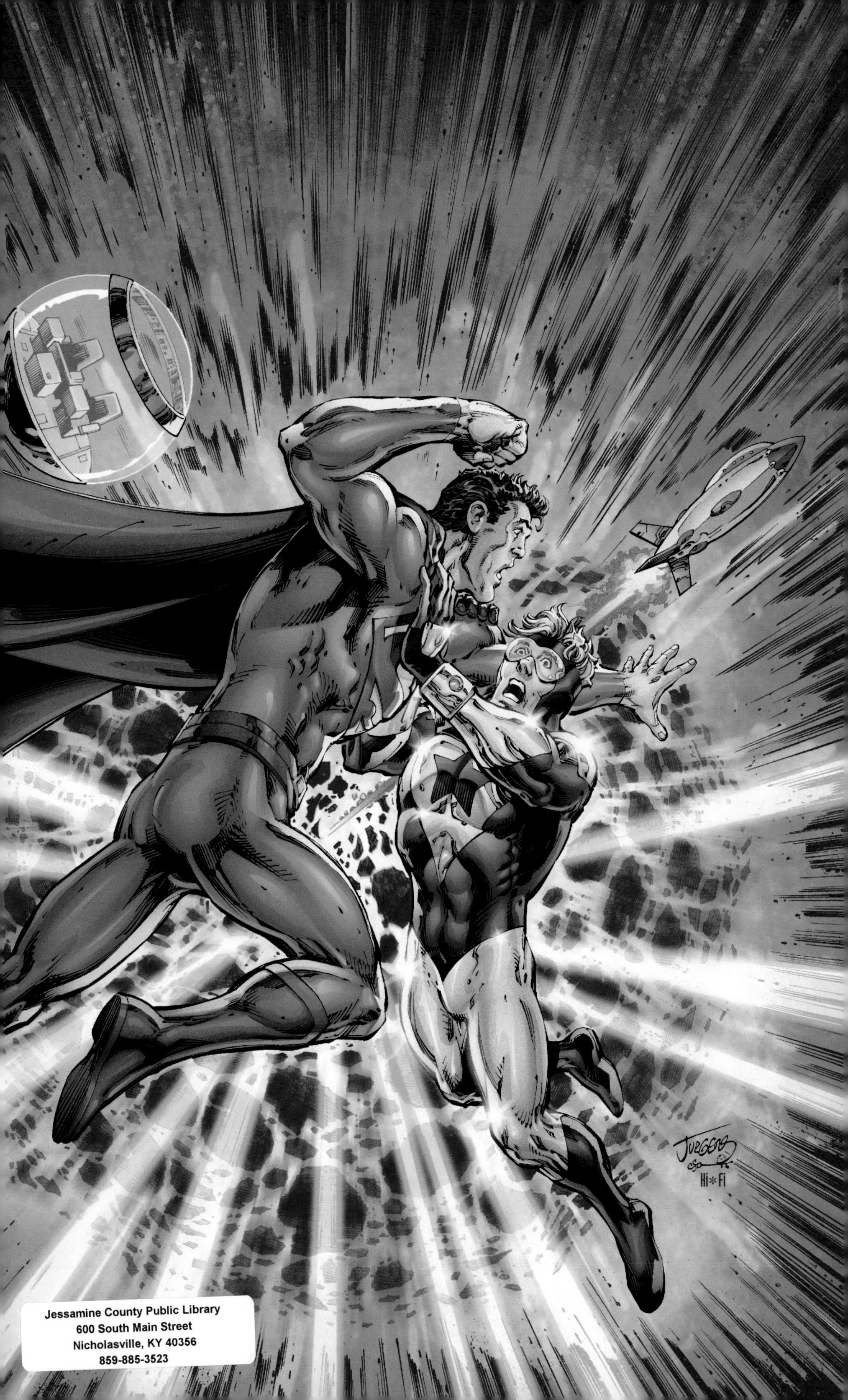
JURGENS
Hi*Fi

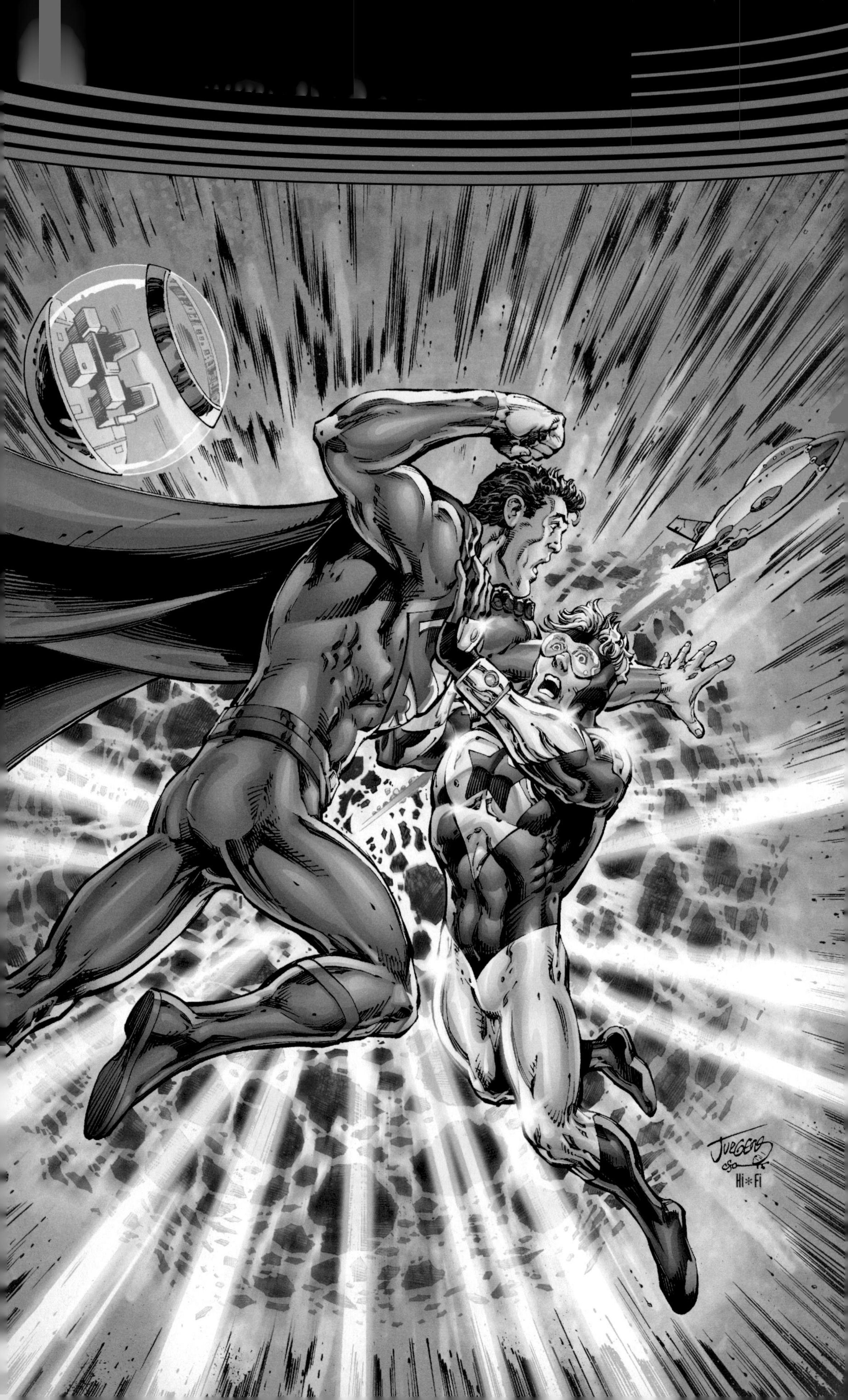
JURGENS
Hi*Fi

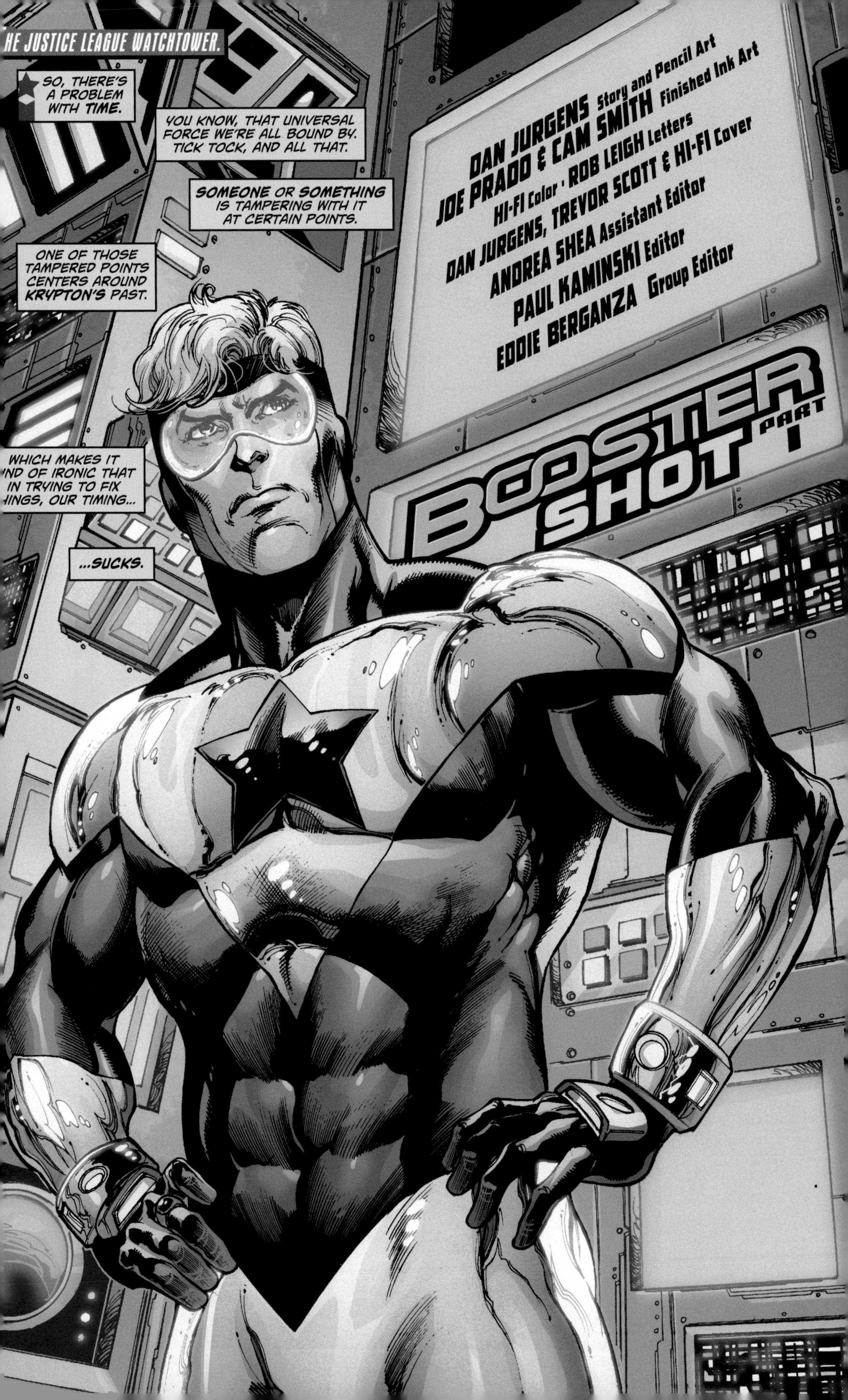
HE JUSTICE LEAGUE WATCHTOWER.
SO, THERE'S A PROBLEM WITH TIME.
YOU KNOW, THAT UNIVERSAL FORCE WE'RE ALL BOUND BY. TICK TOCK, AND ALL THAT.
SOMEONE OR SOMETHING IS TAMPERING WITH IT AT CERTAIN POINTS.
ONE OF THOSE TAMPERED POINTS CENTERS AROUND KRYPTON'S PAST.
DAN JURGENS Story and Pencil Art
JOE PRADO & CAM SMITH Finished Ink Art
HI-FI Color · ROB LEIGH Letters
DAN JURGENS, TREVOR SCOTT & HI-FI Cover
ANDREA SHEA Assistant Editor
PAUL KAMINSKI Editor
EDDIE BERGANZA Group Editor
BOOSTER SHOT PART I
WHICH MAKES IT ND OF IRONIC THAT IN TRYING TO FIX HINGS, OUR TIMING...
...SUCKS.

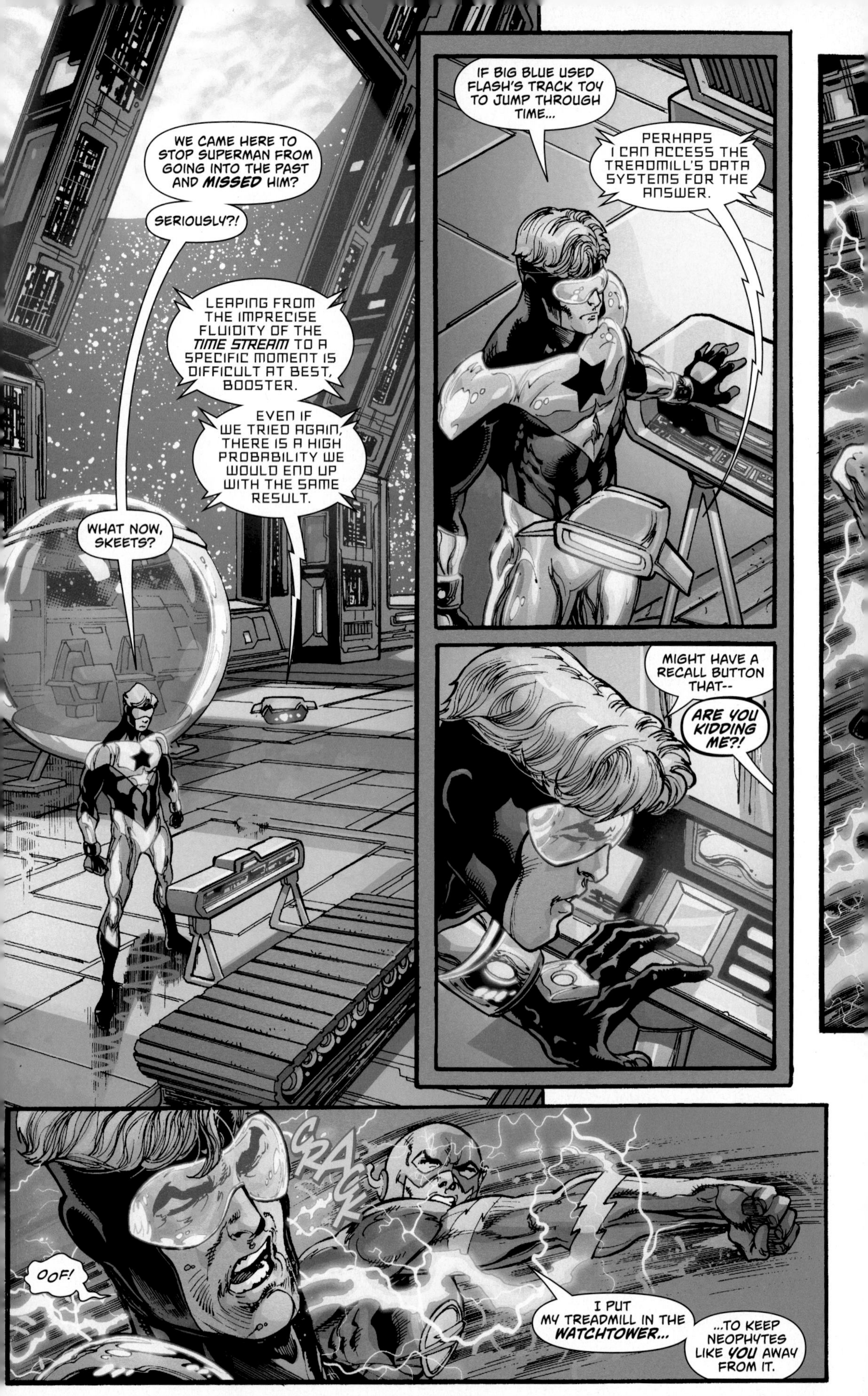
WE CAME HERE TO STOP SUPERMAN FROM GOING INTO THE PAST AND MISSED HIM?
SERIOUSLY?!
LEAPING FROM THE IMPRECISE FLUIDITY OF THE TIME STREAM TO A SPECIFIC MOMENT IS DIFFICULT AT BEST, BOOSTER.
EVEN IF WE TRIED AGAIN, THERE IS A HIGH PROBABILITY WE WOULD END UP WITH THE SAME RESULT.
WHAT NOW, SKEETS?
IF BIG BLUE USED FLASH'S TRACK TOY TO JUMP THROUGH TIME...
PERHAPS I CAN ACCESS THE TREADMILL'S DATA SYSTEMS FOR THE ANSWER.
MIGHT HAVE A RECALL BUTTON THAT--
ARE YOU KIDDING ME?!
CRACK
OOF!
I PUT MY TREADMILL IN THE WATCHTOWER...
...TO KEEP NEOPHYTES LIKE YOU AWAY FROM IT.

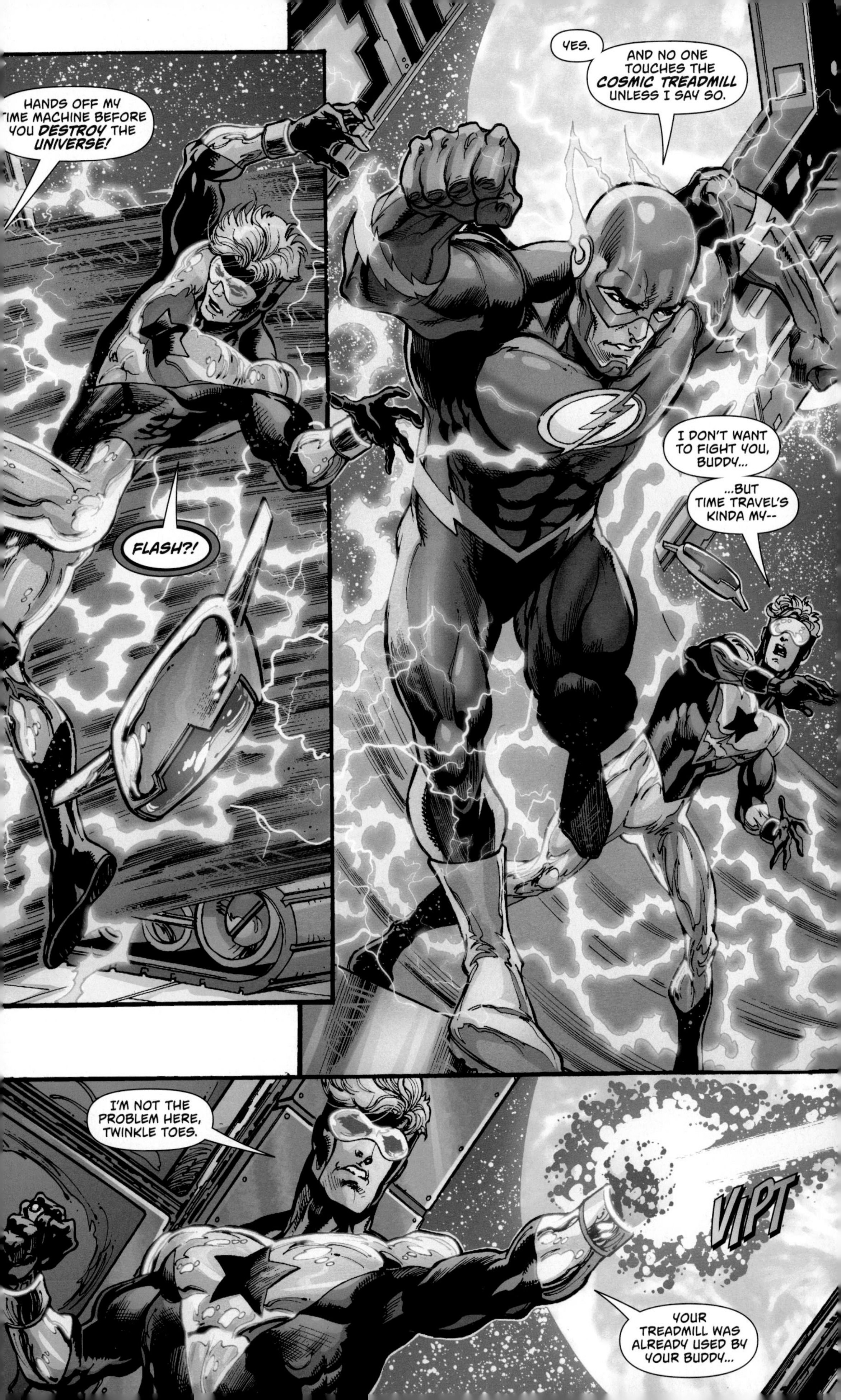
HANDS OFF MY TIME MACHINE BEFORE YOU DESTROY THE UNIVERSE!
FLASH?!
YES.
AND NO ONE TOUCHES THE COSMIC TREADMILL UNLESS I SAY SO.
I DON'T WANT TO FIGHT YOU, BUDDY...
...BUT TIME TRAVEL'S KINDA MY--
I'M NOT THE PROBLEM HERE, TWINKLE TOES.
VIPT
YOUR TREADMILL WAS ALREADY USED BY YOUR BUDDY...

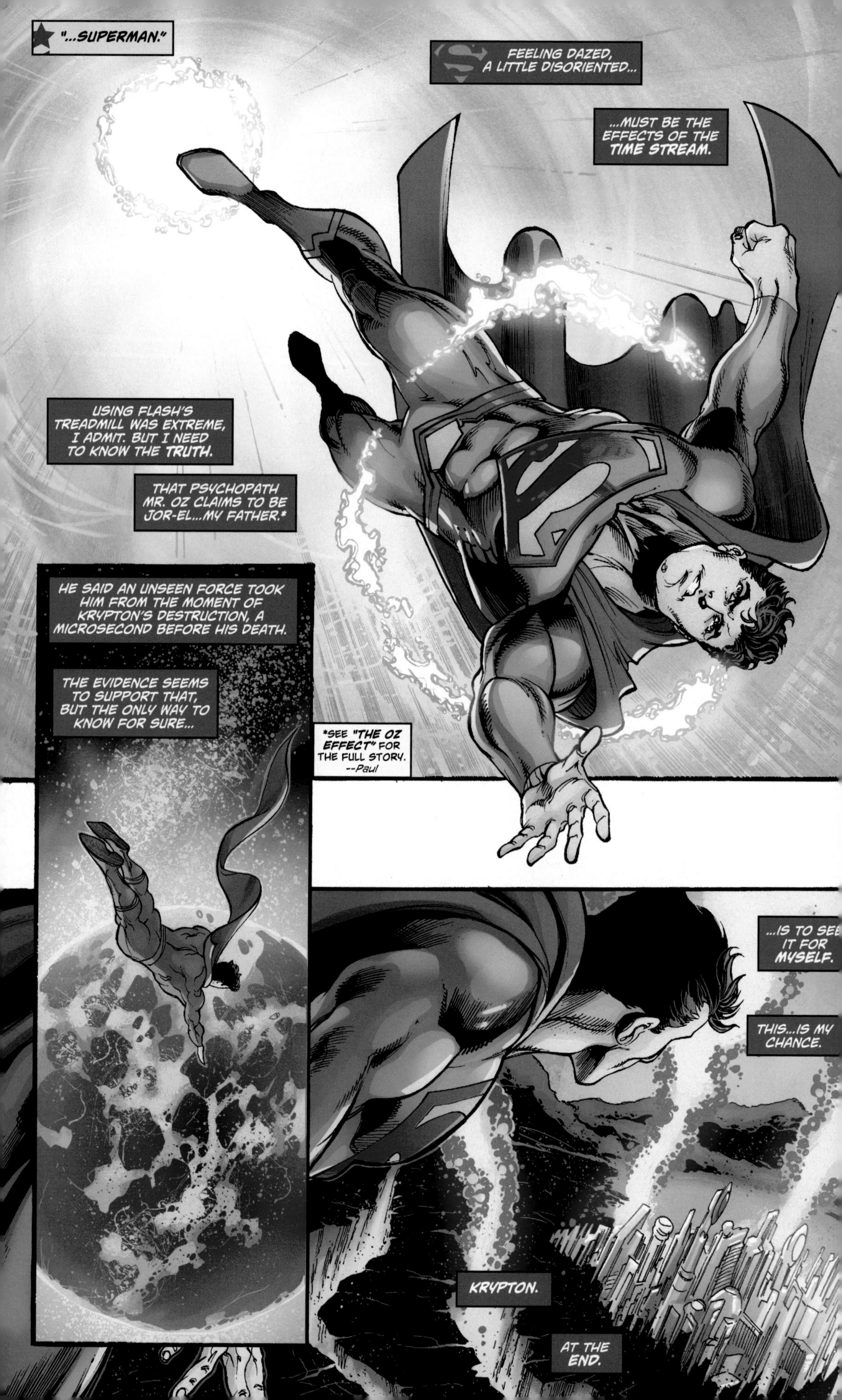

"...SUPERMAN."
FEELING DAZED, A LITTLE DISORIENTED...
...MUST BE THE EFFECTS OF THE TIME STREAM.
USING FLASH'S TREADMILL WAS EXTREME, I ADMIT. BUT I NEED TO KNOW THE TRUTH.
THAT PSYCHOPATH MR. OZ CLAIMS TO BE JOR-EL...MY FATHER.*
HE SAID AN UNSEEN FORCE TOOK HIM FROM THE MOMENT OF KRYPTON'S DESTRUCTION, A MICROSECOND BEFORE HIS DEATH.
THE EVIDENCE SEEMS TO SUPPORT THAT, BUT THE ONLY WAY TO KNOW FOR SURE...
*SEE "THE OZ EFFECT" FOR THE FULL STORY. --Paul
...IS TO SEE IT FOR MYSELF.
THIS...IS MY CHANCE.
KRYPTON.
AT THE END.

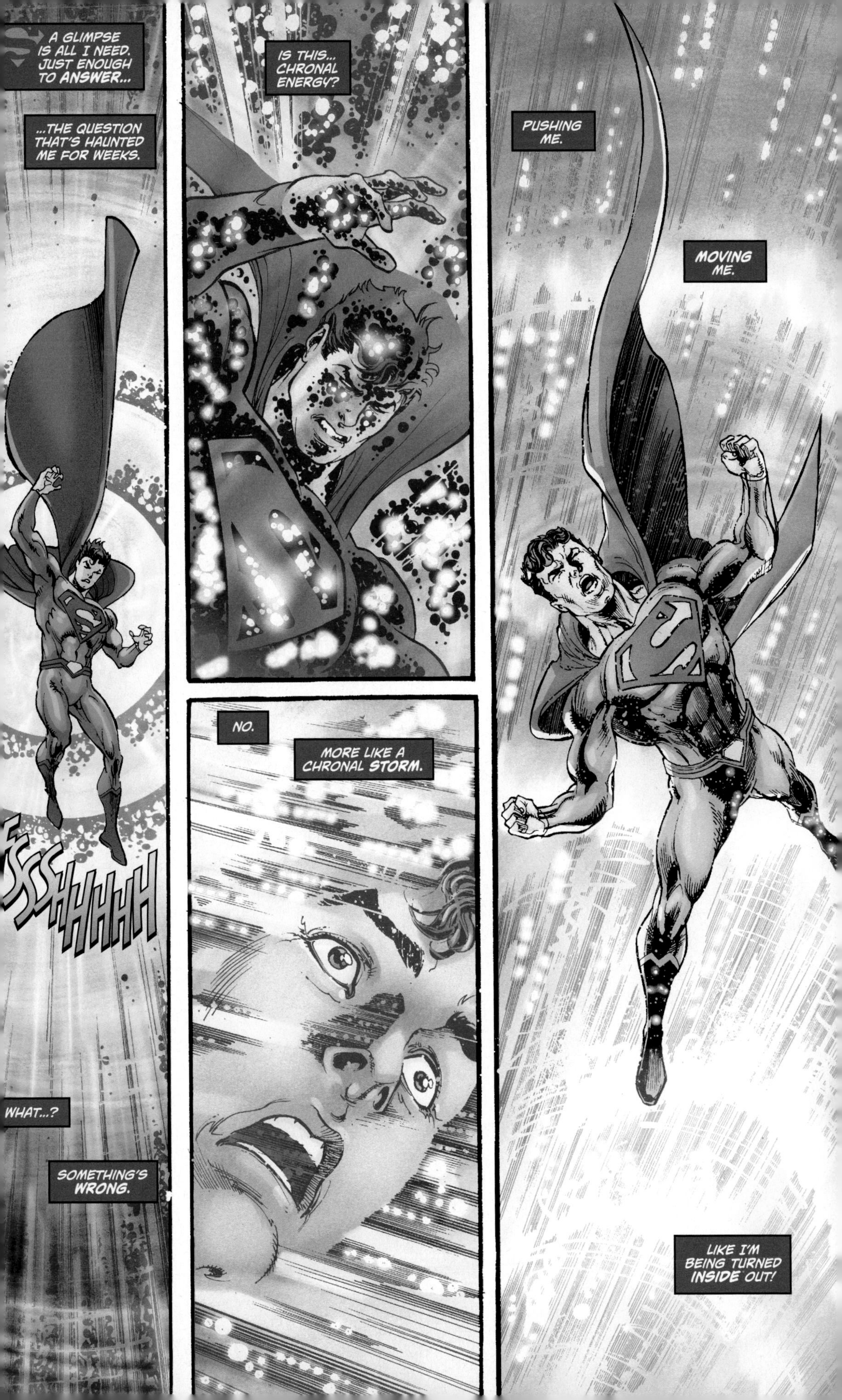
A GLIMPSE IS ALL I NEED. JUST ENOUGH TO ANSWER...
...THE QUESTION THAT'S HAUNTED ME FOR WEEKS.
SSSHHHHH
WHAT...?
SOMETHING'S WRONG.
IS THIS... CHRONAL ENERGY?
NO.
MORE LIKE A CHRONAL STORM.
PUSHING ME.
MOVING ME.
LIKE I'M BEING TURNED INSIDE OUT!

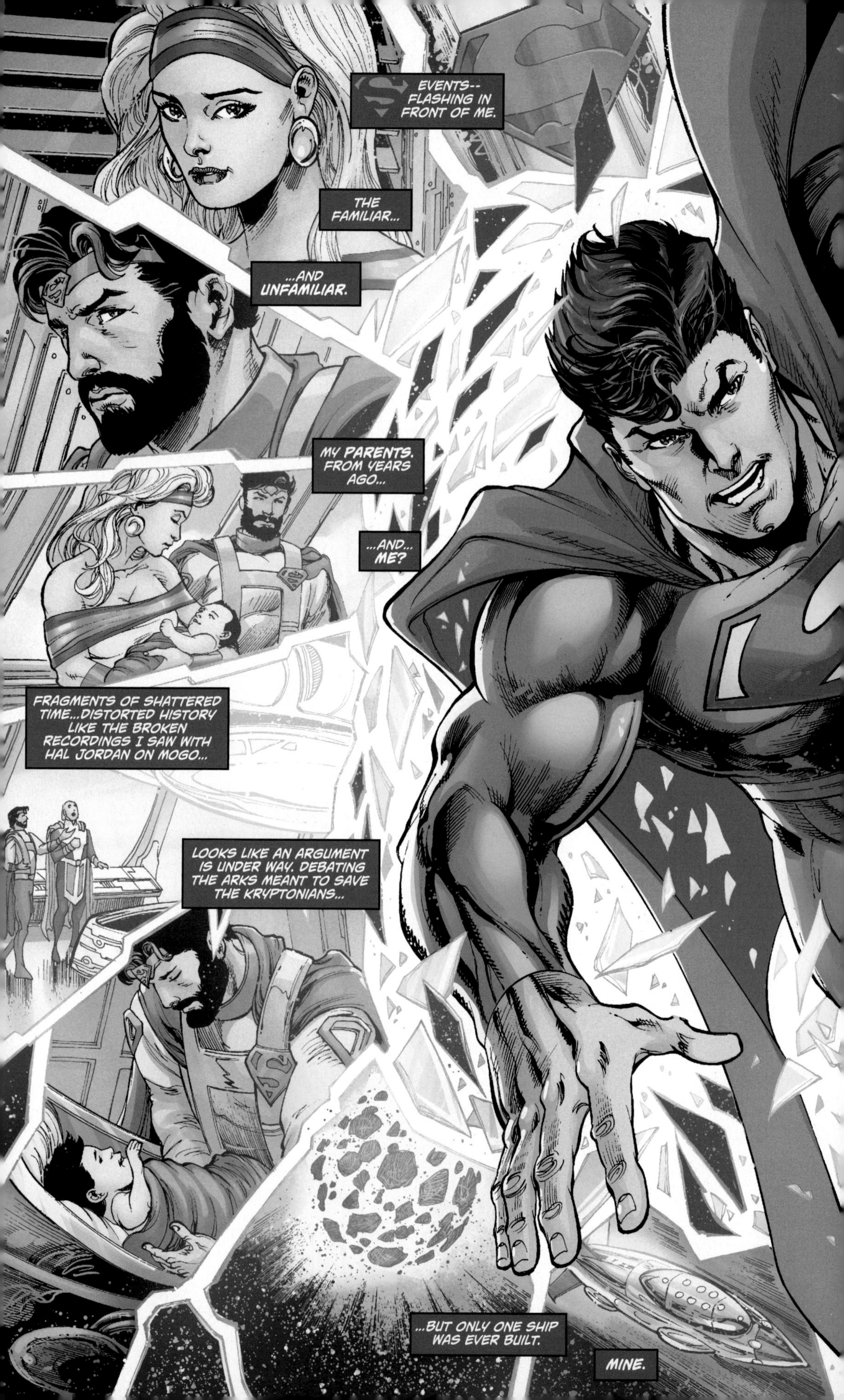
EVENTS--
FLASHING IN
FRONT OF ME.
THE
FAMILIAR...
...AND
UNFAMILIAR.
MY PARENTS.
FROM YEARS
AGO...
...AND...
ME?
FRAGMENTS OF SHATTERED
TIME...DISTORTED HISTORY
LIKE THE BROKEN
RECORDINGS I SAW WITH
HAL JORDAN ON MOGO...
LOOKS LIKE AN ARGUMENT
IS UNDER WAY. DEBATING
THE ARKS MEANT TO SAVE
THE KRYPTONIANS...
...BUT ONLY ONE SHIP
WAS EVER BUILT.
MINE.

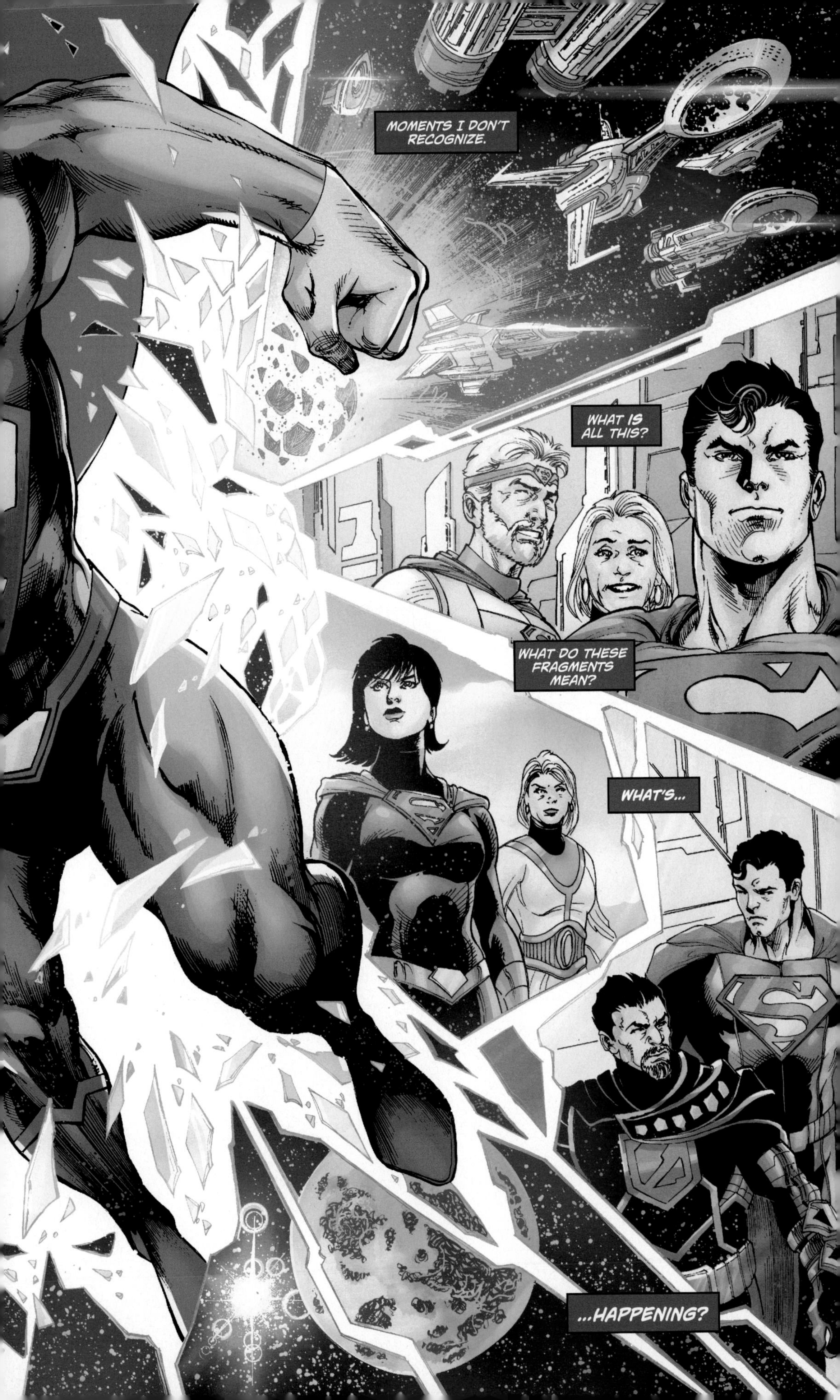
MOMENTS I DON'T RECOGNIZE.
WHAT IS ALL THIS?
WHAT DO THESE FRAGMENTS MEAN?
WHAT'S...
...HAPPENING?

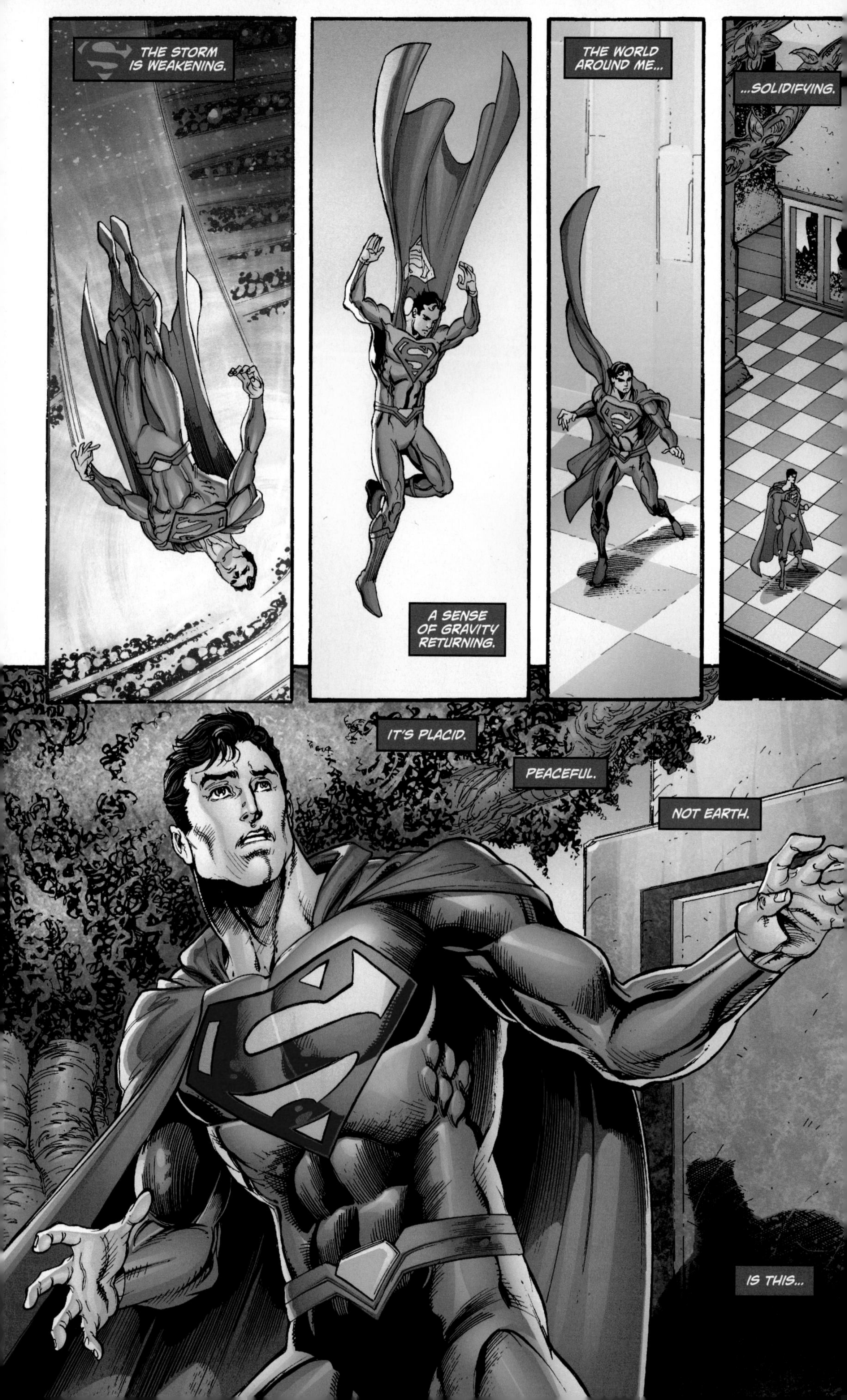
THE STORM IS WEAKENING.
A SENSE OF GRAVITY RETURNING.
THE WORLD AROUND ME...
...SOLIDIFYING.
IT'S PLACID.
PEACEFUL.
NOT EARTH.
IS THIS...

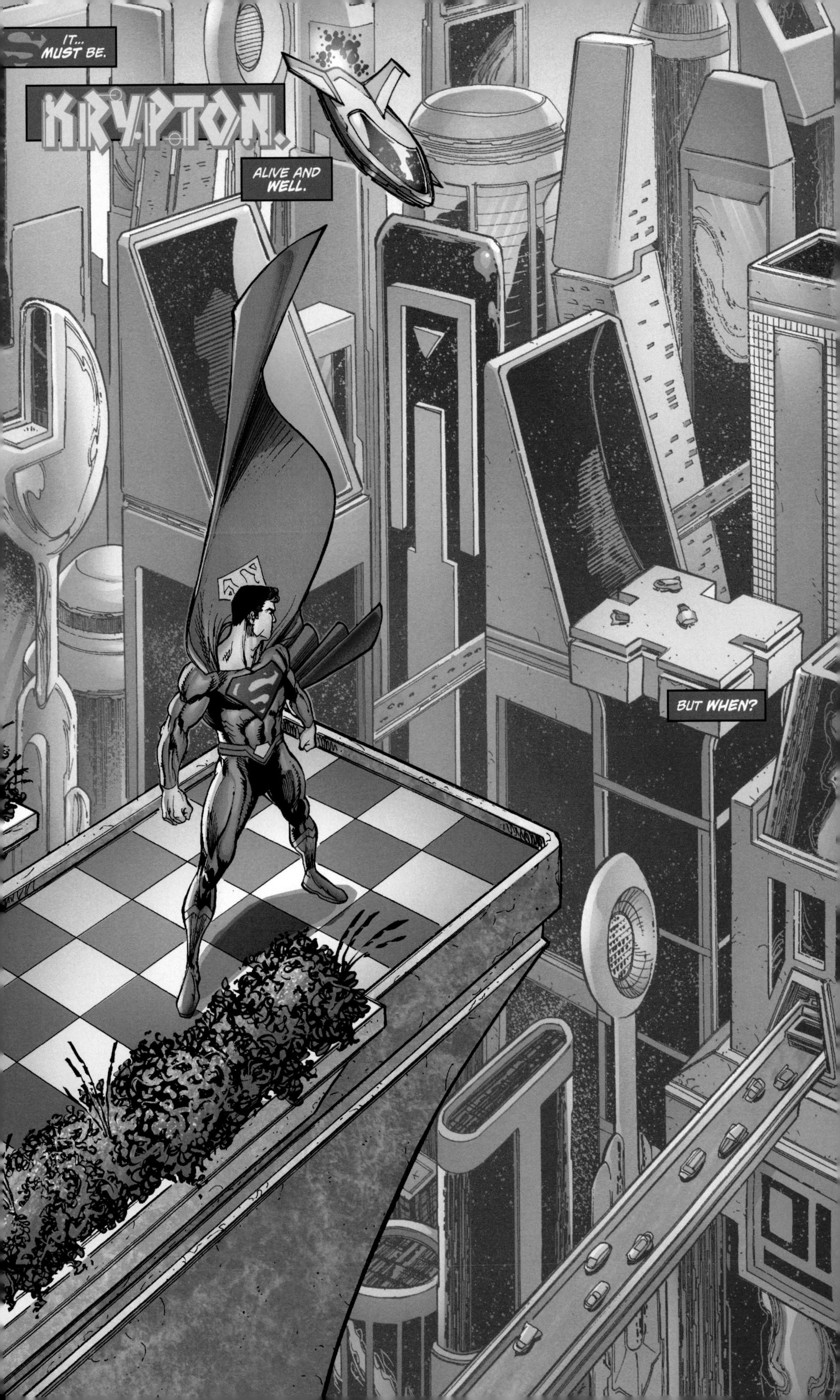
IT... MUST BE.
KRYPTON.
ALIVE AND WELL.
BUT WHEN?

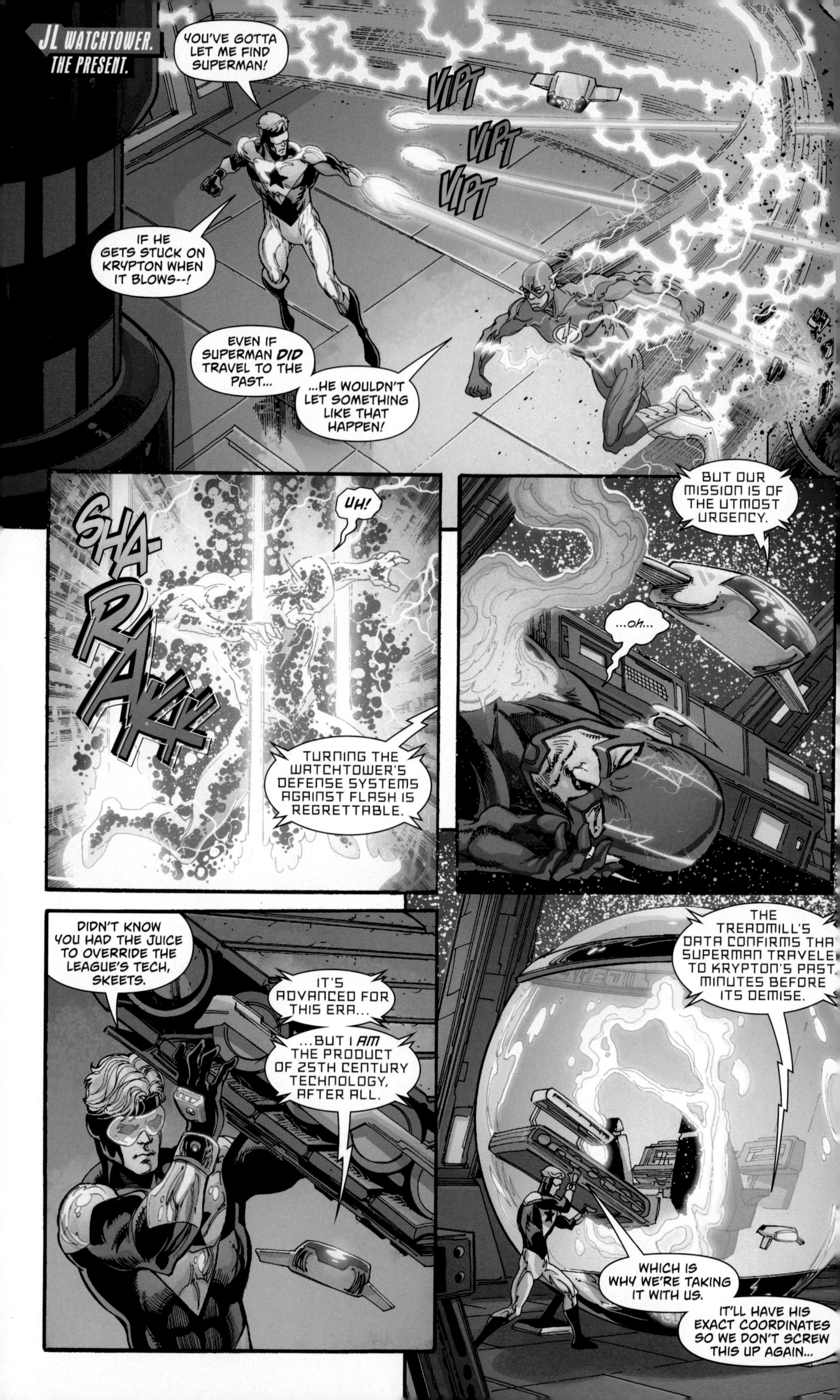

JL WATCHTOWER. THE PRESENT.
YOU'VE GOTTA LET ME FIND SUPERMAN!
VIPT
VIPT
VIPT
IF HE GETS STUCK ON KRYPTON WHEN IT BLOWS--!
EVEN IF SUPERMAN DID TRAVEL TO THE PAST...
...HE WOULDN'T LET SOMETHING LIKE THAT HAPPEN!
SHA-RAKK
UH!
TURNING THE WATCHTOWER'S DEFENSE SYSTEMS AGAINST FLASH IS REGRETTABLE.
BUT OUR MISSION IS OF THE UTMOST URGENCY.
...oh...
DIDN'T KNOW YOU HAD THE JUICE TO OVERRIDE THE LEAGUE'S TECH, SKEETS.
IT'S ADVANCED FOR THIS ERA...
...BUT I AM THE PRODUCT OF 25TH CENTURY TECHNOLOGY, AFTER ALL.
THE TREADMILL'S DATA CONFIRMS THA SUPERMAN TRAVELE TO KRYPTON'S PAST MINUTES BEFORE ITS DEMISE.
WHICH IS WHY WE'RE TAKING IT WITH US.
IT'LL HAVE HIS EXACT COORDINATES SO WE DON'T SCREW THIS UP AGAIN...

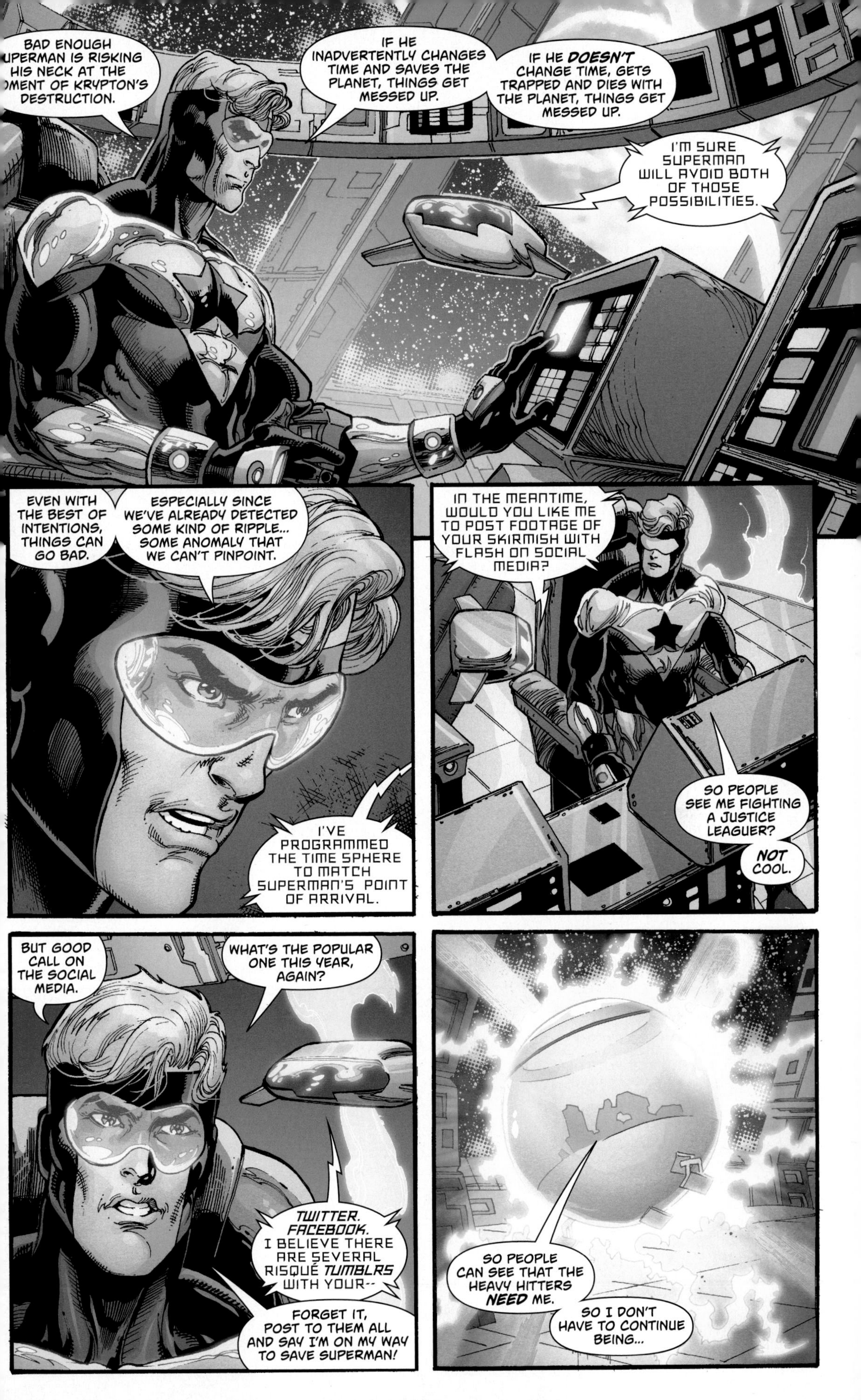

BAD ENOUGH
SUPERMAN IS RISKING HIS NECK AT THE MOMENT OF KRYPTON'S DESTRUCTION.
IF HE INADVERTENTLY CHANGES TIME AND SAVES THE PLANET, THINGS GET MESSED UP.
IF HE DOESN'T CHANGE TIME, GETS TRAPPED AND DIES WITH THE PLANET, THINGS GET MESSED UP.
I'M SURE SUPERMAN WILL AVOID BOTH OF THOSE POSSIBILITIES.
EVEN WITH THE BEST OF INTENTIONS, THINGS CAN GO BAD.
ESPECIALLY SINCE WE'VE ALREADY DETECTED SOME KIND OF RIPPLE... SOME ANOMALY THAT WE CAN'T PINPOINT.
I'VE PROGRAMMED THE TIME SPHERE TO MATCH SUPERMAN'S POINT OF ARRIVAL.
IN THE MEANTIME, WOULD YOU LIKE ME TO POST FOOTAGE OF YOUR SKIRMISH WITH FLASH ON SOCIAL MEDIA?
SO PEOPLE SEE ME FIGHTING A JUSTICE LEAGUER?
NOT COOL.
BUT GOOD CALL ON THE SOCIAL MEDIA.
WHAT'S THE POPULAR ONE THIS YEAR, AGAIN?
TWITTER. FACEBOOK. I BELIEVE THERE ARE SEVERAL RISQUÉ TUMBLRS WITH YOUR--
FORGET IT, POST TO THEM ALL AND SAY I'M ON MY WAY TO SAVE SUPERMAN!
SO PEOPLE CAN SEE THAT THE HEAVY HITTERS NEED ME.
SO I DON'T HAVE TO CONTINUE BEING...

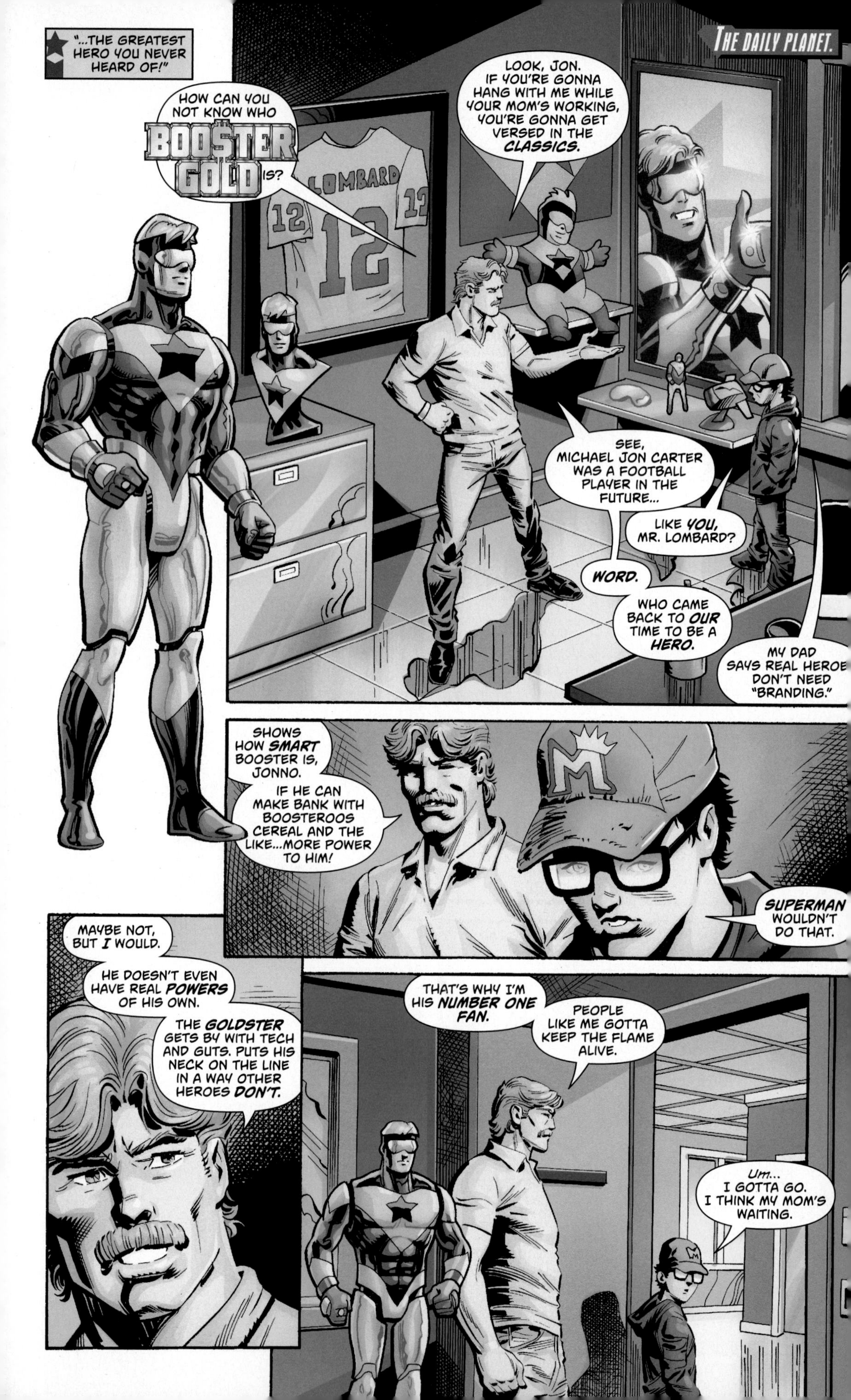

"...THE GREATEST HERO YOU NEVER HEARD OF!"
THE DAILY PLANET.
HOW CAN YOU NOT KNOW WHO BOOSTER GOLD IS?
LOOK, JON. IF YOU'RE GONNA HANG WITH ME WHILE YOUR MOM'S WORKING, YOU'RE GONNA GET VERSED IN THE CLASSICS.
LOMBARD 12
SEE, MICHAEL JON CARTER WAS A FOOTBALL PLAYER IN THE FUTURE...
LIKE YOU, MR. LOMBARD?
WORD.
WHO CAME BACK TO OUR TIME TO BE A HERO.
MY DAD SAYS REAL HEROES DON'T NEED "BRANDING."
SHOWS HOW SMART BOOSTER IS, JONNO.
IF HE CAN MAKE BANK WITH BOOSTEROOS CEREAL AND THE LIKE...MORE POWER TO HIM!
SUPERMAN WOULDN'T DO THAT.
MAYBE NOT, BUT I WOULD.
HE DOESN'T EVEN HAVE REAL POWERS OF HIS OWN.
THE GOLDSTER GETS BY WITH TECH AND GUTS. PUTS HIS NECK ON THE LINE IN A WAY OTHER HEROES DON'T.
THAT'S WHY I'M HIS NUMBER ONE FAN.
PEOPLE LIKE ME GOTTA KEEP THE FLAME ALIVE.
Um... I GOTTA GO. I THINK MY MOM'S WAITING.

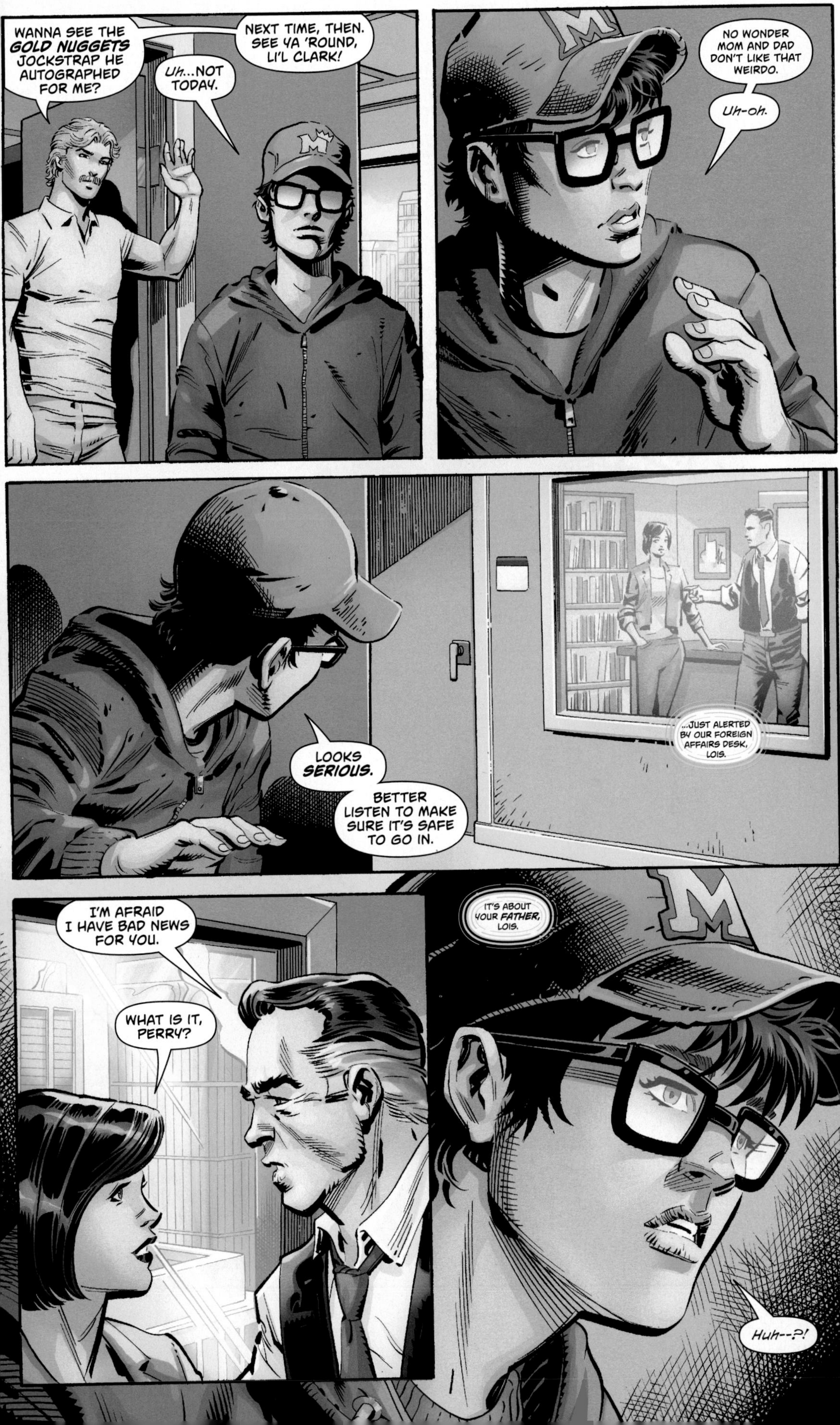
WANNA SEE THE GOLD NUGGETS JOCKSTRAP HE AUTOGRAPHED FOR ME?
Uh...NOT TODAY.
NEXT TIME, THEN. SEE YA 'ROUND, LI'L CLARK!
NO WONDER MOM AND DAD DON'T LIKE THAT WEIRDO.
Uh-oh.
...JUST ALERTED BY OUR FOREIGN AFFAIRS DESK, LOIS.
LOOKS SERIOUS.
BETTER LISTEN TO MAKE SURE IT'S SAFE TO GO IN.
I'M AFRAID I HAVE BAD NEWS FOR YOU.
WHAT IS IT, PERRY?
IT'S ABOUT YOUR FATHER, LOIS.
Huh--?!

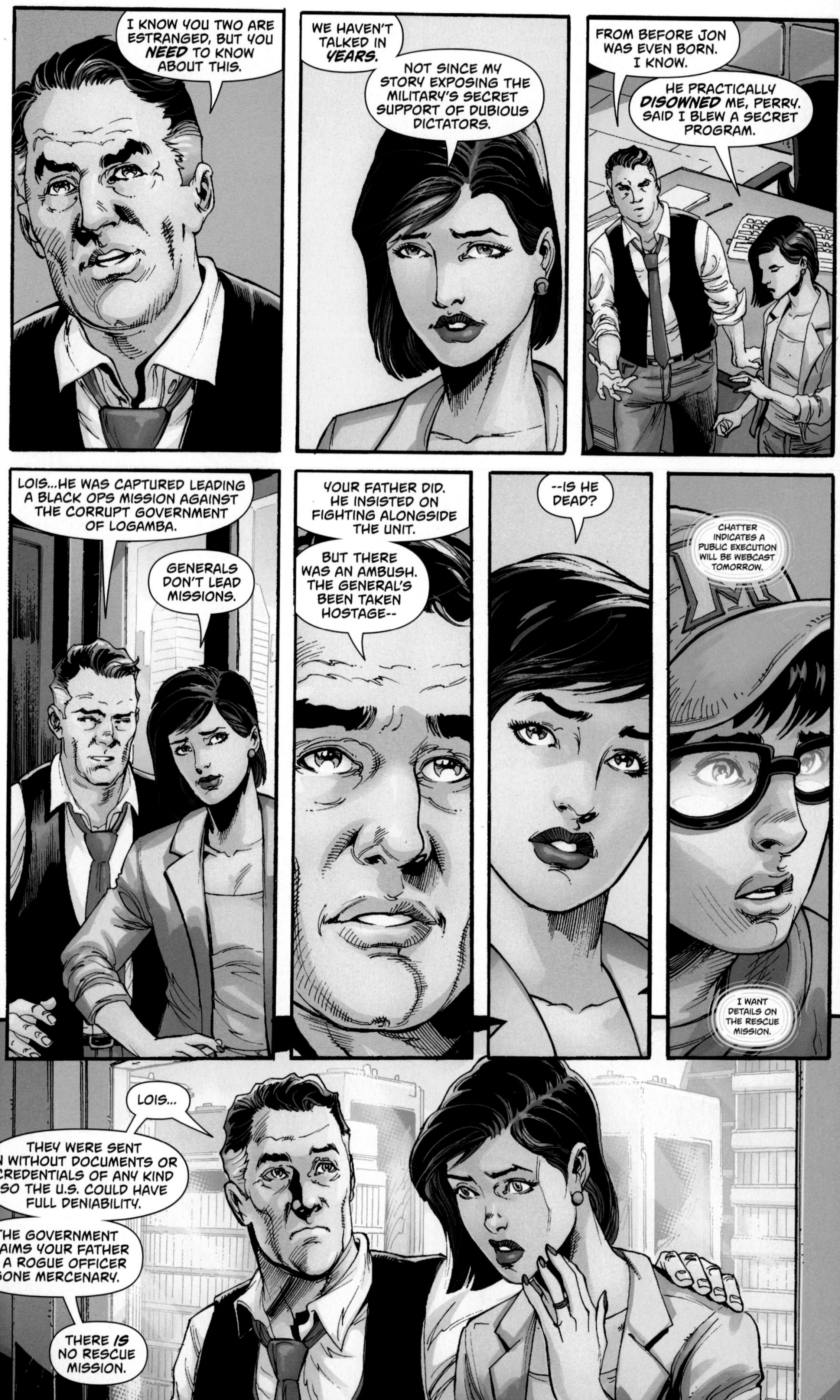
I KNOW YOU TWO ARE ESTRANGED, BUT YOU NEED TO KNOW ABOUT THIS.
WE HAVEN'T TALKED IN YEARS.
NOT SINCE MY STORY EXPOSING THE MILITARY'S SECRET SUPPORT OF DUBIOUS DICTATORS.
FROM BEFORE JON WAS EVEN BORN. I KNOW.
HE PRACTICALLY DISOWNED ME, PERRY. SAID I BLEW A SECRET PROGRAM.
LOIS...HE WAS CAPTURED LEADING A BLACK OPS MISSION AGAINST THE CORRUPT GOVERNMENT OF LOGAMBA.
GENERALS DON'T LEAD MISSIONS.
YOUR FATHER DID. HE INSISTED ON FIGHTING ALONGSIDE THE UNIT.
BUT THERE WAS AN AMBUSH. THE GENERAL'S BEEN TAKEN HOSTAGE--
--IS HE DEAD?
CHATTER INDICATES A PUBLIC EXECUTION WILL BE WEBCAST TOMORROW.
I WANT DETAILS ON THE RESCUE MISSION.
LOIS...
THEY WERE SENT IN WITHOUT DOCUMENTS OR CREDENTIALS OF ANY KIND SO THE U.S. COULD HAVE FULL DENIABILITY.
THE GOVERNMENT CLAIMS YOUR FATHER IS A ROGUE OFFICER GONE MERCENARY.
THERE IS NO RESCUE MISSION.

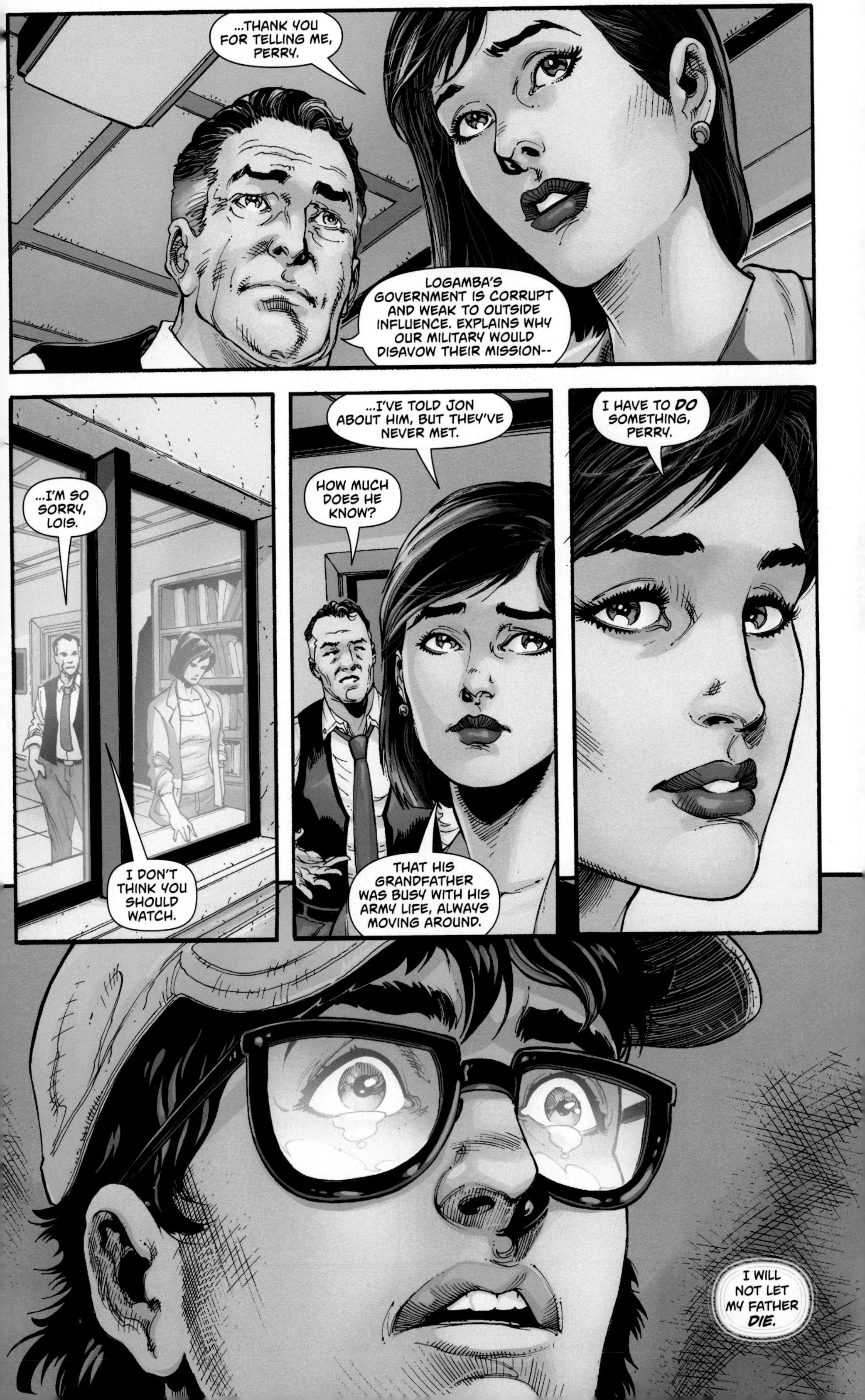
...THANK YOU FOR TELLING ME, PERRY.
LOGAMBA'S GOVERNMENT IS CORRUPT AND WEAK TO OUTSIDE INFLUENCE. EXPLAINS WHY OUR MILITARY WOULD DISAVOW THEIR MISSION--
...I'M SO SORRY, LOIS.
I DON'T THINK YOU SHOULD WATCH.
...I'VE TOLD JON ABOUT HIM, BUT THEY'VE NEVER MET.
HOW MUCH DOES HE KNOW?
THAT HIS GRANDFATHER WAS BUSY WITH HIS ARMY LIFE, ALWAYS MOVING AROUND.
I HAVE TO DO SOMETHING, PERRY.
I WILL NOT LET MY FATHER DIE.

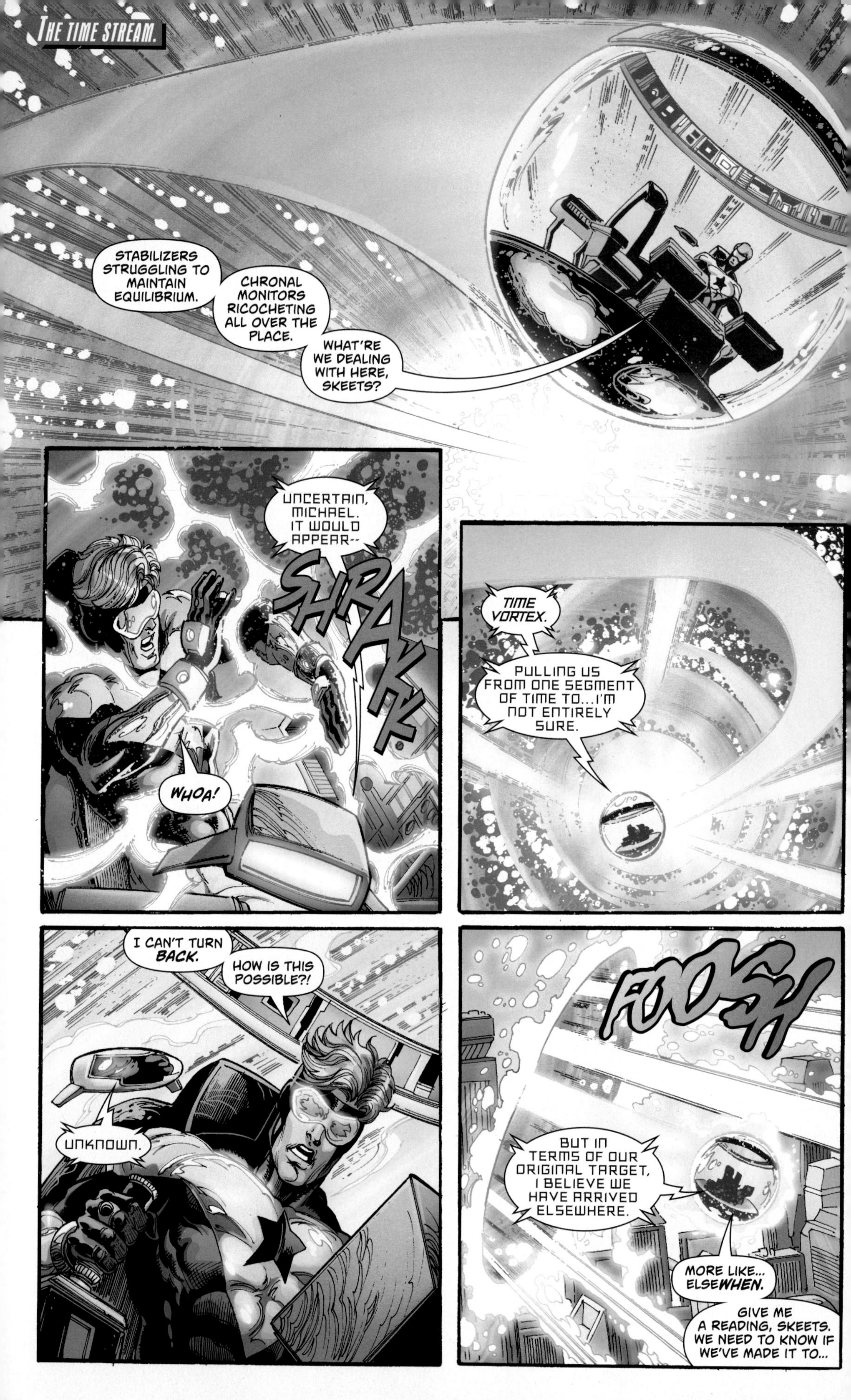
THE TIME STREAM.
STABILIZERS STRUGGLING TO MAINTAIN EQUILIBRIUM.
CHRONAL MONITORS RICOCHETING ALL OVER THE PLACE.
WHAT'RE WE DEALING WITH HERE, SKEETS?
UNCERTAIN, MICHAEL. IT WOULD APPEAR--
SHRAKK
WHOA!
TIME VORTEX.
PULLING US FROM ONE SEGMENT OF TIME TO...I'M NOT ENTIRELY SURE.
I CAN'T TURN BACK.
HOW IS THIS POSSIBLE?!
UNKNOWN.
FOOSH
BUT IN TERMS OF OUR ORIGINAL TARGET, I BELIEVE WE HAVE ARRIVED ELSEWHERE.
MORE LIKE... ELSEWHEN.
GIVE ME A READING, SKEETS. WE NEED TO KNOW IF WE'VE MADE IT TO...

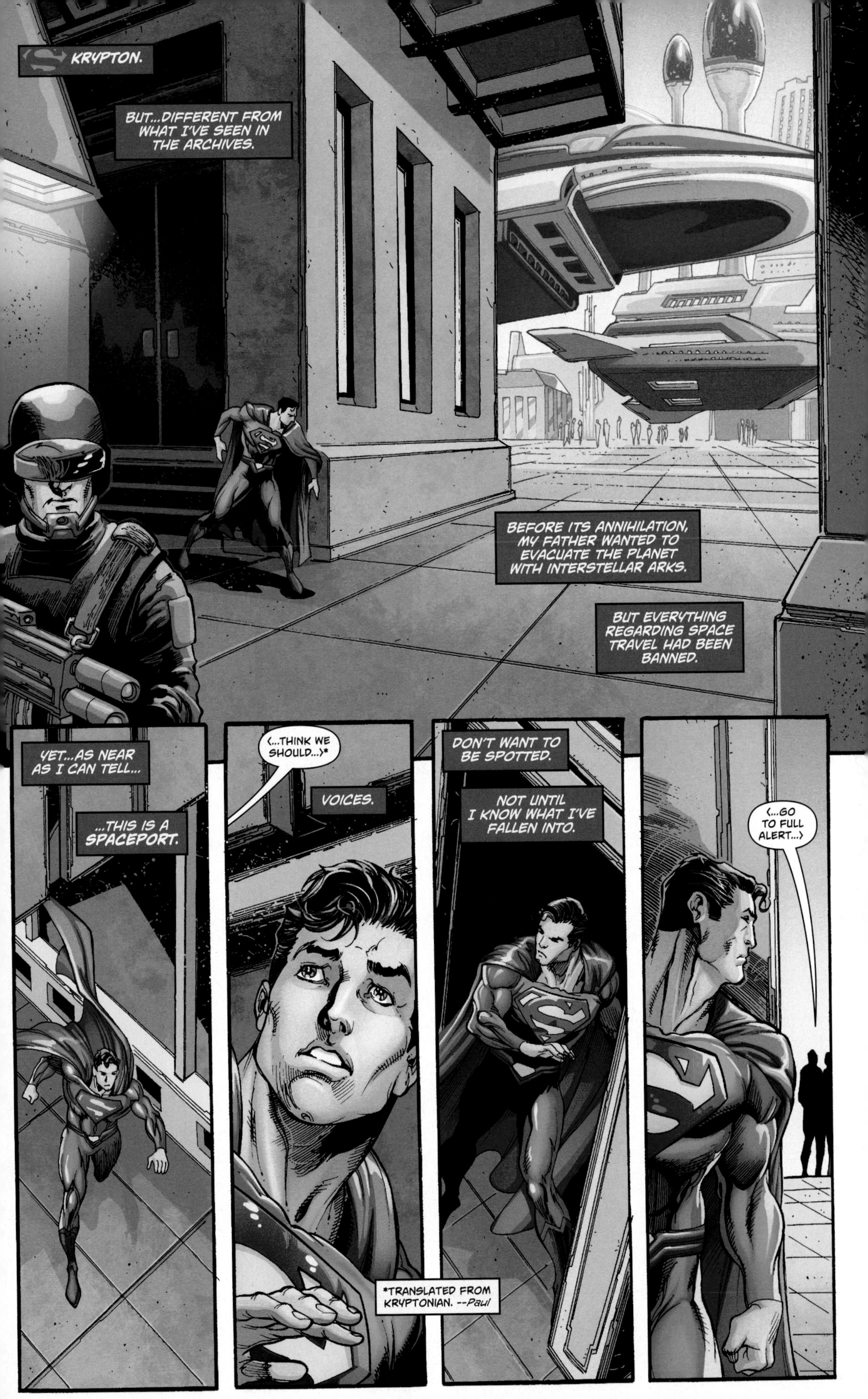
KRYPTON.
BUT...DIFFERENT FROM WHAT I'VE SEEN IN THE ARCHIVES.
BEFORE ITS ANNIHILATION, MY FATHER WANTED TO EVACUATE THE PLANET WITH INTERSTELLAR ARKS.
BUT EVERYTHING REGARDING SPACE TRAVEL HAD BEEN BANNED.
YET...AS NEAR AS I CAN TELL...
...THIS IS A SPACEPORT.
<...THINK WE SHOULD...>*
VOICES.
*TRANSLATED FROM KRYPTONIAN. --Paul
DON'T WANT TO BE SPOTTED.
NOT UNTIL I KNOW WHAT I'VE FALLEN INTO.
<...GO TO FULL ALERT...>

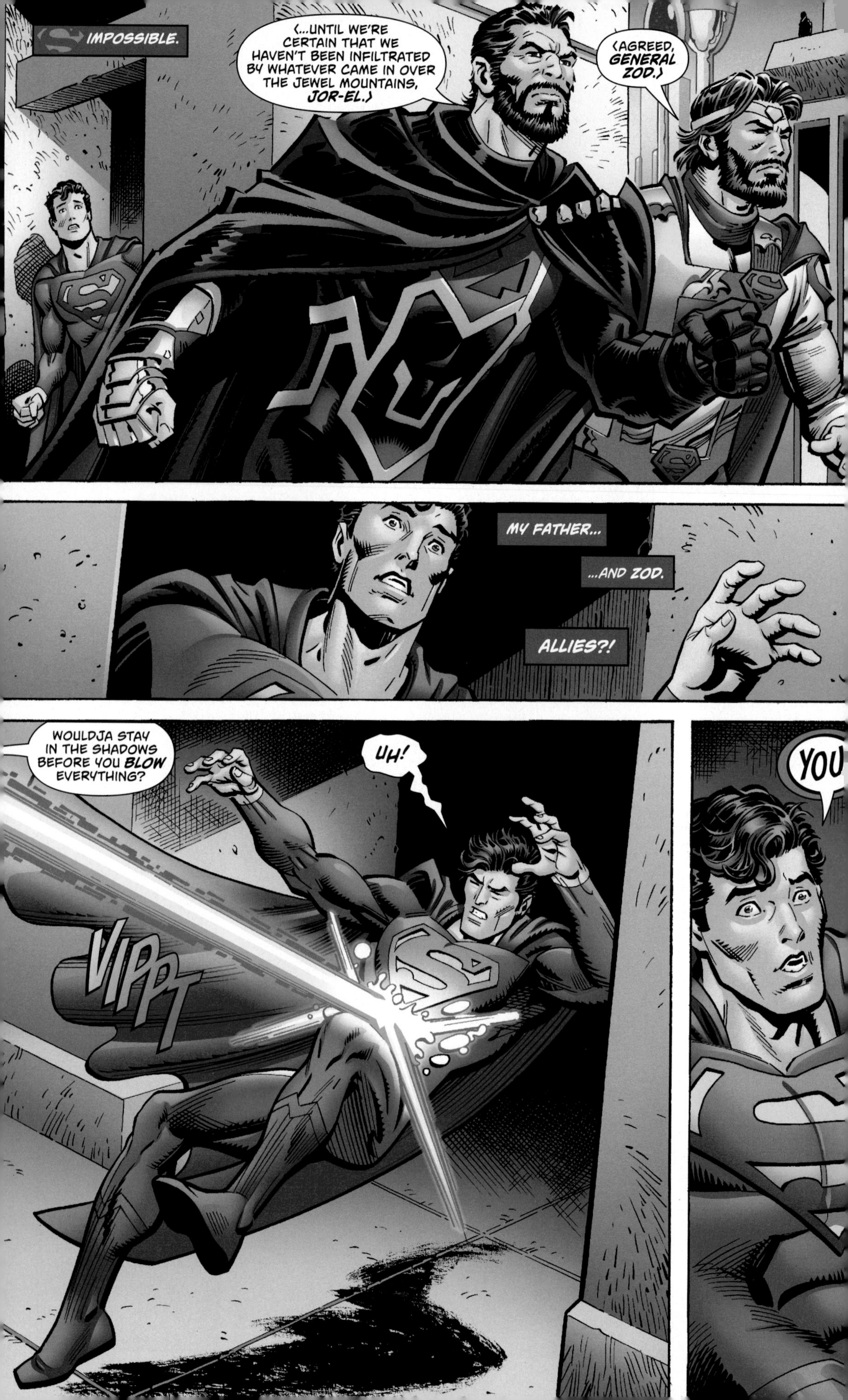
IMPOSSIBLE.
‹...UNTIL WE'RE CERTAIN THAT WE HAVEN'T BEEN INFILTRATED BY WHATEVER CAME IN OVER THE JEWEL MOUNTAINS, JOR-EL.›
‹AGREED, GENERAL ZOD.›
MY FATHER...
...AND ZOD.
ALLIES?!
WOULDJA STAY IN THE SHADOWS BEFORE YOU BLOW EVERYTHING?
UH!
VIPPT
YOU

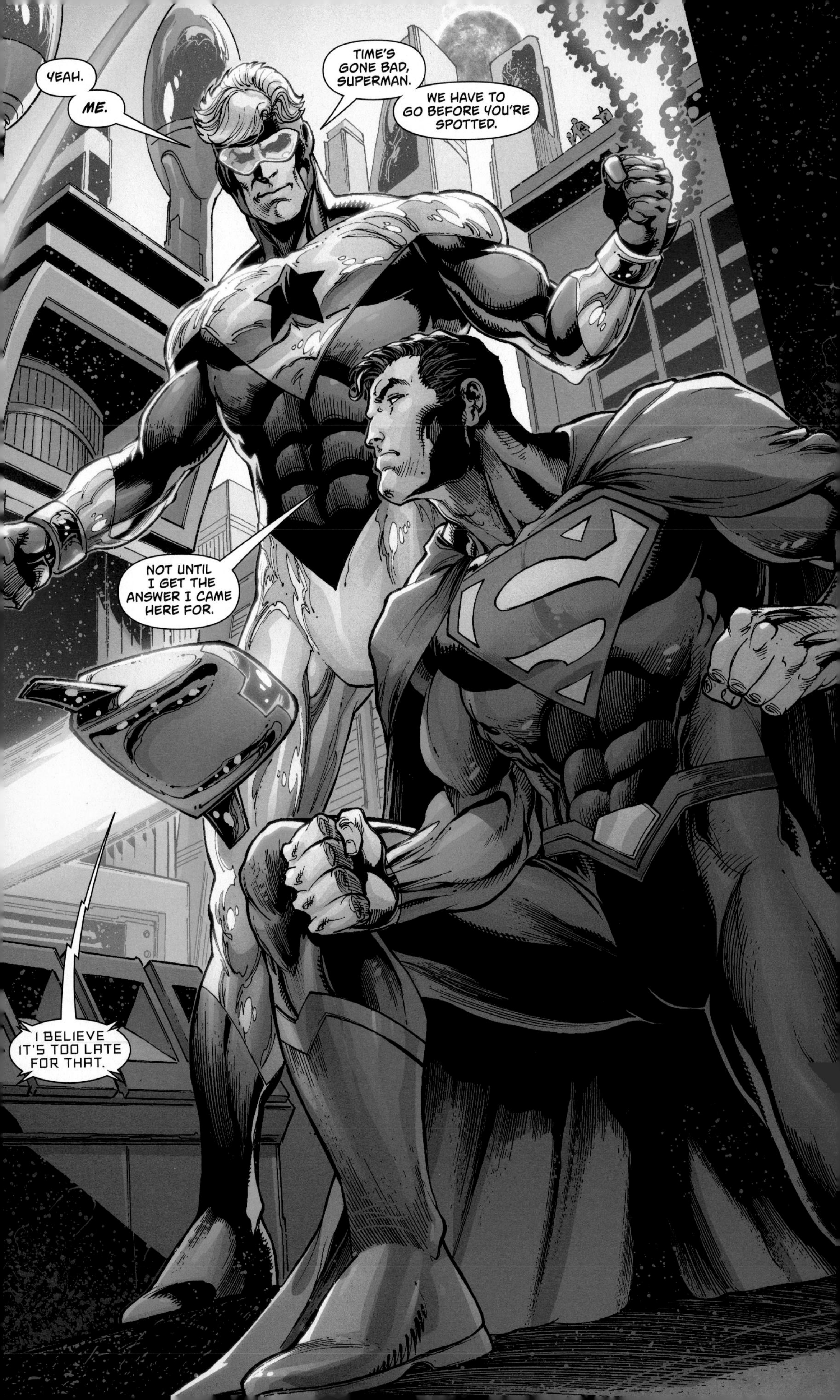
YEAH.
ME.
TIME'S GONE BAD, SUPERMAN.
WE HAVE TO GO BEFORE YOU'RE SPOTTED.
NOT UNTIL I GET THE ANSWER I CAME HERE FOR.
I BELIEVE IT'S TOO LATE FOR THAT.

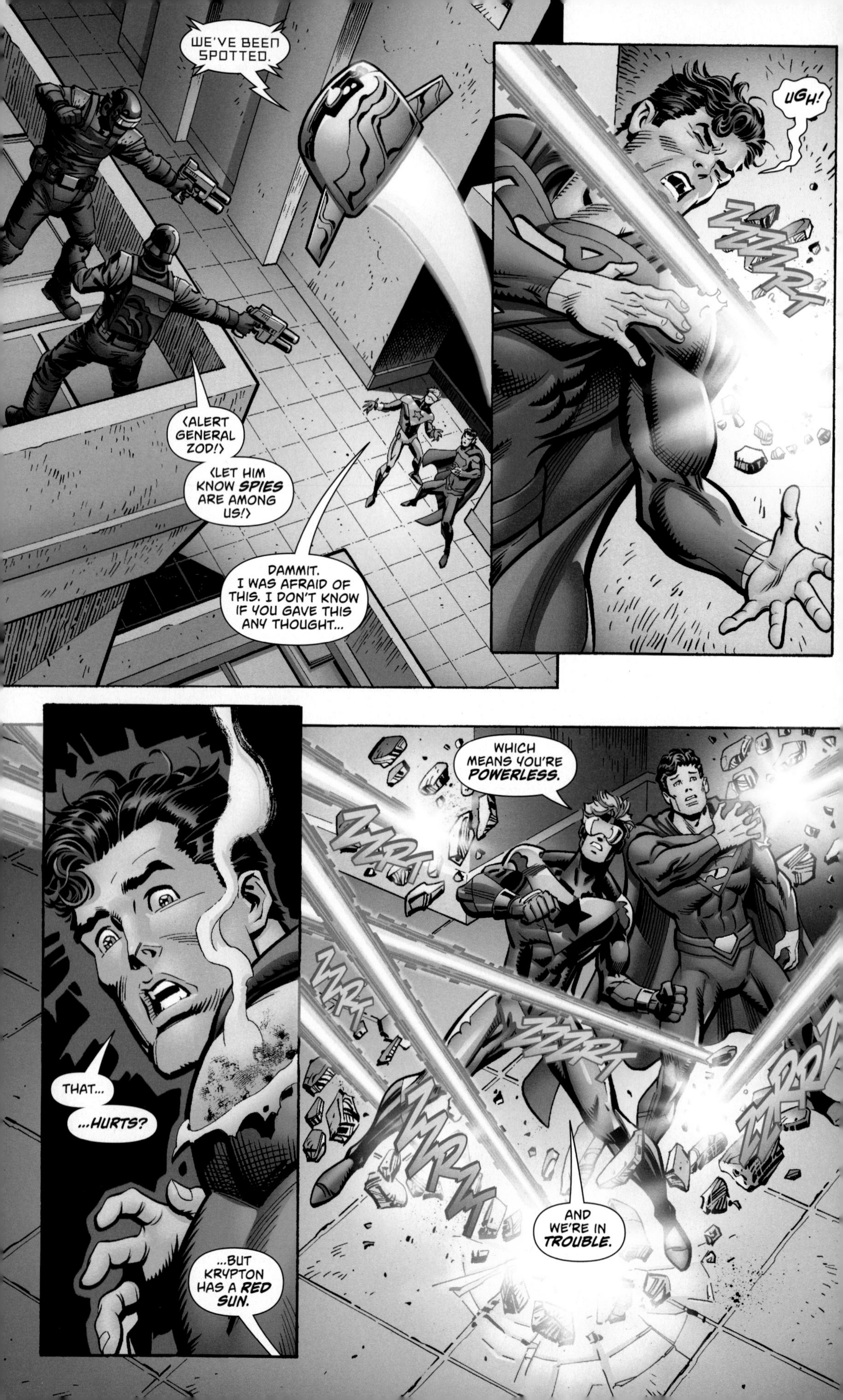
WE'VE BEEN SPOTTED.
UGH!
VZZAARRT
<ALERT GENERAL ZOD!>
<LET HIM KNOW SPIES ARE AMONG US!>
DAMMIT. I WAS AFRAID OF THIS. I DON'T KNOW IF YOU GAVE THIS ANY THOUGHT...
THAT...
...HURTS?
...BUT KRYPTON HAS A RED SUN.
WHICH MEANS YOU'RE POWERLESS.
AND WE'RE IN TROUBLE.
ZZZRK

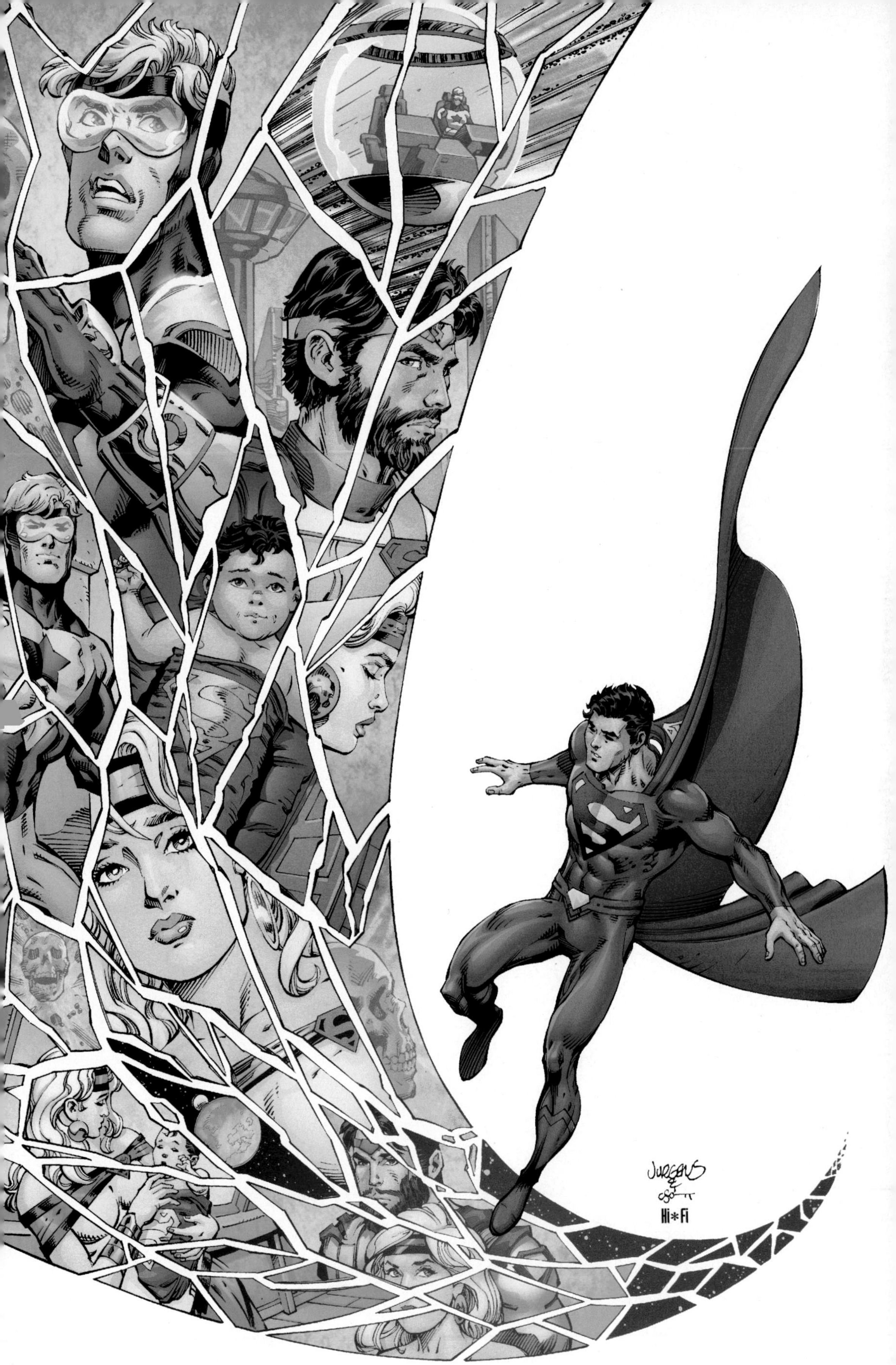
JURGENS
Hi*Fi

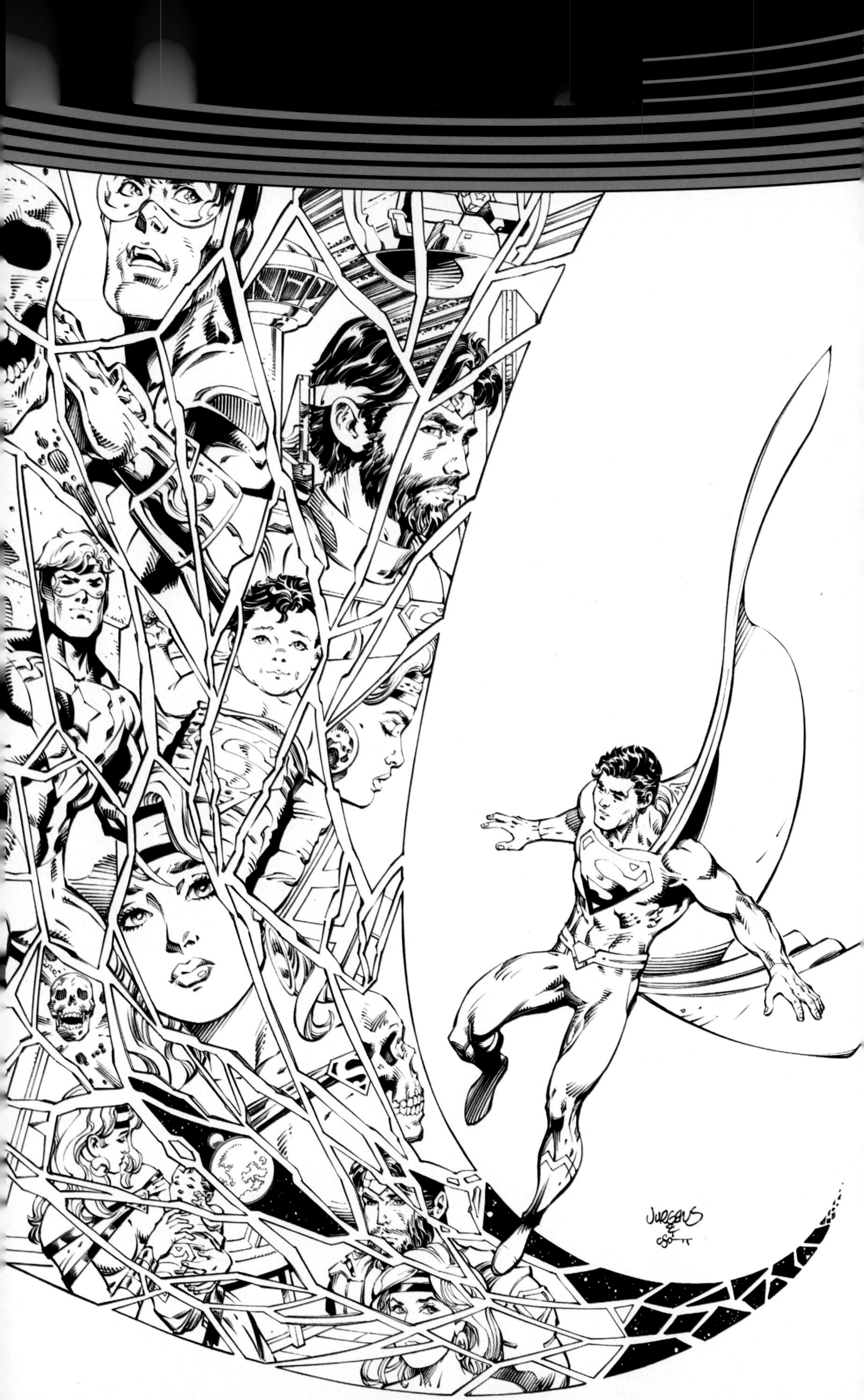
JURGENS

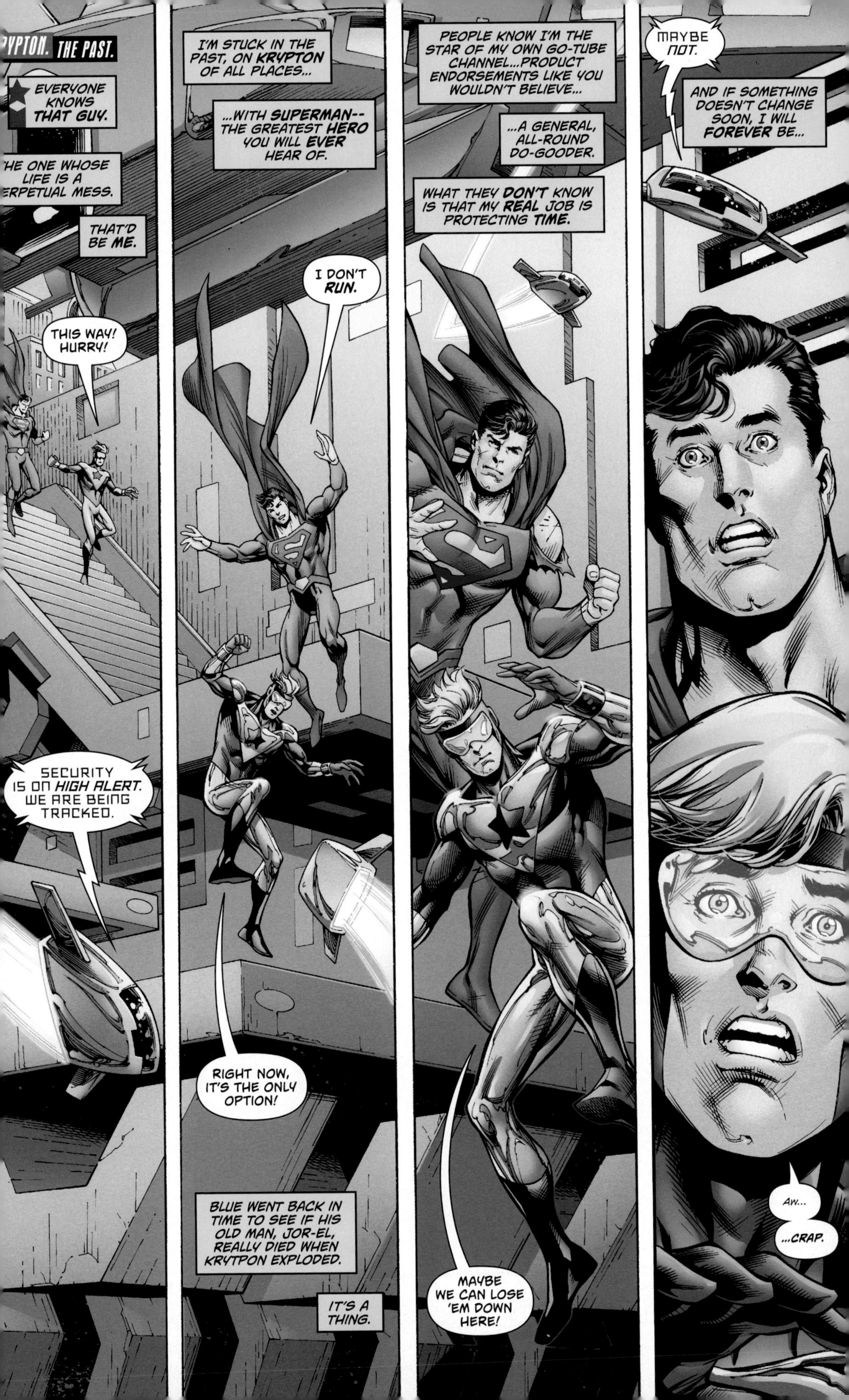

RYPTON. THE PAST.
EVERYONE KNOWS THAT GUY.
THE ONE WHOSE LIFE IS A PERPETUAL MESS.
THAT'D BE ME.
THIS WAY! HURRY!
SECURITY IS ON HIGH ALERT. WE ARE BEING TRACKED.
I'M STUCK IN THE PAST, ON KRYPTON OF ALL PLACES...
...WITH SUPERMAN-- THE GREATEST HERO YOU WILL EVER HEAR OF.
I DON'T RUN.
RIGHT NOW, IT'S THE ONLY OPTION!
BLUE WENT BACK IN TIME TO SEE IF HIS OLD MAN, JOR-EL, REALLY DIED WHEN KRYTPON EXPLODED.
IT'S A THING.
PEOPLE KNOW I'M THE STAR OF MY OWN GO-TUBE CHANNEL...PRODUCT ENDORSEMENTS LIKE YOU WOULDN'T BELIEVE...
...A GENERAL, ALL-ROUND DO-GOODER.
WHAT THEY DON'T KNOW IS THAT MY REAL JOB IS PROTECTING TIME.
MAYBE WE CAN LOSE 'EM DOWN HERE!
MAYBE NOT.
AND IF SOMETHING DOESN'T CHANGE SOON, I WILL FOREVER BE...
AW...
...CRAP.

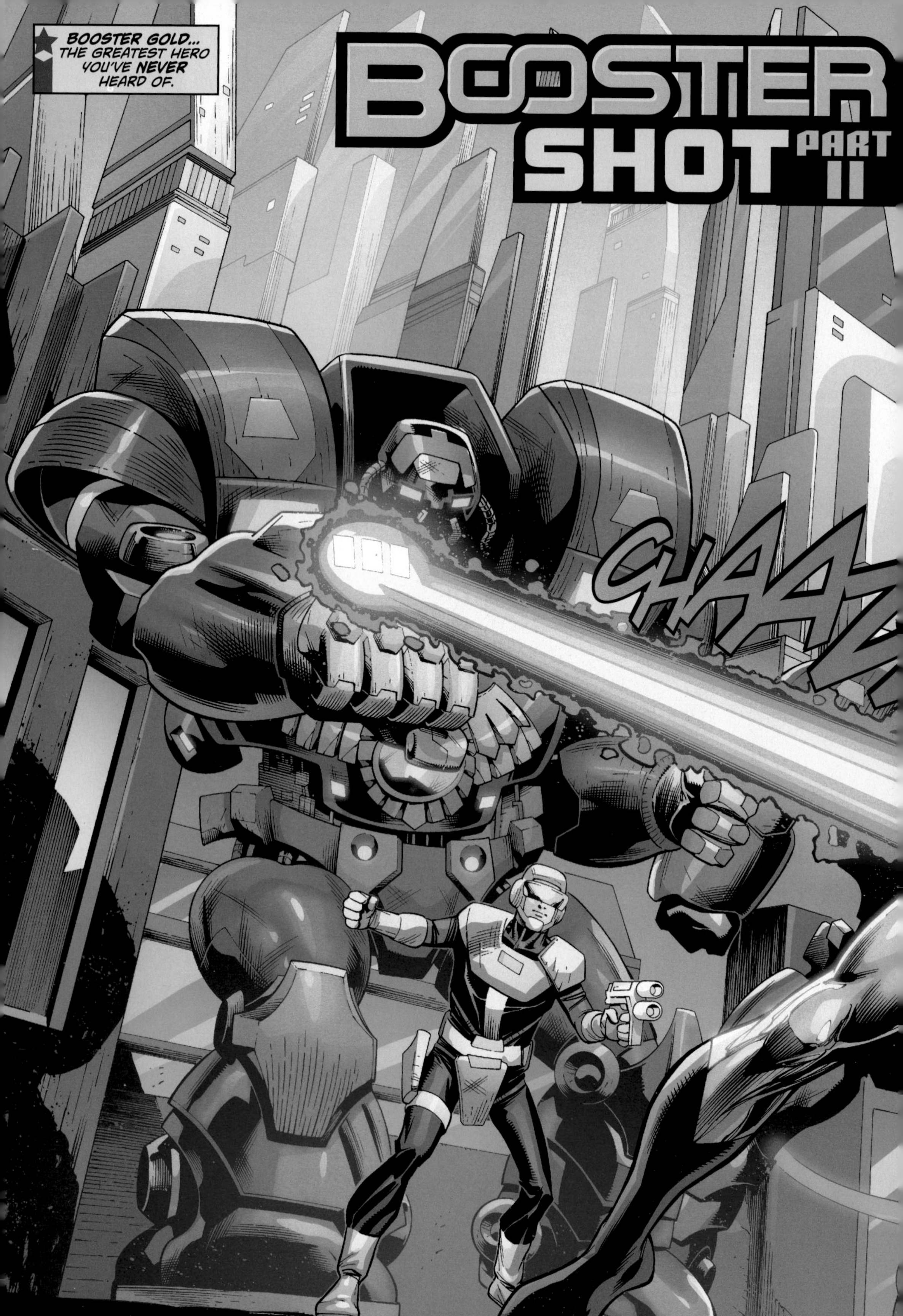
BOOSTER GOLD... THE GREATEST HERO YOU'VE NEVER HEARD OF.
BOOSTER SHOT PART II
CHAAA

DAN JURGENS Story and Pencil Art
ART THIBERT, TREVOR SCOTT, JOHNNY DESJARDINS and JOE PRADO Finished Ink Art
HI-FI Color · **ROB LEIGH** Letters · **DAN JURGENS, TREVOR SCOTT & HI-FI** Cover
ANDREA SHEA Assistant Editor · **PAUL KAMINSKI** Editor · **EDDIE BERGANZA** Group Editor

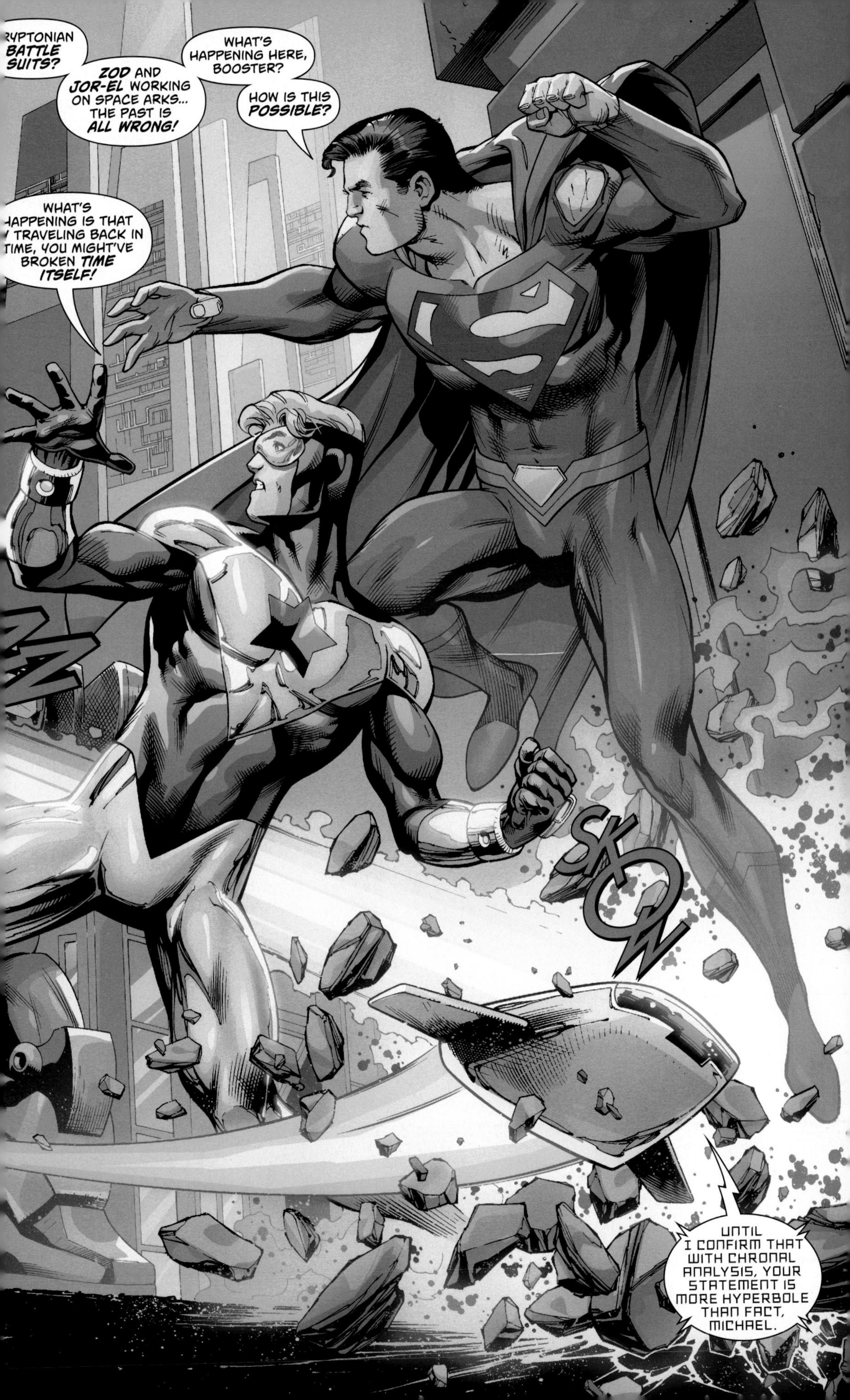
RYPTONIAN BATTLE SUITS?
ZOD AND JOR-EL WORKING ON SPACE ARKS... THE PAST IS ALL WRONG!
WHAT'S HAPPENING HERE, BOOSTER?
HOW IS THIS POSSIBLE?
WHAT'S HAPPENING IS THAT TRAVELING BACK IN TIME, YOU MIGHT'VE BROKEN TIME ITSELF!
UNTIL I CONFIRM THAT WITH CHRONAL ANALYSIS, YOUR STATEMENT IS MORE HYPERBOLE THAN FACT, MICHAEL.

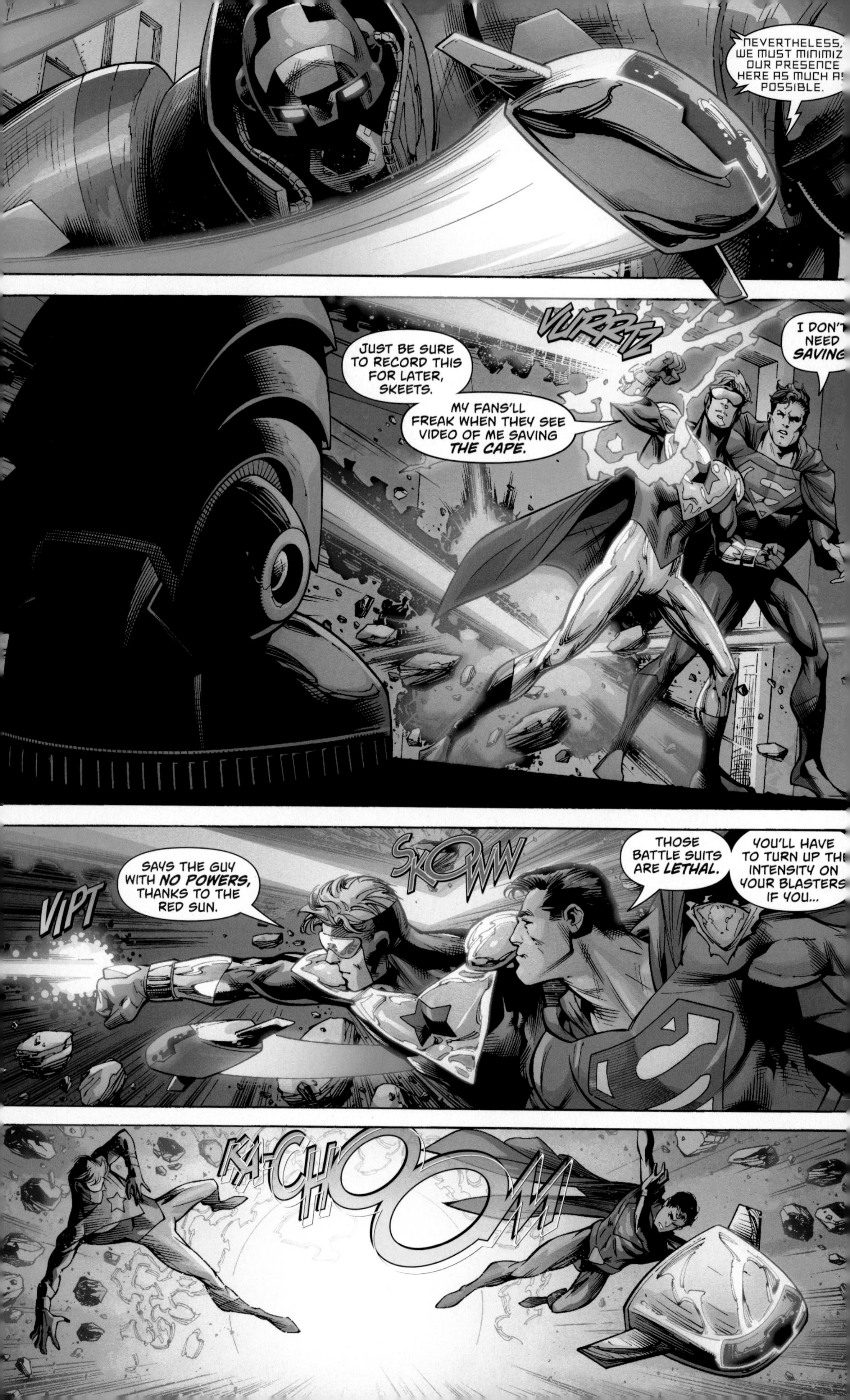
NEVERTHELESS, WE MUST MINIMIZ OUR PRESENCE HERE AS MUCH A: POSSIBLE.
VURRRZ
JUST BE SURE TO RECORD THIS FOR LATER, SKEETS.
MY FANS'LL FREAK WHEN THEY SEE VIDEO OF ME SAVING *THE CAPE.*
I DON'T NEED *SAVING*
SKOWW
VIPT
SAYS THE GUY WITH *NO POWERS,* THANKS TO THE RED SUN.
THOSE BATTLE SUITS ARE *LETHAL.*
YOU'LL HAVE TO TURN UP THE INTENSITY ON YOUR BLASTERS IF YOU...
KA-CHOOOM

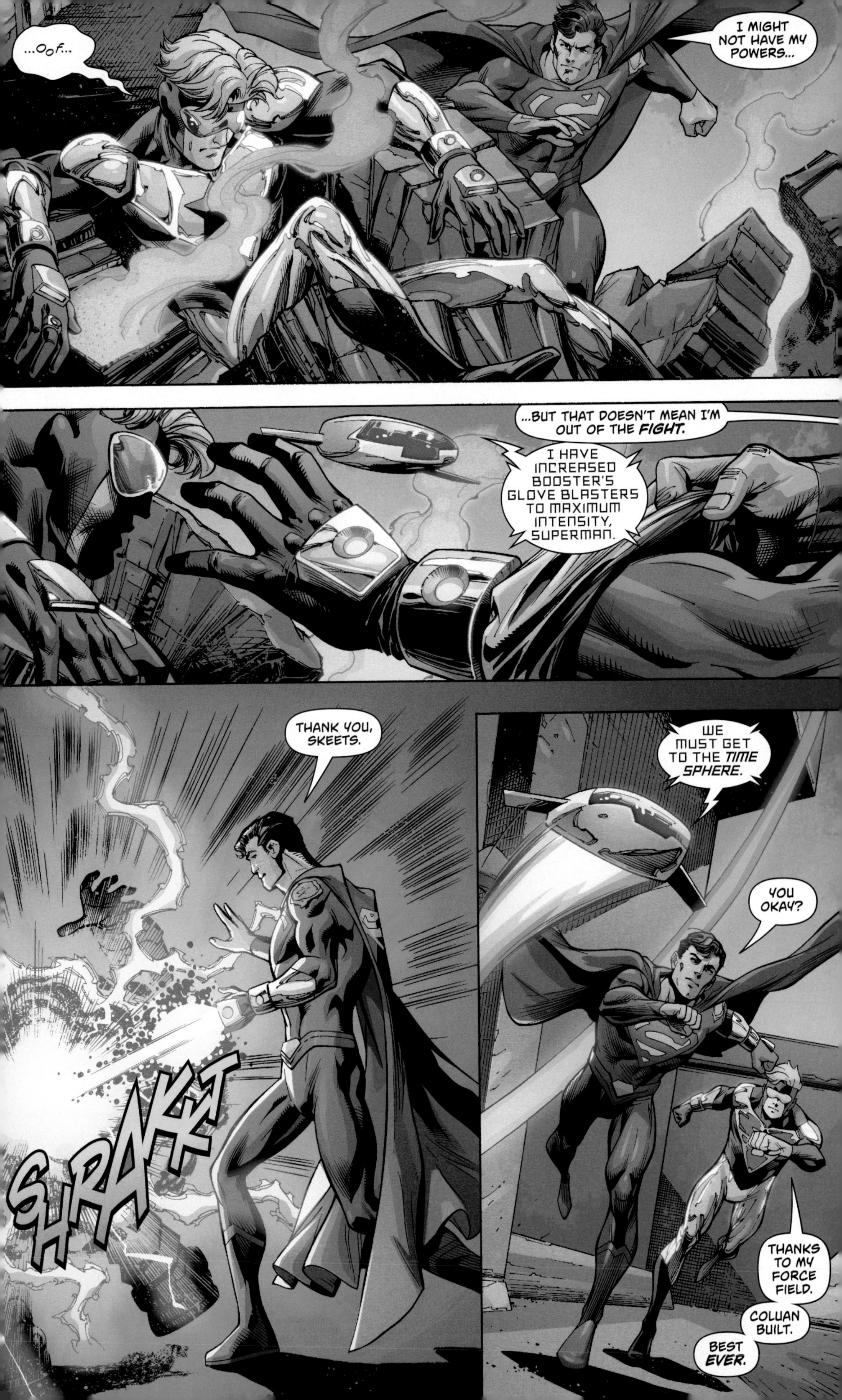
...Oof...
I MIGHT NOT HAVE MY POWERS...
...BUT THAT DOESN'T MEAN I'M OUT OF THE FIGHT.
I HAVE INCREASED BOOSTER'S GLOVE BLASTERS TO MAXIMUM INTENSITY, SUPERMAN.
THANK YOU, SKEETS.
SHRAKT
WE MUST GET TO THE TIME SPHERE.
YOU OKAY?
THANKS TO MY FORCE FIELD.
COLUAN BUILT.
BEST EVER.

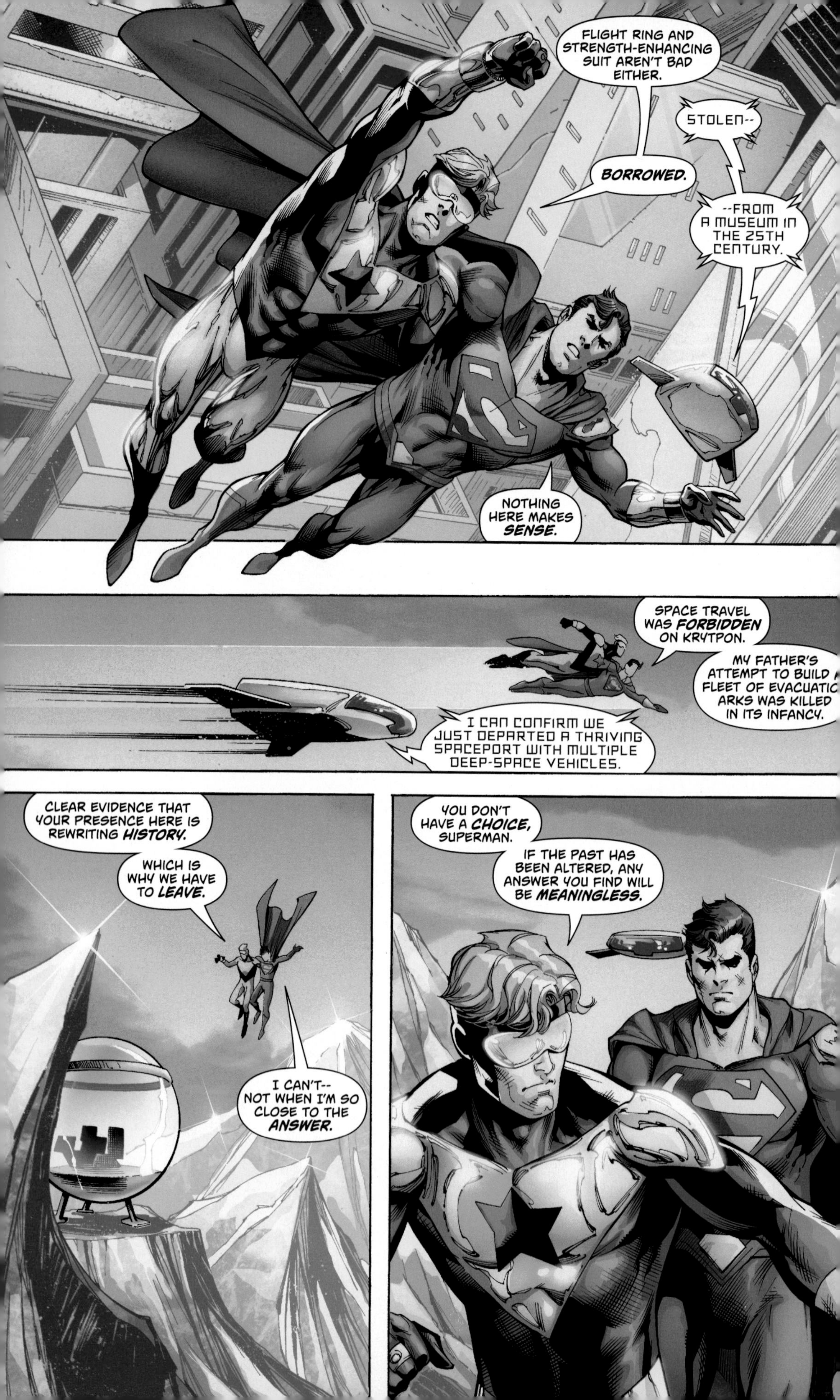
FLIGHT RING AND STRENGTH-ENHANCING SUIT AREN'T BAD EITHER.
BORROWED.
STOLEN--
--FROM A MUSEUM IN THE 25TH CENTURY.
NOTHING HERE MAKES SENSE.
SPACE TRAVEL WAS FORBIDDEN ON KRYTPON.
MY FATHER'S ATTEMPT TO BUILD A FLEET OF EVACUATIO ARKS WAS KILLED IN ITS INFANCY.
I CAN CONFIRM WE JUST DEPARTED A THRIVING SPACEPORT WITH MULTIPLE DEEP-SPACE VEHICLES.
CLEAR EVIDENCE THAT YOUR PRESENCE HERE IS REWRITING HISTORY.
WHICH IS WHY WE HAVE TO LEAVE.
I CAN'T-- NOT WHEN I'M SO CLOSE TO THE ANSWER.
YOU DON'T HAVE A CHOICE, SUPERMAN.
IF THE PAST HAS BEEN ALTERED, ANY ANSWER YOU FIND WILL BE MEANINGLESS.

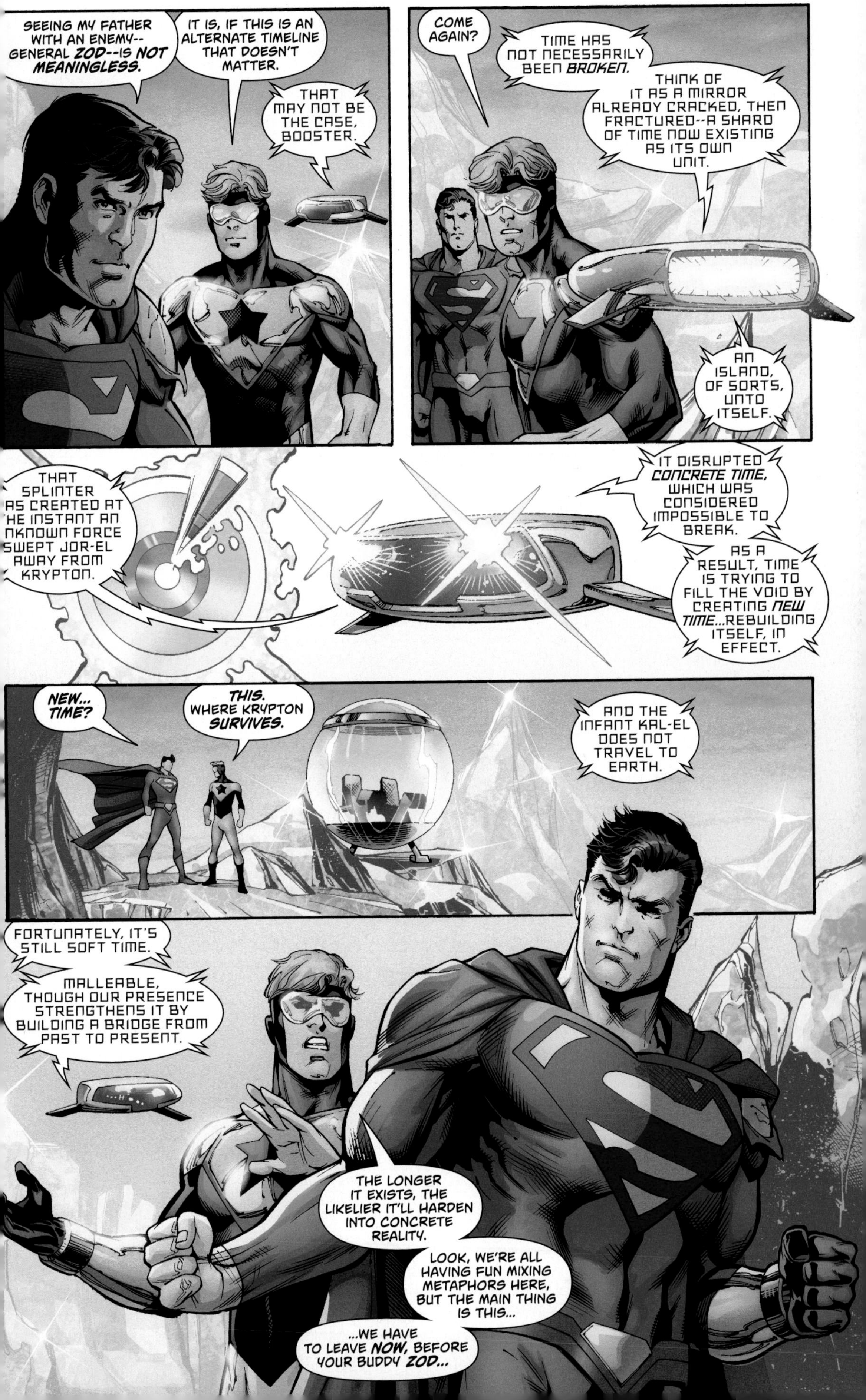

SEEING MY FATHER WITH AN ENEMY--GENERAL ZOD--IS NOT MEANINGLESS.
IT IS, IF THIS IS AN ALTERNATE TIMELINE THAT DOESN'T MATTER.
THAT MAY NOT BE THE CASE, BOOSTER.
COME AGAIN?
TIME HAS NOT NECESSARILY BEEN BROKEN.
THINK OF IT AS A MIRROR ALREADY CRACKED, THEN FRACTURED--A SHARD OF TIME NOW EXISTING AS ITS OWN UNIT.
AN ISLAND, OF SORTS, UNTO ITSELF.
THAT SPLINTER AS CREATED AT HE INSTANT AN NKNOWN FORCE SWEPT JOR-EL AWAY FROM KRYPTON.
IT DISRUPTED CONCRETE TIME, WHICH WAS CONSIDERED IMPOSSIBLE TO BREAK.
AS A RESULT, TIME IS TRYING TO FILL THE VOID BY CREATING NEW TIME...REBUILDING ITSELF, IN EFFECT.
NEW... TIME?
THIS. WHERE KRYPTON SURVIVES.
AND THE INFANT KAL-EL DOES NOT TRAVEL TO EARTH.
FORTUNATELY, IT'S STILL SOFT TIME.
MALLEABLE, THOUGH OUR PRESENCE STRENGTHENS IT BY BUILDING A BRIDGE FROM PAST TO PRESENT.
THE LONGER IT EXISTS, THE LIKELIER IT'LL HARDEN INTO CONCRETE REALITY.
LOOK, WE'RE ALL HAVING FUN MIXING METAPHORS HERE, BUT THE MAIN THING IS THIS...
...WE HAVE TO LEAVE NOW, BEFORE YOUR BUDDY ZOD...

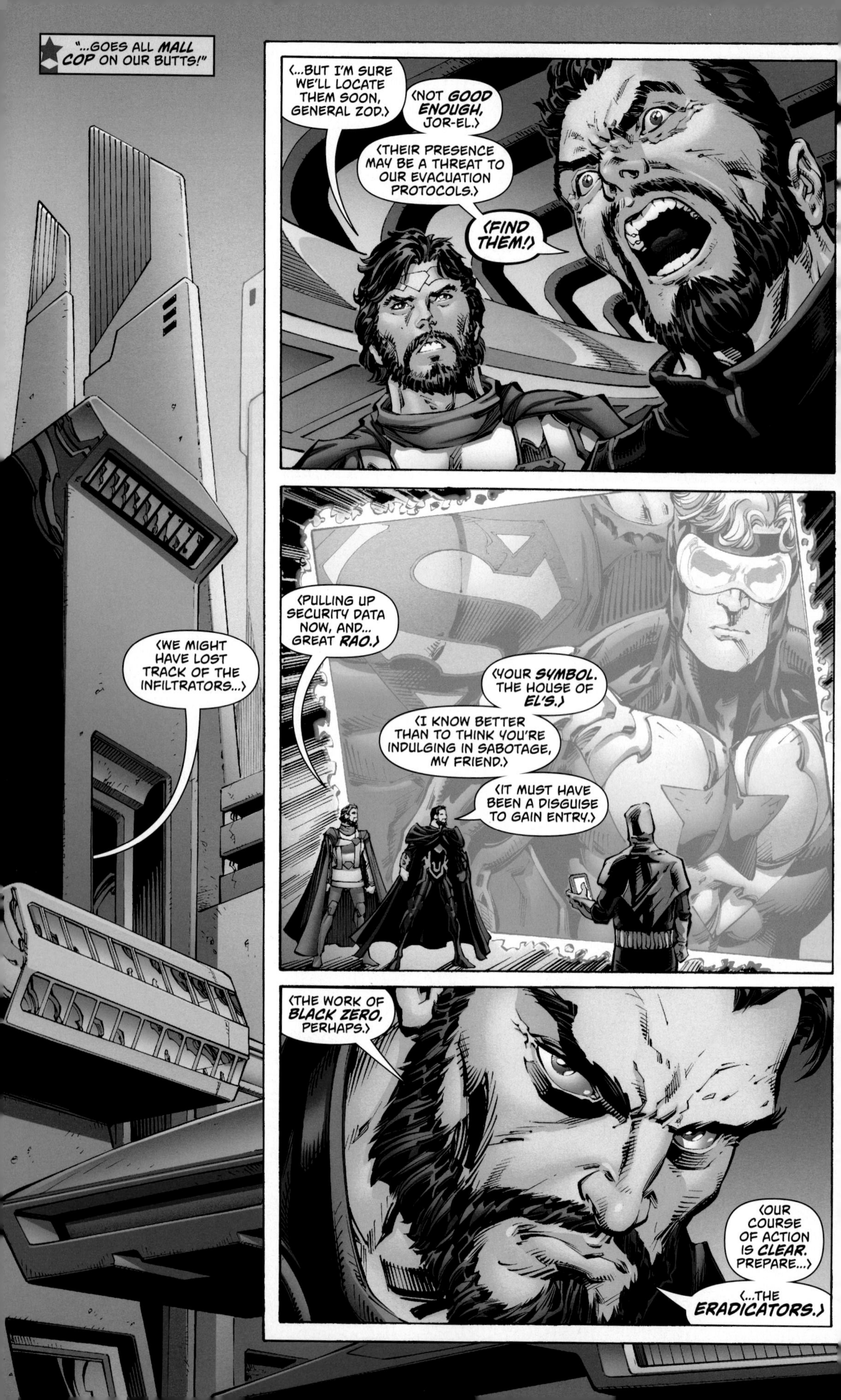
"...GOES ALL MALL COP ON OUR BUTTS!"
‹...BUT I'M SURE WE'LL LOCATE THEM SOON, GENERAL ZOD.›
‹NOT GOOD ENOUGH, JOR-EL.›
‹THEIR PRESENCE MAY BE A THREAT TO OUR EVACUATION PROTOCOLS.›
‹FIND THEM!›
‹WE MIGHT HAVE LOST TRACK OF THE INFILTRATORS...›
‹PULLING UP SECURITY DATA NOW, AND... GREAT RAO.›
‹YOUR SYMBOL. THE HOUSE OF EL'S.›
‹I KNOW BETTER THAN TO THINK YOU'RE INDULGING IN SABOTAGE, MY FRIEND.›
‹IT MUST HAVE BEEN A DISGUISE TO GAIN ENTRY.›
‹THE WORK OF BLACK ZERO, PERHAPS.›
‹OUR COURSE OF ACTION IS CLEAR. PREPARE...›
‹...THE ERADICATORS.›

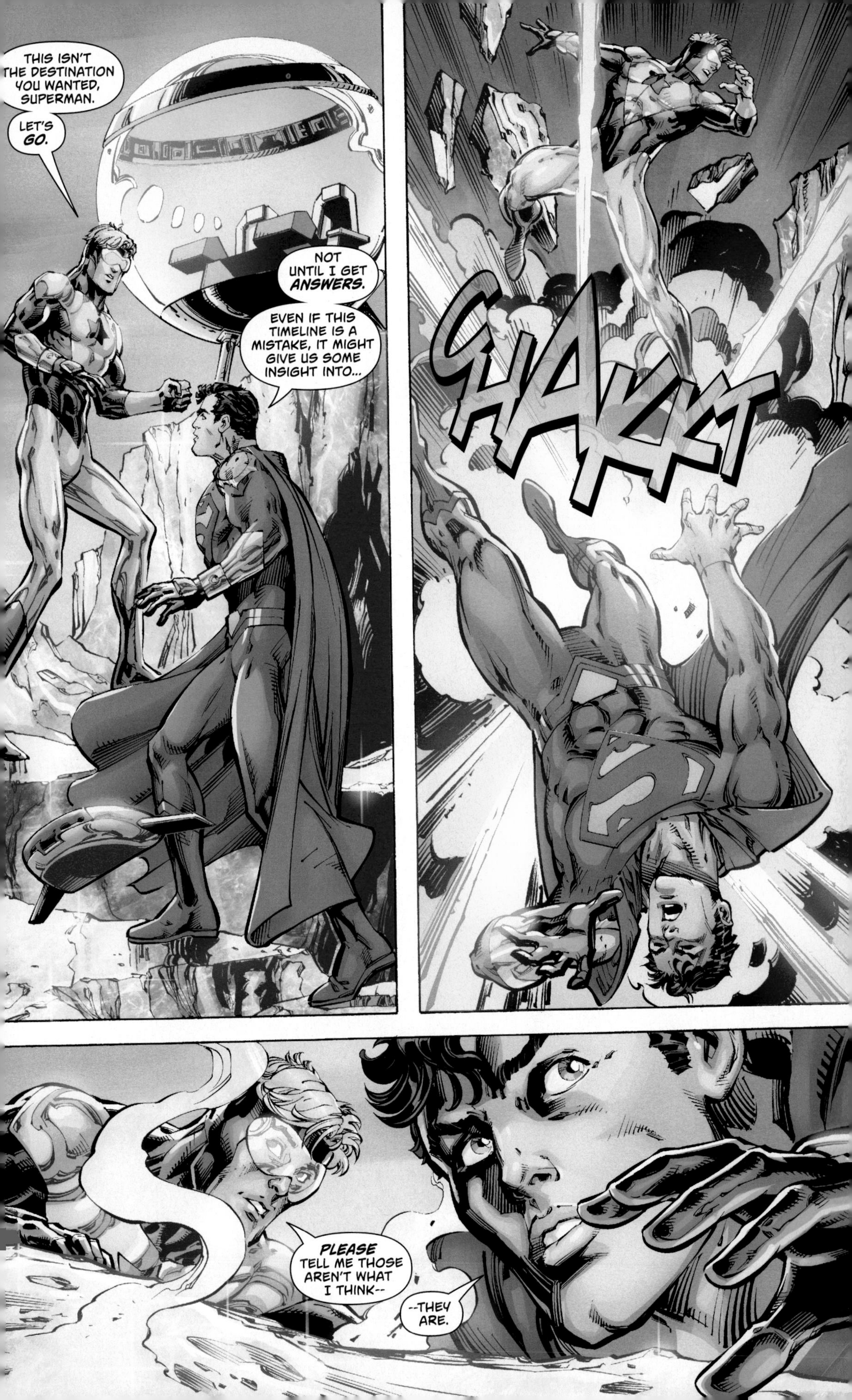
THIS ISN'T THE DESTINATION YOU WANTED, SUPERMAN.
LET'S *GO*.
NOT UNTIL I GET ***ANSWERS***.
EVEN IF THIS TIMELINE IS A MISTAKE, IT MIGHT GIVE US SOME INSIGHT INTO...
CHAKKT
PLEASE TELL ME THOSE AREN'T WHAT I THINK--
--THEY ARE.

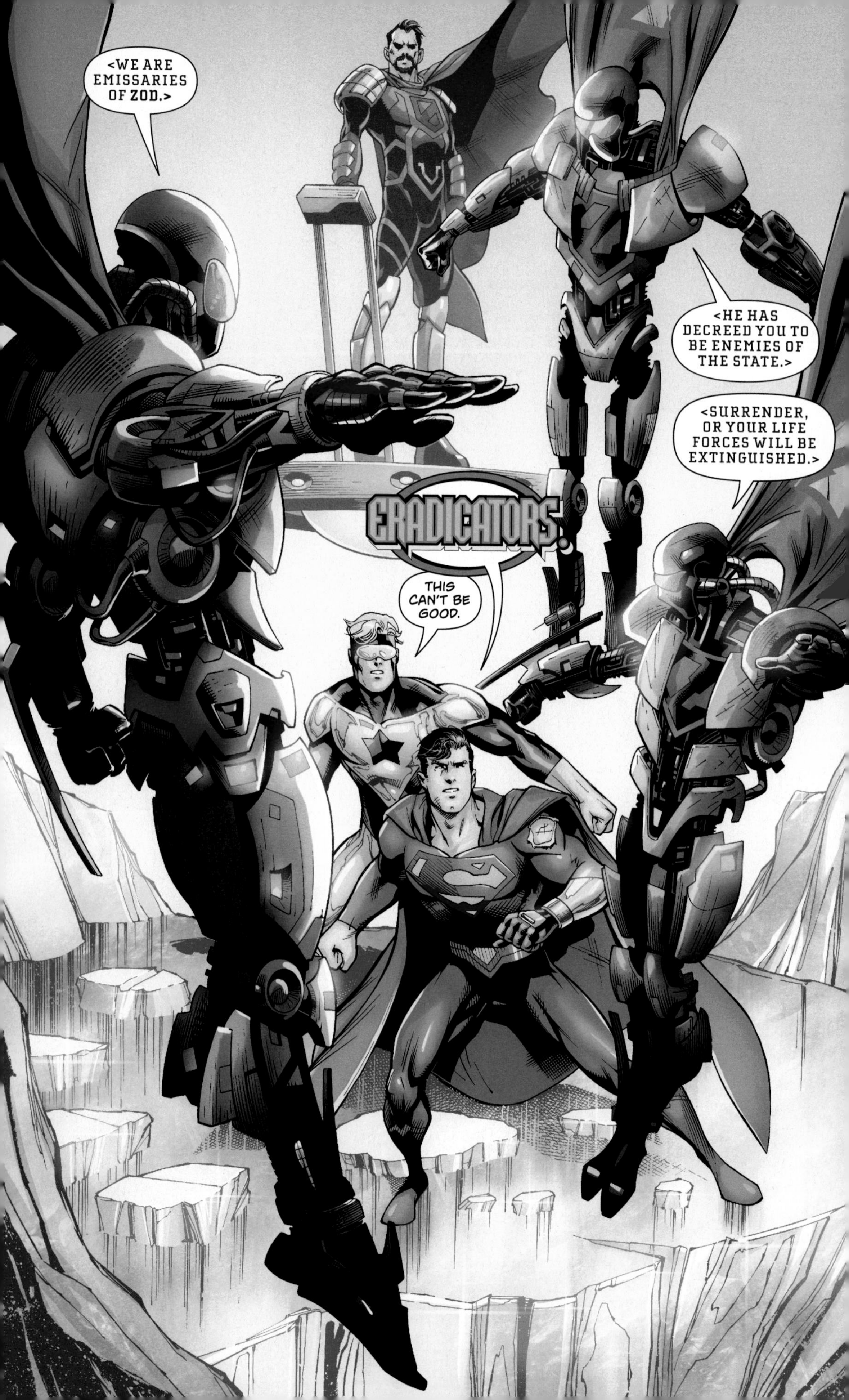
<WE ARE EMISSARIES OF ZOD.>
<HE HAS DECREED YOU TO BE ENEMIES OF THE STATE.>
<SURRENDER, OR YOUR LIFE FORCES WILL BE EXTINGUISHED.>
ERADICATORS.
THIS CAN'T BE GOOD.

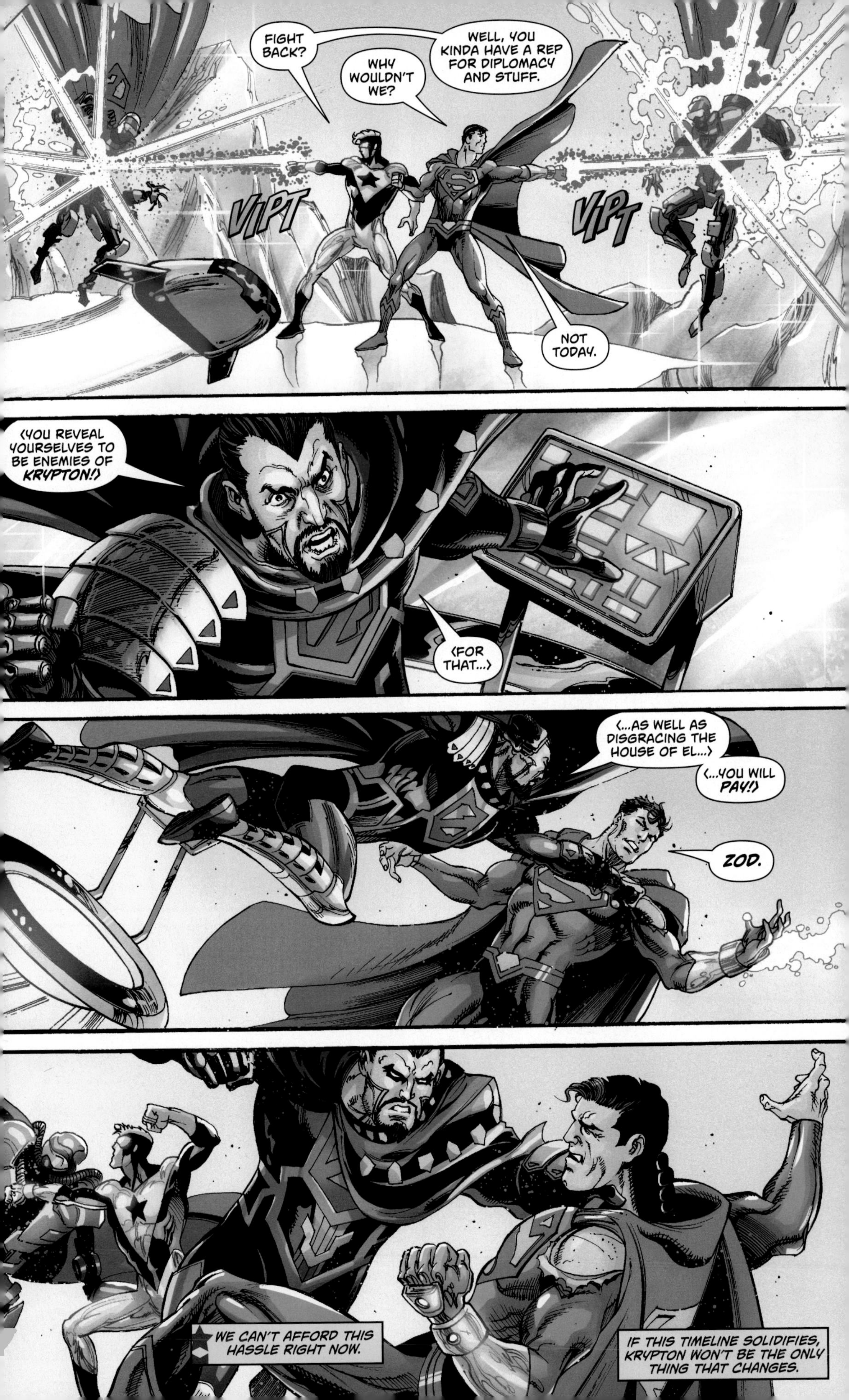
FIGHT BACK?
WHY WOULDN'T WE?
WELL, YOU KINDA HAVE A REP FOR DIPLOMACY AND STUFF.
VIPT
VIPT
NOT TODAY.
‹YOU REVEAL YOURSELVES TO BE ENEMIES OF KRYPTON!›
‹FOR THAT...›
‹...AS WELL AS DISGRACING THE HOUSE OF EL...›
‹...YOU WILL PAY!›
ZOD.
WE CAN'T AFFORD THIS HASSLE RIGHT NOW.
IF THIS TIMELINE SOLIDIFIES, KRYPTON WON'T BE THE ONLY THING THAT CHANGES.

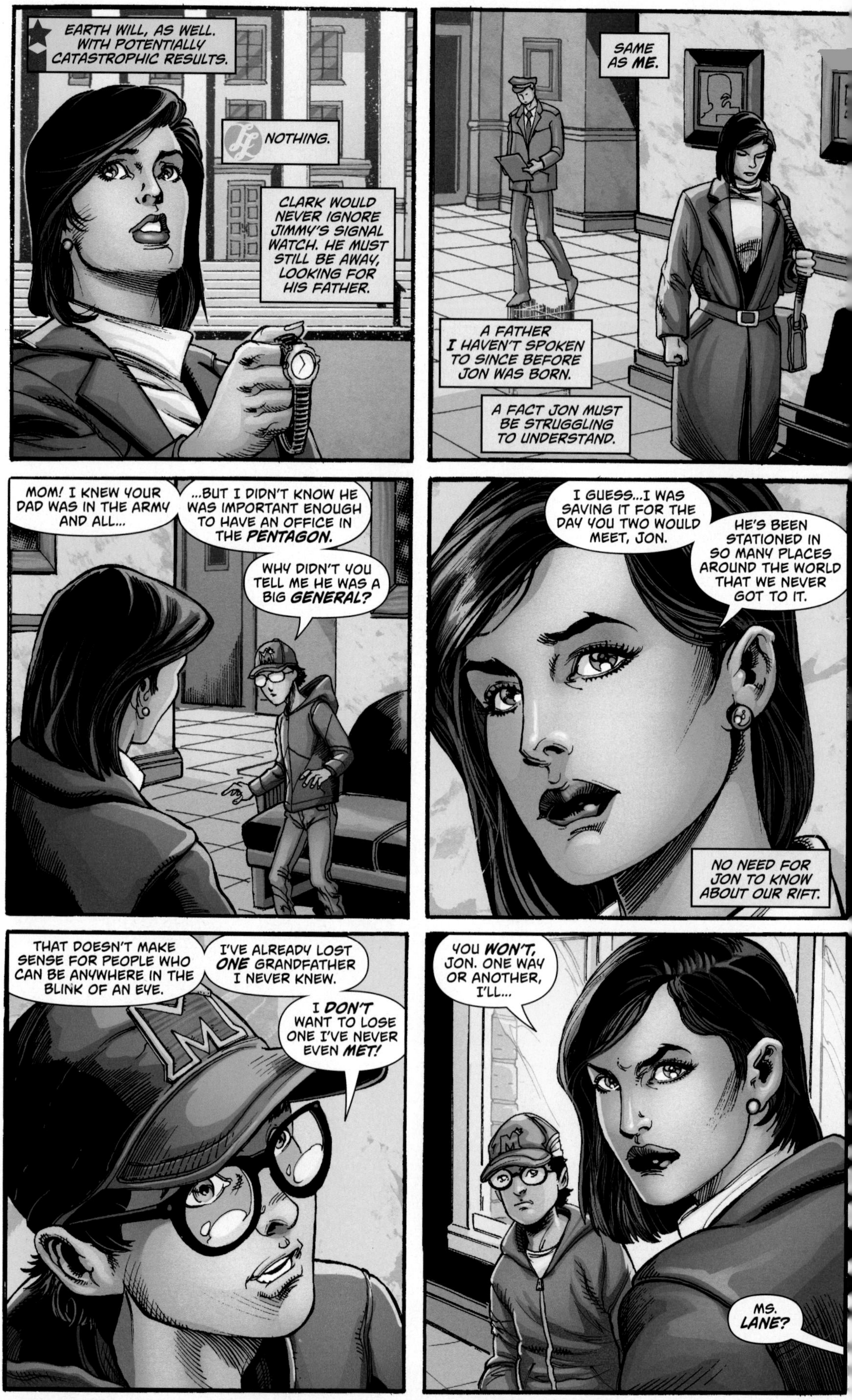
EARTH WILL, AS WELL. WITH POTENTIALLY CATASTROPHIC RESULTS.
NOTHING.
CLARK WOULD NEVER IGNORE JIMMY'S SIGNAL WATCH. HE MUST STILL BE AWAY, LOOKING FOR HIS FATHER.
SAME AS ME.
A FATHER I HAVEN'T SPOKEN TO SINCE BEFORE JON WAS BORN.
A FACT JON MUST BE STRUGGLING TO UNDERSTAND.
MOM! I KNEW YOUR DAD WAS IN THE ARMY AND ALL...
...BUT I DIDN'T KNOW HE WAS IMPORTANT ENOUGH TO HAVE AN OFFICE IN THE PENTAGON.
WHY DIDN'T YOU TELL ME HE WAS A BIG GENERAL?
I GUESS...I WAS SAVING IT FOR THE DAY YOU TWO WOULD MEET, JON.
HE'S BEEN STATIONED IN SO MANY PLACES AROUND THE WORLD THAT WE NEVER GOT TO IT.
NO NEED FOR JON TO KNOW ABOUT OUR RIFT.
THAT DOESN'T MAKE SENSE FOR PEOPLE WHO CAN BE ANYWHERE IN THE BLINK OF AN EYE.
I'VE ALREADY LOST ONE GRANDFATHER I NEVER KNEW.
I DON'T WANT TO LOSE ONE I'VE NEVER EVEN MET!
YOU WON'T, JON. ONE WAY OR ANOTHER, I'LL...
MS. LANE?

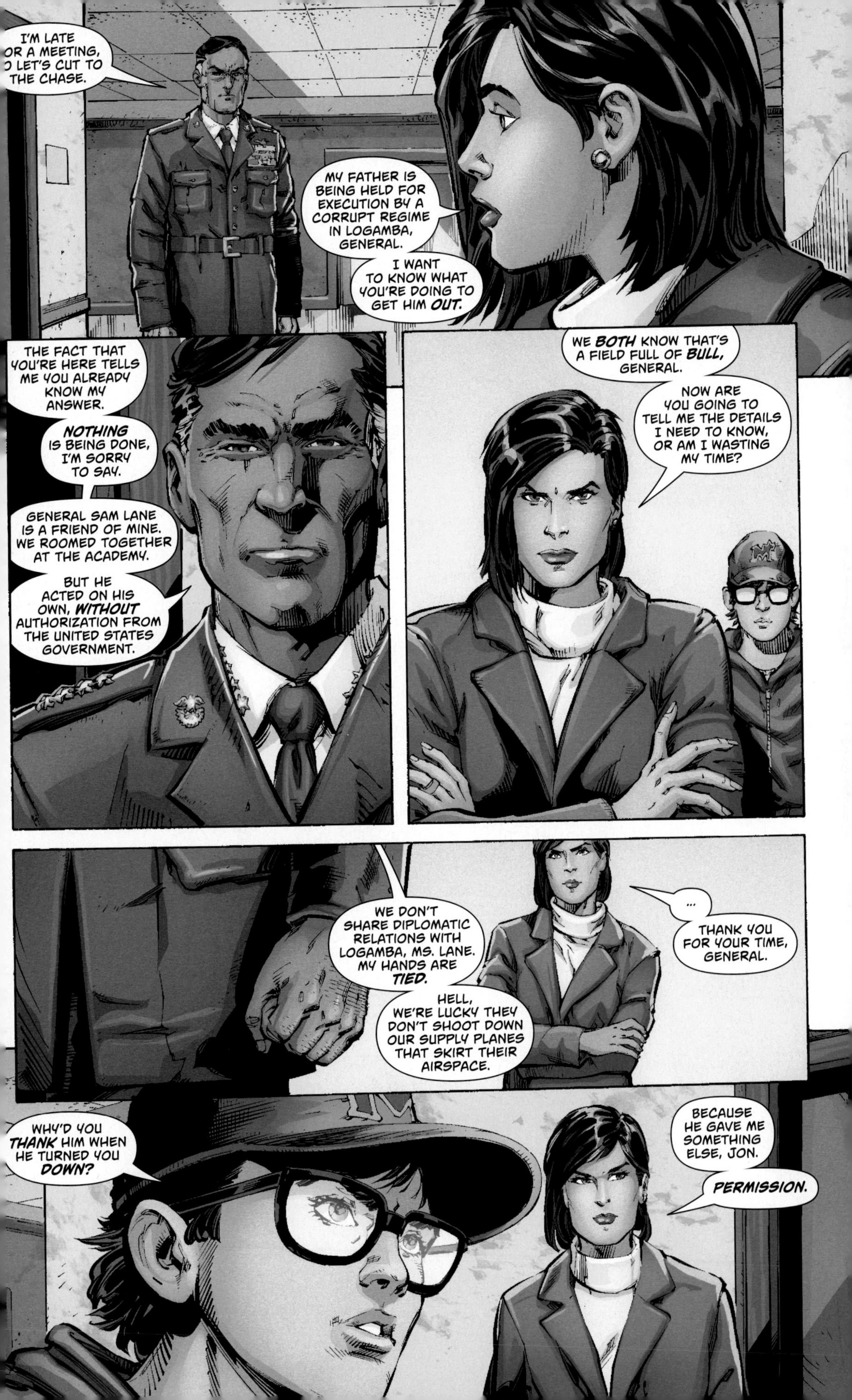

I'M LATE
OR A MEETING,
O LET'S CUT TO
THE CHASE.
MY FATHER IS BEING HELD FOR EXECUTION BY A CORRUPT REGIME IN LOGAMBA, GENERAL.
I WANT TO KNOW WHAT YOU'RE DOING TO GET HIM OUT.
THE FACT THAT YOU'RE HERE TELLS ME YOU ALREADY KNOW MY ANSWER.
NOTHING IS BEING DONE, I'M SORRY TO SAY.
GENERAL SAM LANE IS A FRIEND OF MINE. WE ROOMED TOGETHER AT THE ACADEMY.
BUT HE ACTED ON HIS OWN, WITHOUT AUTHORIZATION FROM THE UNITED STATES GOVERNMENT.
WE BOTH KNOW THAT'S A FIELD FULL OF BULL, GENERAL.
NOW ARE YOU GOING TO TELL ME THE DETAILS I NEED TO KNOW, OR AM I WASTING MY TIME?
WE DON'T SHARE DIPLOMATIC RELATIONS WITH LOGAMBA, MS. LANE. MY HANDS ARE TIED.
HELL, WE'RE LUCKY THEY DON'T SHOOT DOWN OUR SUPPLY PLANES THAT SKIRT THEIR AIRSPACE.
...
THANK YOU FOR YOUR TIME, GENERAL.
WHY'D YOU THANK HIM WHEN HE TURNED YOU DOWN?
BECAUSE HE GAVE ME SOMETHING ELSE, JON.
PERMISSION.

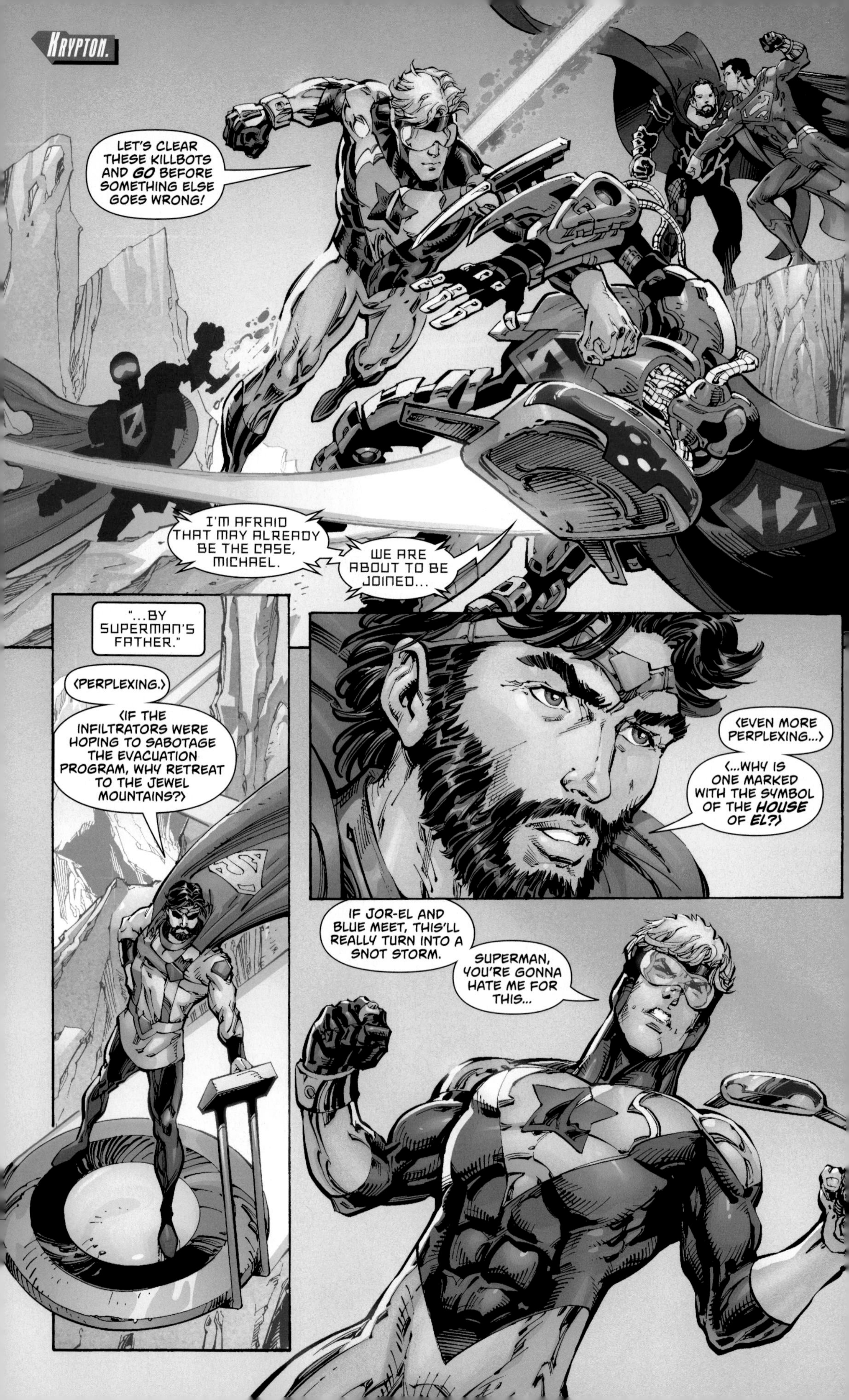
KRYPTON.
LET'S CLEAR THESE KILLBOTS AND GO BEFORE SOMETHING ELSE GOES WRONG!
I'M AFRAID THAT MAY ALREADY BE THE CASE, MICHAEL.
WE ARE ABOUT TO BE JOINED...
"...BY SUPERMAN'S FATHER."
‹PERPLEXING.›
‹IF THE INFILTRATORS WERE HOPING TO SABOTAGE THE EVACUATION PROGRAM, WHY RETREAT TO THE JEWEL MOUNTAINS?›
‹EVEN MORE PERPLEXING...›
‹...WHY IS ONE MARKED WITH THE SYMBOL OF THE HOUSE OF EL?›
IF JOR-EL AND BLUE MEET, THIS'LL REALLY TURN INTO A SNOT STORM.
SUPERMAN, YOU'RE GONNA HATE ME FOR THIS...

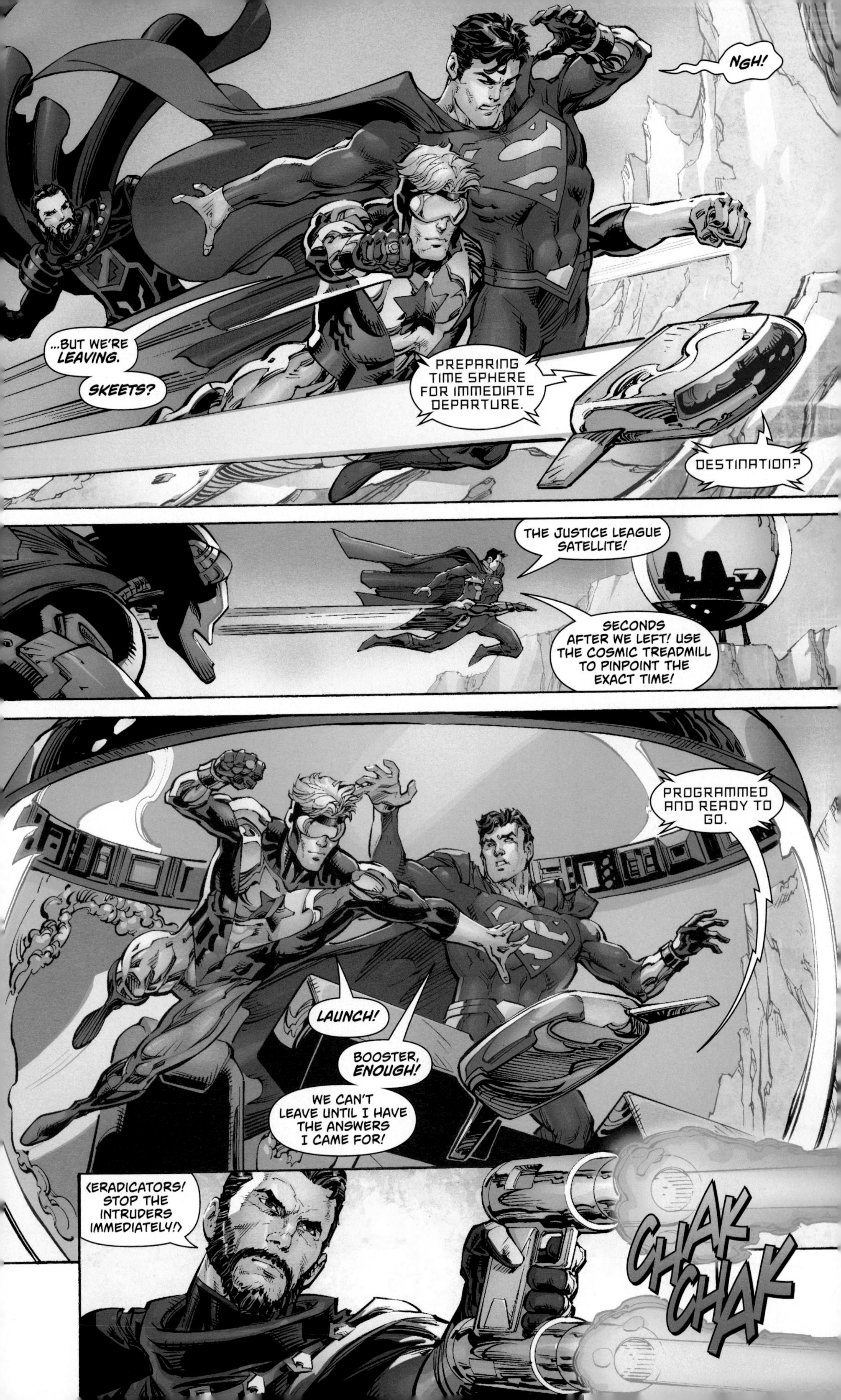
NGH!
...BUT WE'RE LEAVING.
SKEETS?
PREPARING TIME SPHERE FOR IMMEDIATE DEPARTURE.
DESTINATION?
THE JUSTICE LEAGUE SATELLITE!
SECONDS AFTER WE LEFT! USE THE COSMIC TREADMILL TO PINPOINT THE EXACT TIME!
PROGRAMMED AND READY TO GO.
LAUNCH!
BOOSTER, ENOUGH!
WE CAN'T LEAVE UNTIL I HAVE THE ANSWERS I CAME FOR!
‹ERADICATORS! STOP THE INTRUDERS IMMEDIATELY!›
CHAK CHAK

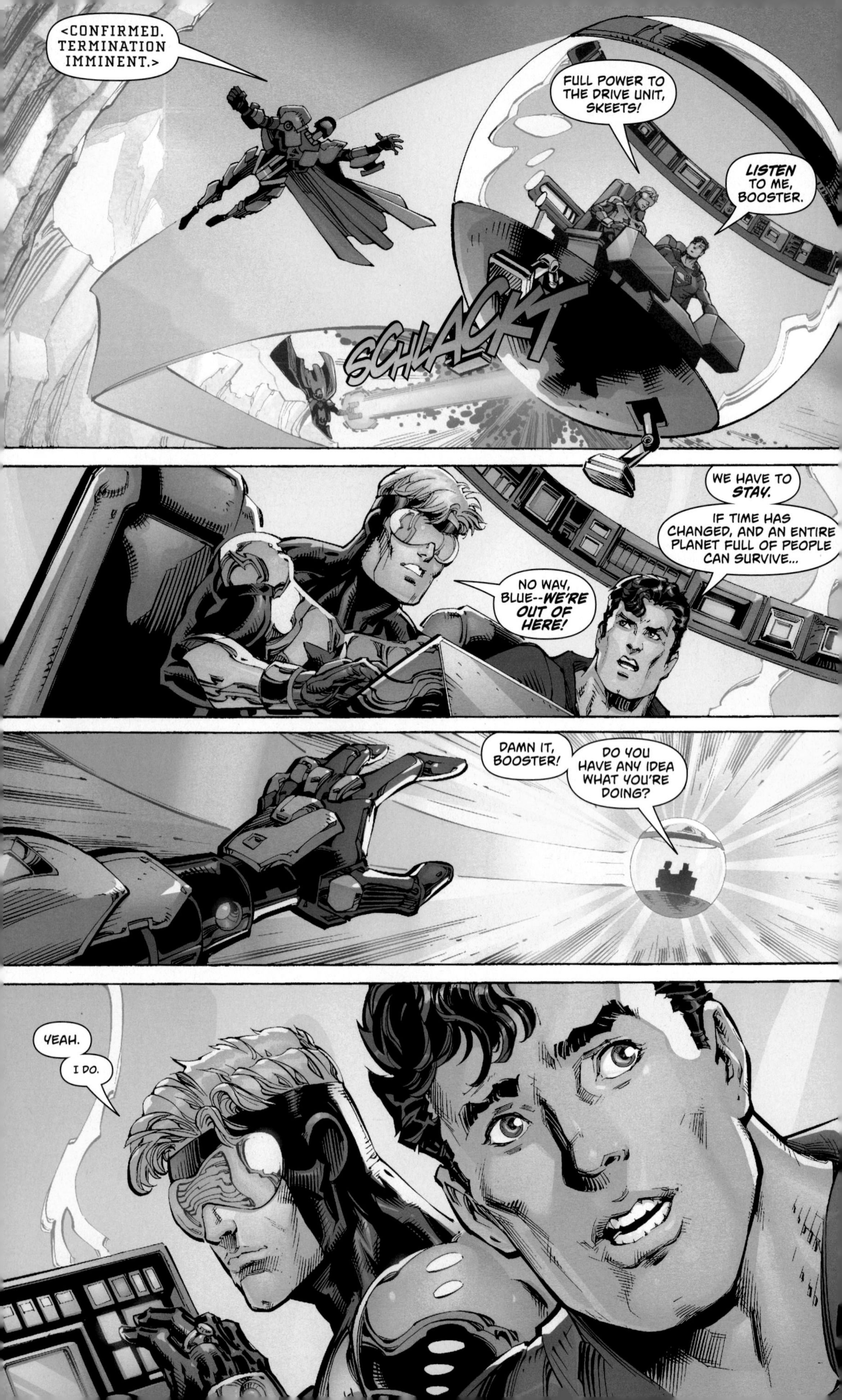
<CONFIRMED. TERMINATION IMMINENT.>
FULL POWER TO THE DRIVE UNIT, SKEETS!
LISTEN TO ME, BOOSTER.
SCHLACK!
WE HAVE TO STAY.
IF TIME HAS CHANGED, AND AN ENTIRE PLANET FULL OF PEOPLE CAN SURVIVE...
NO WAY, BLUE--WE'RE OUT OF HERE!
DAMN IT, BOOSTER!
DO YOU HAVE ANY IDEA WHAT YOU'RE DOING?
YEAH.
I DO.

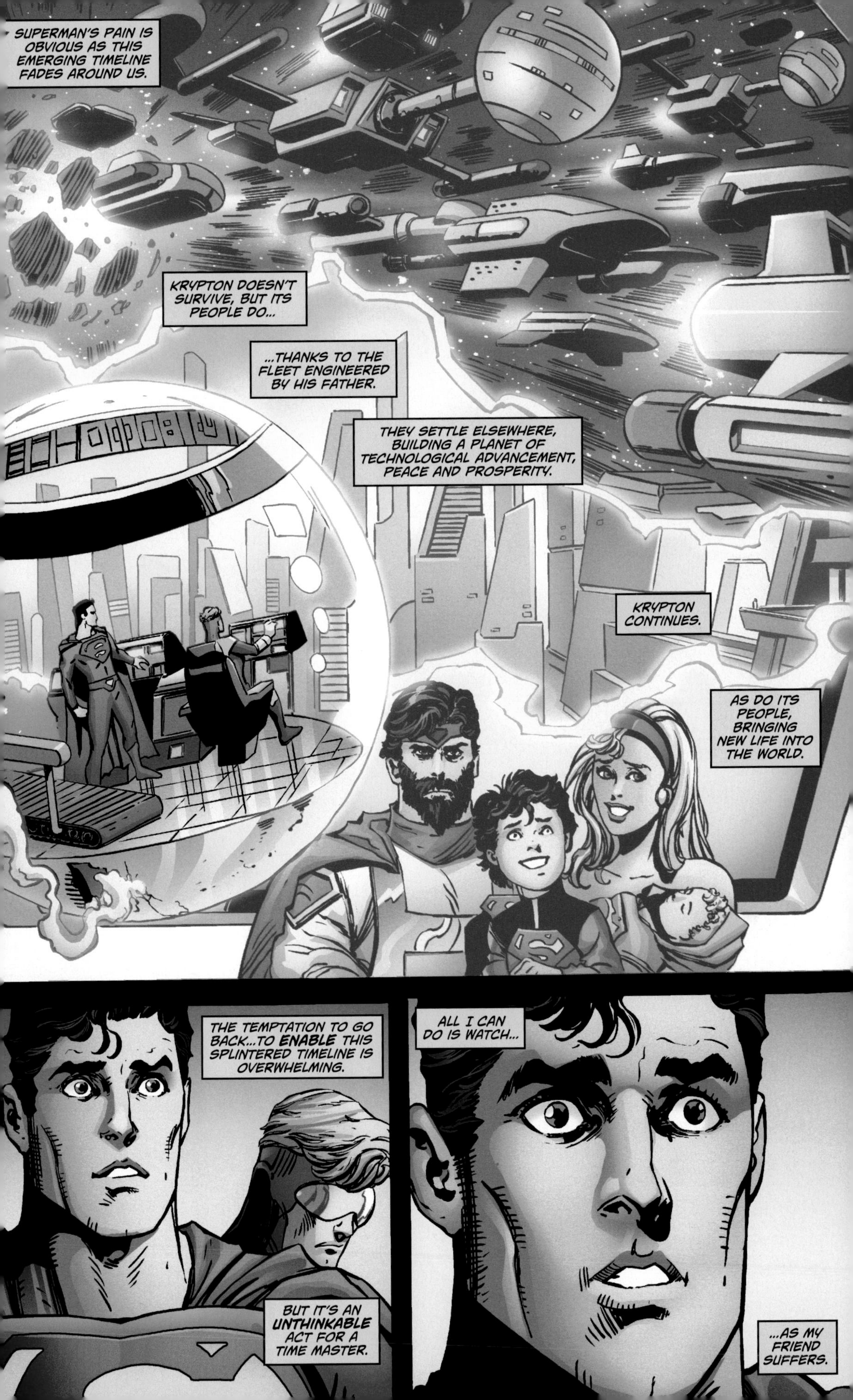
SUPERMAN'S PAIN IS OBVIOUS AS THIS EMERGING TIMELINE FADES AROUND US.
KRYPTON DOESN'T SURVIVE, BUT ITS PEOPLE DO...
...THANKS TO THE FLEET ENGINEERED BY HIS FATHER.
THEY SETTLE ELSEWHERE, BUILDING A PLANET OF TECHNOLOGICAL ADVANCEMENT, PEACE AND PROSPERITY.
KRYPTON CONTINUES.
AS DO ITS PEOPLE, BRINGING NEW LIFE INTO THE WORLD.
THE TEMPTATION TO GO BACK...TO **ENABLE** THIS SPLINTERED TIMELINE IS OVERWHELMING.
BUT IT'S AN ***UNTHINKABLE*** ACT FOR A TIME MASTER.
ALL I CAN DO IS WATCH...
...AS MY FRIEND SUFFERS.

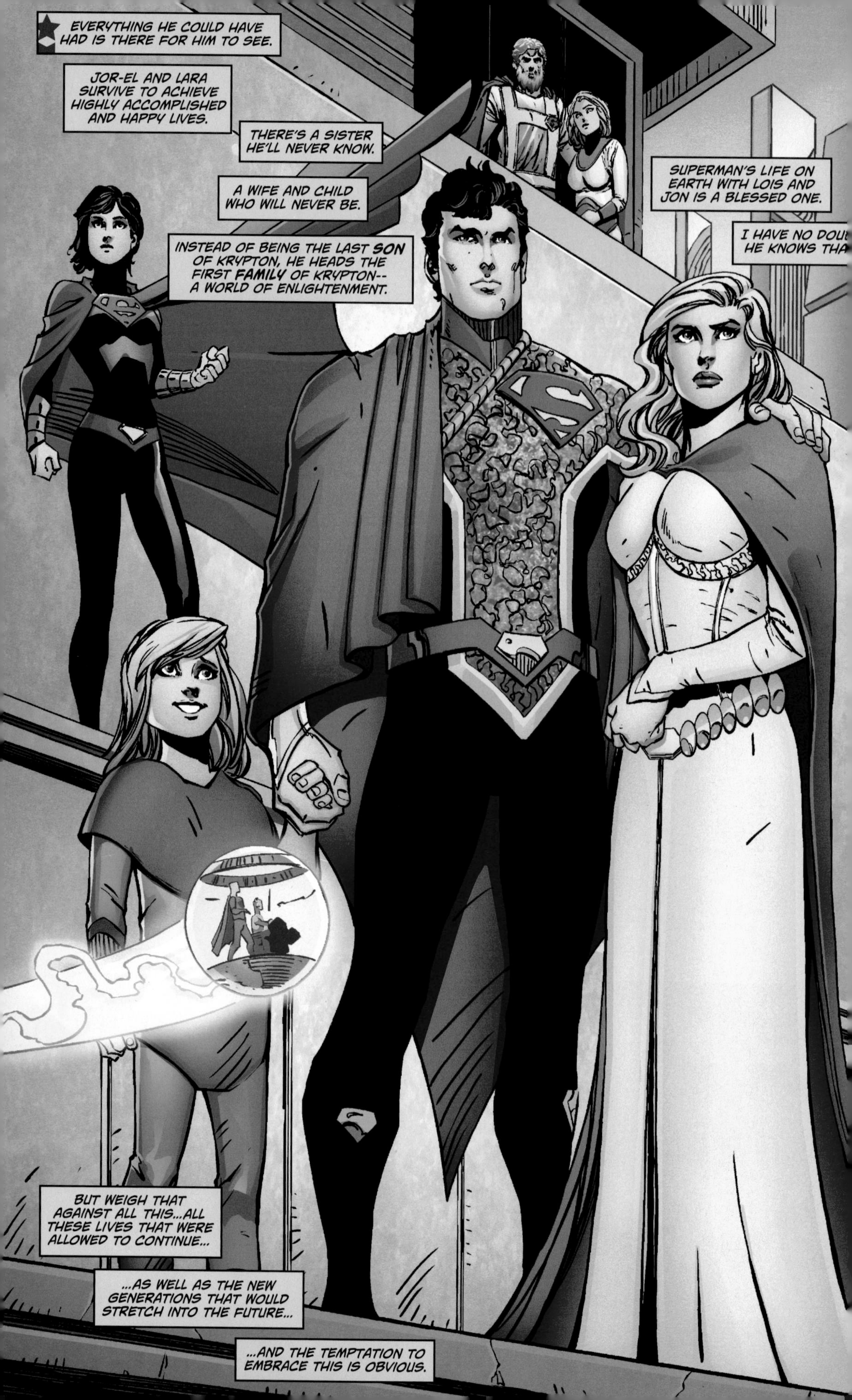
EVERYTHING HE COULD HAVE HAD IS THERE FOR HIM TO SEE.
JOR-EL AND LARA SURVIVE TO ACHIEVE HIGHLY ACCOMPLISHED AND HAPPY LIVES.
THERE'S A SISTER HE'LL NEVER KNOW.
A WIFE AND CHILD WHO WILL NEVER BE.
INSTEAD OF BEING THE LAST SON OF KRYPTON, HE HEADS THE FIRST FAMILY OF KRYPTON-- A WORLD OF ENLIGHTENMENT.
SUPERMAN'S LIFE ON EARTH WITH LOIS AND JON IS A BLESSED ONE.
I HAVE NO DOU HE KNOWS THA
BUT WEIGH THAT AGAINST ALL THIS...ALL THESE LIVES THAT WERE ALLOWED TO CONTINUE...
...AS WELL AS THE NEW GENERATIONS THAT WOULD STRETCH INTO THE FUTURE...
...AND THE TEMPTATION TO EMBRACE THIS IS OBVIOUS.

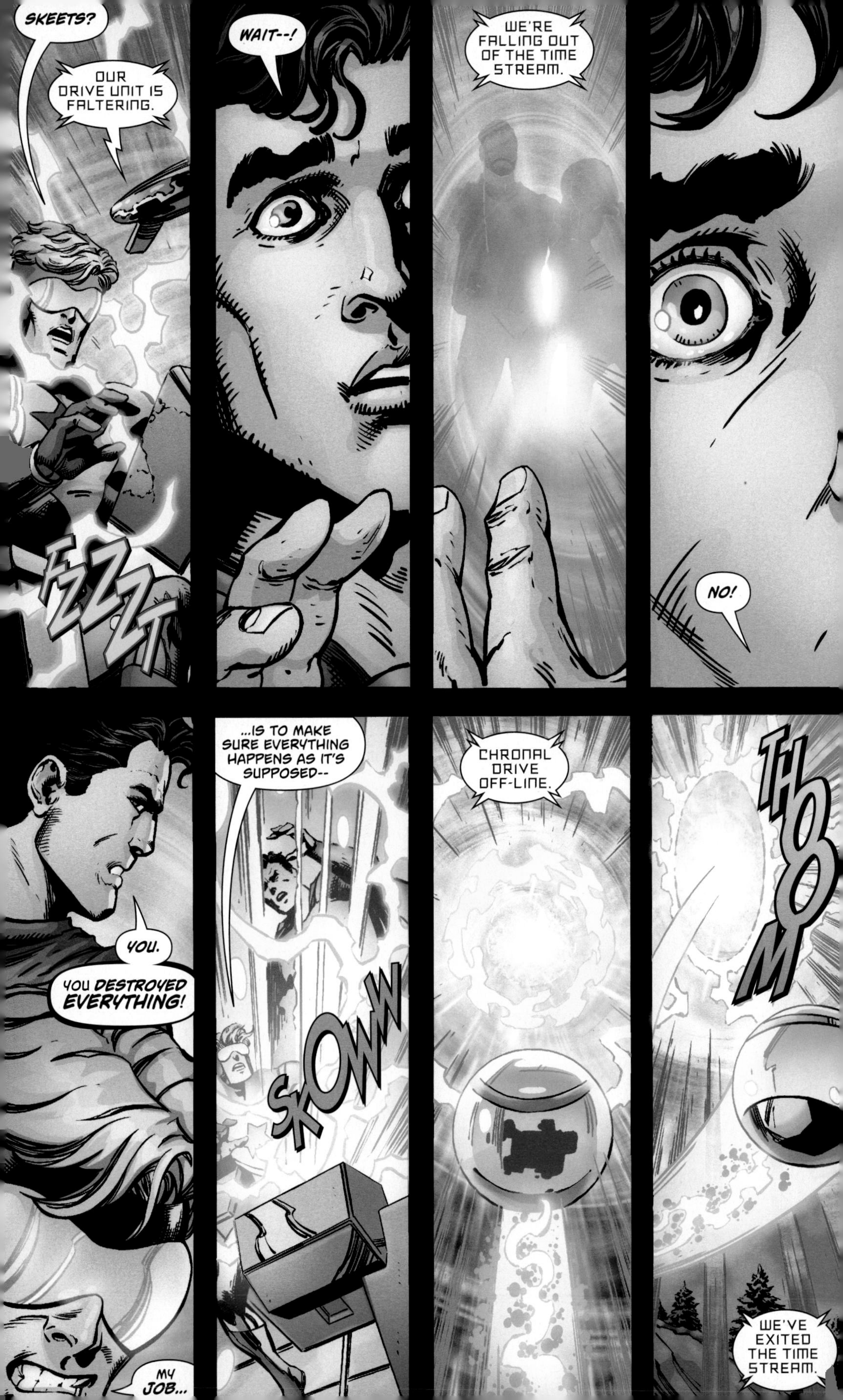
SKEETS?
OUR DRIVE UNIT IS FALTERING.
FZZZZT
WAIT--!
WE'RE FALLING OUT OF THE TIME STREAM.
NO!
YOU.
YOU DESTROYED EVERYTHING!
MY JOB...
...IS TO MAKE SURE EVERYTHING HAPPENS AS IT'S SUPPOSED--
SKOWW
CHRONAL DRIVE OFF-LINE.
THOOM
WE'VE EXITED THE TIME STREAM.

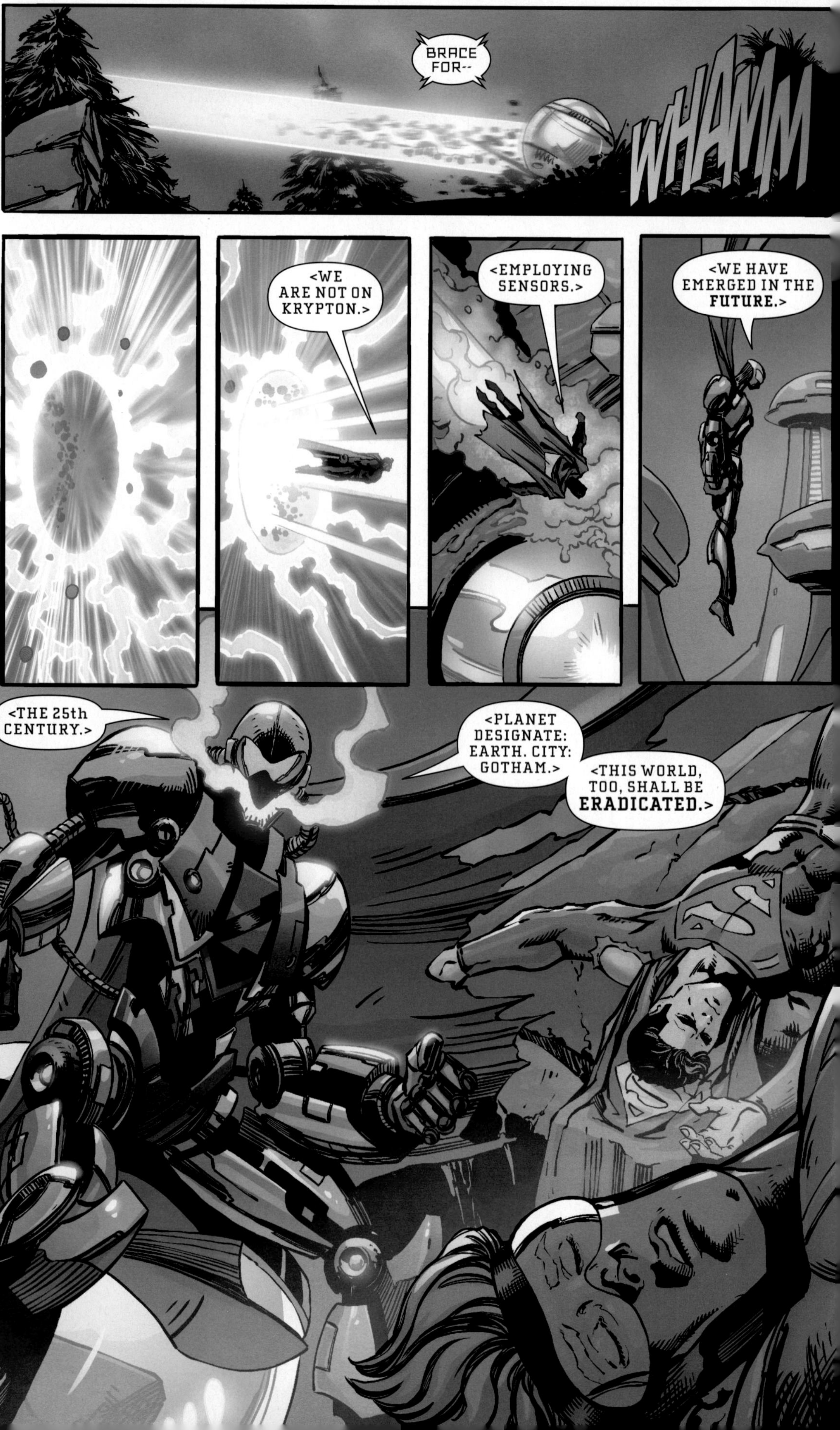
BRACE FOR--
WHAMM
<WE ARE NOT ON KRYPTON.>
<EMPLOYING SENSORS.>
<WE HAVE EMERGED IN THE FUTURE.>
<THE 25th CENTURY.>
<PLANET DESIGNATE: EARTH. CITY: GOTHAM.>
<THIS WORLD, TOO, SHALL BE ERADICATED.>

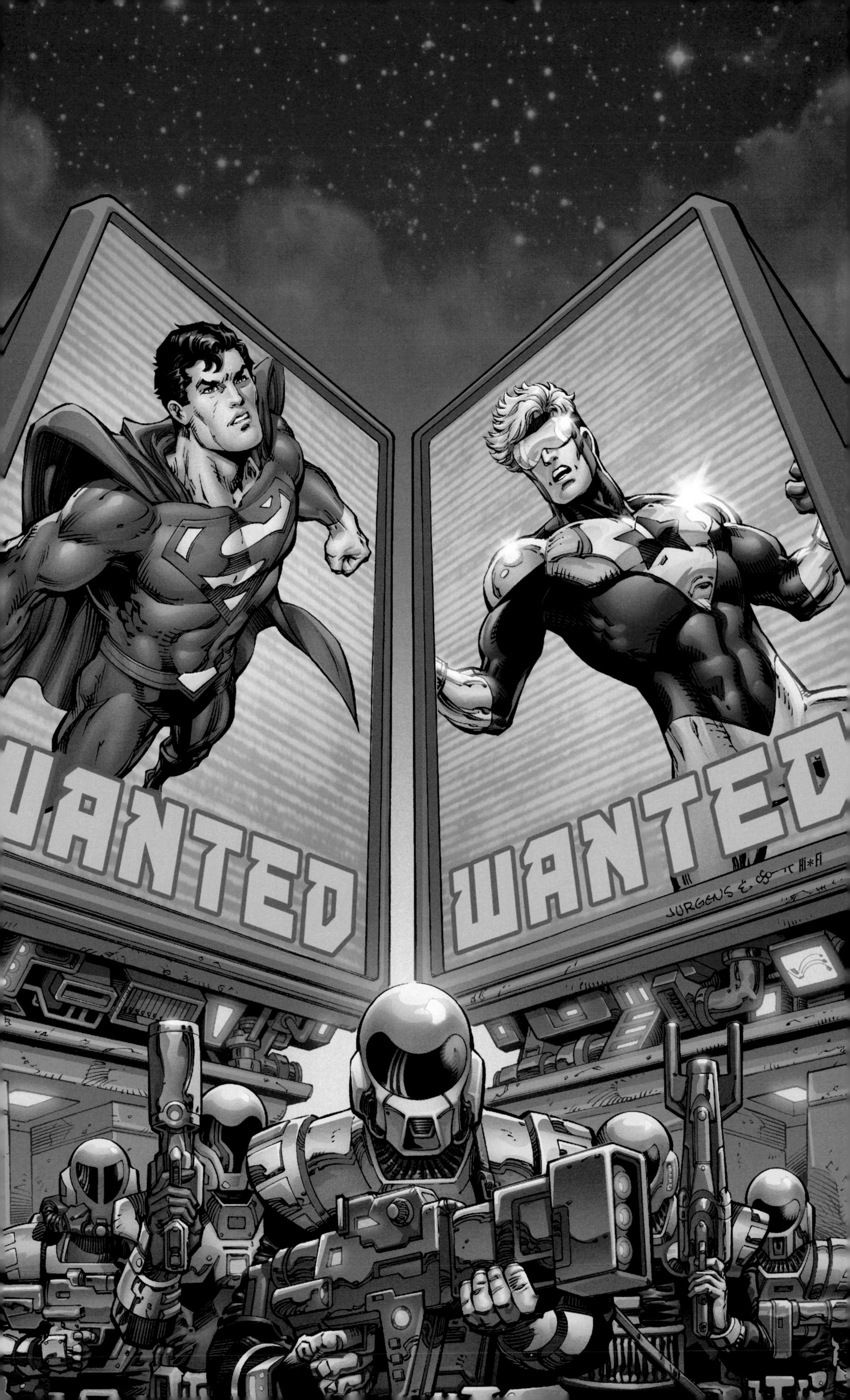
WANTED
JURGENS
Hi*Fi

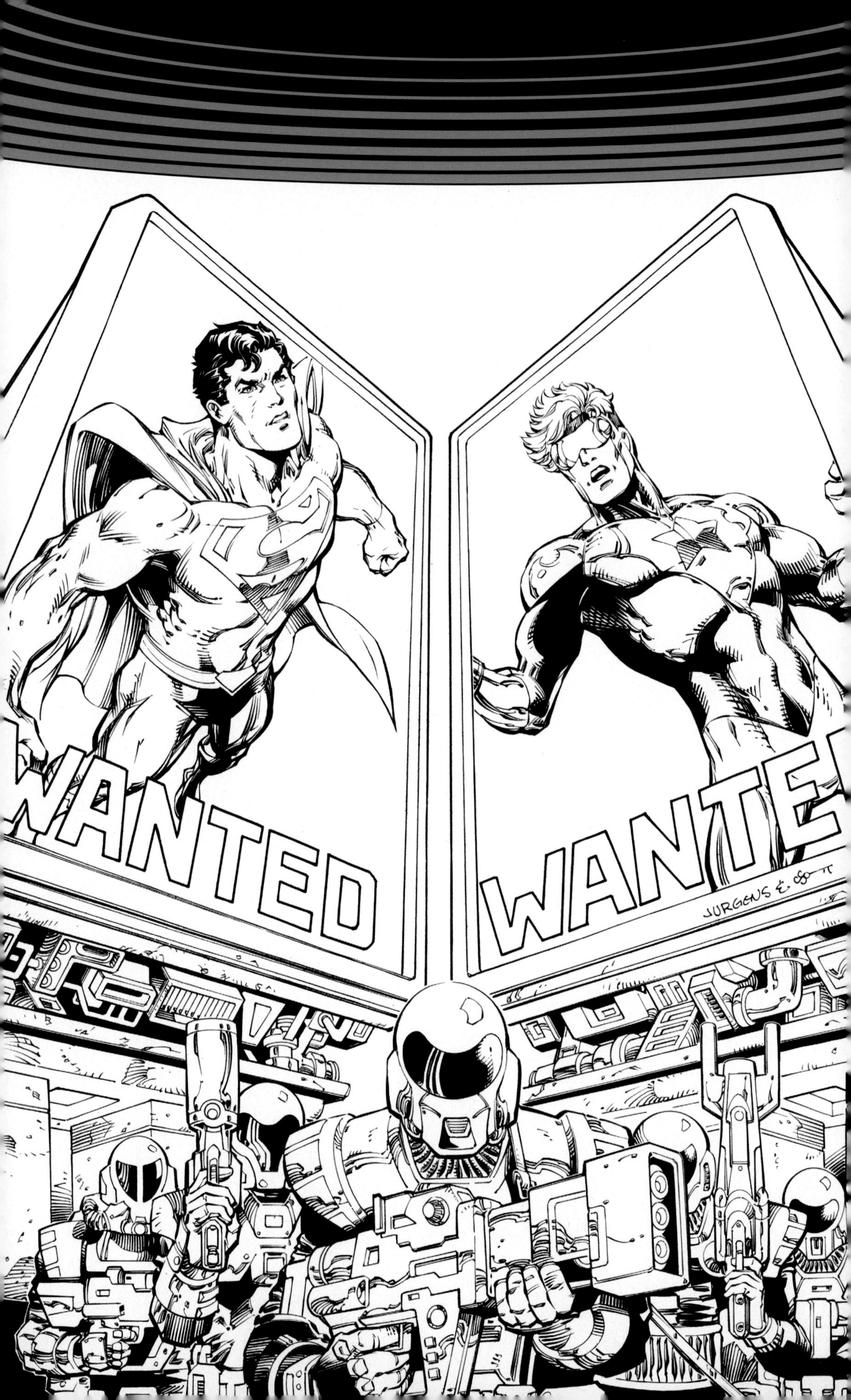
WANTED
WANTE
JURGENS

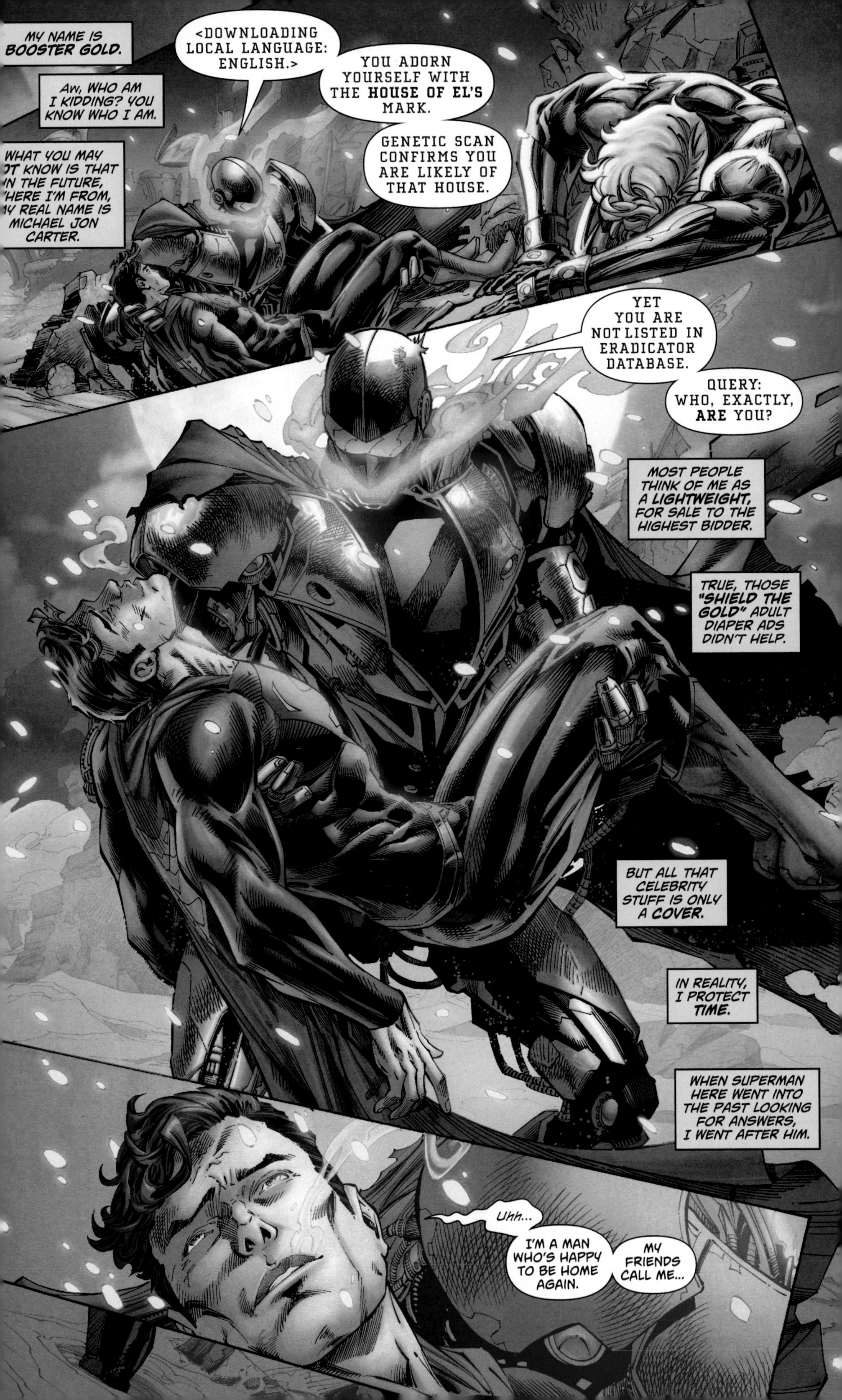
MY NAME IS BOOSTER GOLD.
<DOWNLOADING LOCAL LANGUAGE: ENGLISH.>
YOU ADORN YOURSELF WITH THE HOUSE OF EL'S MARK.
AW, WHO AM I KIDDING? YOU KNOW WHO I AM.
GENETIC SCAN CONFIRMS YOU ARE LIKELY OF THAT HOUSE.
YET YOU ARE NOT LISTED IN ERADICATOR DATABASE.
QUERY: WHO, EXACTLY, ARE YOU?
MOST PEOPLE THINK OF ME AS A LIGHTWEIGHT, FOR SALE TO THE HIGHEST BIDDER.
TRUE, THOSE "SHIELD THE GOLD" ADULT DIAPER ADS DIDN'T HELP.
BUT ALL THAT CELEBRITY STUFF IS ONLY A COVER.
IN REALITY, I PROTECT TIME.
WHEN SUPERMAN HERE WENT INTO THE PAST LOOKING FOR ANSWERS, I WENT AFTER HIM.
Uhh...
I'M A MAN WHO'S HAPPY TO BE HOME AGAIN.
MY FRIENDS CALL ME...

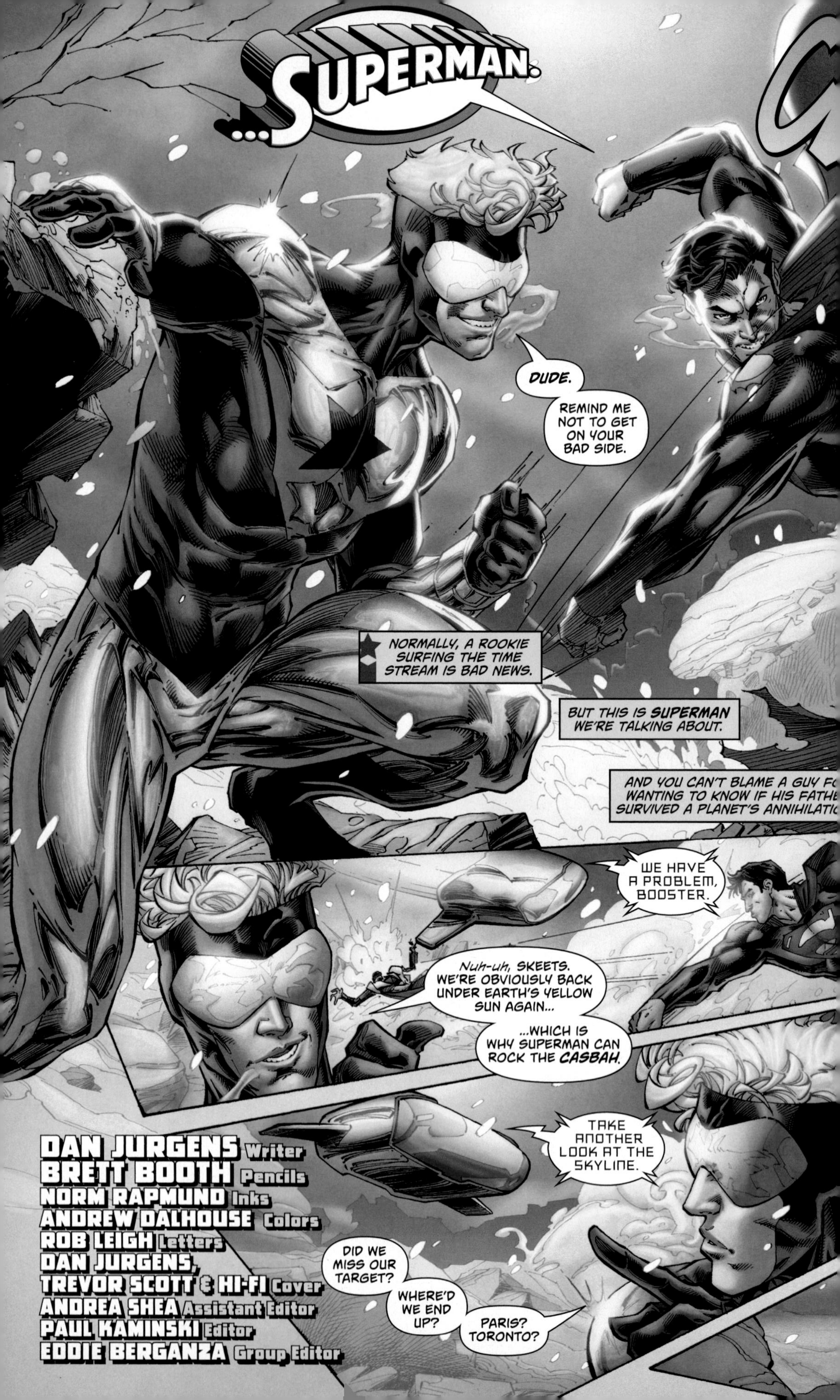

...SUPERMAN.
DUDE.
REMIND ME NOT TO GET ON YOUR BAD SIDE.
NORMALLY, A ROOKIE SURFING THE TIME STREAM IS BAD NEWS.
BUT THIS IS SUPERMAN WE'RE TALKING ABOUT.
AND YOU CAN'T BLAME A GUY F
WANTING TO KNOW IF HIS FATH
SURVIVED A PLANET'S ANNIHILATI
WE HAVE A PROBLEM, BOOSTER.
Nuh-uh, SKEETS. WE'RE OBVIOUSLY BACK UNDER EARTH'S YELLOW SUN AGAIN...
...WHICH IS WHY SUPERMAN CAN ROCK THE CASBAH.
TAKE ANOTHER LOOK AT THE SKYLINE.
DID WE MISS OUR TARGET?
WHERE'D WE END UP?
PARIS? TORONTO?
DAN JURGENS Writer
BRETT BOOTH Pencils
NORM RAPMUND Inks
ANDREW DALHOUSE Colors
ROB LEIGH Letters
DAN JURGENS, TREVOR SCOTT & HI-FI Cover
ANDREA SHEA Assistant Editor
PAUL KAMINSKI Editor
EDDIE BERGANZA Group Editor

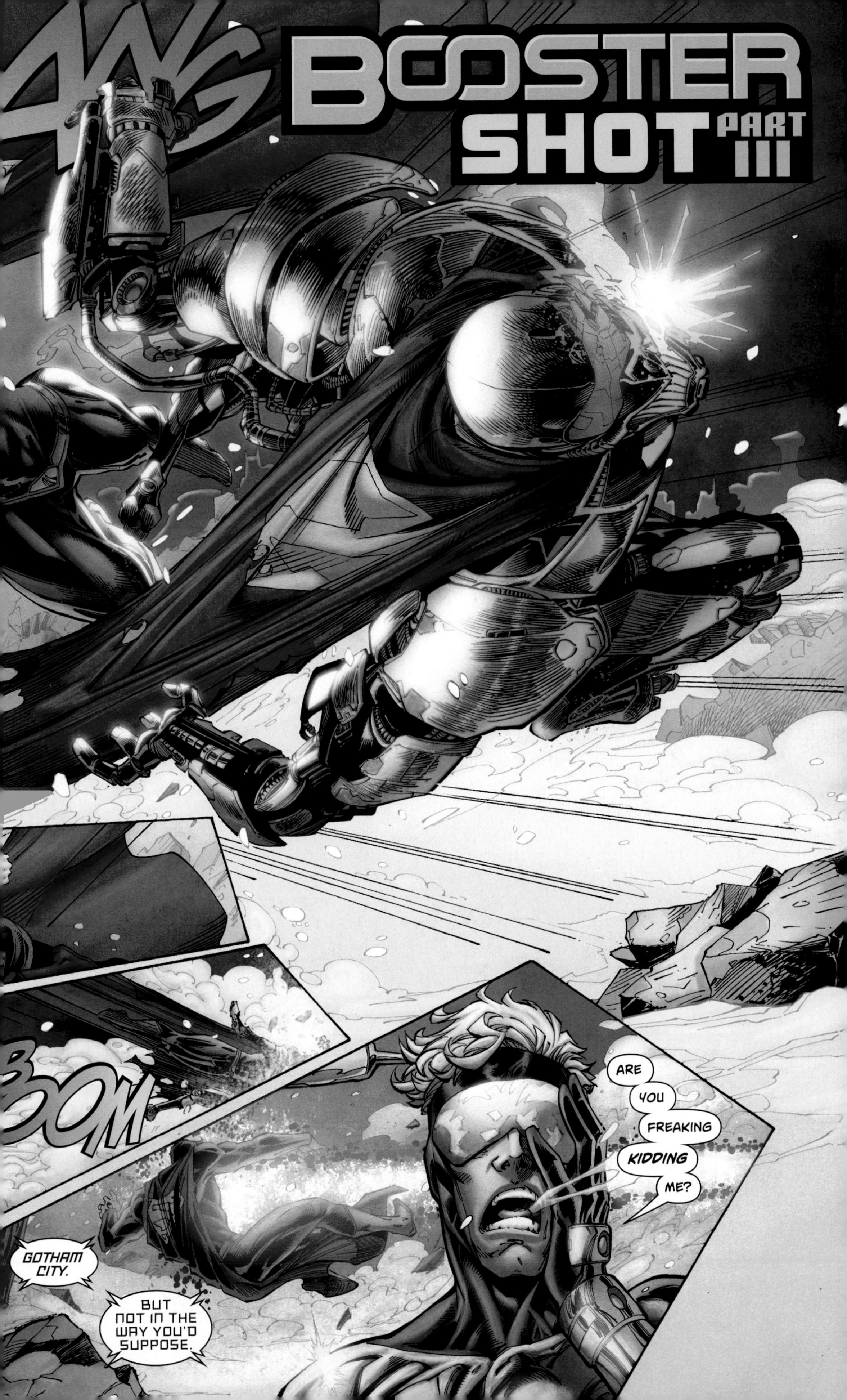

BOOSTER SHOT PART III
ARE YOU FREAKING KIDDING ME?
GOTHAM CITY.
BUT NOT IN THE WAY YOU'D SUPPOSE.

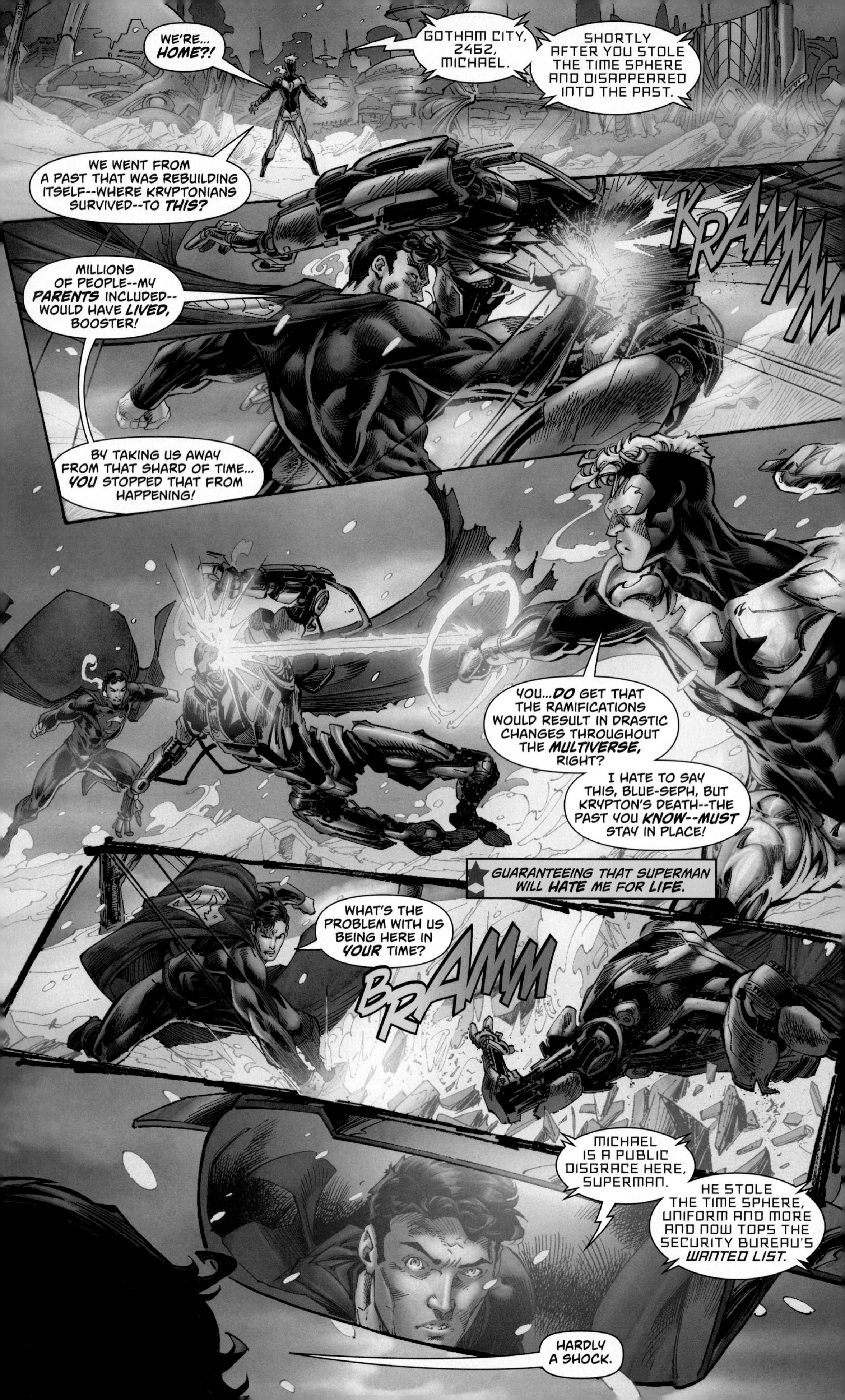
WE'RE... HOME?!
GOTHAM CITY, 2462, MICHAEL.
SHORTLY AFTER YOU STOLE THE TIME SPHERE AND DISAPPEARED INTO THE PAST.
WE WENT FROM A PAST THAT WAS REBUILDING ITSELF--WHERE KRYPTONIANS SURVIVED--TO THIS?
KRAMMM
MILLIONS OF PEOPLE--MY PARENTS INCLUDED--WOULD HAVE LIVED, BOOSTER!
BY TAKING US AWAY FROM THAT SHARD OF TIME... YOU STOPPED THAT FROM HAPPENING!
YOU...DO GET THAT THE RAMIFICATIONS WOULD RESULT IN DRASTIC CHANGES THROUGHOUT THE MULTIVERSE, RIGHT?
I HATE TO SAY THIS, BLUE-SEPH, BUT KRYPTON'S DEATH--THE PAST YOU KNOW--MUST STAY IN PLACE!
GUARANTEEING THAT SUPERMAN WILL HATE ME FOR LIFE.
WHAT'S THE PROBLEM WITH US BEING HERE IN YOUR TIME?
BRAMM
MICHAEL IS A PUBLIC DISGRACE HERE, SUPERMAN.
HE STOLE THE TIME SPHERE, UNIFORM AND MORE AND NOW TOPS THE SECURITY BUREAU'S WANTED LIST.
HARDLY A SHOCK.

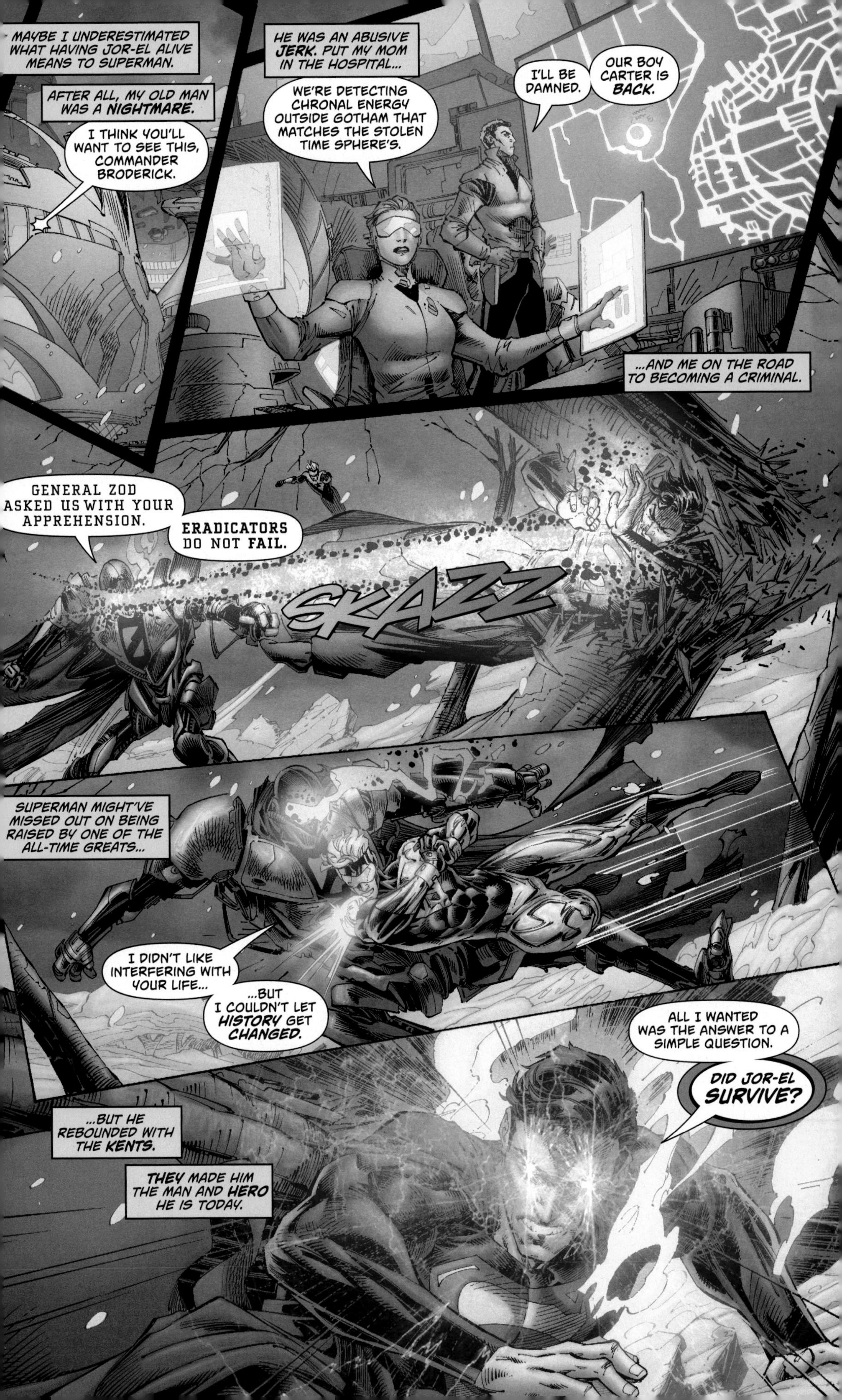
MAYBE I UNDERESTIMATED WHAT HAVING JOR-EL ALIVE MEANS TO SUPERMAN.
AFTER ALL, MY OLD MAN WAS A NIGHTMARE.
I THINK YOU'LL WANT TO SEE THIS, COMMANDER BRODERICK.
HE WAS AN ABUSIVE JERK. PUT MY MOM IN THE HOSPITAL...
WE'RE DETECTING CHRONAL ENERGY OUTSIDE GOTHAM THAT MATCHES THE STOLEN TIME SPHERE'S.
I'LL BE DAMNED.
OUR BOY CARTER IS BACK.
...AND ME ON THE ROAD TO BECOMING A CRIMINAL.
GENERAL ZOD ASKED US WITH YOUR APPREHENSION.
ERADICATORS DO NOT FAIL.
SKAZZ
SUPERMAN MIGHT'VE MISSED OUT ON BEING RAISED BY ONE OF THE ALL-TIME GREATS...
I DIDN'T LIKE INTERFERING WITH YOUR LIFE...
...BUT I COULDN'T LET HISTORY GET CHANGED.
ALL I WANTED WAS THE ANSWER TO A SIMPLE QUESTION.
DID JOR-EL SURVIVE?
...BUT HE REBOUNDED WITH THE KENTS.
THEY MADE HIM THE MAN AND HERO HE IS TODAY.

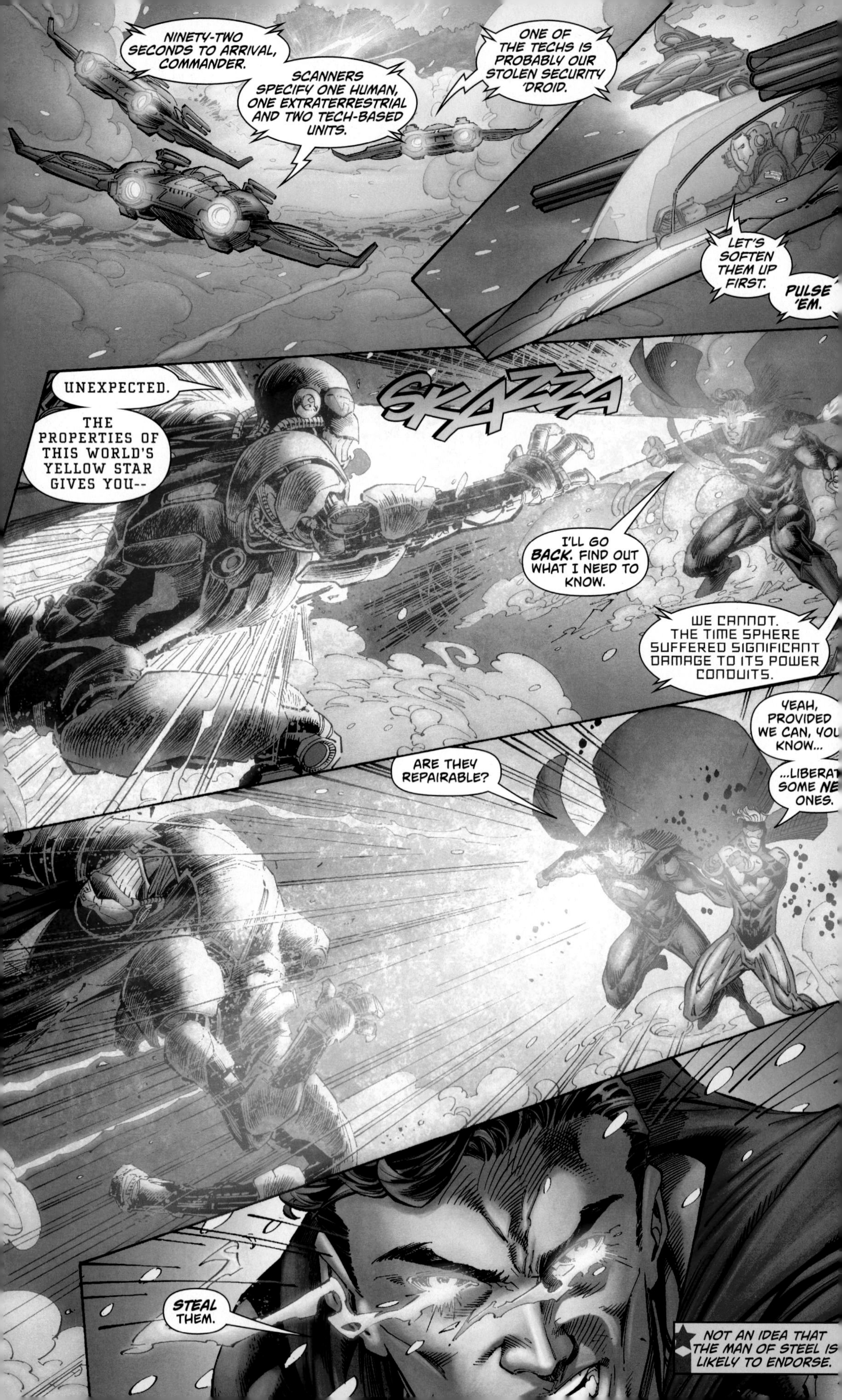
NINETY-TWO SECONDS TO ARRIVAL, COMMANDER.
SCANNERS SPECIFY ONE HUMAN, ONE EXTRATERRESTRIAL AND TWO TECH-BASED UNITS.
ONE OF THE TECHS IS PROBABLY OUR STOLEN SECURITY 'DROID.
LET'S SOFTEN THEM UP FIRST.
PULSE 'EM.
SKAZZA
UNEXPECTED.
THE PROPERTIES OF THIS WORLD'S YELLOW STAR GIVES YOU--
I'LL GO BACK. FIND OUT WHAT I NEED TO KNOW.
WE CANNOT. THE TIME SPHERE SUFFERED SIGNIFICANT DAMAGE TO ITS POWER CONDUITS.
ARE THEY REPAIRABLE?
YEAH, PROVIDED WE CAN, YOU KNOW...
STEAL THEM.
NOT AN IDEA THAT THE MAN OF STEEL IS LIKELY TO ENDORSE.

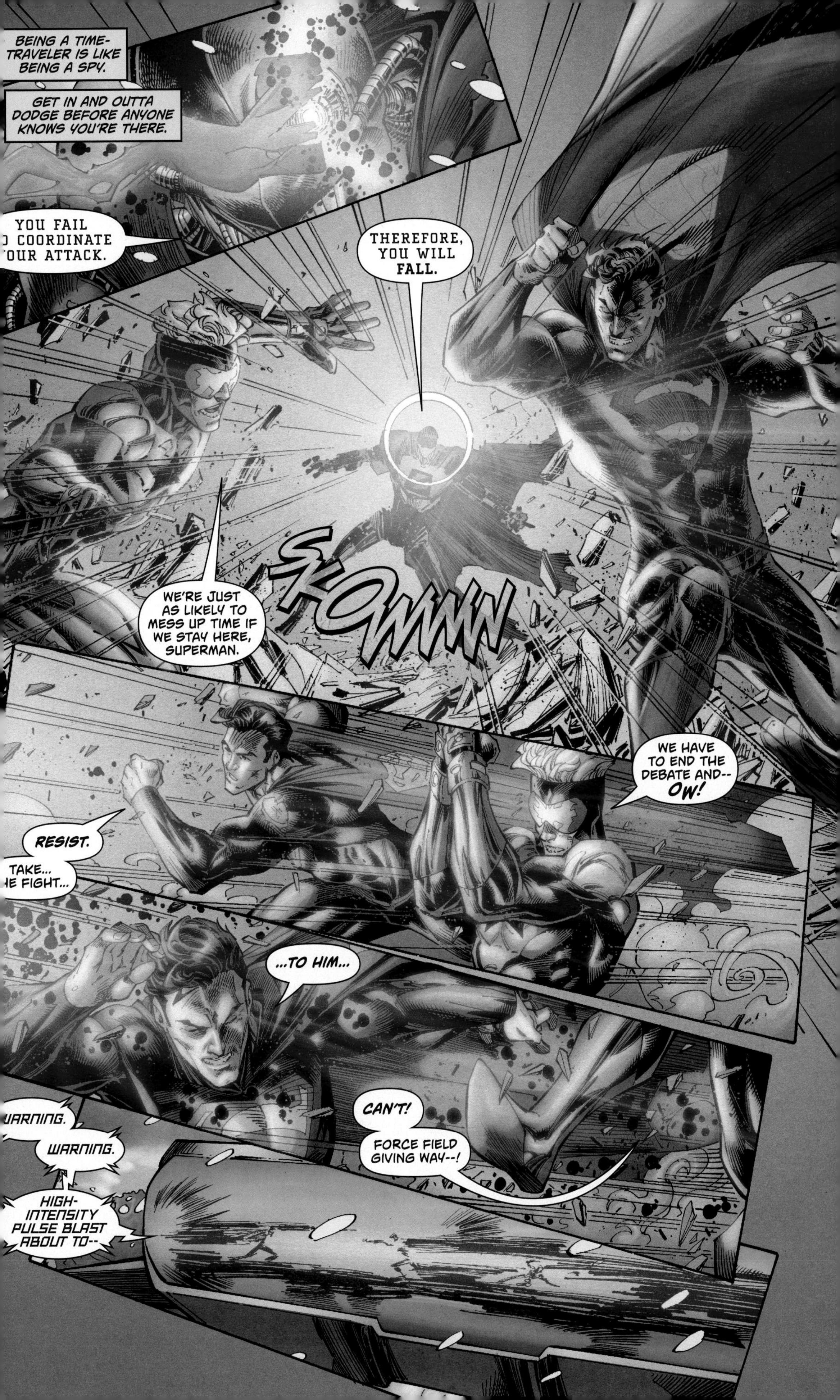
BEING A TIME-TRAVELER IS LIKE BEING A SPY.
GET IN AND OUTTA DODGE BEFORE ANYONE KNOWS YOU'RE THERE.
YOU FAIL
O COORDINATE
OUR ATTACK.
THEREFORE, YOU WILL FALL.
WE'RE JUST AS LIKELY TO MESS UP TIME IF WE STAY HERE, SUPERMAN.
SKOMMN
WE HAVE TO END THE DEBATE AND-- OW!
RESIST.
TAKE...
E FIGHT...
...TO HIM...
CAN'T!
FORCE FIELD GIVING WAY--!
ARNING.
WARNING.
HIGH-INTENSITY PULSE BLAST ABOUT TO--

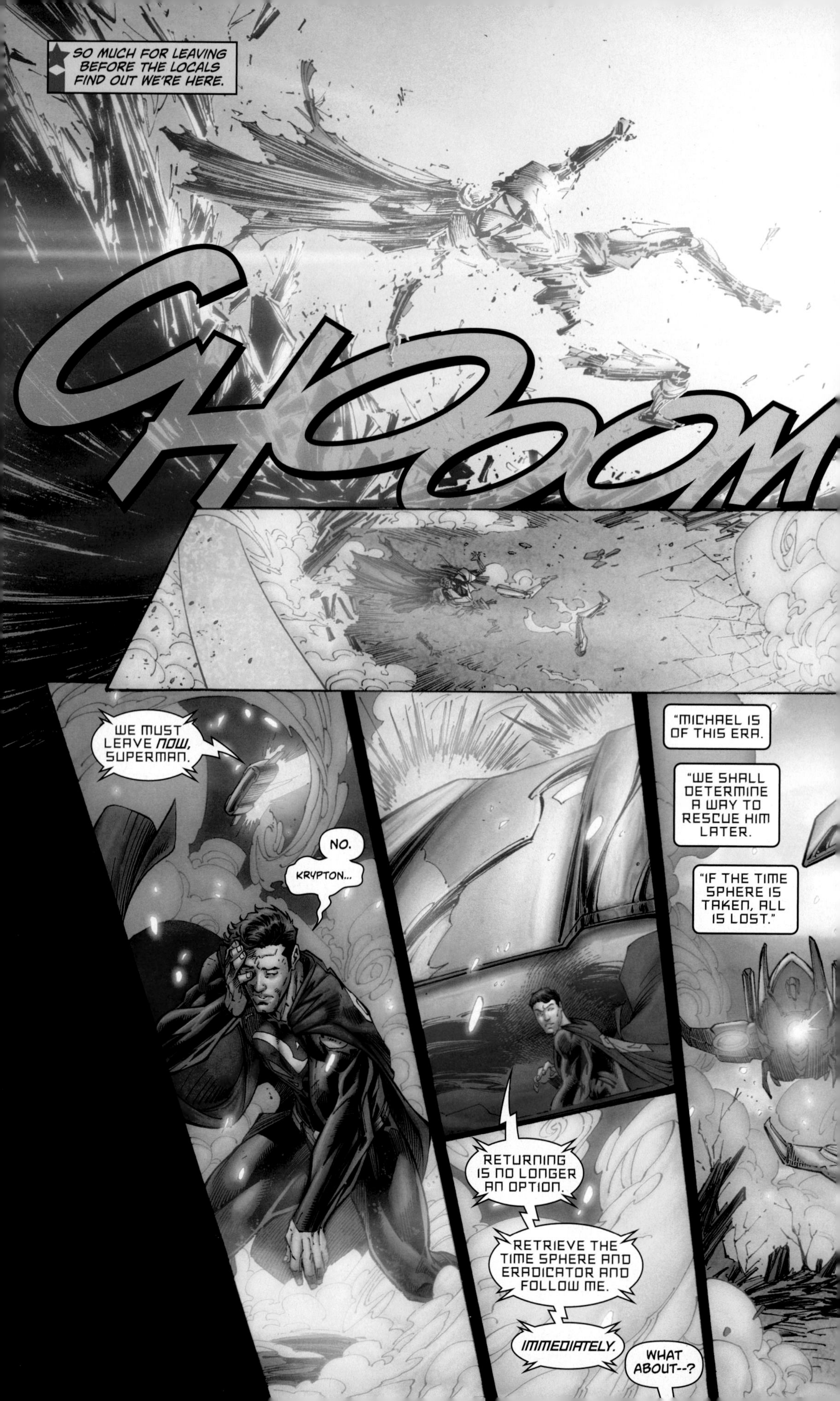

SO MUCH FOR LEAVING BEFORE THE LOCALS FIND OUT WE'RE HERE.
GKOOOM
WE MUST LEAVE *NOW*, SUPERMAN.
NO.
KRYPTON...
"MICHAEL IS OF THIS ERA.
"WE SHALL DETERMINE A WAY TO RESCUE HIM LATER.
"IF THE TIME SPHERE IS TAKEN, ALL IS LOST."
RETURNING IS NO LONGER AN OPTION.
RETRIEVE THE TIME SPHERE AND ERADICATOR AND FOLLOW ME.
IMMEDIATELY.
WHAT ABOUT--?

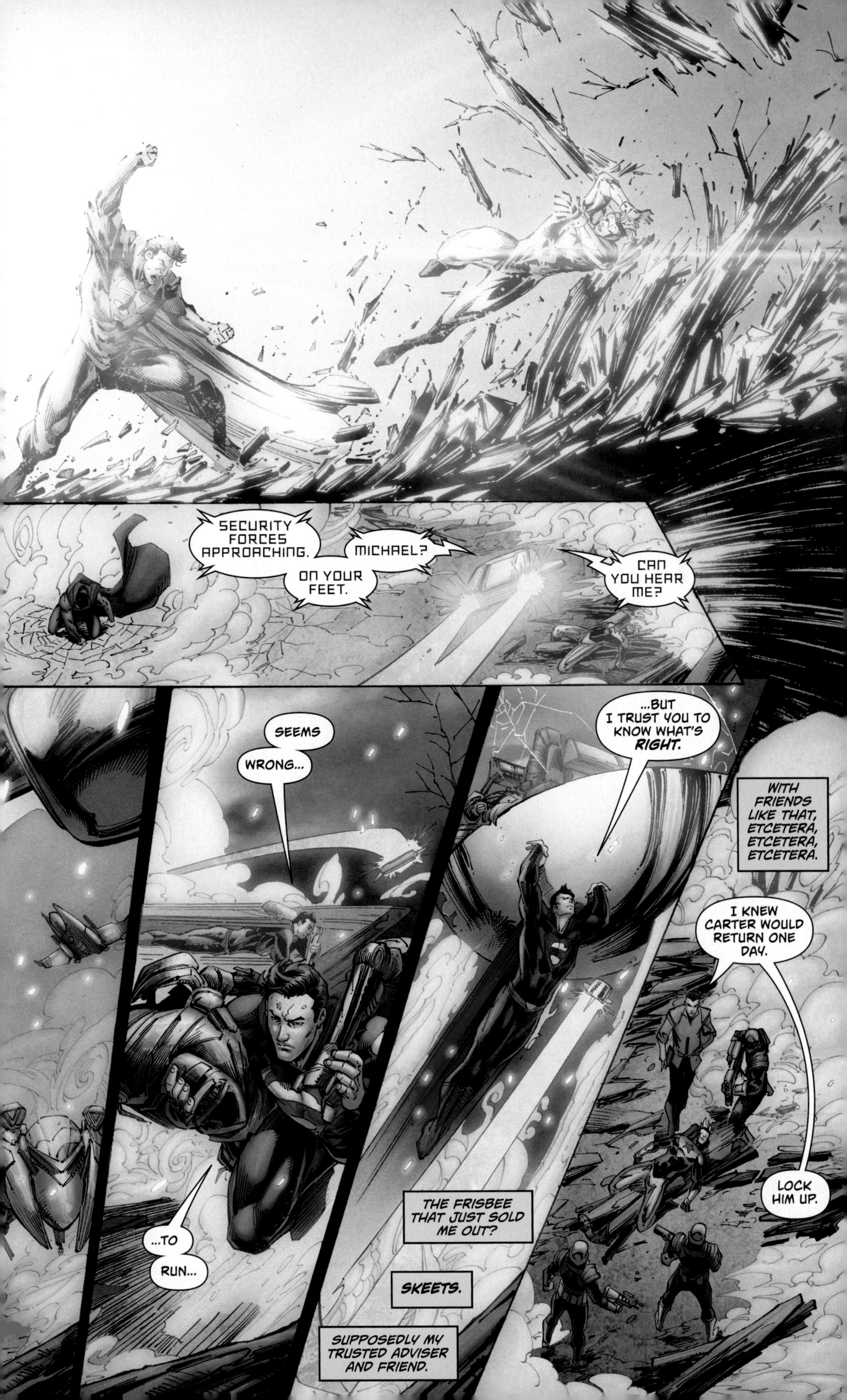
SECURITY FORCES APPROACHING.
ON YOUR FEET.
MICHAEL?
CAN YOU HEAR ME?
SEEMS
WRONG...
...TO
RUN...
...BUT I TRUST YOU TO KNOW WHAT'S **RIGHT.**
THE FRISBEE THAT JUST SOLD ME OUT?
SKEETS.
SUPPOSEDLY MY TRUSTED ADVISER AND FRIEND.
WITH FRIENDS LIKE THAT, ETCETERA, ETCETERA, ETCETERA.
I KNEW CARTER WOULD RETURN ONE DAY.
LOCK HIM UP.

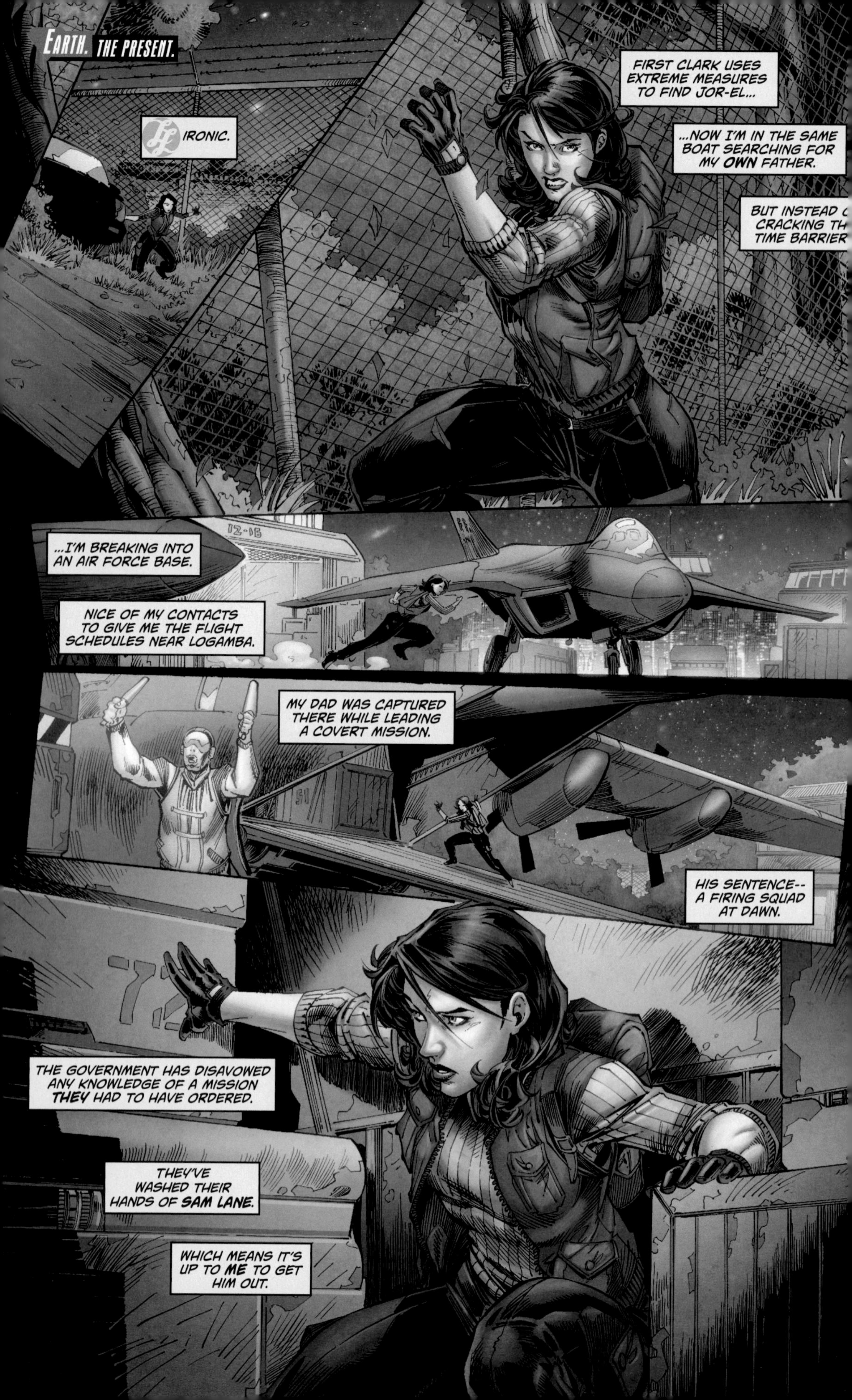
EARTH. THE PRESENT.
IRONIC.
FIRST CLARK USES EXTREME MEASURES TO FIND JOR-EL...
...NOW I'M IN THE SAME BOAT SEARCHING FOR MY OWN FATHER.
BUT INSTEAD
CRACKING TH
TIME BARRIER
...I'M BREAKING INTO AN AIR FORCE BASE.
NICE OF MY CONTACTS TO GIVE ME THE FLIGHT SCHEDULES NEAR LOGAMBA.
MY DAD WAS CAPTURED THERE WHILE LEADING A COVERT MISSION.
HIS SENTENCE-- A FIRING SQUAD AT DAWN.
THE GOVERNMENT HAS DISAVOWED ANY KNOWLEDGE OF A MISSION THEY HAD TO HAVE ORDERED.
THEY'VE WASHED THEIR HANDS OF SAM LANE.
WHICH MEANS IT'S UP TO ME TO GET HIM OUT.

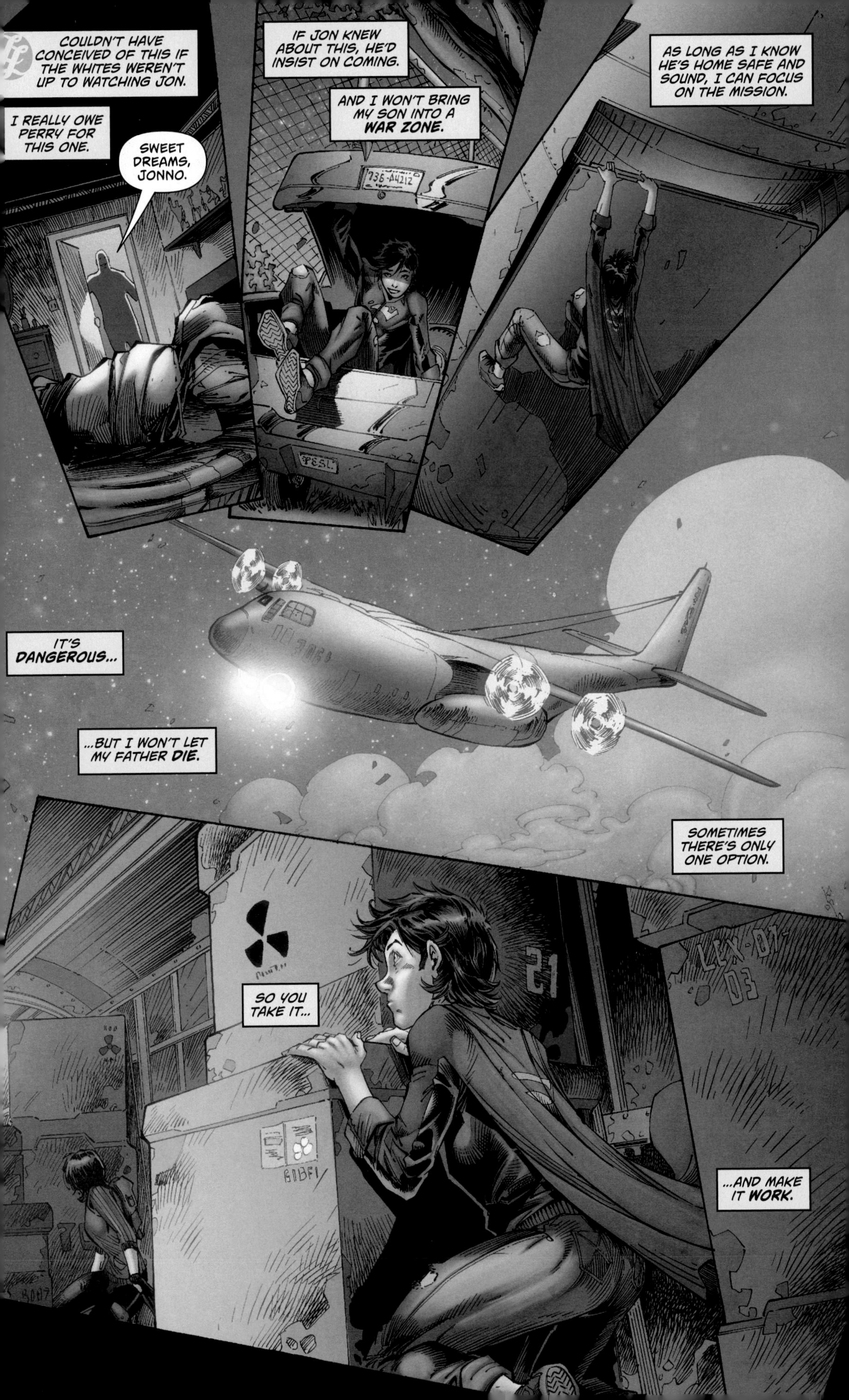
COULDN'T HAVE CONCEIVED OF THIS IF THE WHITES WEREN'T UP TO WATCHING JON.
I REALLY OWE PERRY FOR THIS ONE.
SWEET DREAMS, JONNO.
IF JON KNEW ABOUT THIS, HE'D INSIST ON COMING.
AND I WON'T BRING MY SON INTO A WAR ZONE.
AS LONG AS I KNOW HE'S HOME SAFE AND SOUND, I CAN FOCUS ON THE MISSION.
IT'S DANGEROUS...
...BUT I WON'T LET MY FATHER DIE.
SOMETIMES THERE'S ONLY ONE OPTION.
SO YOU TAKE IT...
...AND MAKE IT WORK.

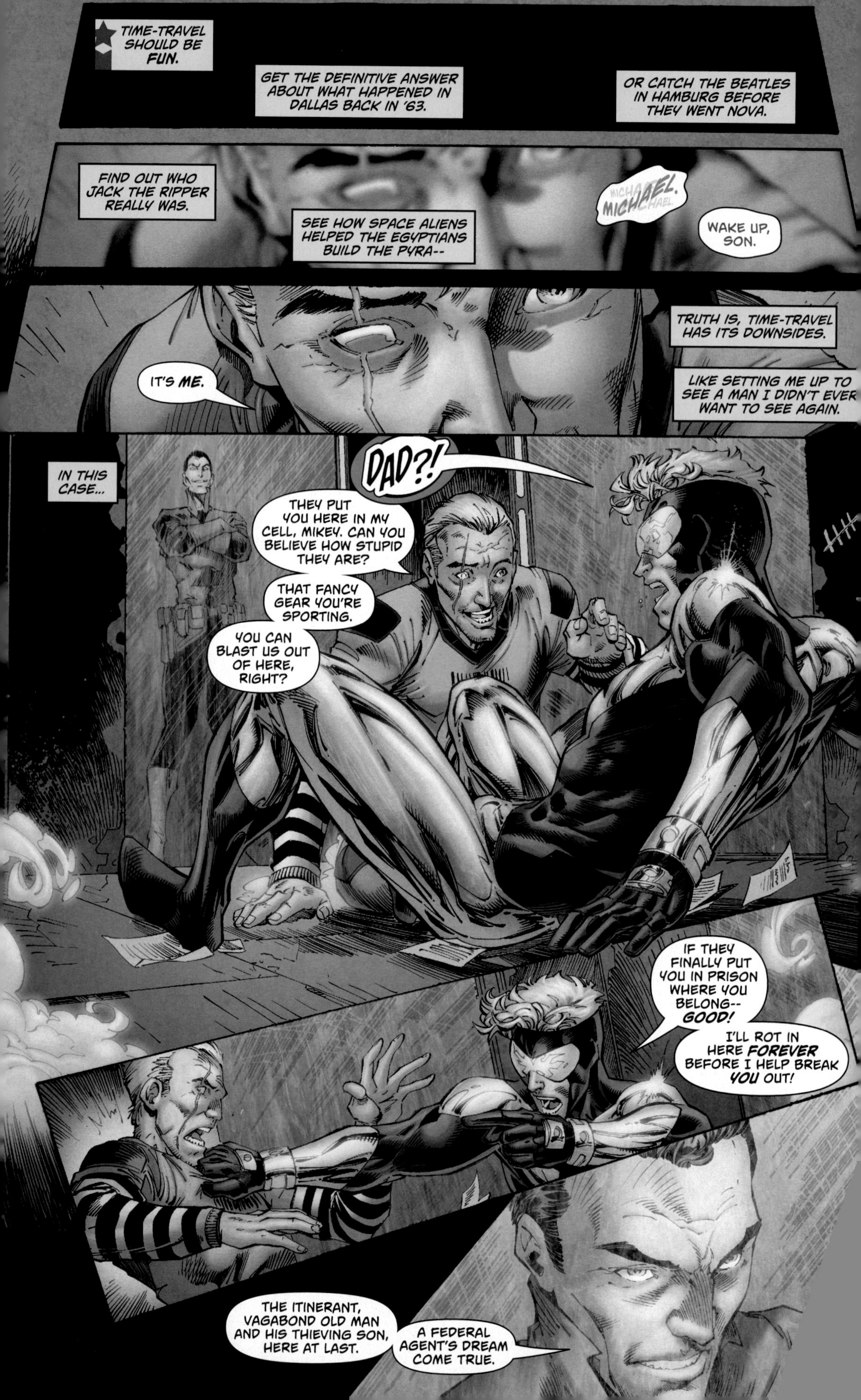
TIME-TRAVEL SHOULD BE FUN.
GET THE DEFINITIVE ANSWER ABOUT WHAT HAPPENED IN DALLAS BACK IN '63.
OR CATCH THE BEATLES IN HAMBURG BEFORE THEY WENT NOVA.
FIND OUT WHO JACK THE RIPPER REALLY WAS.
SEE HOW SPACE ALIENS HELPED THE EGYPTIANS BUILD THE PYRA--
MICHAEL. MICHAEL.
WAKE UP, SON.
TRUTH IS, TIME-TRAVEL HAS ITS DOWNSIDES.
IT'S ME.
LIKE SETTING ME UP TO SEE A MAN I DIDN'T EVER WANT TO SEE AGAIN.
IN THIS CASE...
DAD?!
THEY PUT YOU HERE IN MY CELL, MIKEY. CAN YOU BELIEVE HOW STUPID THEY ARE?
THAT FANCY GEAR YOU'RE SPORTING.
YOU CAN BLAST US OUT OF HERE, RIGHT?
IF THEY FINALLY PUT YOU IN PRISON WHERE YOU BELONG-- GOOD!
I'LL ROT IN HERE FOREVER BEFORE I HELP BREAK YOU OUT!
THE ITINERANT, VAGABOND OLD MAN AND HIS THIEVING SON, HERE AT LAST.
A FEDERAL AGENT'S DREAM COME TRUE.

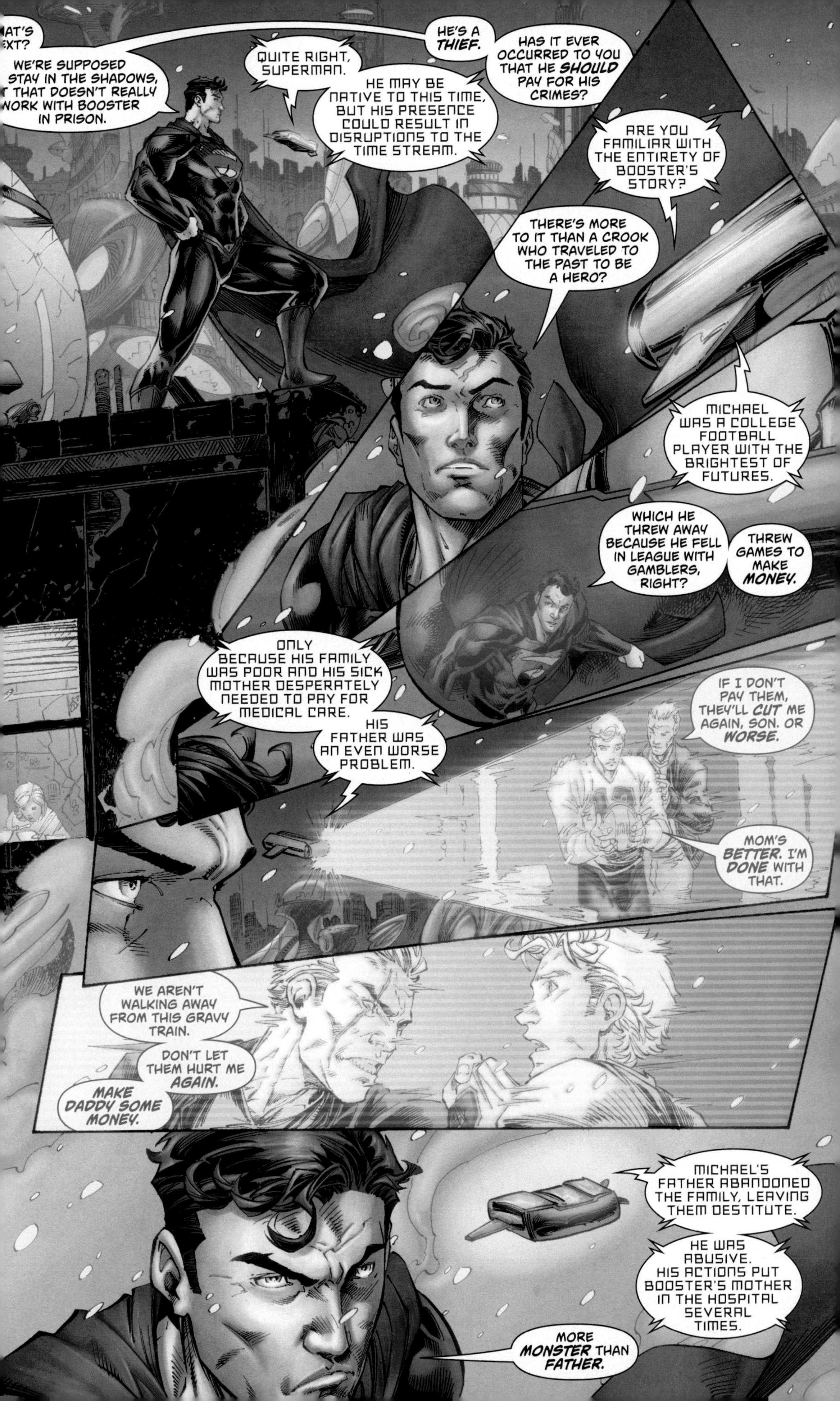

WE'RE SUPPOSED STAY IN THE SHADOWS, T THAT DOESN'T REALLY WORK WITH BOOSTER IN PRISON.
HE'S A THIEF.
QUITE RIGHT, SUPERMAN.
HE MAY BE NATIVE TO THIS TIME, BUT HIS PRESENCE COULD RESULT IN DISRUPTIONS TO THE TIME STREAM.
HAS IT EVER OCCURRED TO YOU THAT HE SHOULD PAY FOR HIS CRIMES?
ARE YOU FAMILIAR WITH THE ENTIRETY OF BOOSTER'S STORY?
THERE'S MORE TO IT THAN A CROOK WHO TRAVELED TO THE PAST TO BE A HERO?
MICHAEL WAS A COLLEGE FOOTBALL PLAYER WITH THE BRIGHTEST OF FUTURES.
WHICH HE THREW AWAY BECAUSE HE FELL IN LEAGUE WITH GAMBLERS, RIGHT?
THREW GAMES TO MAKE MONEY.
ONLY BECAUSE HIS FAMILY WAS POOR AND HIS SICK MOTHER DESPERATELY NEEDED TO PAY FOR MEDICAL CARE.
HIS FATHER WAS AN EVEN WORSE PROBLEM.
IF I DON'T PAY THEM, THEY'LL CUT ME AGAIN, SON. OR WORSE.
MOM'S BETTER. I'M DONE WITH THAT.
WE AREN'T WALKING AWAY FROM THIS GRAVY TRAIN.
DON'T LET THEM HURT ME AGAIN.
MAKE DADDY SOME MONEY.
MICHAEL'S FATHER ABANDONED THE FAMILY, LEAVING THEM DESTITUTE.
HE WAS ABUSIVE. HIS ACTIONS PUT BOOSTER'S MOTHER IN THE HOSPITAL SEVERAL TIMES.
MORE MONSTER THAN FATHER.

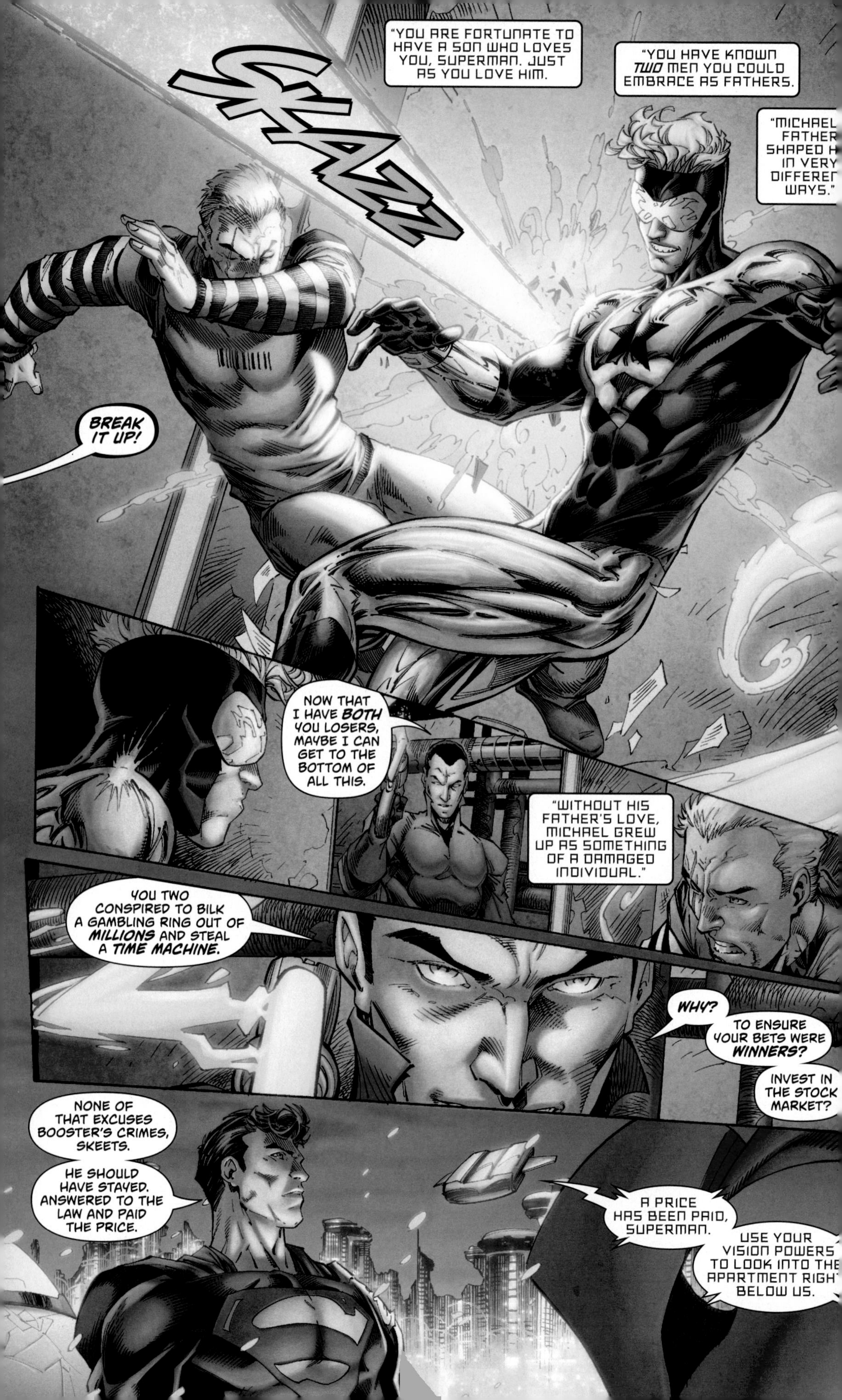
SKAZZ
"YOU ARE FORTUNATE TO HAVE A SON WHO LOVES YOU, SUPERMAN. JUST AS YOU LOVE HIM.
"YOU HAVE KNOWN TWO MEN YOU COULD EMBRACE AS FATHERS.
"MICHAEL FATHER SHAPED H IN VERY DIFFEREN WAYS."
BREAK IT UP!
NOW THAT I HAVE BOTH YOU LOSERS, MAYBE I CAN GET TO THE BOTTOM OF ALL THIS.
"WITHOUT HIS FATHER'S LOVE, MICHAEL GREW UP AS SOMETHING OF A DAMAGED INDIVIDUAL."
YOU TWO CONSPIRED TO BILK A GAMBLING RING OUT OF MILLIONS AND STEAL A TIME MACHINE.
WHY?
TO ENSURE YOUR BETS WERE WINNERS?
INVEST IN THE STOCK MARKET?
NONE OF THAT EXCUSES BOOSTER'S CRIMES, SKEETS.
HE SHOULD HAVE STAYED. ANSWERED TO THE LAW AND PAID THE PRICE.
A PRICE HAS BEEN PAID, SUPERMAN.
USE YOUR VISION POWERS TO LOOK INTO THE APARTMENT RIGH BELOW US.

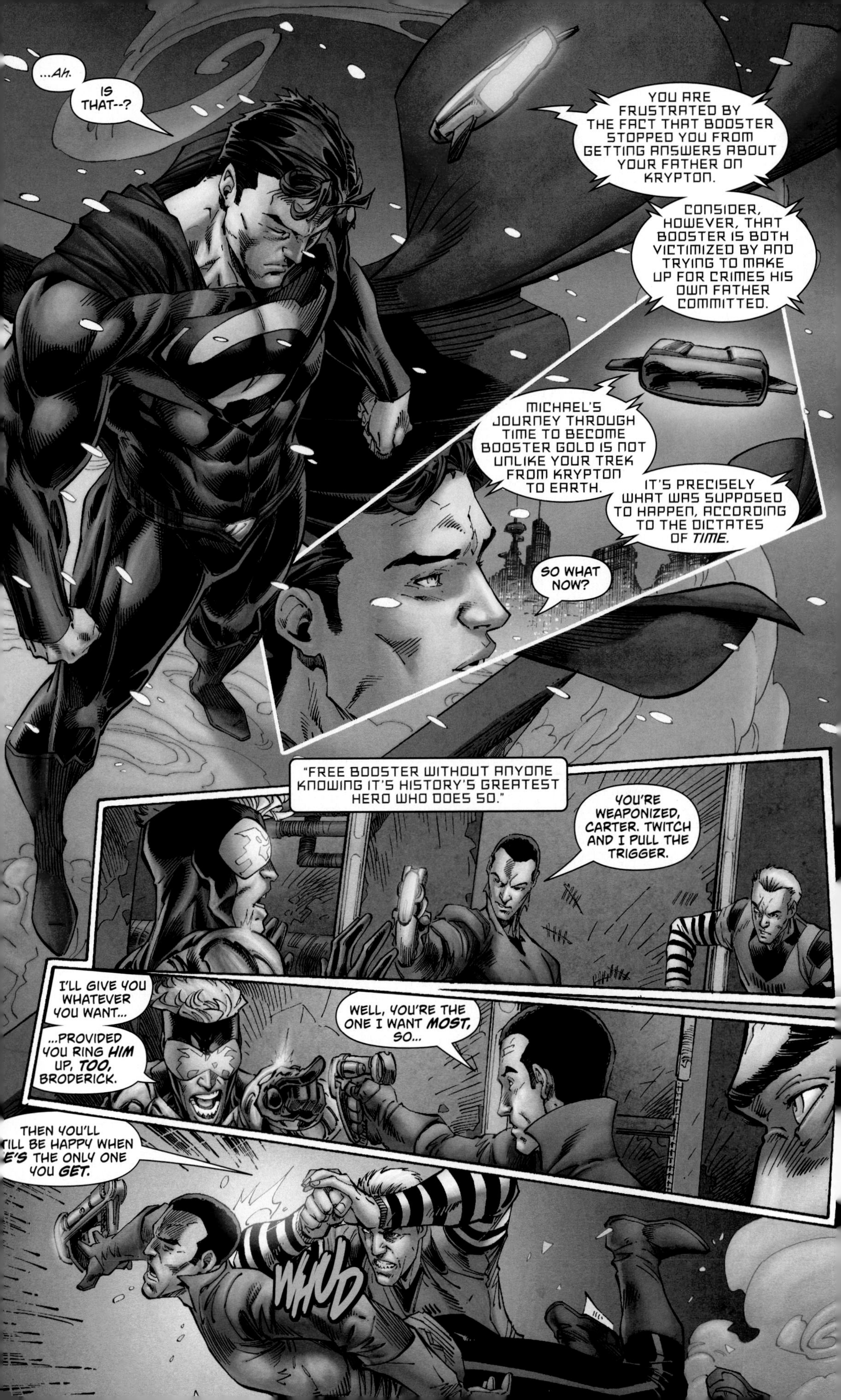

...Ah.
IS THAT--?
YOU ARE FRUSTRATED BY THE FACT THAT BOOSTER STOPPED YOU FROM GETTING ANSWERS ABOUT YOUR FATHER ON KRYPTON.
CONSIDER, HOWEVER, THAT BOOSTER IS BOTH VICTIMIZED BY AND TRYING TO MAKE UP FOR CRIMES HIS OWN FATHER COMMITTED.
MICHAEL'S JOURNEY THROUGH TIME TO BECOME BOOSTER GOLD IS NOT UNLIKE YOUR TREK FROM KRYPTON TO EARTH.
IT'S PRECISELY WHAT WAS SUPPOSED TO HAPPEN, ACCORDING TO THE DICTATES OF TIME.
SO WHAT NOW?
"FREE BOOSTER WITHOUT ANYONE KNOWING IT'S HISTORY'S GREATEST HERO WHO DOES SO."
YOU'RE WEAPONIZED, CARTER. TWITCH AND I PULL THE TRIGGER.
I'LL GIVE YOU WHATEVER YOU WANT...
...PROVIDED YOU RING HIM UP, TOO, BRODERICK.
WELL, YOU'RE THE ONE I WANT MOST, SO...
THEN YOU'LL STILL BE HAPPY WHEN HE'S THE ONLY ONE YOU GET.
WHUD

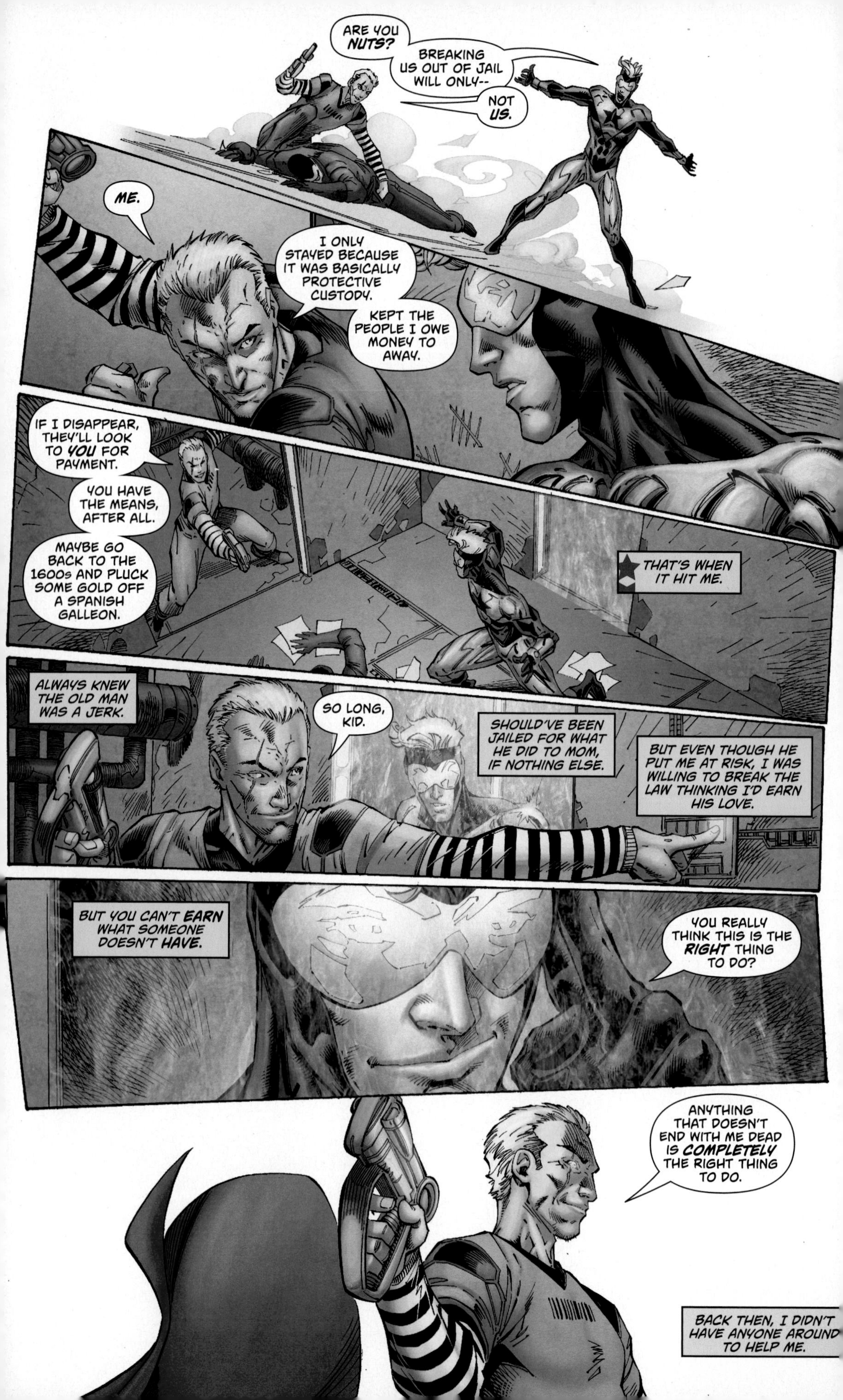
ARE YOU NUTS?
BREAKING US OUT OF JAIL WILL ONLY--
NOT US.
ME.
I ONLY STAYED BECAUSE IT WAS BASICALLY PROTECTIVE CUSTODY.
KEPT THE PEOPLE I OWE MONEY TO AWAY.
IF I DISAPPEAR, THEY'LL LOOK TO YOU FOR PAYMENT.
YOU HAVE THE MEANS, AFTER ALL.
MAYBE GO BACK TO THE 1600s AND PLUCK SOME GOLD OFF A SPANISH GALLEON.
THAT'S WHEN IT HIT ME.
ALWAYS KNEW THE OLD MAN WAS A JERK.
SO LONG, KID.
SHOULD'VE BEEN JAILED FOR WHAT HE DID TO MOM, IF NOTHING ELSE.
BUT EVEN THOUGH HE PUT ME AT RISK, I WAS WILLING TO BREAK THE LAW THINKING I'D EARN HIS LOVE.
BUT YOU CAN'T EARN WHAT SOMEONE DOESN'T HAVE.
YOU REALLY THINK THIS IS THE RIGHT THING TO DO?
ANYTHING THAT DOESN'T END WITH ME DEAD IS COMPLETELY THE RIGHT THING TO DO.
BACK THEN, I DIDN'T HAVE ANYONE AROUND TO HELP ME.

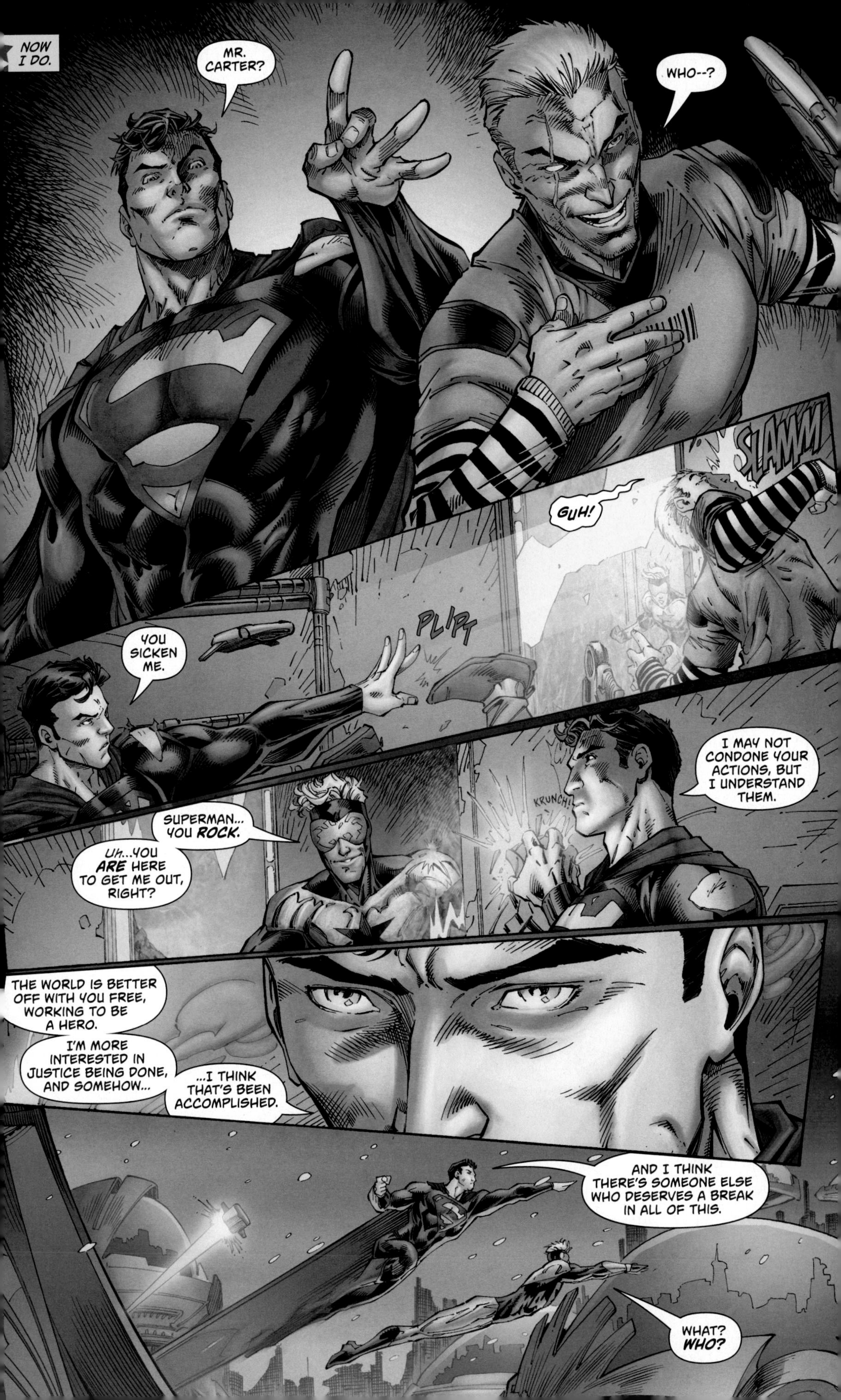

NOW I DO.
MR. CARTER?
WHO--?
SLAMM!
GUH!
PLIPT
YOU SICKEN ME.
I MAY NOT CONDONE YOUR ACTIONS, BUT I UNDERSTAND THEM.
KRUNCH!
SUPERMAN... YOU ROCK.
Uh...YOU ARE HERE TO GET ME OUT, RIGHT?
THE WORLD IS BETTER OFF WITH YOU FREE, WORKING TO BE A HERO.
I'M MORE INTERESTED IN JUSTICE BEING DONE, AND SOMEHOW...
...I THINK THAT'S BEEN ACCOMPLISHED.
AND I THINK THERE'S SOMEONE ELSE WHO DESERVES A BREAK IN ALL OF THIS.
WHAT? WHO?

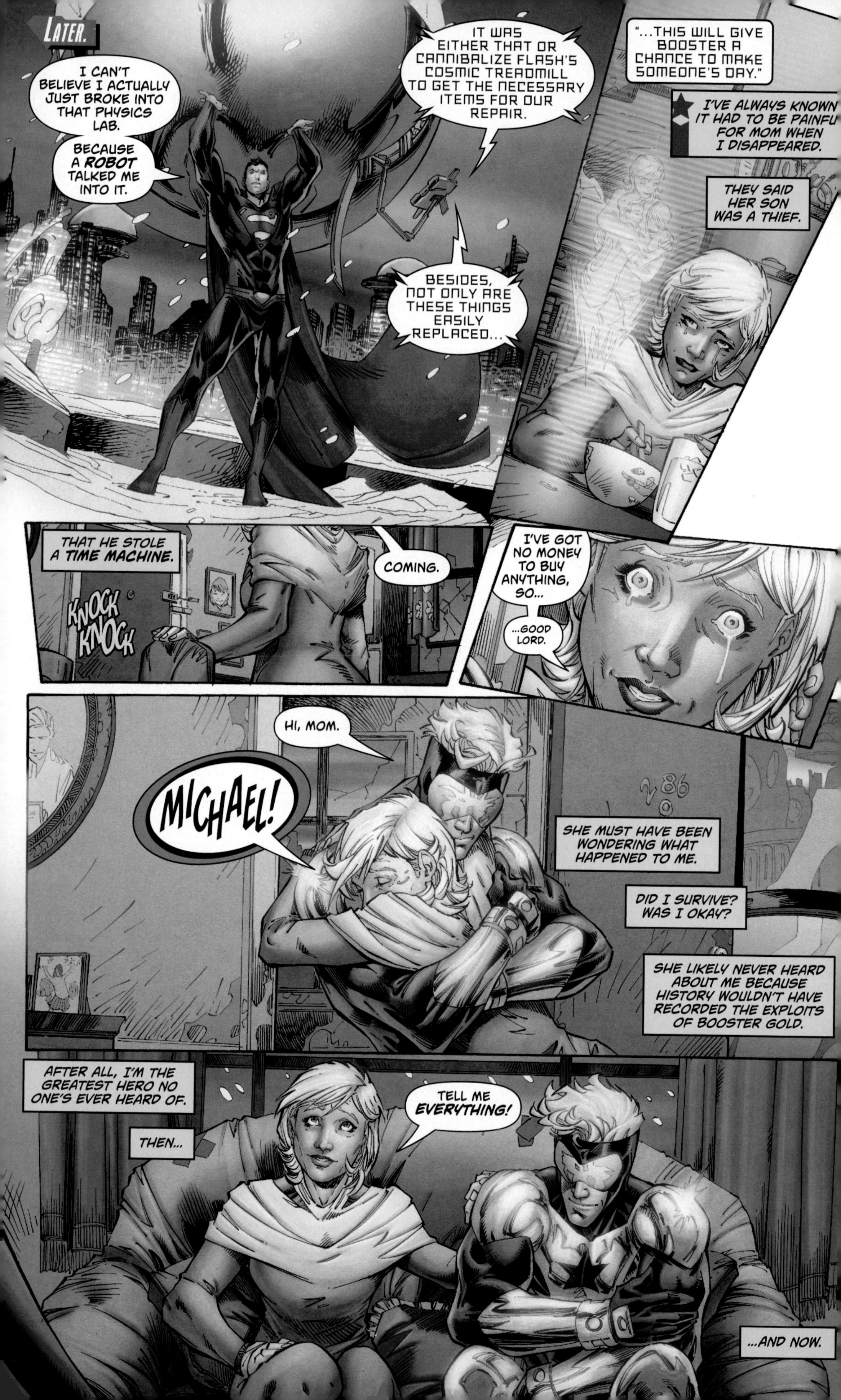
LATER.
I CAN'T BELIEVE I ACTUALLY JUST BROKE INTO THAT PHYSICS LAB.
BECAUSE A ROBOT TALKED ME INTO IT.
IT WAS EITHER THAT OR CANNIBALIZE FLASH'S COSMIC TREADMILL TO GET THE NECESSARY ITEMS FOR OUR REPAIR.
BESIDES, NOT ONLY ARE THESE THINGS EASILY REPLACED...
"...THIS WILL GIVE BOOSTER A CHANCE TO MAKE SOMEONE'S DAY."
I'VE ALWAYS KNOWN IT HAD TO BE PAINFU FOR MOM WHEN I DISAPPEARED.
THEY SAID HER SON WAS A THIEF.
THAT HE STOLE A TIME MACHINE.
KNOCK KNOCK
COMING.
I'VE GOT NO MONEY TO BUY ANYTHING, SO...
...GOOD LORD.
HI, MOM.
MICHAEL!
SHE MUST HAVE BEEN WONDERING WHAT HAPPENED TO ME.
DID I SURVIVE? WAS I OKAY?
SHE LIKELY NEVER HEARD ABOUT ME BECAUSE HISTORY WOULDN'T HAVE RECORDED THE EXPLOITS OF BOOSTER GOLD.
AFTER ALL, I'M THE GREATEST HERO NO ONE'S EVER HEARD OF.
THEN...
TELL ME EVERYTHING!
...AND NOW.

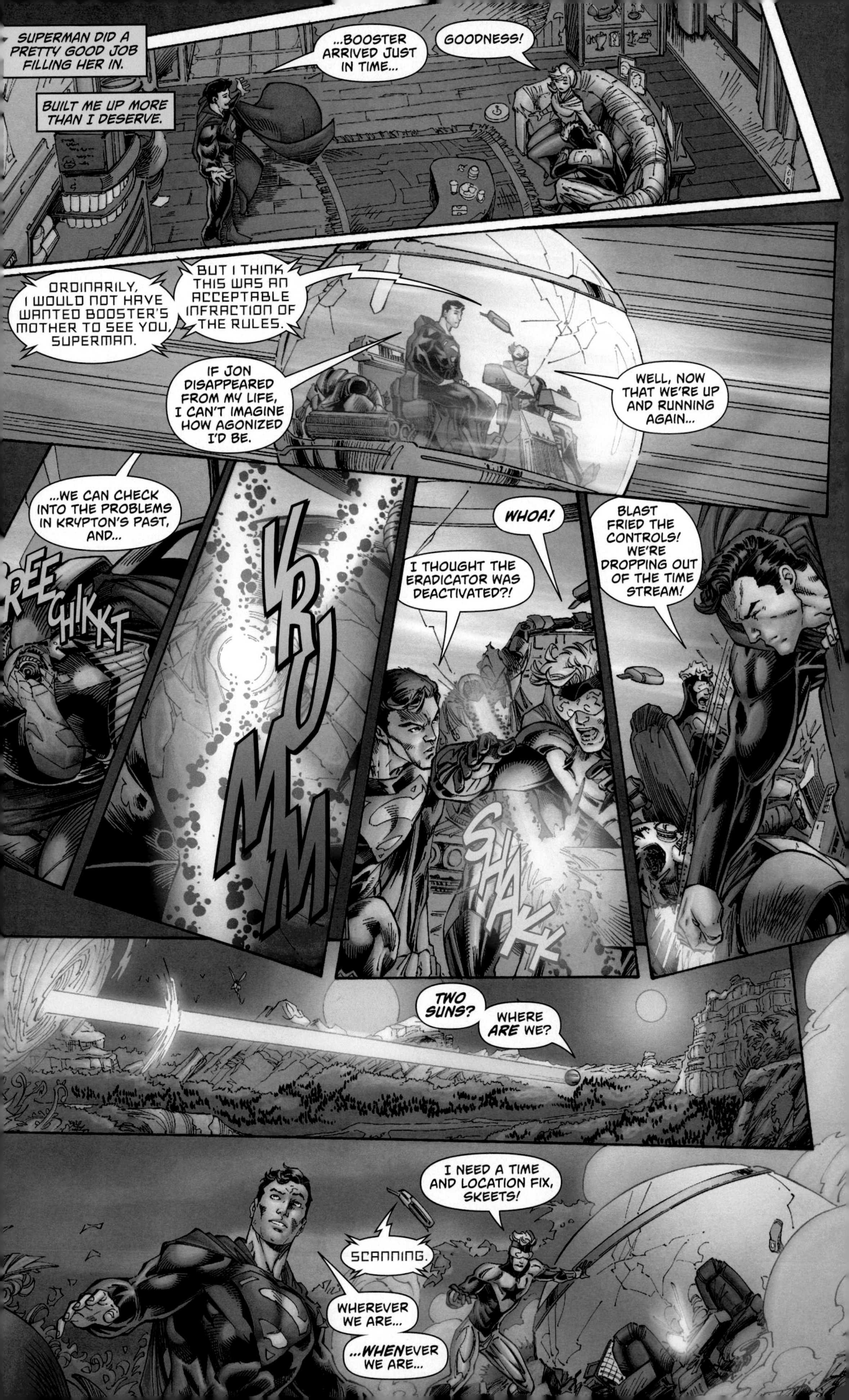
SUPERMAN DID A PRETTY GOOD JOB FILLING HER IN.
...BOOSTER ARRIVED JUST IN TIME...
GOODNESS!
BUILT ME UP MORE THAN I DESERVE.
ORDINARILY, I WOULD NOT HAVE WANTED BOOSTER'S MOTHER TO SEE YOU, SUPERMAN.
BUT I THINK THIS WAS AN ACCEPTABLE INFRACTION OF THE RULES.
IF JON DISAPPEARED FROM MY LIFE, I CAN'T IMAGINE HOW AGONIZED I'D BE.
WELL, NOW THAT WE'RE UP AND RUNNING AGAIN...
...WE CAN CHECK INTO THE PROBLEMS IN KRYPTON'S PAST, AND...
REEEE CHIKKKT
VRUMMM
I THOUGHT THE ERADICATOR WAS DEACTIVATED?!
WHOA!
SHAKKK
BLAST FRIED THE CONTROLS! WE'RE DROPPING OUT OF THE TIME STREAM!
TWO SUNS?
WHERE ARE WE?
I NEED A TIME AND LOCATION FIX, SKEETS!
SCANNING.
WHEREVER WE ARE...
...WHENEVER WE ARE...

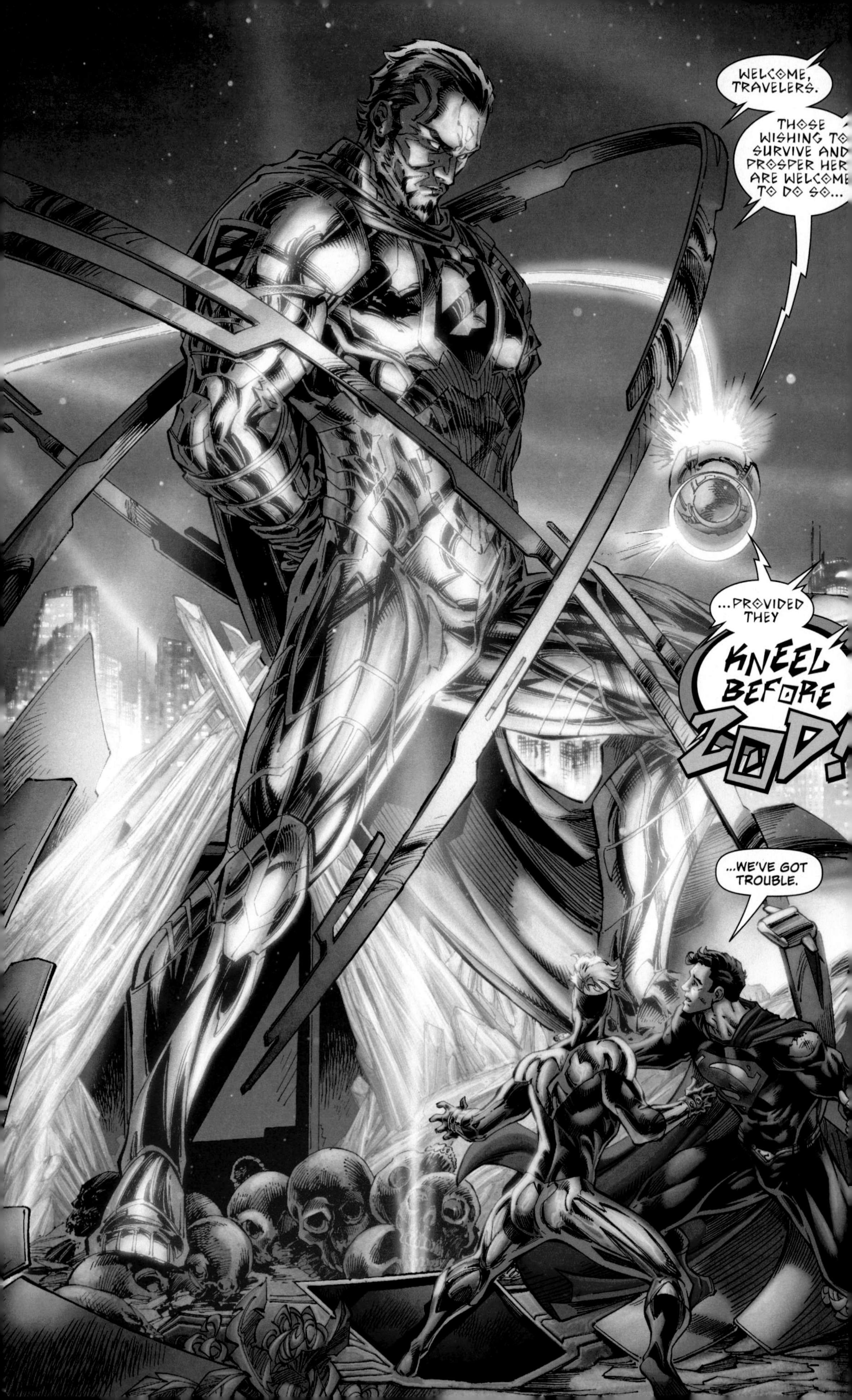
WELCOME, TRAVELERS.
THOSE WISHING TO SURVIVE AND PROSPER HER ARE WELCOME TO DO SO...
...PROVIDED THEY KNEEL BEFORE ZOD!
...WE'VE GOT TROUBLE.

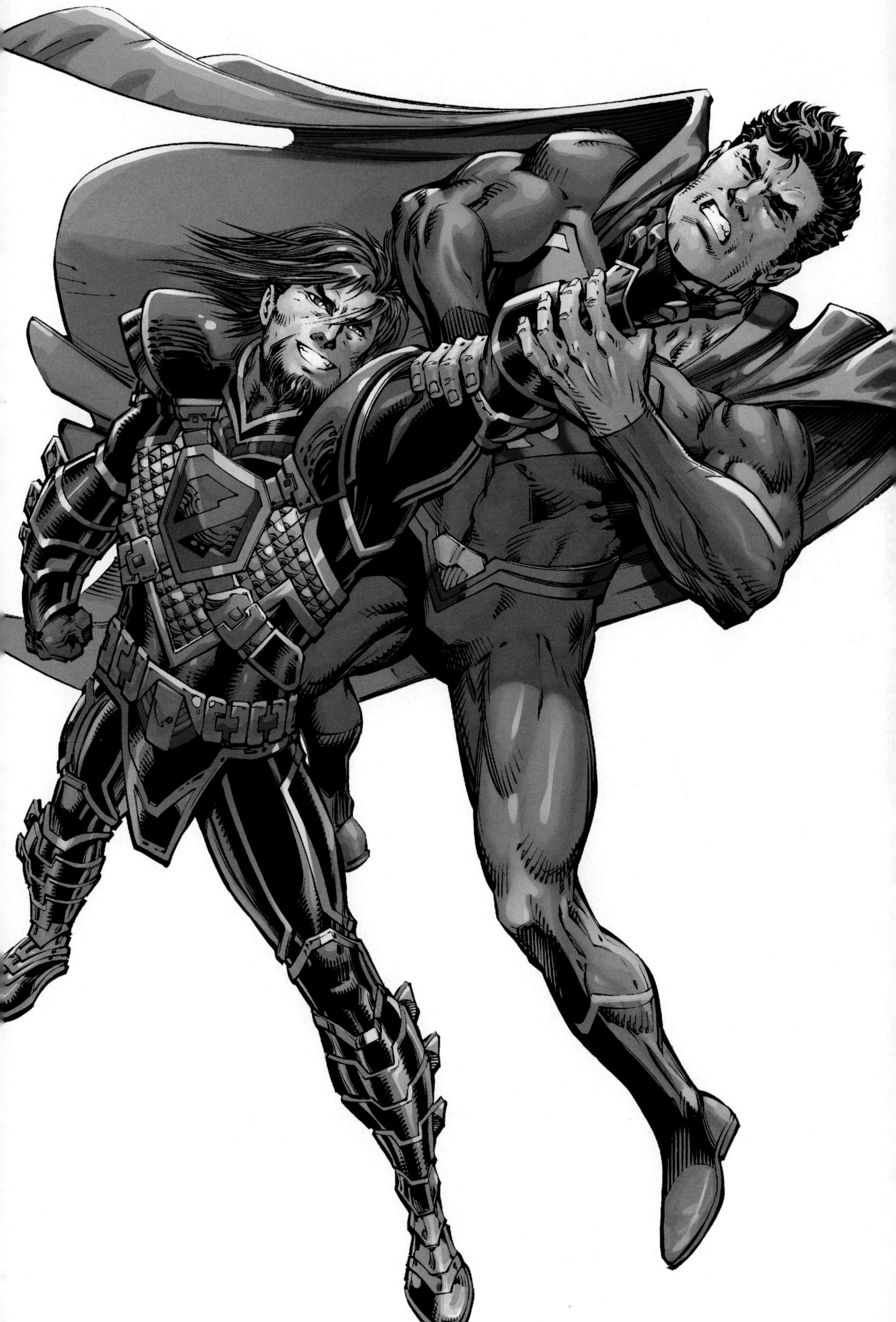

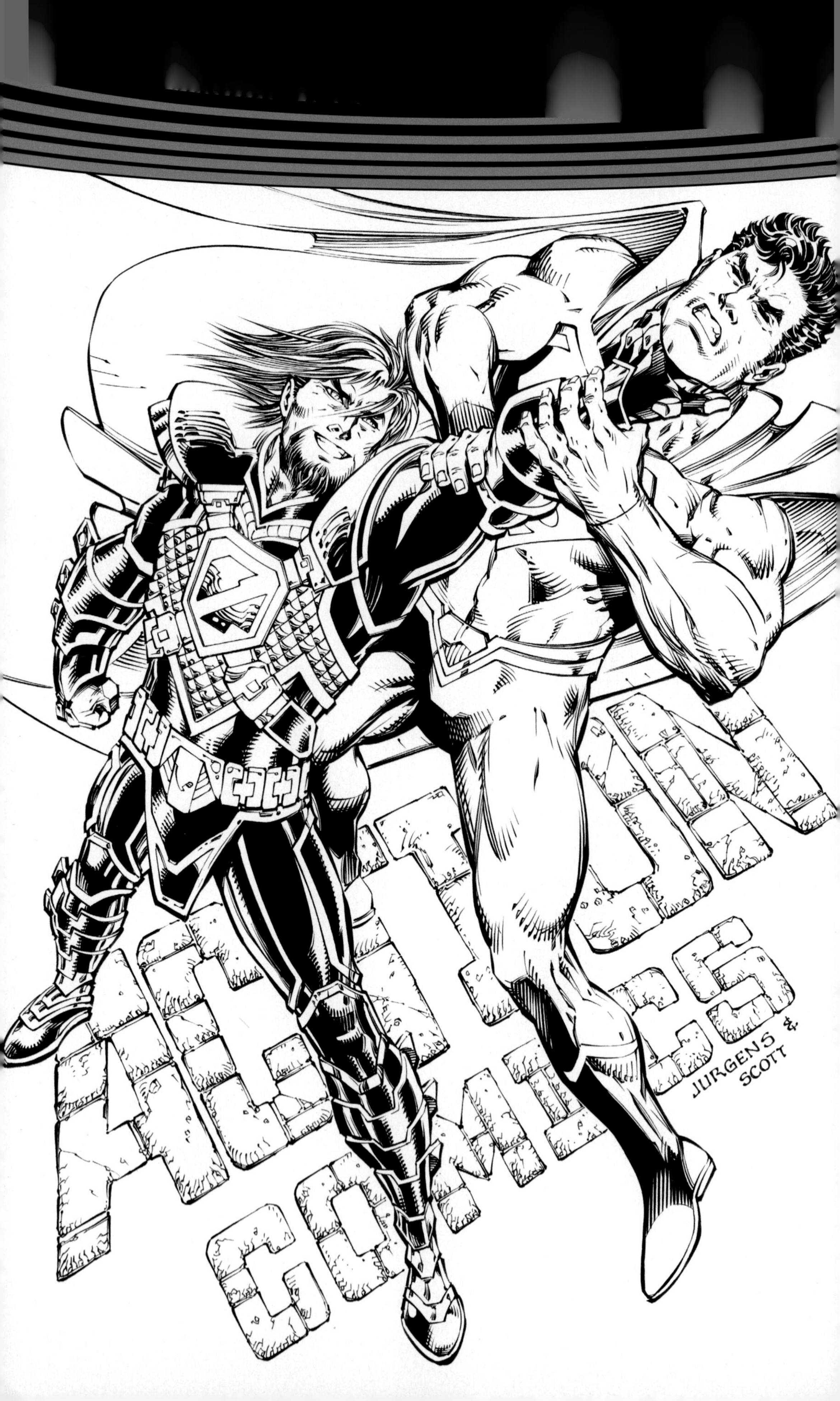
ACTION COMICS
JURGENS & SCOTT

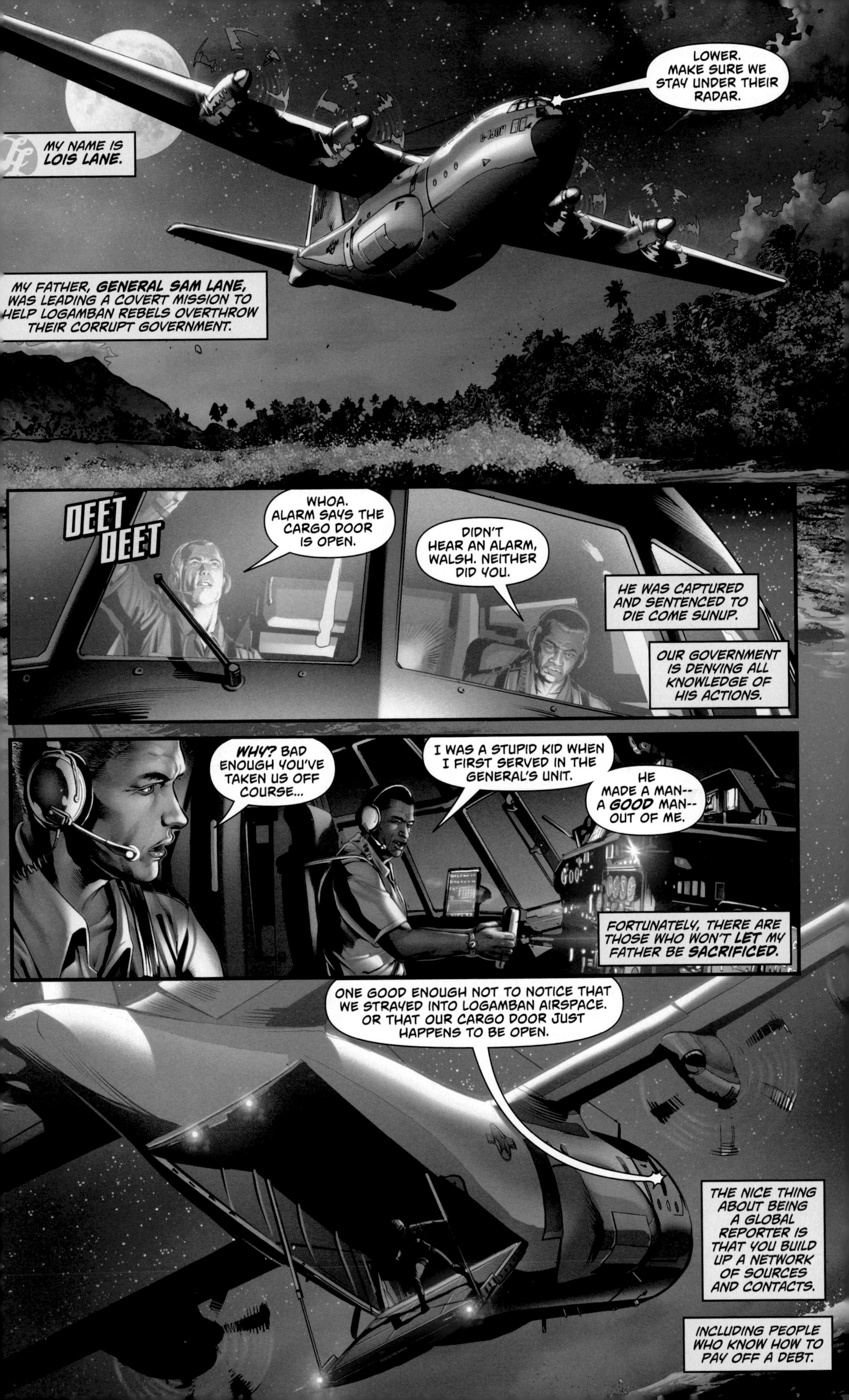
MY NAME IS LOIS LANE.
LOWER. MAKE SURE WE STAY UNDER THEIR RADAR.
MY FATHER, GENERAL SAM LANE, WAS LEADING A COVERT MISSION TO HELP LOGAMBAN REBELS OVERTHROW THEIR CORRUPT GOVERNMENT.
DEET DEET
WHOA. ALARM SAYS THE CARGO DOOR IS OPEN.
DIDN'T HEAR AN ALARM, WALSH. NEITHER DID YOU.
HE WAS CAPTURED AND SENTENCED TO DIE COME SUNUP.
OUR GOVERNMENT IS DENYING ALL KNOWLEDGE OF HIS ACTIONS.
WHY? BAD ENOUGH YOU'VE TAKEN US OFF COURSE...
I WAS A STUPID KID WHEN I FIRST SERVED IN THE GENERAL'S UNIT.
HE MADE A MAN-- A GOOD MAN-- OUT OF ME.
FORTUNATELY, THERE ARE THOSE WHO WON'T LET MY FATHER BE SACRIFICED.
ONE GOOD ENOUGH NOT TO NOTICE THAT WE STRAYED INTO LOGAMBAN AIRSPACE. OR THAT OUR CARGO DOOR JUST HAPPENS TO BE OPEN.
THE NICE THING ABOUT BEING A GLOBAL REPORTER IS THAT YOU BUILD UP A NETWORK OF SOURCES AND CONTACTS.
INCLUDING PEOPLE WHO KNOW HOW TO PAY OFF A DEBT.

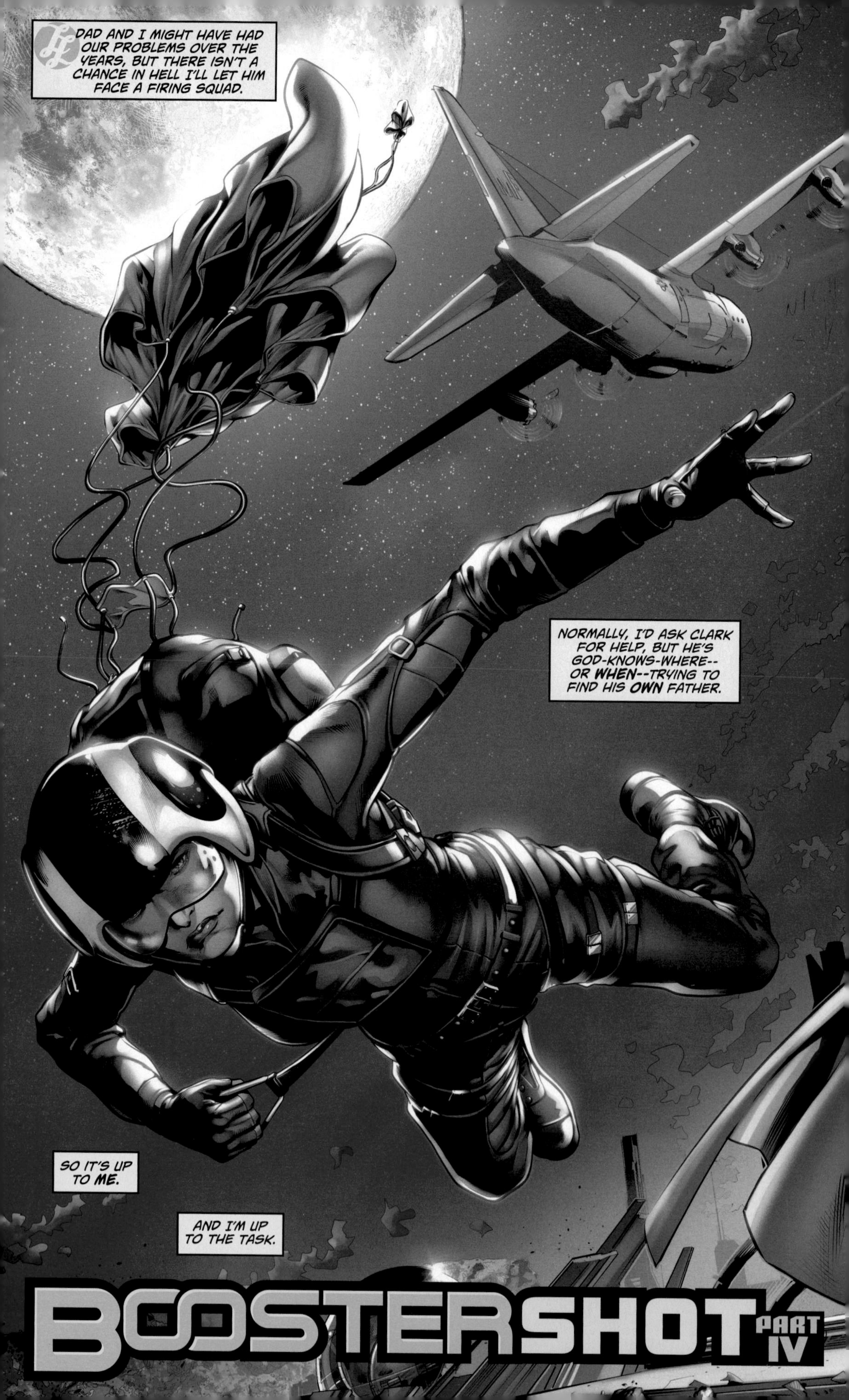
DAD AND I MIGHT HAVE HAD OUR PROBLEMS OVER THE YEARS, BUT THERE ISN'T A CHANCE IN HELL I'LL LET HIM FACE A FIRING SQUAD.
NORMALLY, I'D ASK CLARK FOR HELP, BUT HE'S GOD-KNOWS-WHERE-- OR WHEN--TRYING TO FIND HIS OWN FATHER.
SO IT'S UP TO ME.
AND I'M UP TO THE TASK.
BOOSTERSHOT PART IV

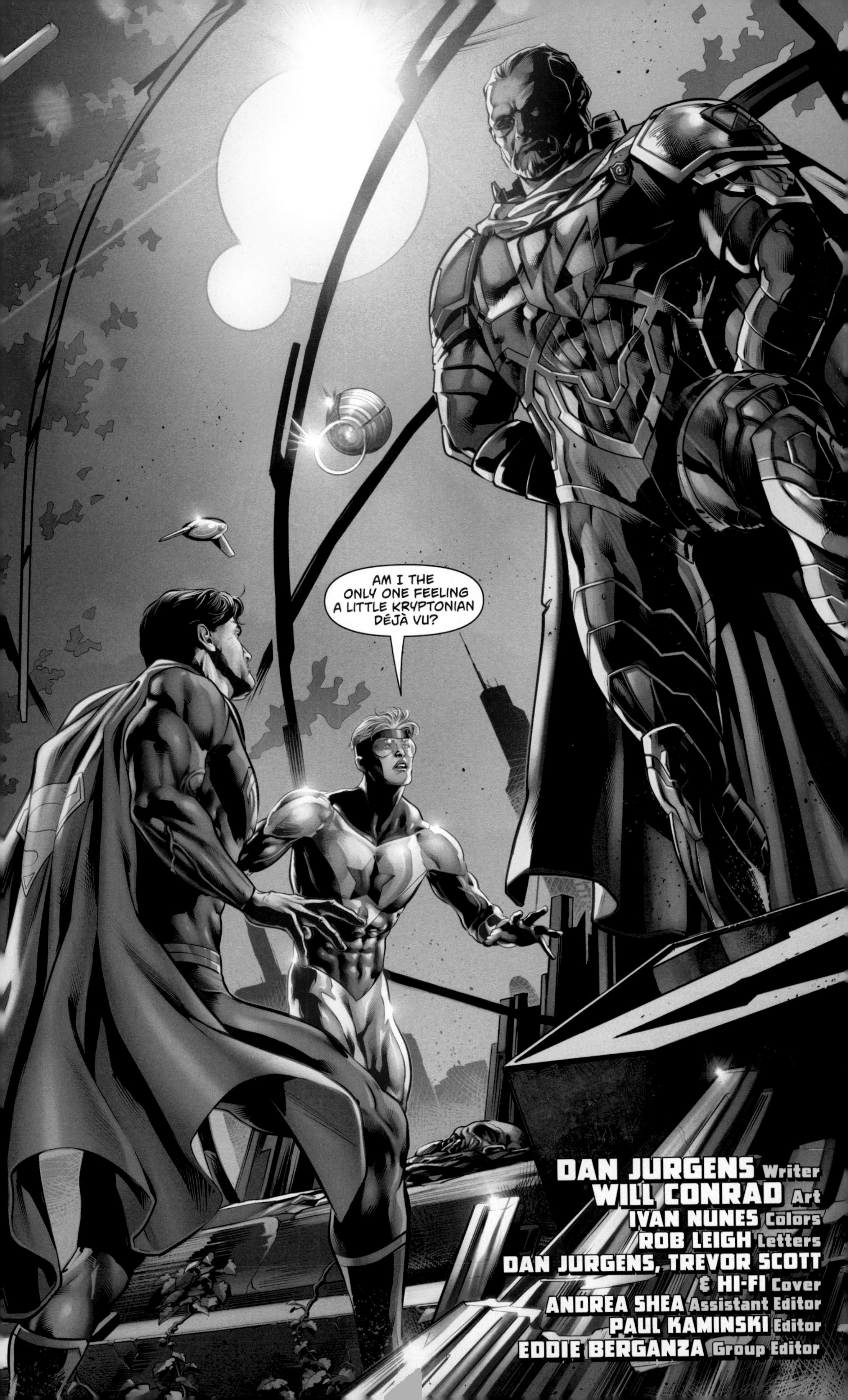
AM I THE ONLY ONE FEELING A LITTLE KRYPTONIAN DÉJÀ VU?
DAN JURGENS Writer
WILL CONRAD Art
IVAN NUNES Colors
ROB LEIGH Letters
DAN JURGENS, TREVOR SCOTT & HI-FI Cover
ANDREA SHEA Assistant Editor
PAUL KAMINSKI Editor
EDDIE BERGANZA Group Editor

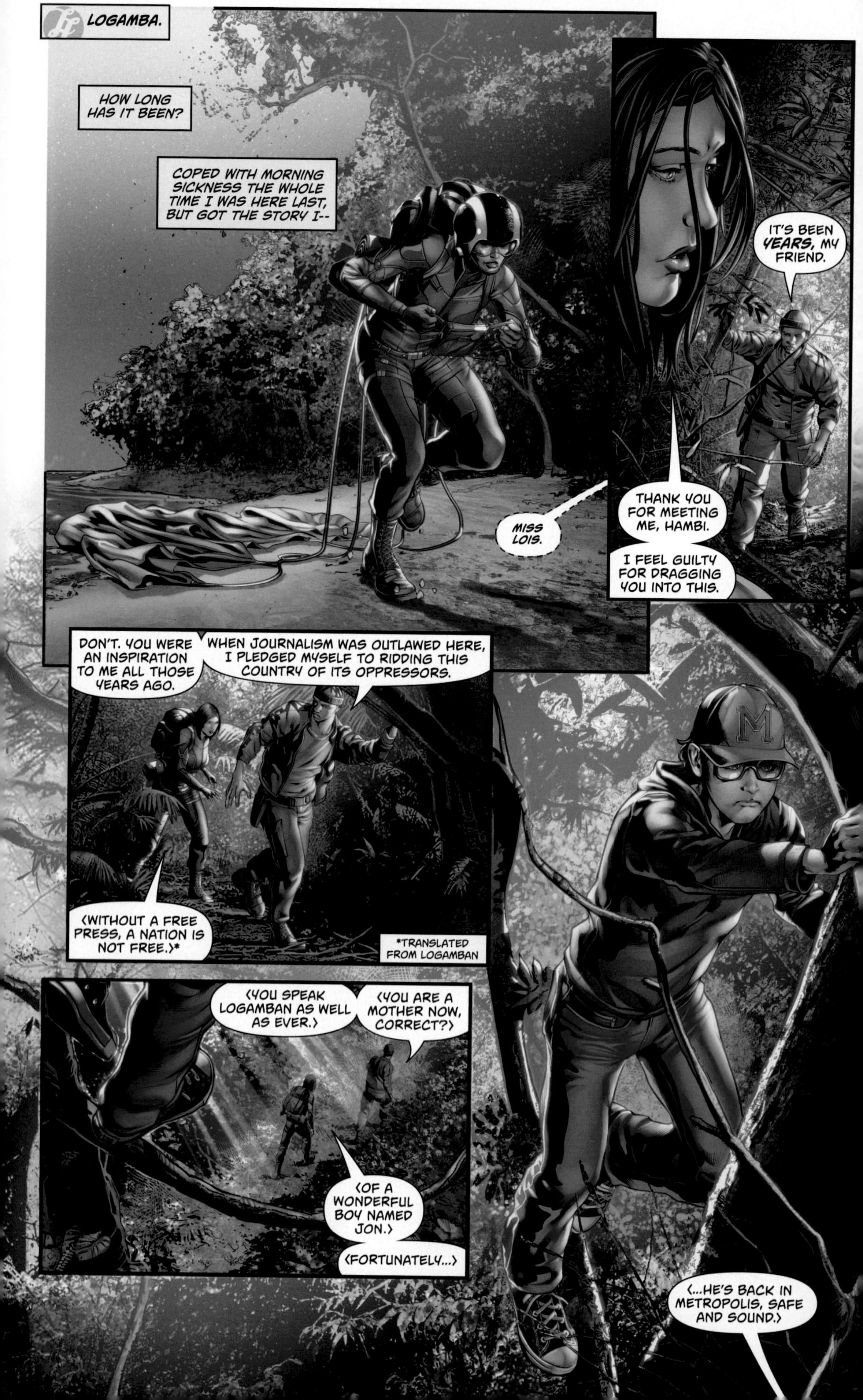
LOGAMBA.
HOW LONG HAS IT BEEN?
COPED WITH MORNING SICKNESS THE WHOLE TIME I WAS HERE LAST, BUT GOT THE STORY I--
MISS LOIS.
IT'S BEEN YEARS, MY FRIEND.
THANK YOU FOR MEETING ME, HAMBI.
I FEEL GUILTY FOR DRAGGING YOU INTO THIS.
DON'T. YOU WERE AN INSPIRATION TO ME ALL THOSE YEARS AGO.
WHEN JOURNALISM WAS OUTLAWED HERE, I PLEDGED MYSELF TO RIDDING THIS COUNTRY OF ITS OPPRESSORS.
(WITHOUT A FREE PRESS, A NATION IS NOT FREE.)*
*TRANSLATED FROM LOGAMBAN
(YOU SPEAK LOGAMBAN AS WELL AS EVER.)
(YOU ARE A MOTHER NOW, CORRECT?)
(OF A WONDERFUL BOY NAMED JON.)
(FORTUNATELY...)
(...HE'S BACK IN METROPOLIS, SAFE AND SOUND.)

YOU ARE COMMANDED ONCE MORE TO *KNEEL*, TRAVELERS.

PROVE TO NEW KRYPTON'S SECURITY FORCES THAT YOU ARE LOYAL SUBJECTS OF ZOD.

NEW KRYPTON? WHY'S THAT THING SPEAKING ENGLISH, THEN?

IT SEEMS TO SCAN NEW ENTITIES FOR THEIR NATIVE LANGUAGE.

AND THAT STATUE IS OBVIOUSLY ZOD.

WHERE *ARE* WE, BOOSTER?

NOT.

MAYBE NOT EVEN THE PRESENT.

CONFIRMED. STILL WORKING TO PINPOINT OUR SPECIFIC TIME AND LOCATION.

FOR THE LAST TIME. *KNEEL.*

NEVER.

THEN YOU WILL BE *REPORTED.*

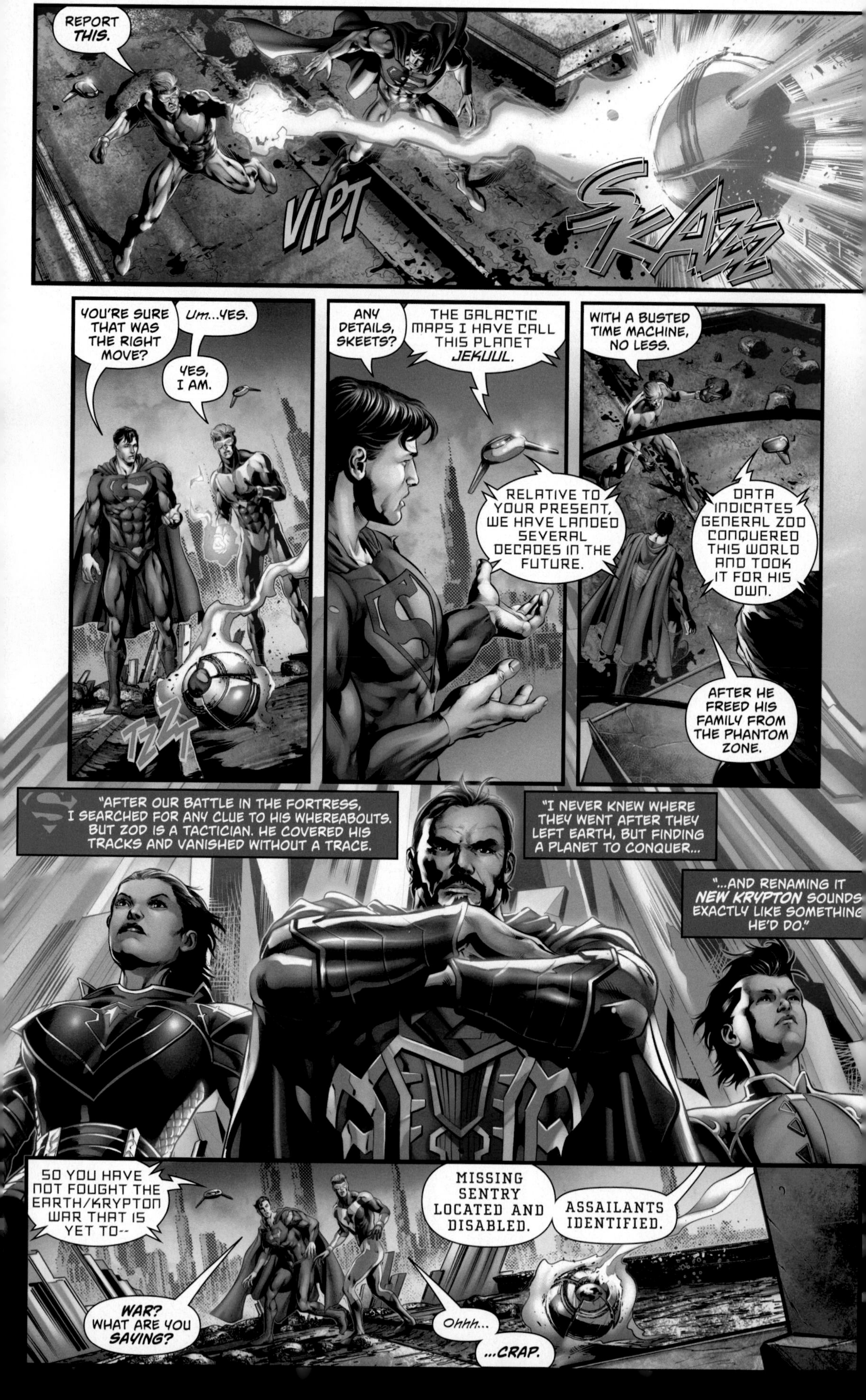
REPORT THIS.
VIPT
SKAZZ
YOU'RE SURE THAT WAS THE RIGHT MOVE?
Um...YES.
YES, I AM.
TZZT
ANY DETAILS, SKEETS?
THE GALACTIC MAPS I HAVE CALL THIS PLANET JEKUUL.
RELATIVE TO YOUR PRESENT, WE HAVE LANDED SEVERAL DECADES IN THE FUTURE.
WITH A BUSTED TIME MACHINE, NO LESS.
DATA INDICATES GENERAL ZOD CONQUERED THIS WORLD AND TOOK IT FOR HIS OWN.
AFTER HE FREED HIS FAMILY FROM THE PHANTOM ZONE.
"AFTER OUR BATTLE IN THE FORTRESS, I SEARCHED FOR ANY CLUE TO HIS WHEREABOUTS. BUT ZOD IS A TACTICIAN. HE COVERED HIS TRACKS AND VANISHED WITHOUT A TRACE.
"I NEVER KNEW WHERE THEY WENT AFTER THEY LEFT EARTH, BUT FINDING A PLANET TO CONQUER...
"...AND RENAMING IT NEW KRYPTON SOUNDS EXACTLY LIKE SOMETHING HE'D DO."
SO YOU HAVE NOT FOUGHT THE EARTH/KRYPTON WAR THAT IS YET TO--
WAR? WHAT ARE YOU SAYING?
MISSING SENTRY LOCATED AND DISABLED.
ASSAILANTS IDENTIFIED.
Ohhh...
...CRAP.

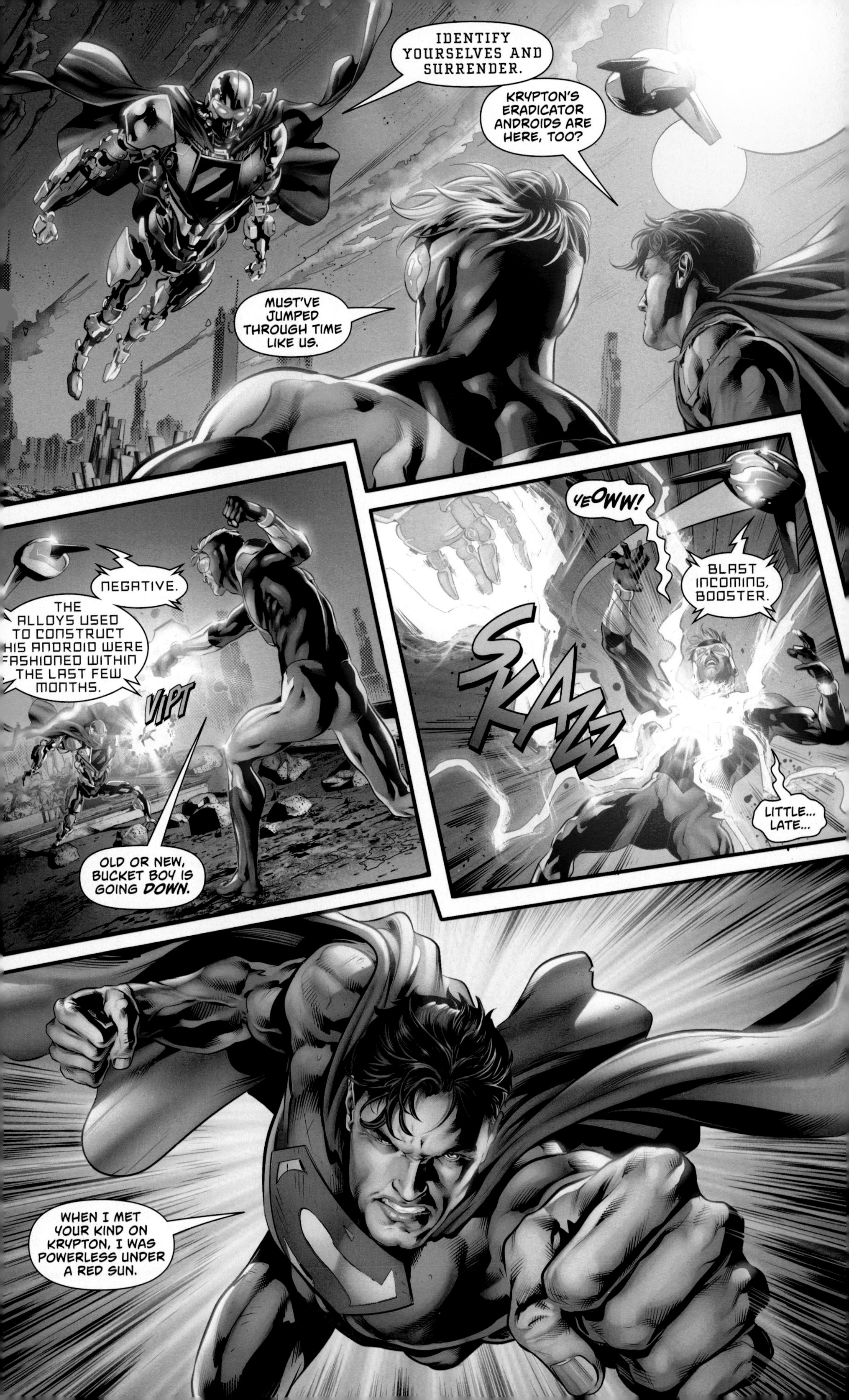
IDENTIFY YOURSELVES AND SURRENDER.
KRYPTON'S ERADICATOR ANDROIDS ARE HERE, TOO?
MUST'VE JUMPED THROUGH TIME LIKE US.
NEGATIVE.
THE ALLOYS USED TO CONSTRUCT HIS ANDROID WERE FASHIONED WITHIN THE LAST FEW MONTHS.
VIPT
OLD OR NEW, BUCKET BOY IS GOING DOWN.
YEOWW!
BLAST INCOMING, BOOSTER.
SKAZZ
LITTLE... LATE...
WHEN I MET YOUR KIND ON KRYPTON, I WAS POWERLESS UNDER A RED SUN.

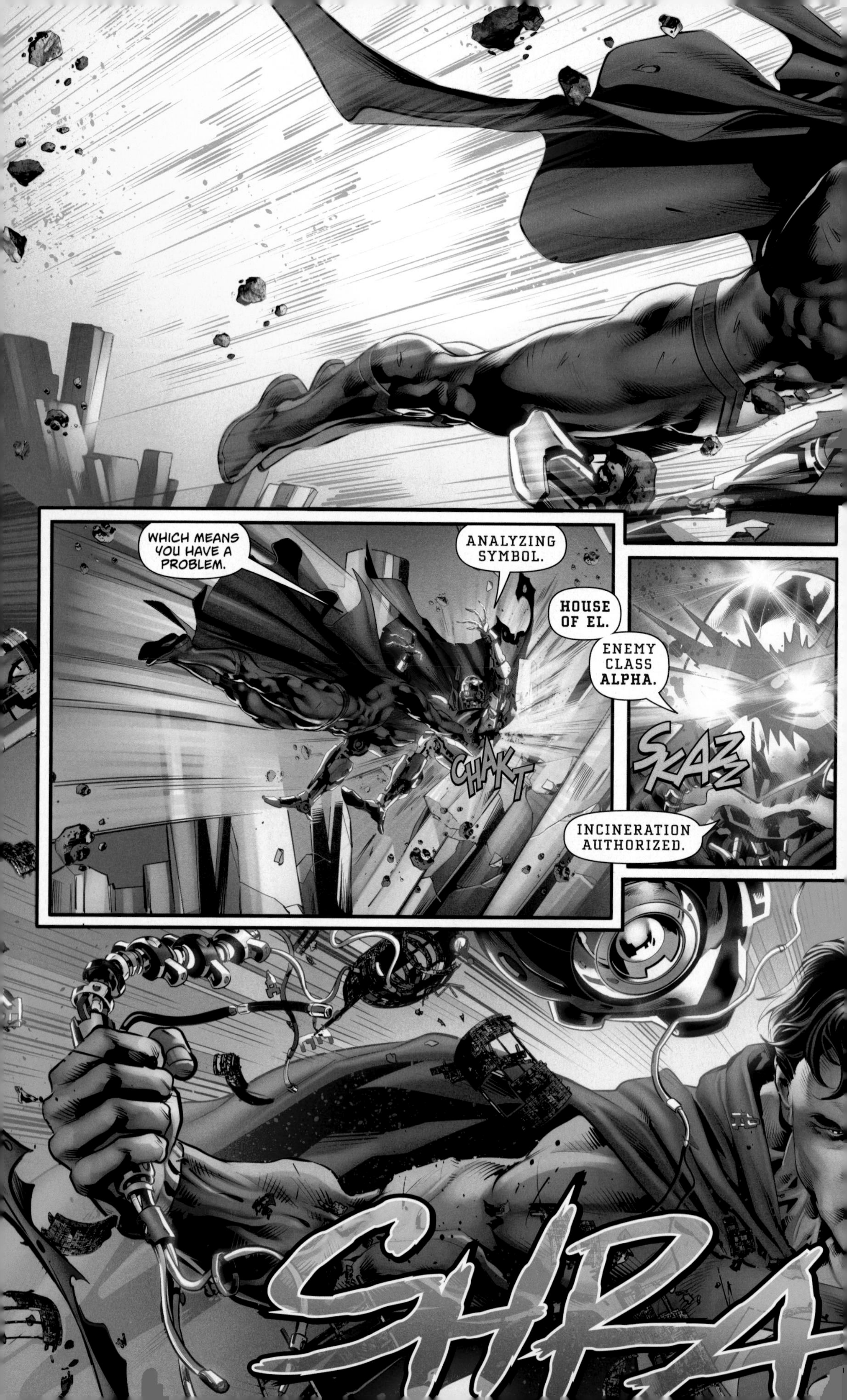

WHICH MEANS YOU HAVE A PROBLEM.
ANALYZING SYMBOL.
HOUSE OF EL.
ENEMY CLASS ALPHA.
CHAKT
SKAZZ
INCINERATION AUTHORIZED.
SHRA

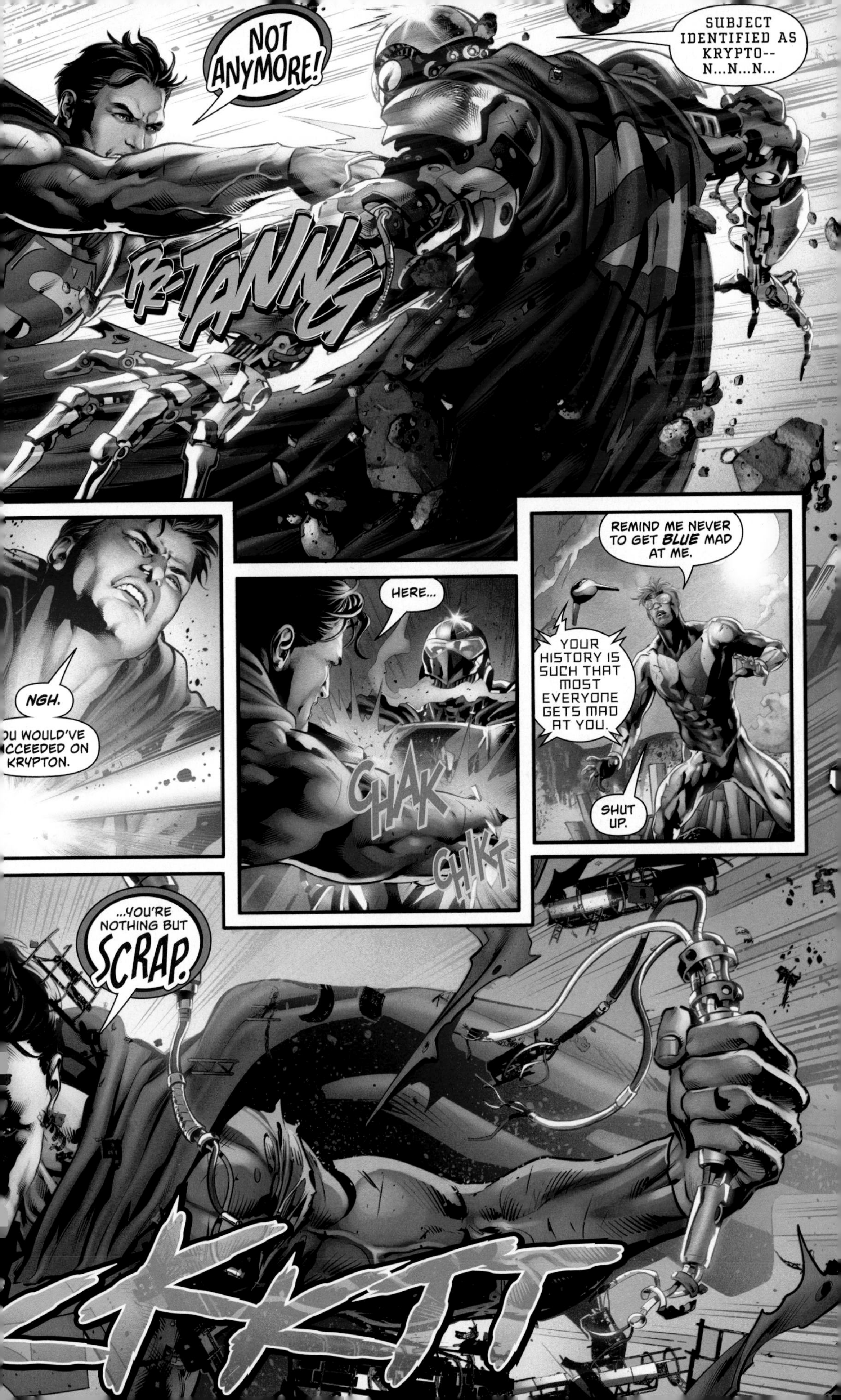
NOT ANYMORE!
SUBJECT IDENTIFIED AS KRYPTO-- N...N...N...
RR-TANNNG
NGH.
OU WOULD'VE CCEEDED ON KRYPTON.
HERE...
CHAK
CHIKT
REMIND ME NEVER TO GET BLUE MAD AT ME.
YOUR HISTORY IS SUCH THAT MOST EVERYONE GETS MAD AT YOU.
SHUT UP.
...YOU'RE NOTHING BUT SCRAP.
KKTT

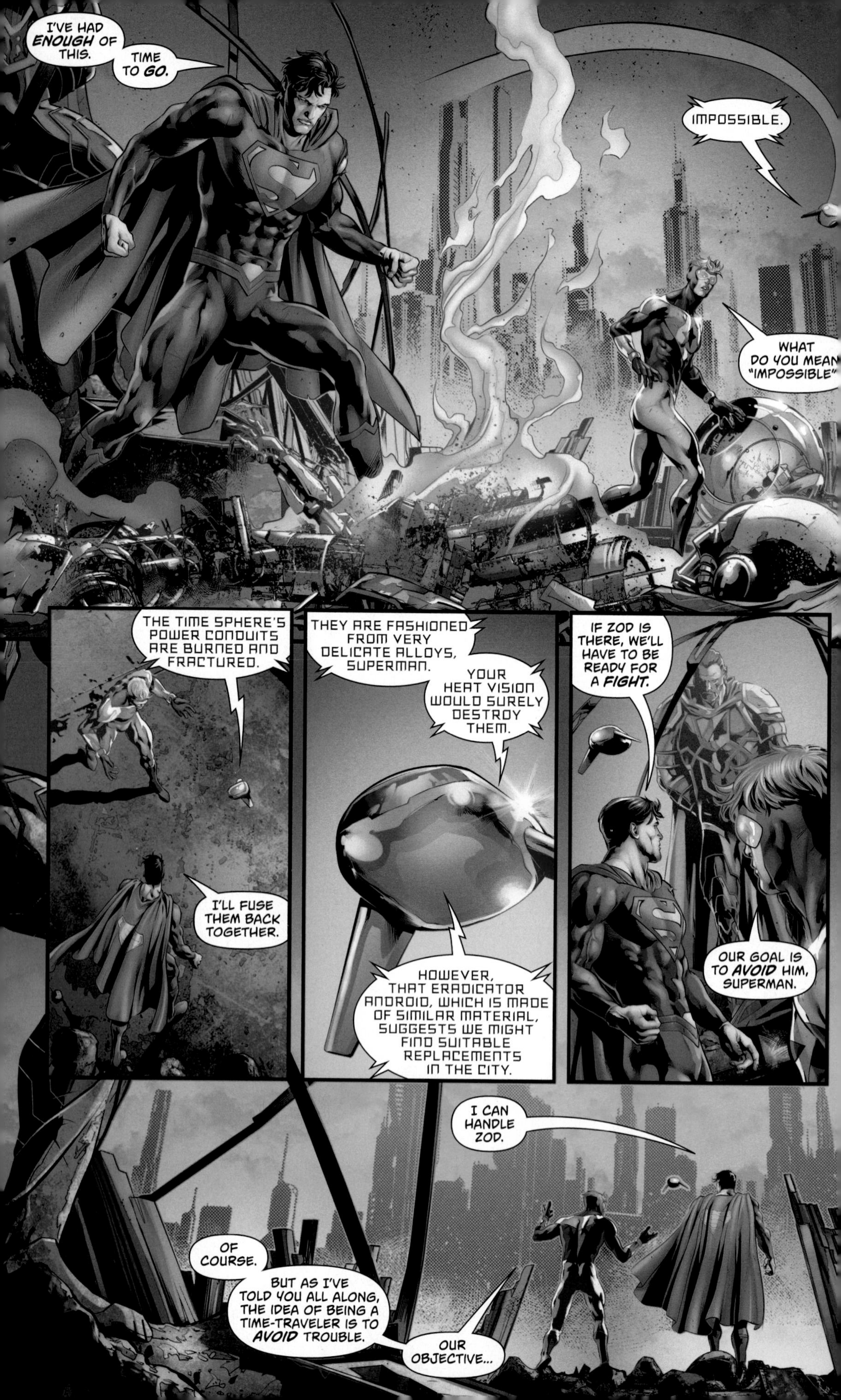
I'VE HAD ENOUGH OF THIS.
TIME TO GO.
IMPOSSIBLE.
WHAT DO YOU MEAN "IMPOSSIBLE"
THE TIME SPHERE'S POWER CONDUITS ARE BURNED AND FRACTURED.
I'LL FUSE THEM BACK TOGETHER.
THEY ARE FASHIONED FROM VERY DELICATE ALLOYS, SUPERMAN.
YOUR HEAT VISION WOULD SURELY DESTROY THEM.
HOWEVER, THAT ERADICATOR ANDROID, WHICH IS MADE OF SIMILAR MATERIAL, SUGGESTS WE MIGHT FIND SUITABLE REPLACEMENTS IN THE CITY.
IF ZOD IS THERE, WE'LL HAVE TO BE READY FOR A FIGHT.
OUR GOAL IS TO AVOID HIM, SUPERMAN.
I CAN HANDLE ZOD.
OF COURSE.
BUT AS I'VE TOLD YOU ALL ALONG, THE IDEA OF BEING A TIME-TRAVELER IS TO AVOID TROUBLE.
OUR OBJECTIVE...

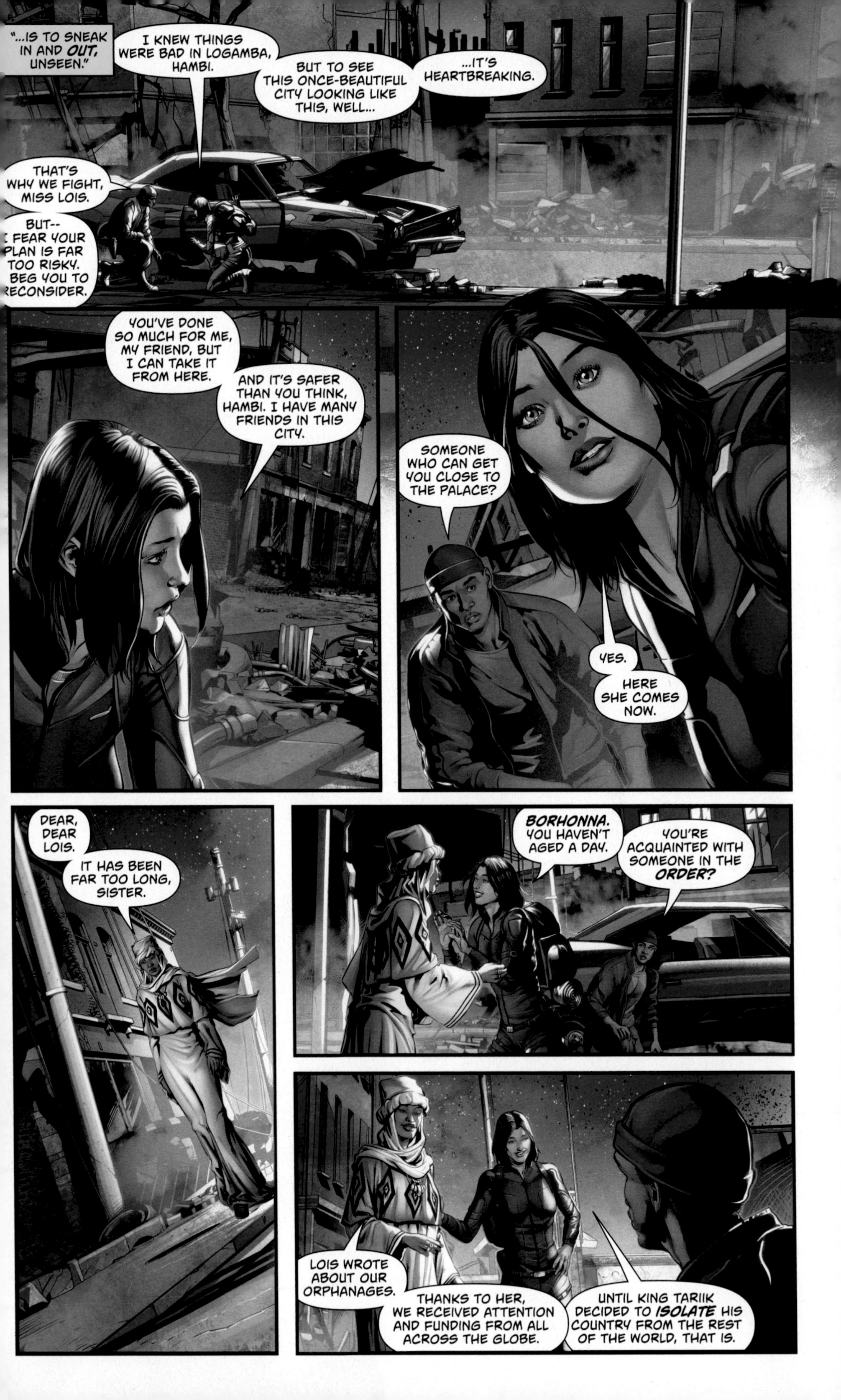
"...IS TO SNEAK IN AND *OUT*, UNSEEN."
I KNEW THINGS WERE BAD IN LOGAMBA, HAMBI.
BUT TO SEE THIS ONCE-BEAUTIFUL CITY LOOKING LIKE THIS, WELL...
...IT'S HEARTBREAKING.
THAT'S WHY WE FIGHT, MISS LOIS.
BUT-- I FEAR YOUR PLAN IS FAR TOO RISKY. I BEG YOU TO RECONSIDER.
YOU'VE DONE SO MUCH FOR ME, MY FRIEND, BUT I CAN TAKE IT FROM HERE.
AND IT'S SAFER THAN YOU THINK, HAMBI. I HAVE MANY FRIENDS IN THIS CITY.
SOMEONE WHO CAN GET YOU CLOSE TO THE PALACE?
YES.
HERE SHE COMES NOW.
DEAR, DEAR LOIS.
IT HAS BEEN FAR TOO LONG, SISTER.
BORHONNA. YOU HAVEN'T AGED A DAY.
YOU'RE ACQUAINTED WITH SOMEONE IN THE *ORDER?*
LOIS WROTE ABOUT OUR ORPHANAGES.
THANKS TO HER, WE RECEIVED ATTENTION AND FUNDING FROM ALL ACROSS THE GLOBE.
UNTIL KING TARIIK DECIDED TO *ISOLATE* HIS COUNTRY FROM THE REST OF THE WORLD, THAT IS.

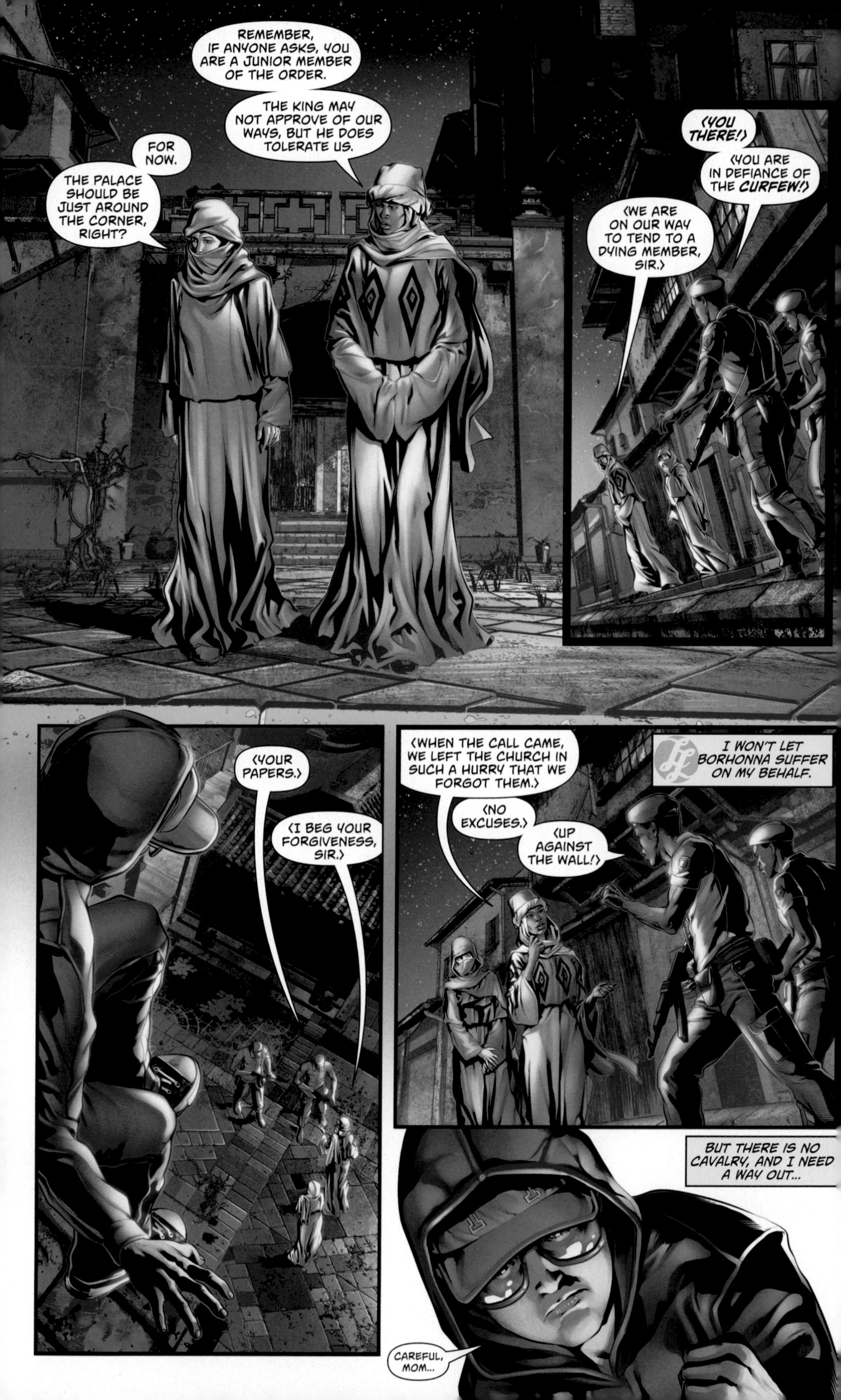

REMEMBER, IF ANYONE ASKS, YOU ARE A JUNIOR MEMBER OF THE ORDER.
THE KING MAY NOT APPROVE OF OUR WAYS, BUT HE DOES TOLERATE US.
FOR NOW.
THE PALACE SHOULD BE JUST AROUND THE CORNER, RIGHT?
‹YOU THERE!›
‹YOU ARE IN DEFIANCE OF THE CURFEW!›
‹WE ARE ON OUR WAY TO TEND TO A DYING MEMBER, SIR.›
‹YOUR PAPERS.›
‹I BEG YOUR FORGIVENESS, SIR.›
‹WHEN THE CALL CAME, WE LEFT THE CHURCH IN SUCH A HURRY THAT WE FORGOT THEM.›
‹NO EXCUSES.›
‹UP AGAINST THE WALL!›
I WON'T LET BORHONNA SUFFER ON MY BEHALF.
BUT THERE IS NO CAVALRY, AND I NEED A WAY OUT...
CAREFUL, MOM...

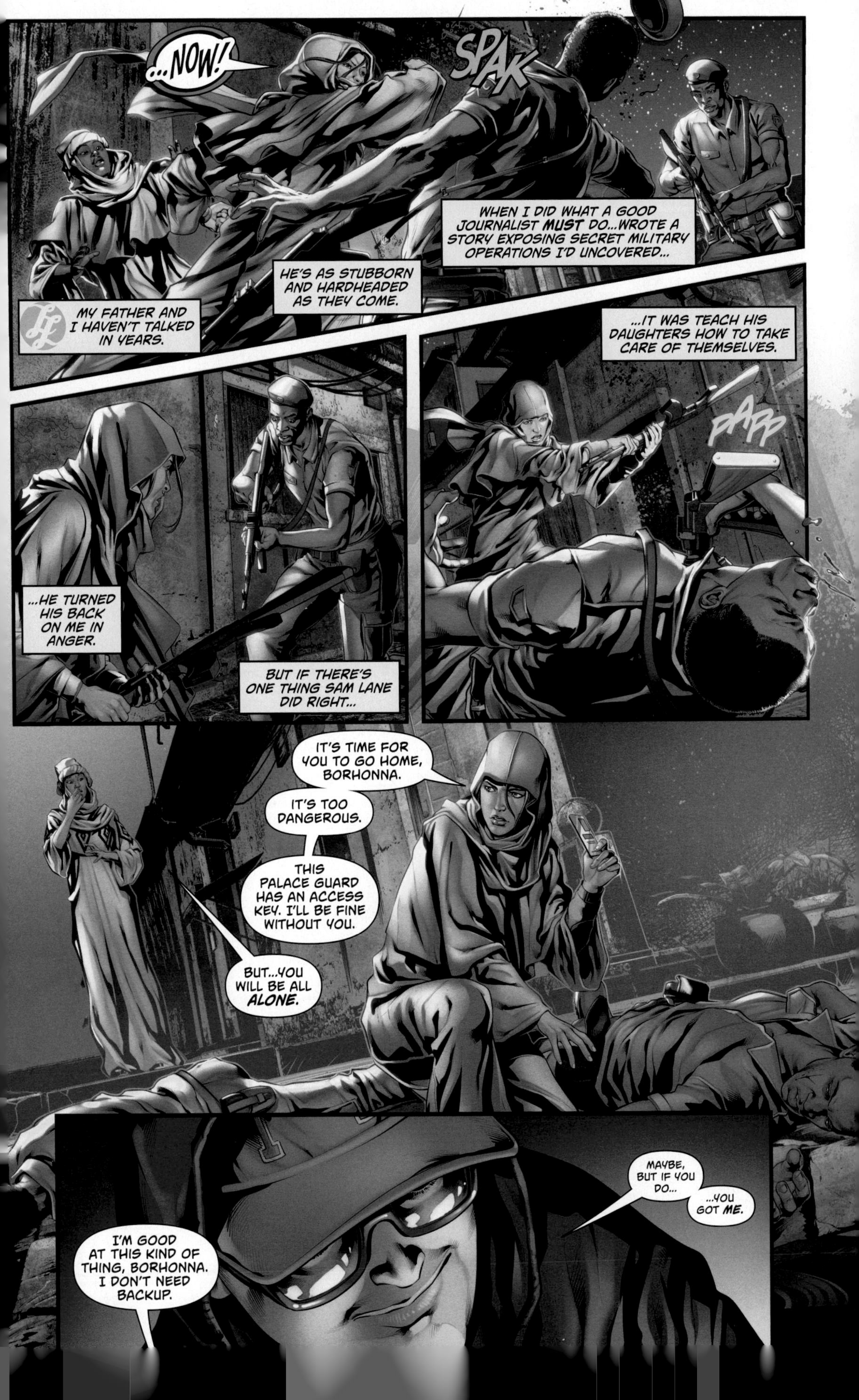
...NOW!
SPAK
MY FATHER AND I HAVEN'T TALKED IN YEARS.
HE'S AS STUBBORN AND HARDHEADED AS THEY COME.
WHEN I DID WHAT A GOOD JOURNALIST MUST DO...WROTE A STORY EXPOSING SECRET MILITARY OPERATIONS I'D UNCOVERED...
...HE TURNED HIS BACK ON ME IN ANGER.
BUT IF THERE'S ONE THING SAM LANE DID RIGHT...
...IT WAS TEACH HIS DAUGHTERS HOW TO TAKE CARE OF THEMSELVES.
PAPP
IT'S TIME FOR YOU TO GO HOME, BORHONNA.
IT'S TOO DANGEROUS.
THIS PALACE GUARD HAS AN ACCESS KEY. I'LL BE FINE WITHOUT YOU.
BUT...YOU WILL BE ALL ALONE.
I'M GOOD AT THIS KIND OF THING, BORHONNA. I DON'T NEED BACKUP.
MAYBE, BUT IF YOU DO...
...YOU GOT ME.

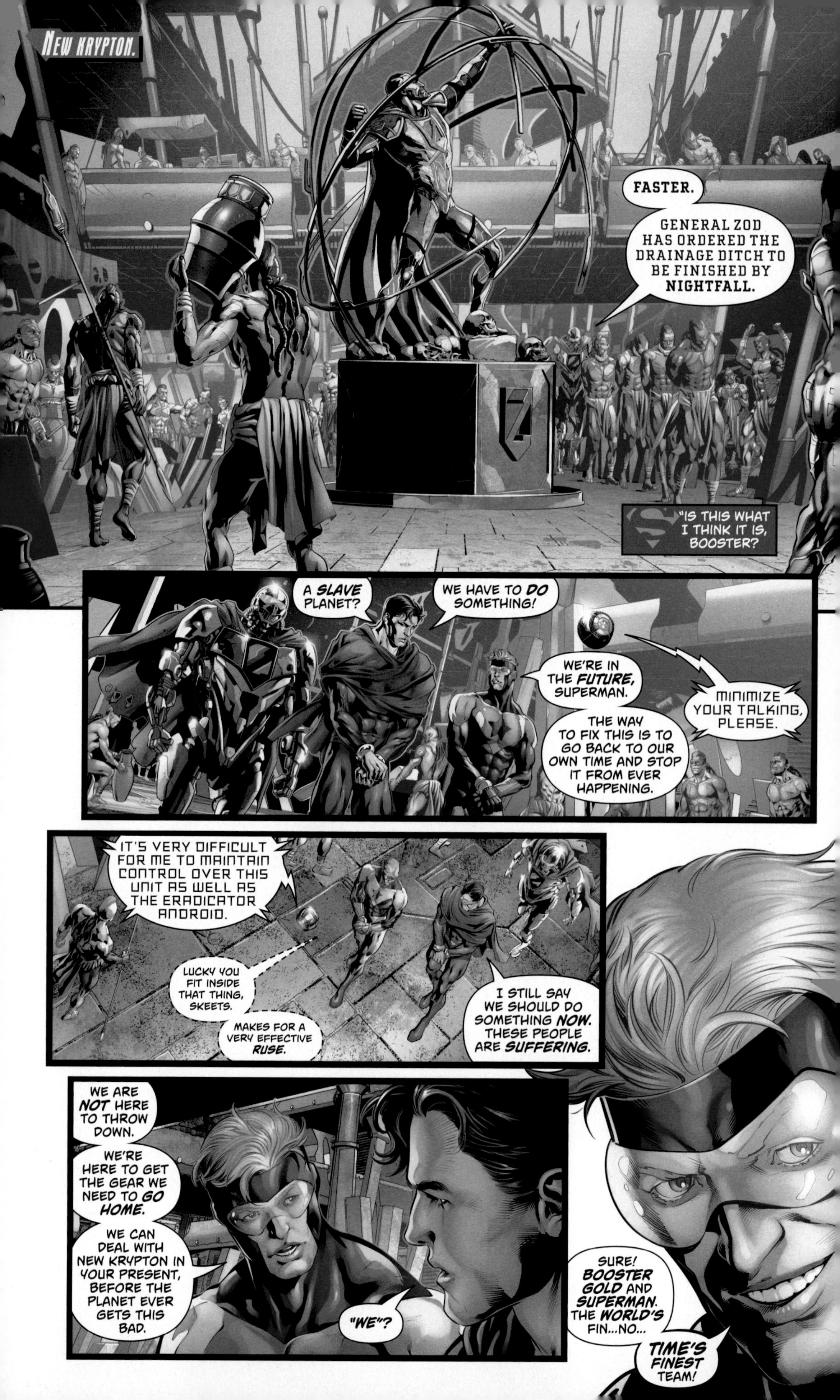
NEW KRYPTON.
FASTER.
GENERAL ZOD HAS ORDERED THE DRAINAGE DITCH TO BE FINISHED BY NIGHTFALL.
"IS THIS WHAT I THINK IT IS, BOOSTER?
A SLAVE PLANET?
WE HAVE TO DO SOMETHING!
WE'RE IN THE FUTURE, SUPERMAN.
THE WAY TO FIX THIS IS TO GO BACK TO OUR OWN TIME AND STOP IT FROM EVER HAPPENING.
MINIMIZE YOUR TALKING, PLEASE.
IT'S VERY DIFFICULT FOR ME TO MAINTAIN CONTROL OVER THIS UNIT AS WELL AS THE ERADICATOR ANDROID.
LUCKY YOU FIT INSIDE THAT THING, SKEETS.
MAKES FOR A VERY EFFECTIVE RUSE.
I STILL SAY WE SHOULD DO SOMETHING NOW. THESE PEOPLE ARE SUFFERING.
WE ARE NOT HERE TO THROW DOWN.
WE'RE HERE TO GET THE GEAR WE NEED TO GO HOME.
WE CAN DEAL WITH NEW KRYPTON IN YOUR PRESENT, BEFORE THE PLANET EVER GETS THIS BAD.
"WE"?
SURE! BOOSTER GOLD AND SUPERMAN. THE WORLD'S FIN...NO...
TIME'S FINEST TEAM!

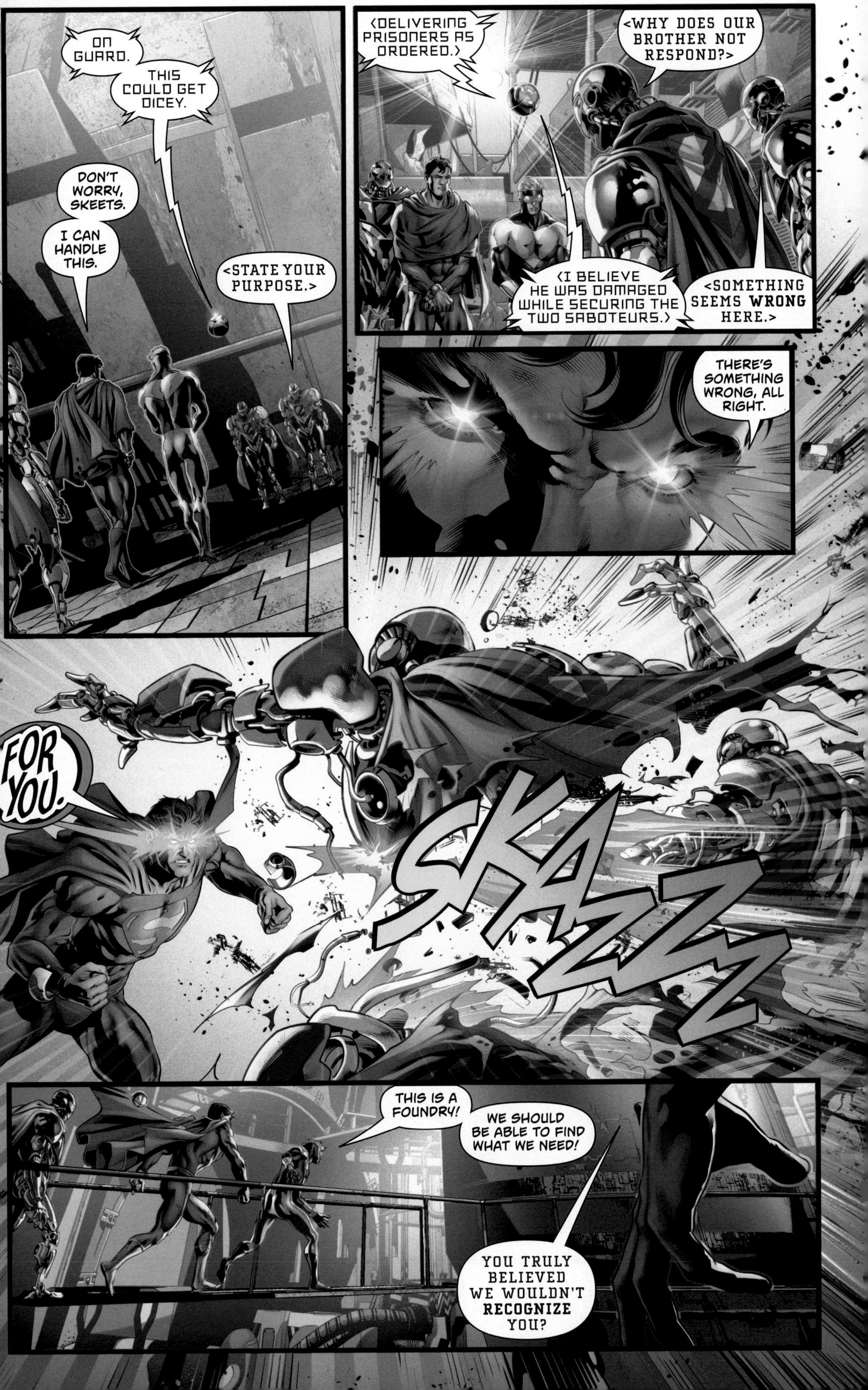
ON GUARD.
THIS COULD GET DICEY.
DON'T WORRY, SKEETS.
I CAN HANDLE THIS.
<STATE YOUR PURPOSE.>
<DELIVERING PRISONERS AS ORDERED.>
<WHY DOES OUR BROTHER NOT RESPOND?>
<I BELIEVE HE WAS DAMAGED WHILE SECURING THE TWO SABOTEURS.>
<SOMETHING SEEMS WRONG HERE.>
THERE'S SOMETHING WRONG, ALL RIGHT.
FOR YOU.
SKAZZM
THIS IS A FOUNDRY!
WE SHOULD BE ABLE TO FIND WHAT WE NEED!
YOU TRULY BELIEVED WE WOULDN'T RECOGNIZE YOU?

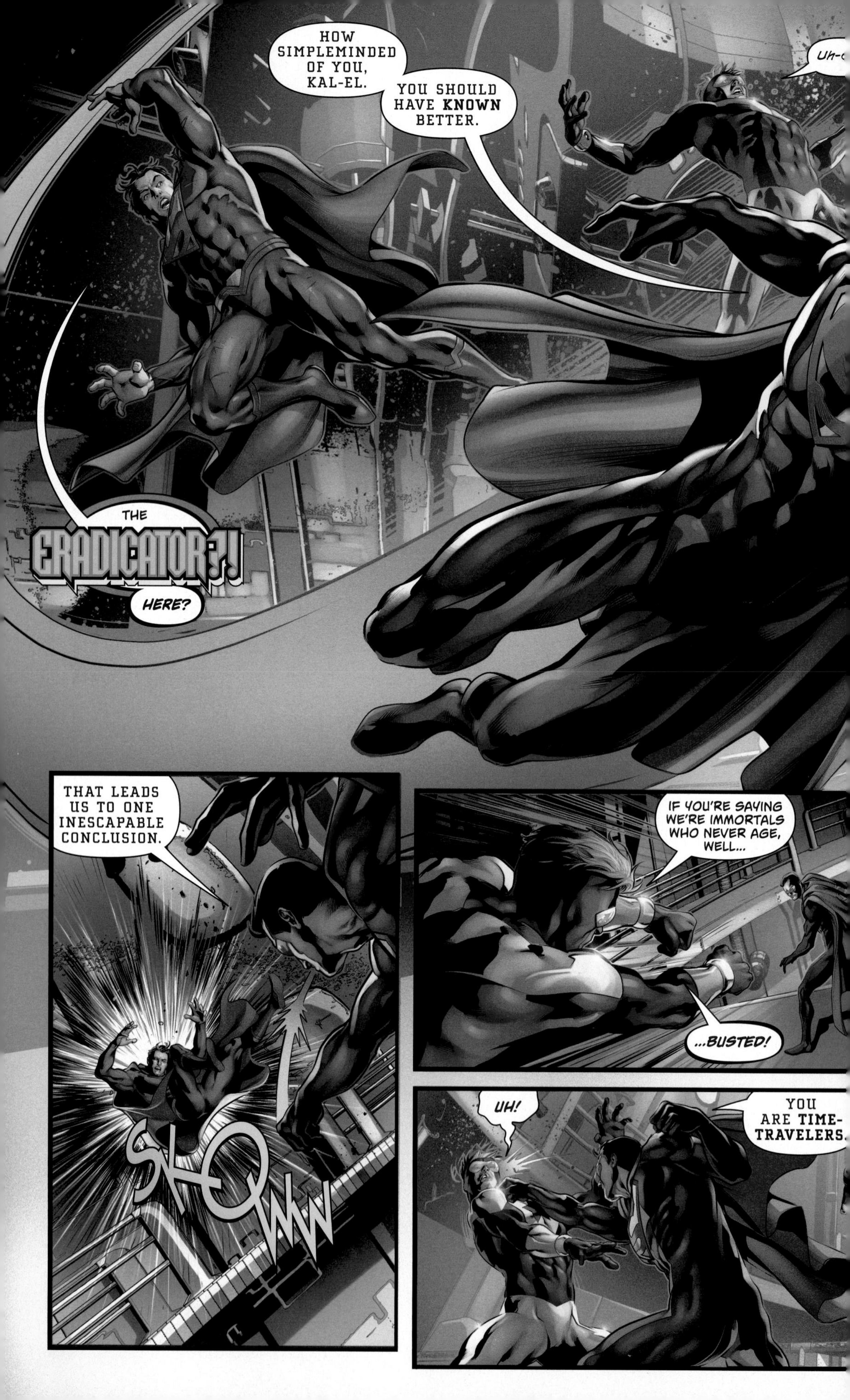
HOW SIMPLEMINDED OF YOU, KAL-EL.
YOU SHOULD HAVE **KNOWN** BETTER.
THE ERADICATOR?!
HERE?
THAT LEADS US TO ONE INESCAPABLE CONCLUSION.
SHOWW
IF YOU'RE SAYING WE'RE IMMORTALS WHO NEVER AGE, WELL...
...BUSTED!
UH!
YOU ARE **TIME-TRAVELERS.**

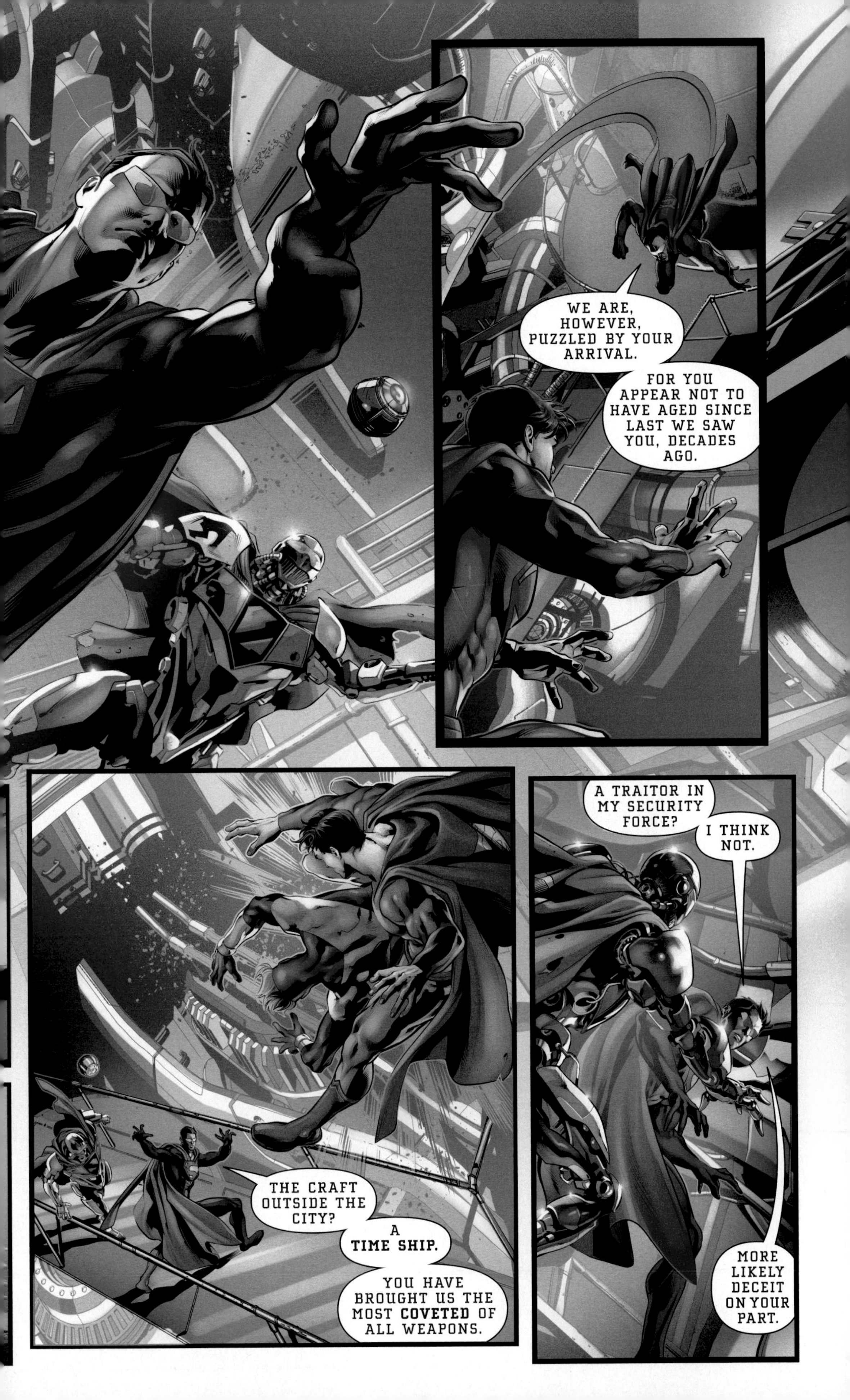
WE ARE, HOWEVER, PUZZLED BY YOUR ARRIVAL.
FOR YOU APPEAR NOT TO HAVE AGED SINCE LAST WE SAW YOU, DECADES AGO.
THE CRAFT OUTSIDE THE CITY?
A TIME SHIP.
YOU HAVE BROUGHT US THE MOST COVETED OF ALL WEAPONS.
A TRAITOR IN MY SECURITY FORCE?
I THINK NOT.
MORE LIKELY DECEIT ON YOUR PART.

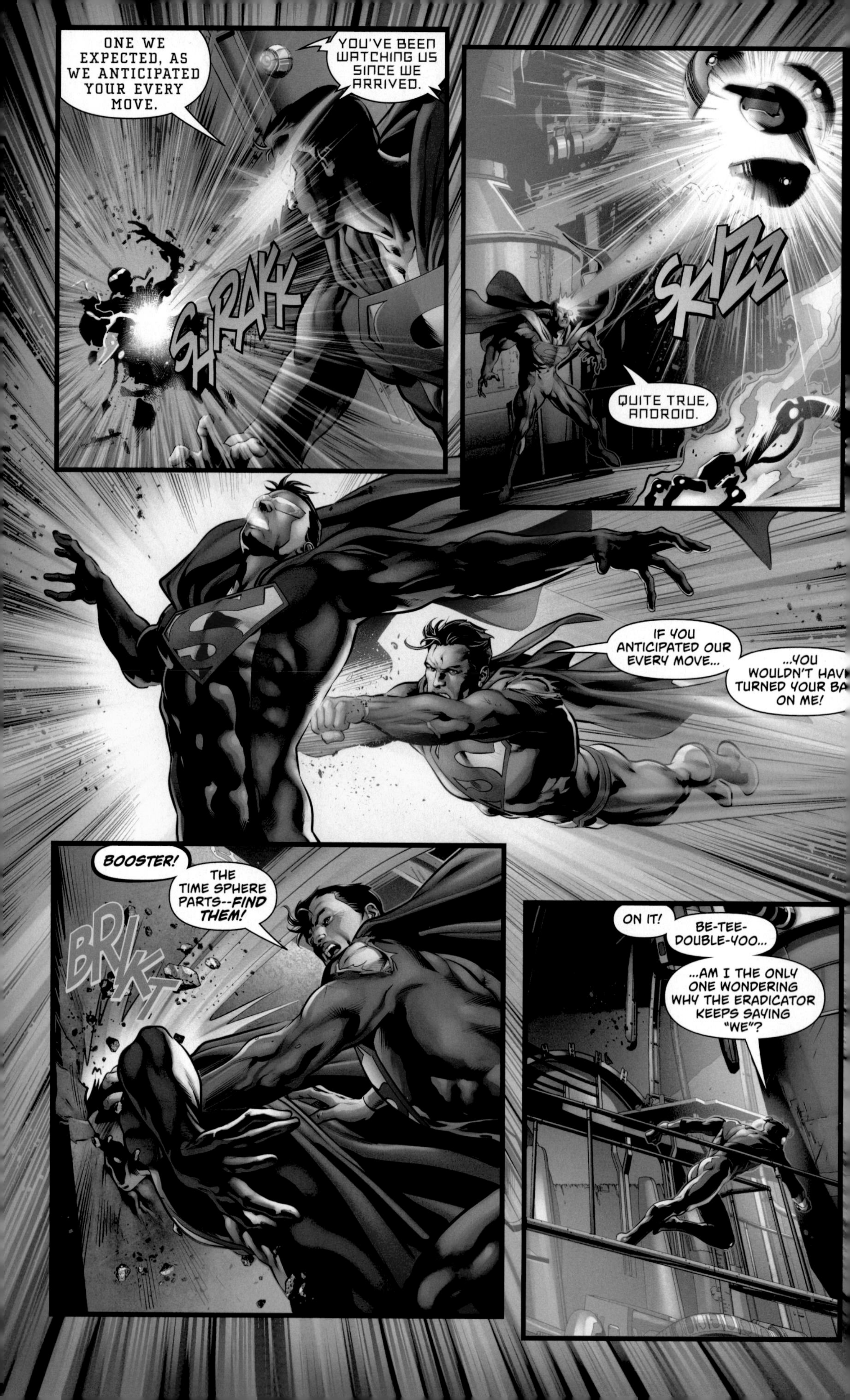
ONE WE EXPECTED, AS WE ANTICIPATED YOUR EVERY MOVE.
YOU'VE BEEN WATCHING US SINCE WE ARRIVED.
SHRAKK
SKIZZ
QUITE TRUE, ANDROID.
IF YOU ANTICIPATED OUR EVERY MOVE...
...YOU WOULDN'T HAV TURNED YOUR BA ON ME!
BOOSTER!
THE TIME SPHERE PARTS--FIND THEM!
BRAKT
ON IT!
BE-TEE-DOUBLE-YOO...
...AM I THE ONLY ONE WONDERING WHY THE ERADICATOR KEEPS SAYING "WE"?

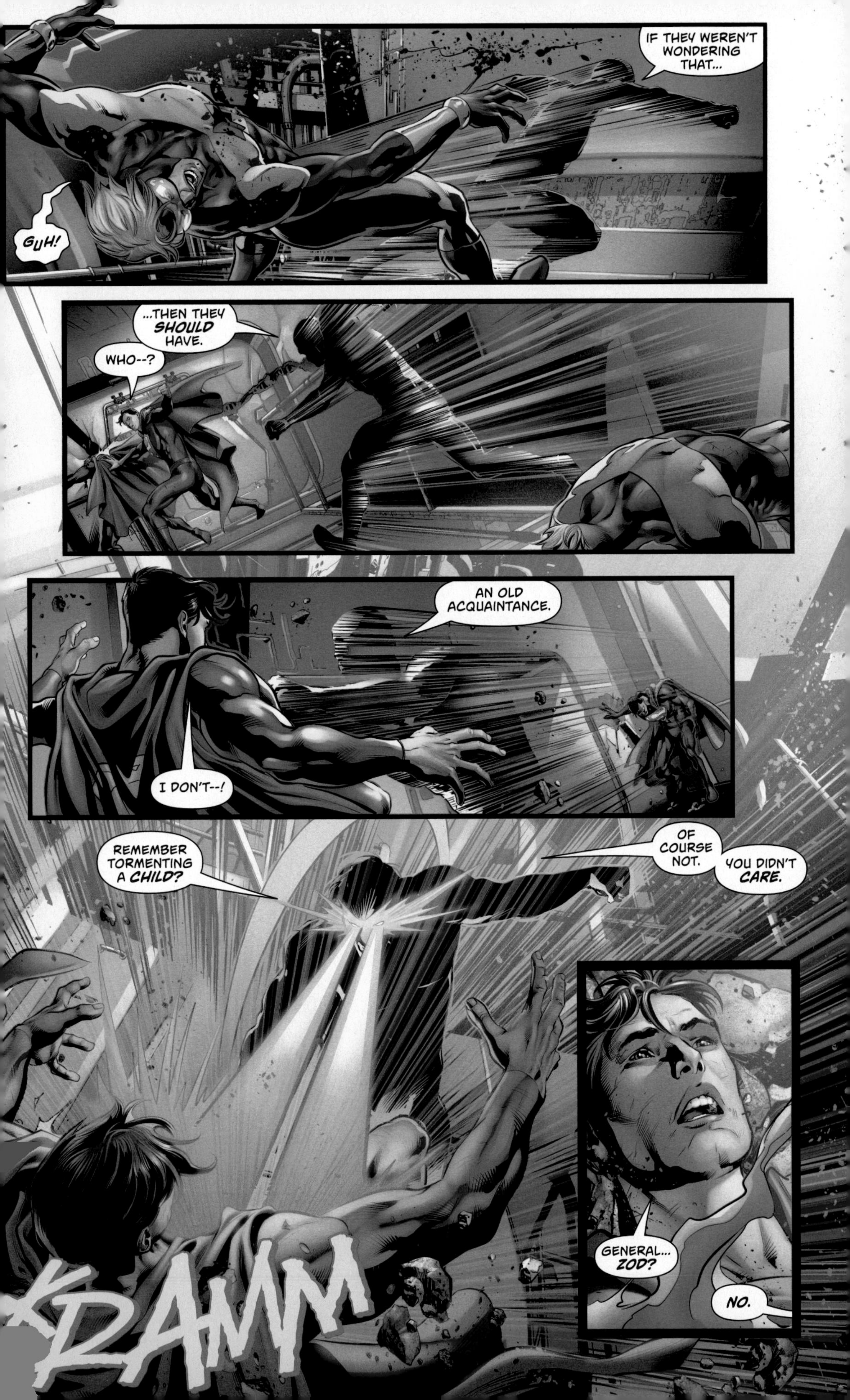
IF THEY WEREN'T WONDERING THAT...
GUH!
...THEN THEY SHOULD HAVE.
WHO--?
AN OLD ACQUAINTANCE.
I DON'T--!
REMEMBER TORMENTING A CHILD?
OF COURSE NOT.
YOU DIDN'T CARE.
KRAMM
GENERAL... ZOD?
NO.

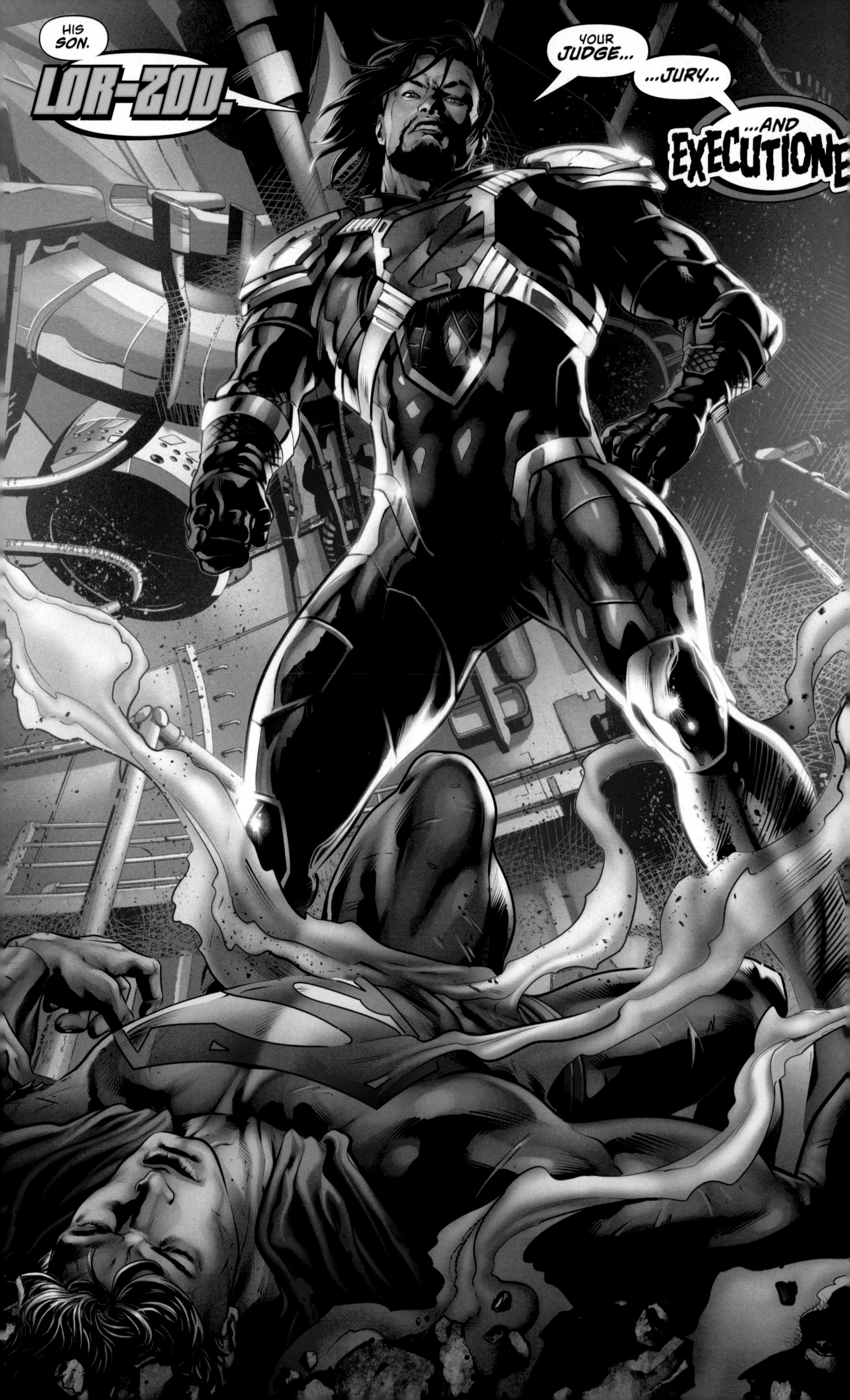
HIS SON.
LOR-ZOD.
YOUR JUDGE...
...JURY...
...AND EXECUTIONE

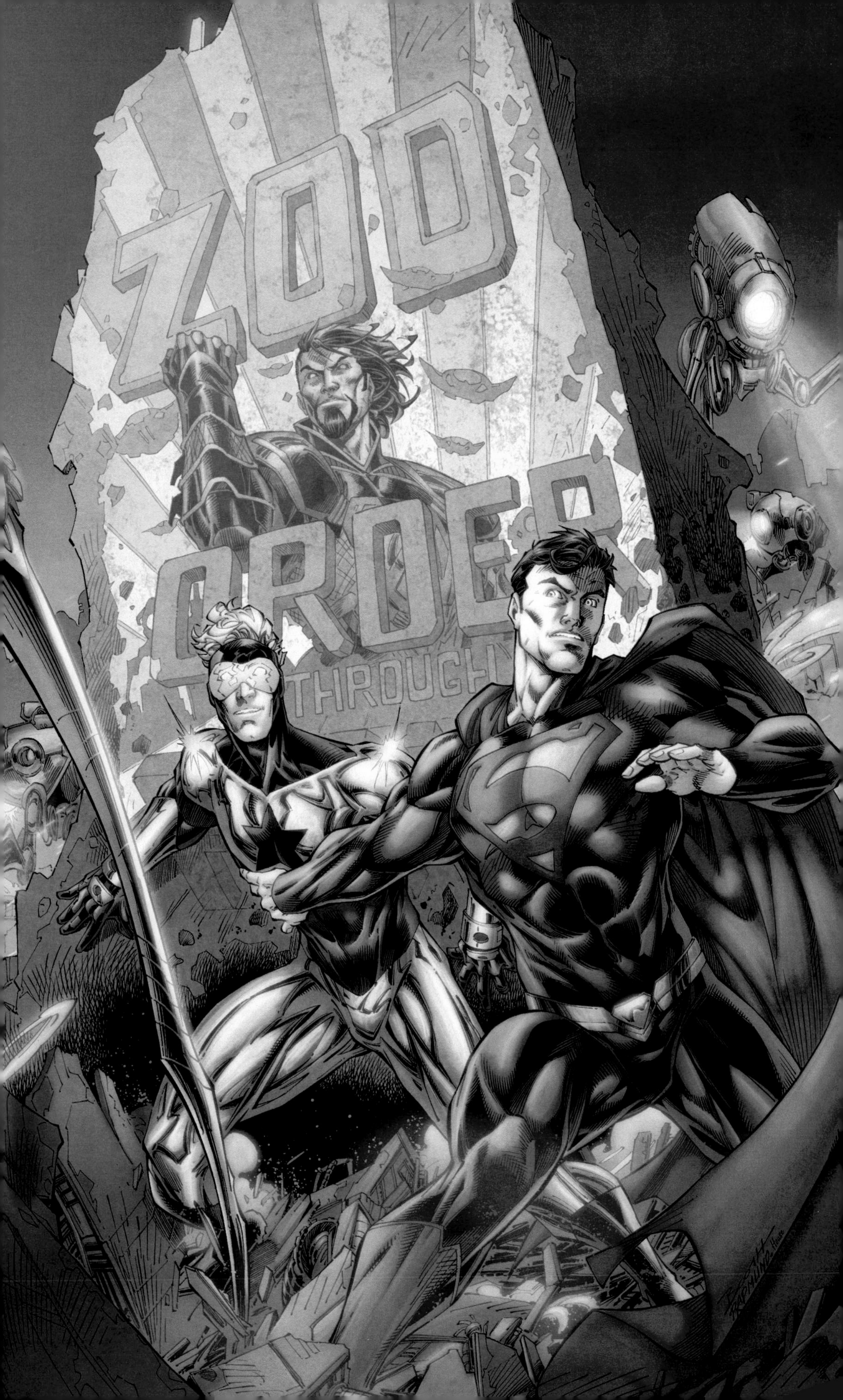
ZOD
ORDER
THROUGH

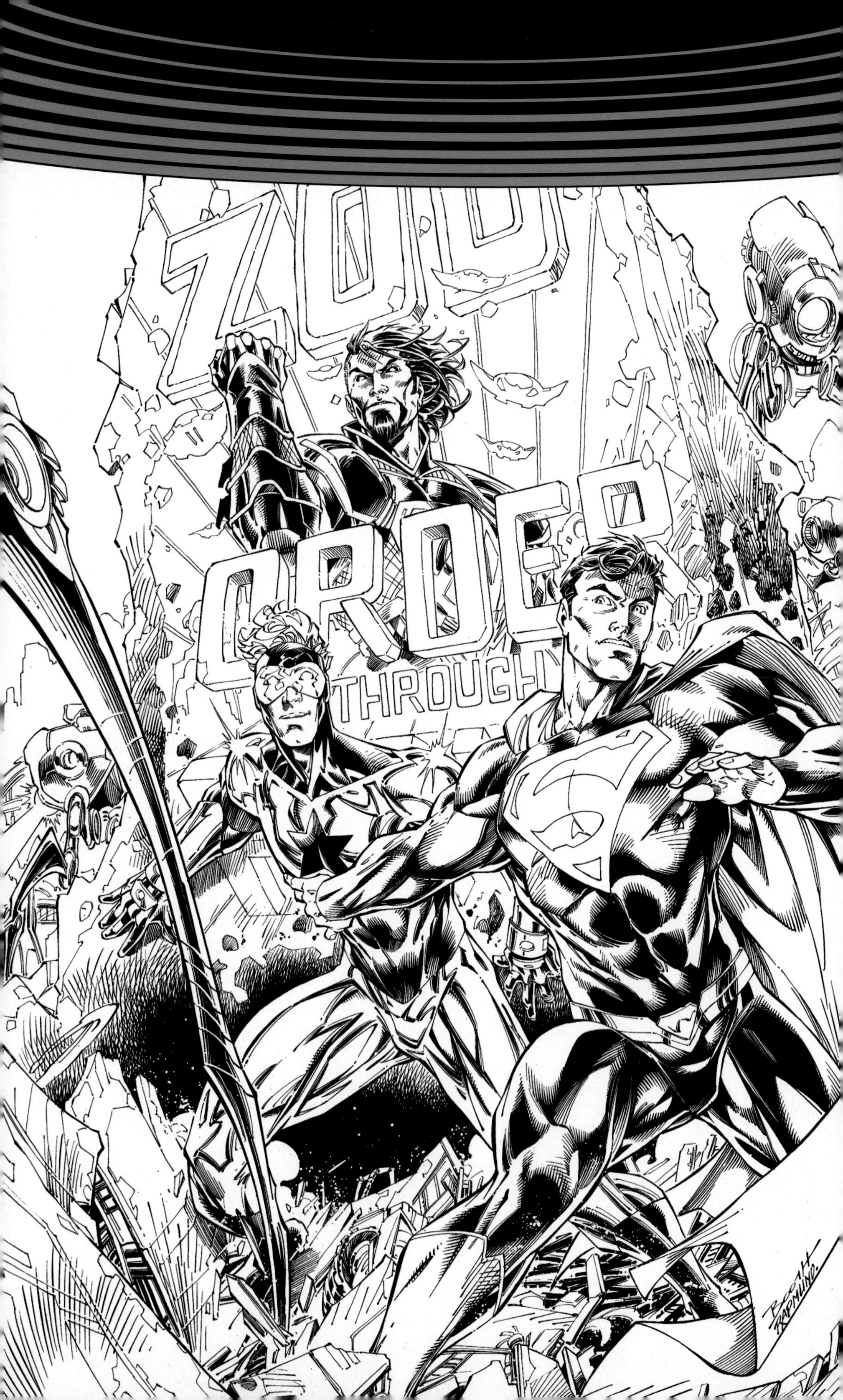
ZOD
ORDER
THROUGH

IT BEGAN WITH **MR. OZ.**

HE CLAIMED TO BE MY FATHER, **JOR-EL.**

SAID A MYSTERIOUS FORCE SWEPT HIM AWAY FROM KRYPTON'S DESTRUCTION AT THE LAST POSSIBLE SECOND.

SO I USED FLASH'S COSMIC TREADMILL TO GO BACK IN TIME TO SEE THE TRUTH FOR MYSELF.

BUT THE PAST-- TIME ITSELF--WAS **FRACTURED.**

I ENDED UP IN A [SH]ARD OF THE PAST [T]HAT WAS **WRONG.**

WHERE JOR-EL AND ALL KRYPTONIANS SURVIVED.

I NEVER GOT THE ANSWER I WAS LOOKING FOR BECAUSE THE SELF-APPOINTED GUARDIAN OF TIME...

...BOOSTER GOLD...

[T]OOK ME AWAY BEFORE THAT [M]ERGING PAST COULD SOLIDIFY [IN]TO PERMANENT REALITY.

BEFORE ALL THAT, **GENERAL ZOD** WAS AN ENTIRELY DIFFERENT PROBLEM.

[AF]TER A HARSH BATTLE, [Z]OD, HIS WIFE **URSA** AND SON **LOR-ZOD** [IM]PRISONED ME IN THE [PH]ANTOM ZONE BEFORE [E]SCAPING TO PARTS UNKNOWN.

IMPOSSIBLE AS IT SEEMS, ALL OF THAT HAS COME TOGETHER **HERE.**

THIS **SECOND.**

THIS **FUTURE** ON AN ALIEN WORLD...

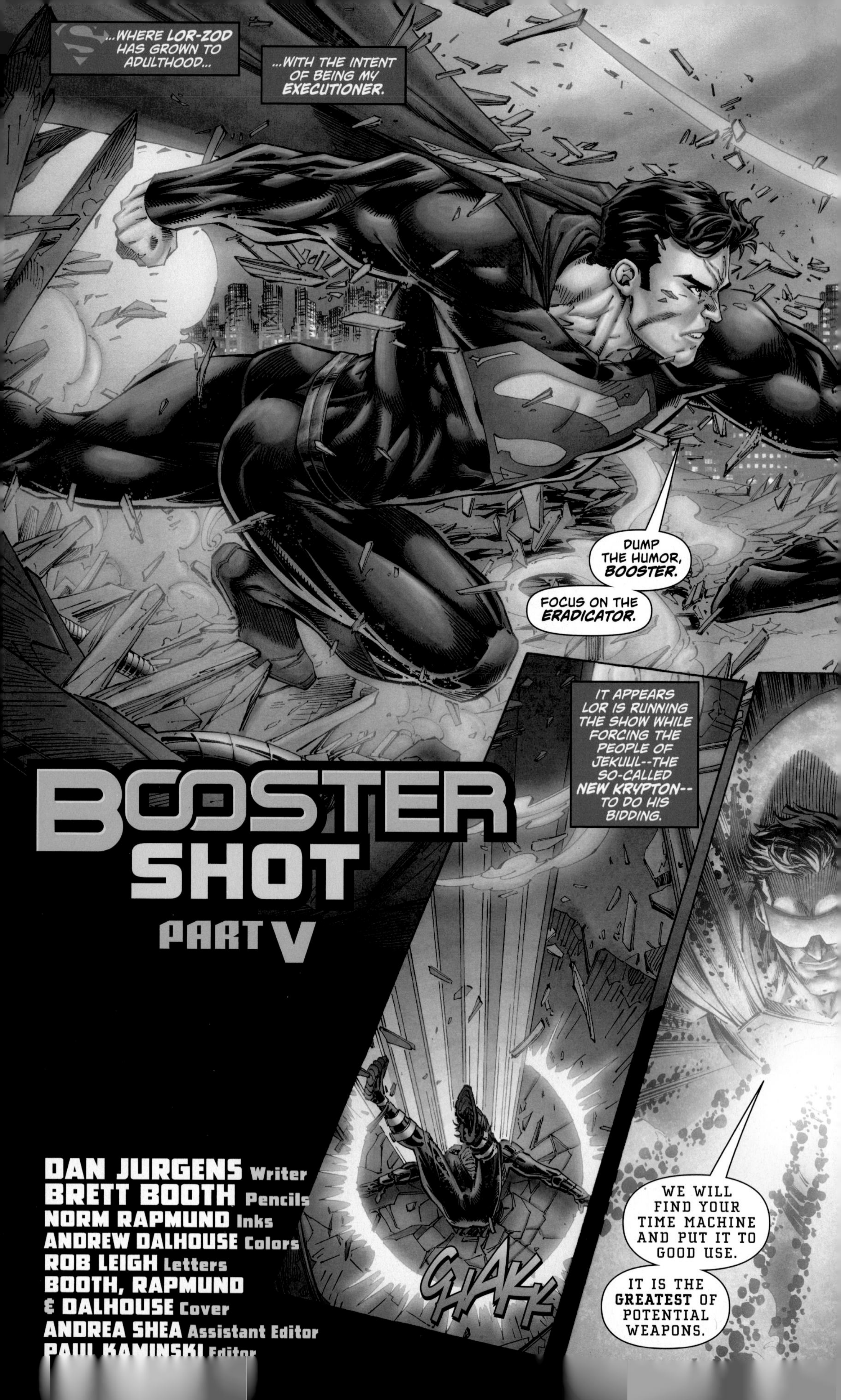

...WHERE LOR-ZOD HAS GROWN TO ADULTHOOD...
...WITH THE INTENT OF BEING MY EXECUTIONER.
DUMP THE HUMOR, BOOSTER.
FOCUS ON THE ERADICATOR.
BOOSTER SHOT PART V
IT APPEARS LOR IS RUNNING THE SHOW WHILE FORCING THE PEOPLE OF JEKUUL--THE SO-CALLED NEW KRYPTON--TO DO HIS BIDDING.
DAN JURGENS Writer
BRETT BOOTH Pencils
NORM RAPMUND Inks
ANDREW DALHOUSE Colors
ROB LEIGH Letters
BOOTH, RAPMUND & DALHOUSE Cover
ANDREA SHEA Assistant Editor
PAUL KAMINSKI Editor
CHAKK
WE WILL FIND YOUR TIME MACHINE AND PUT IT TO GOOD USE.
IT IS THE GREATEST OF POTENTIAL WEAPONS.

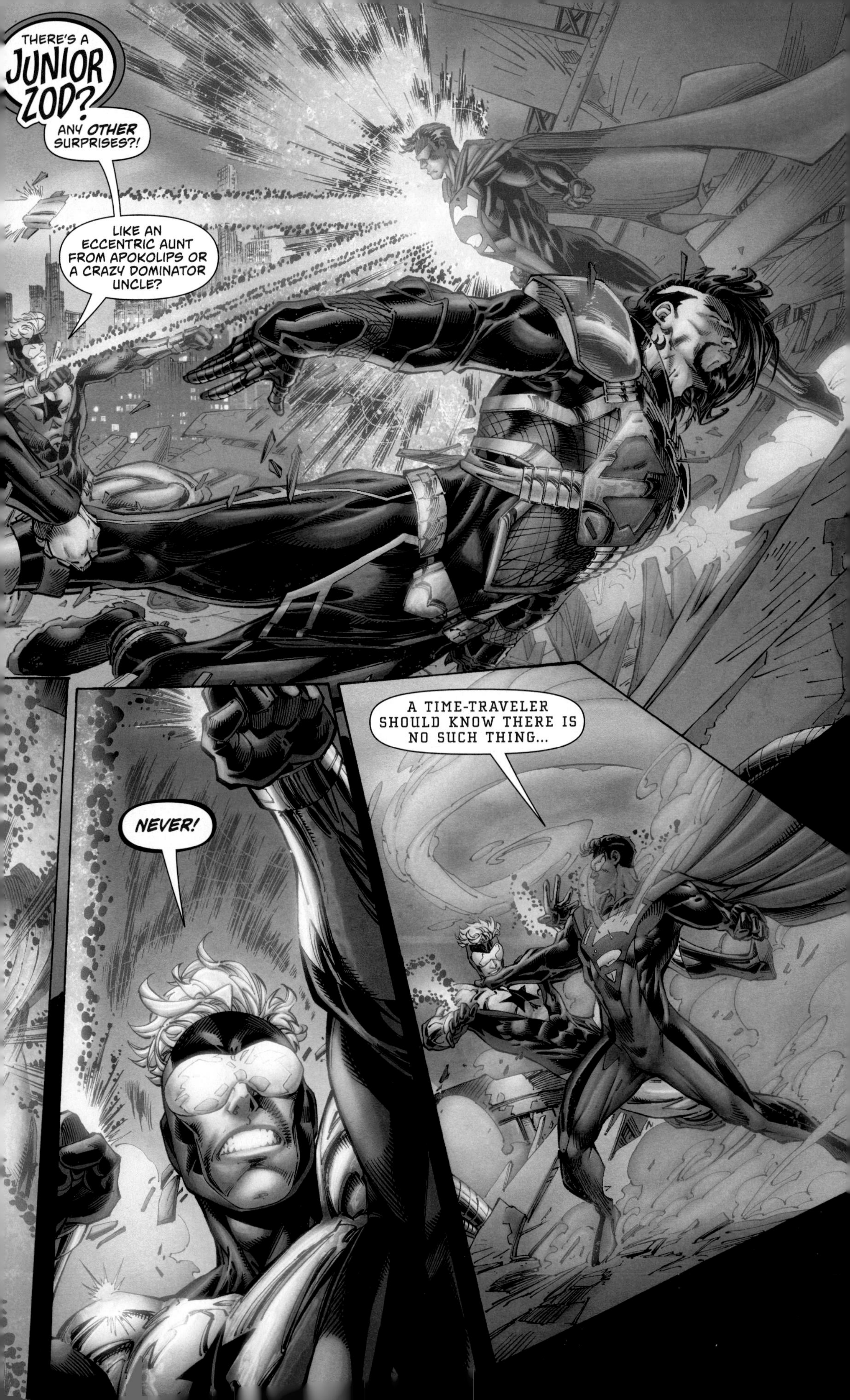
THERE'S A JUNIOR ZOD?
ANY OTHER SURPRISES?!
LIKE AN ECCENTRIC AUNT FROM APOKOLIPS OR A CRAZY DOMINATOR UNCLE?
A TIME-TRAVELER SHOULD KNOW THERE IS NO SUCH THING...
NEVER!

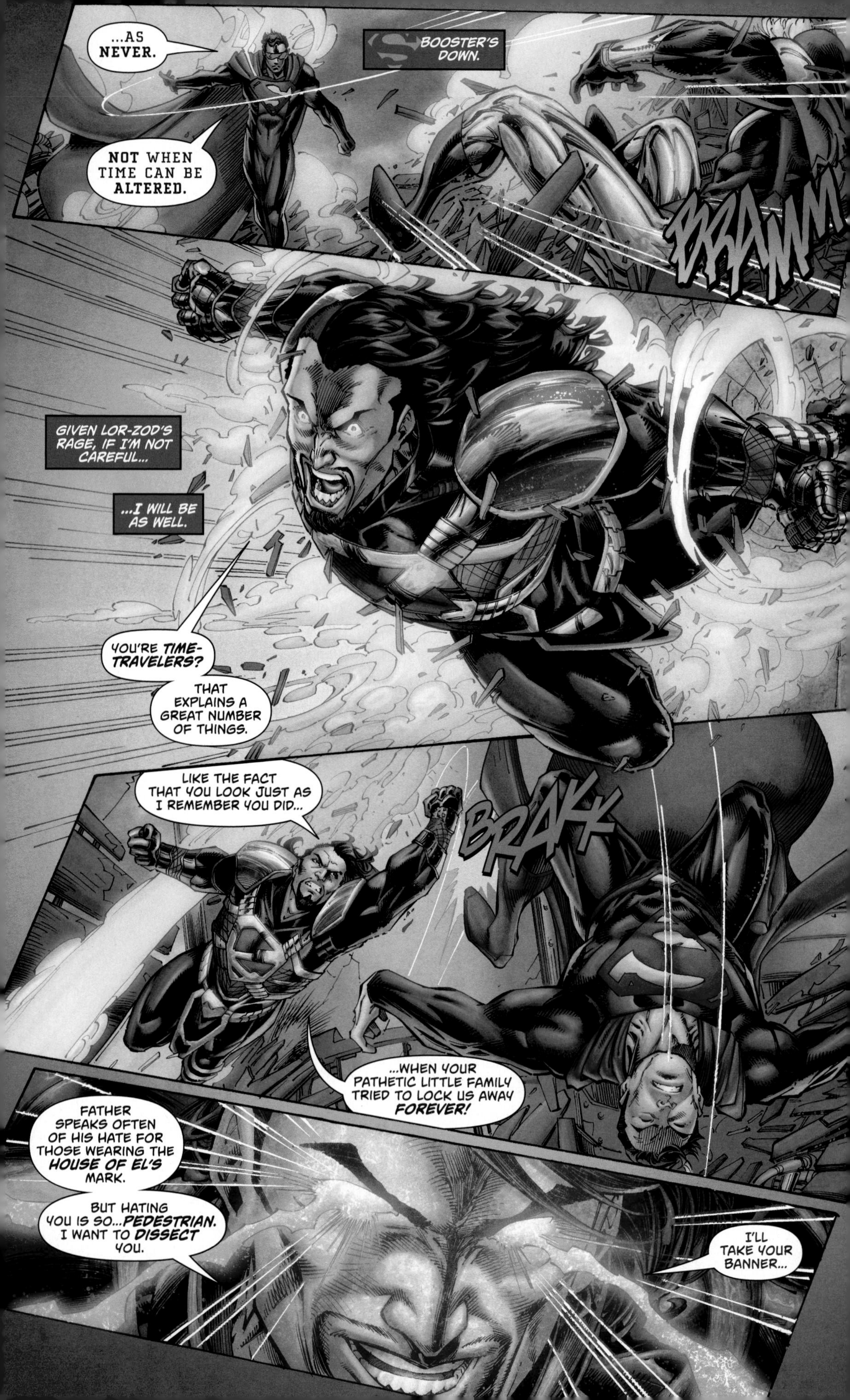

...AS NEVER.
BOOSTER'S DOWN.
NOT WHEN TIME CAN BE ALTERED.
BRAMM
GIVEN LOR-ZOD'S RAGE, IF I'M NOT CAREFUL...
...I WILL BE AS WELL.
YOU'RE TIME-TRAVELERS?
THAT EXPLAINS A GREAT NUMBER OF THINGS.
LIKE THE FACT THAT YOU LOOK JUST AS I REMEMBER YOU DID...
BRAKK
...WHEN YOUR PATHETIC LITTLE FAMILY TRIED TO LOCK US AWAY FOREVER!
FATHER SPEAKS OFTEN OF HIS HATE FOR THOSE WEARING THE HOUSE OF EL'S MARK.
BUT HATING YOU IS SO...PEDESTRIAN. I WANT TO DISSECT YOU.
I'LL TAKE YOUR BANNER...

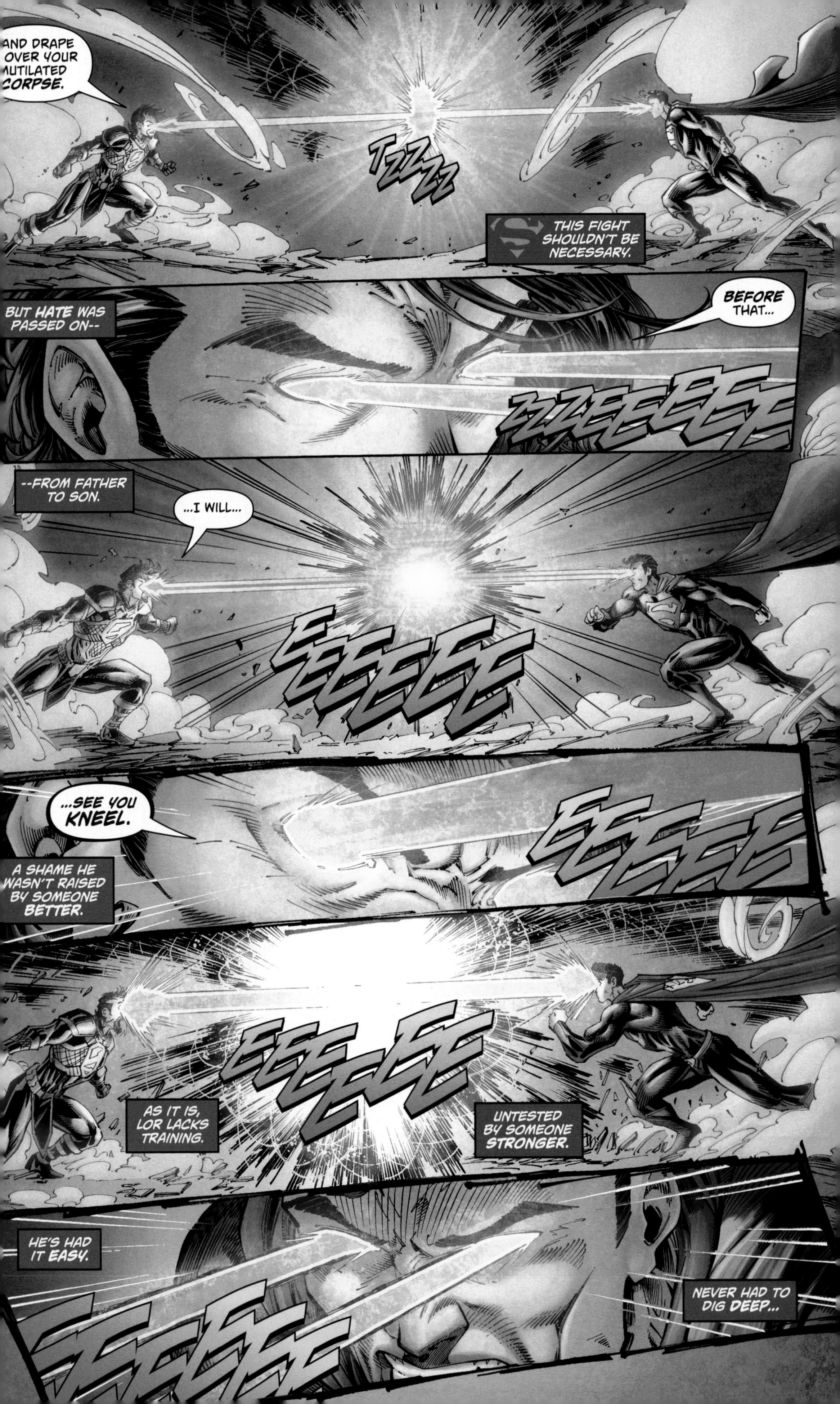
AND DRAPE OVER YOUR MUTILATED CORPSE.
TZZZZ
THIS FIGHT SHOULDN'T BE NECESSARY.
BUT HATE WAS PASSED ON--
BEFORE THAT...
ZZZEEEEEEE
--FROM FATHER TO SON.
...I WILL...
EEEEEEE
...SEE YOU KNEEL.
EEEEEEE
A SHAME HE WASN'T RAISED BY SOMEONE BETTER.
EEEEEEE
AS IT IS, LOR LACKS TRAINING.
UNTESTED BY SOMEONE STRONGER.
HE'S HAD IT EASY.
NEVER HAD TO DIG DEEP...
EEEEE

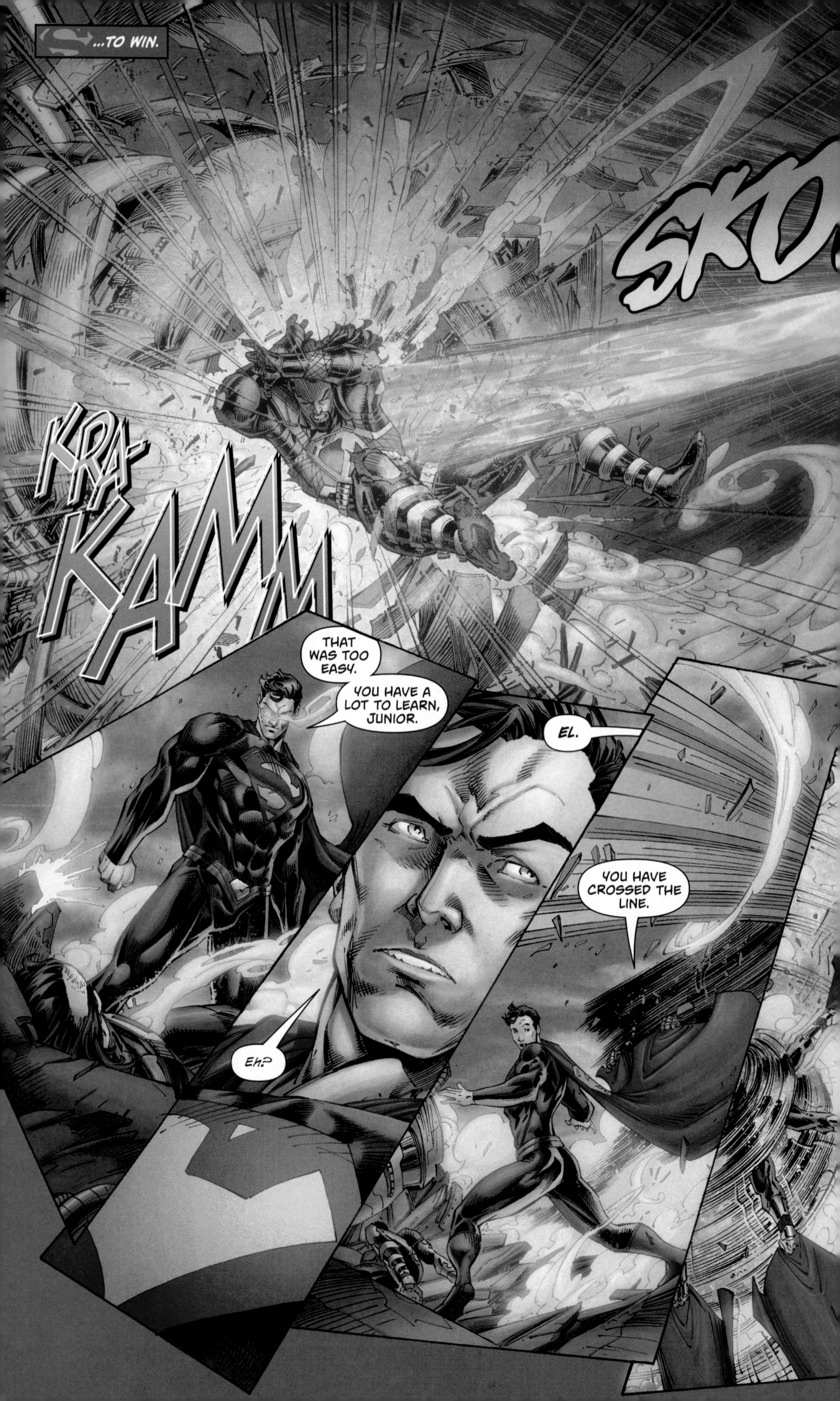
...TO WIN.
SKO
KRA-KAMM
THAT WAS TOO EASY.
YOU HAVE A LOT TO LEARN, JUNIOR.
EL.
Eh?
YOU HAVE CROSSED THE LINE.

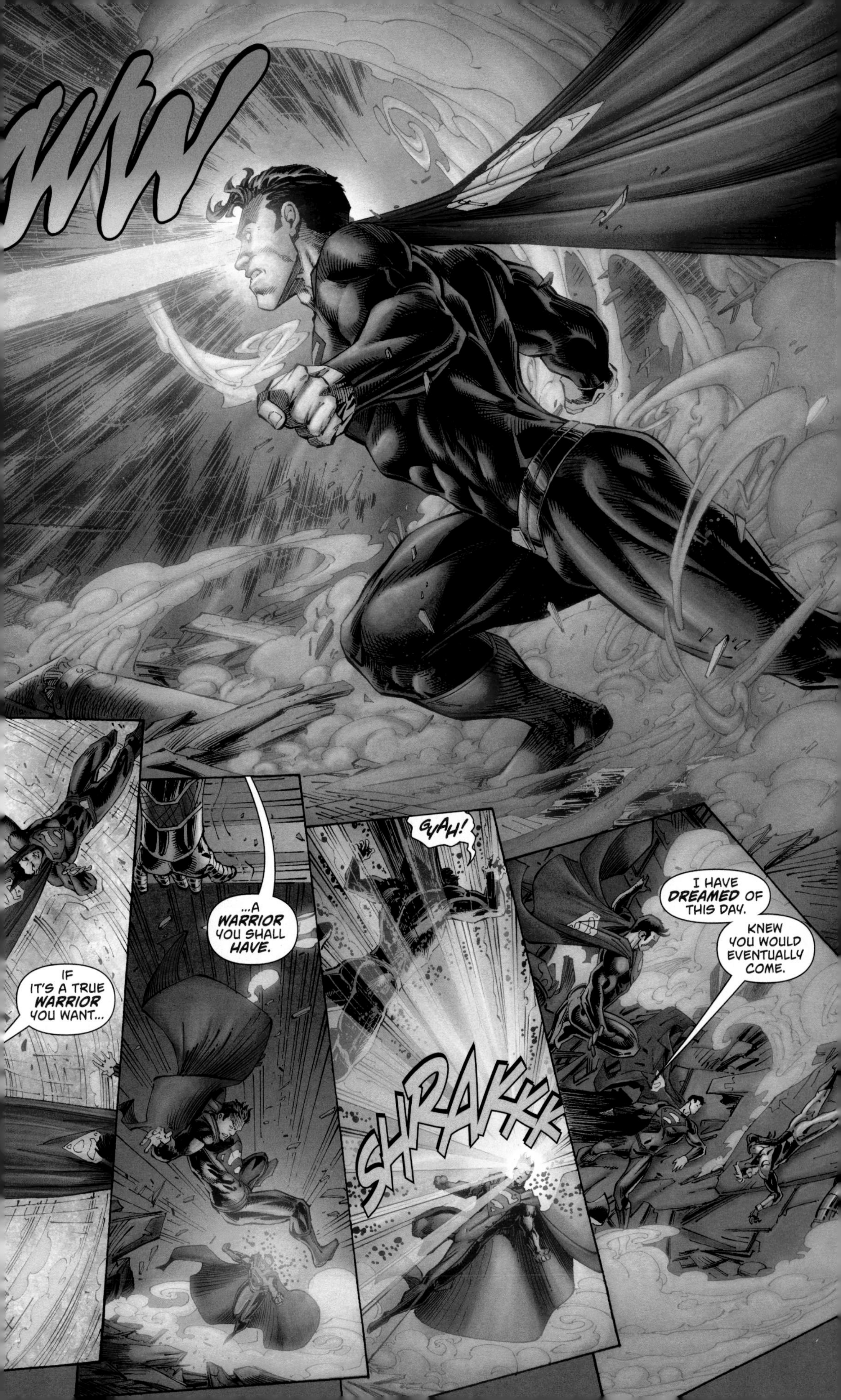

IF IT'S A TRUE WARRIOR YOU WANT...
...A WARRIOR YOU SHALL HAVE.
GYAH!
SHRAKKK
I HAVE DREAMED OF THIS DAY.
KNEW YOU WOULD EVENTUALLY COME.

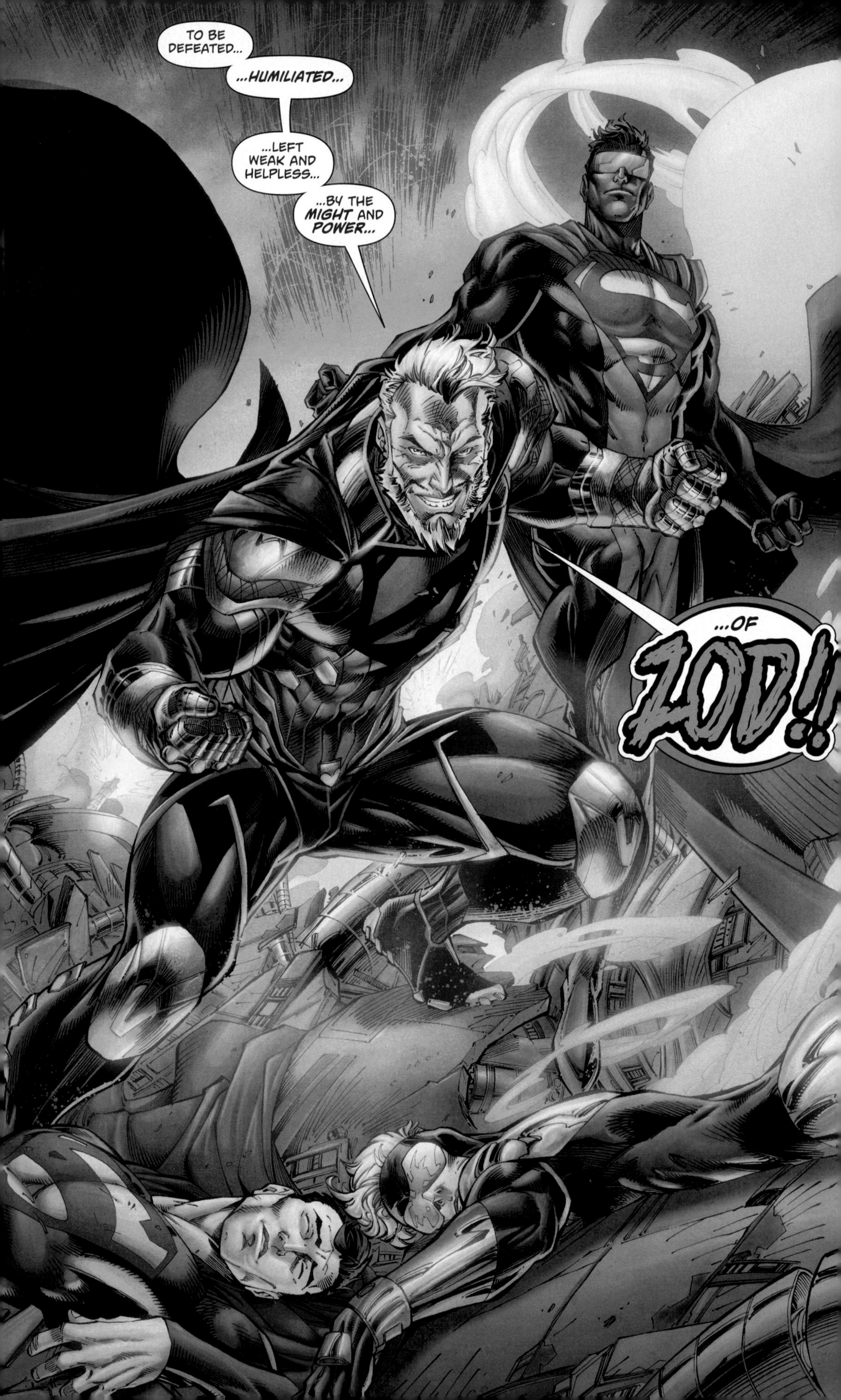
TO BE DEFEATED...
...HUMILIATED...
...LEFT WEAK AND HELPLESS...
...BY THE MIGHT AND POWER...
...OF ZOD!!

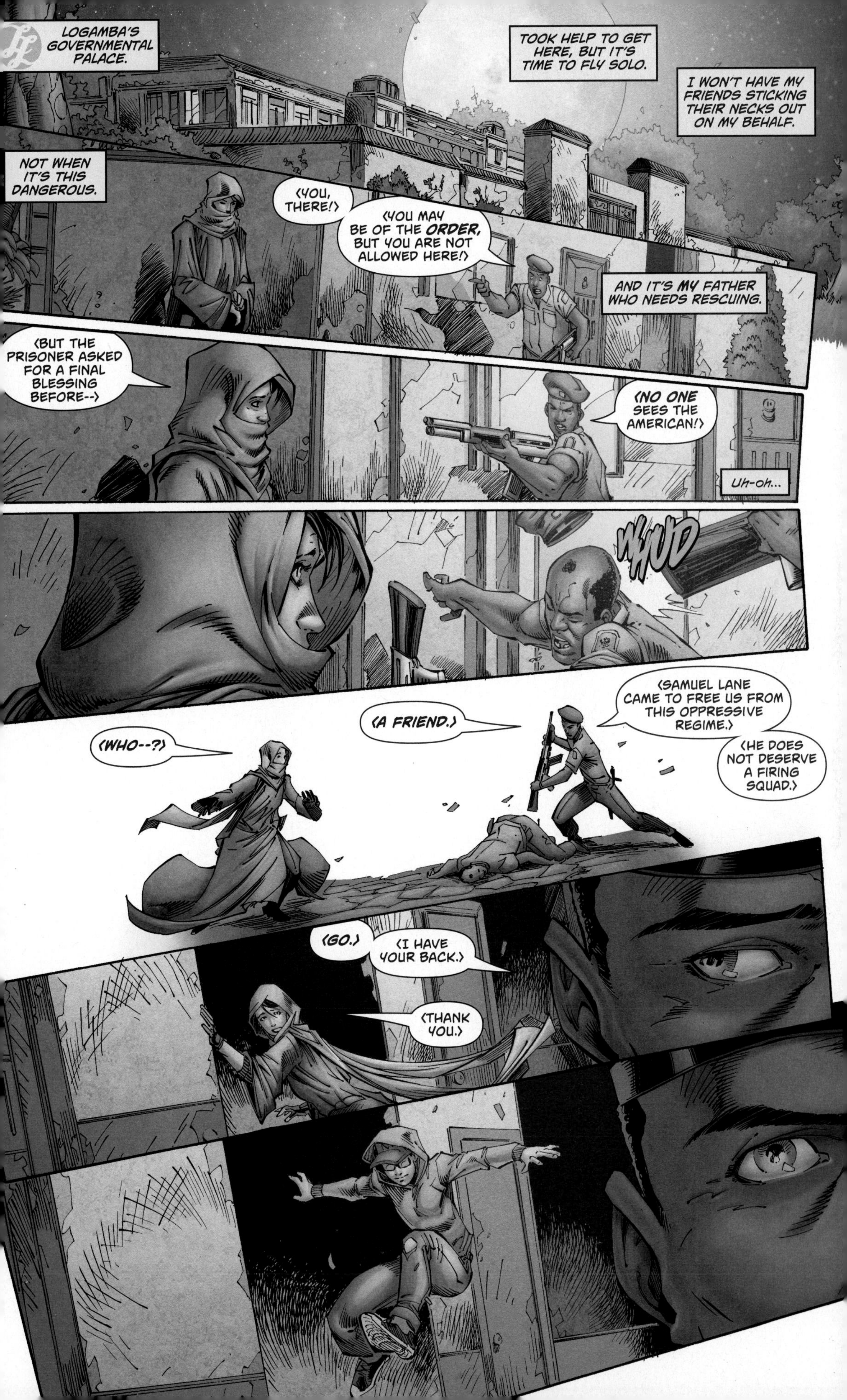
LOGAMBA'S GOVERNMENTAL PALACE.
TOOK HELP TO GET HERE, BUT IT'S TIME TO FLY SOLO.
I WON'T HAVE MY FRIENDS STICKING THEIR NECKS OUT ON MY BEHALF.
NOT WHEN IT'S THIS DANGEROUS.
‹YOU, THERE!›
‹YOU MAY BE OF THE ORDER, BUT YOU ARE NOT ALLOWED HERE!›
AND IT'S MY FATHER WHO NEEDS RESCUING.
‹BUT THE PRISONER ASKED FOR A FINAL BLESSING BEFORE--›
‹NO ONE SEES THE AMERICAN!›
Uh-oh...
WHUD
‹WHO--?›
‹A FRIEND.›
‹SAMUEL LANE CAME TO FREE US FROM THIS OPPRESSIVE REGIME.›
‹HE DOES NOT DESERVE A FIRING SQUAD.›
‹GO.›
‹I HAVE YOUR BACK.›
‹THANK YOU.›

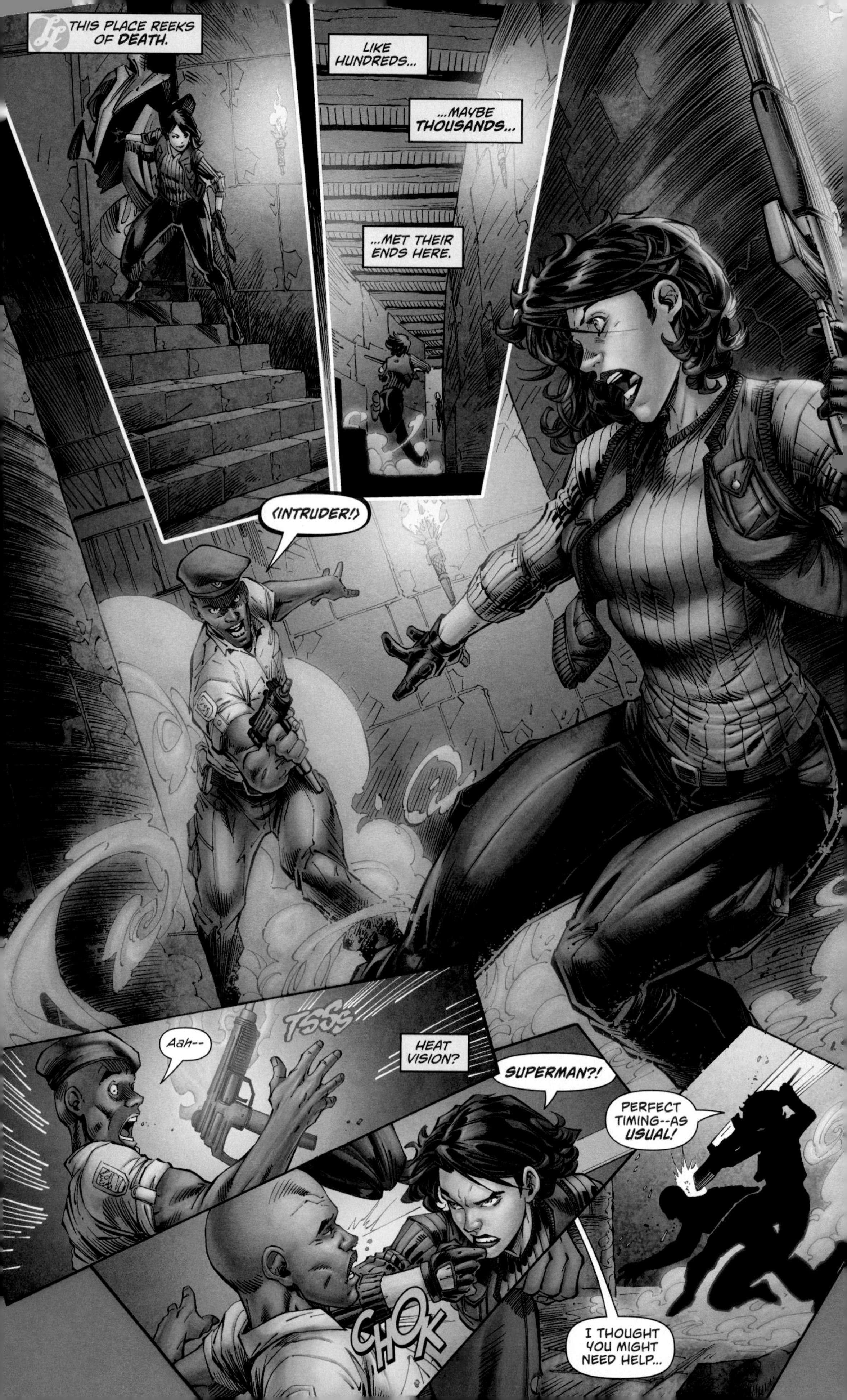
THIS PLACE REEKS OF DEATH.
LIKE HUNDREDS...
...MAYBE THOUSANDS...
...MET THEIR ENDS HERE.
<INTRUDER!>
Aah--
TSSS
HEAT VISION?
SUPERMAN?!
PERFECT TIMING--AS USUAL!
CHOK
I THOUGHT YOU MIGHT NEED HELP...

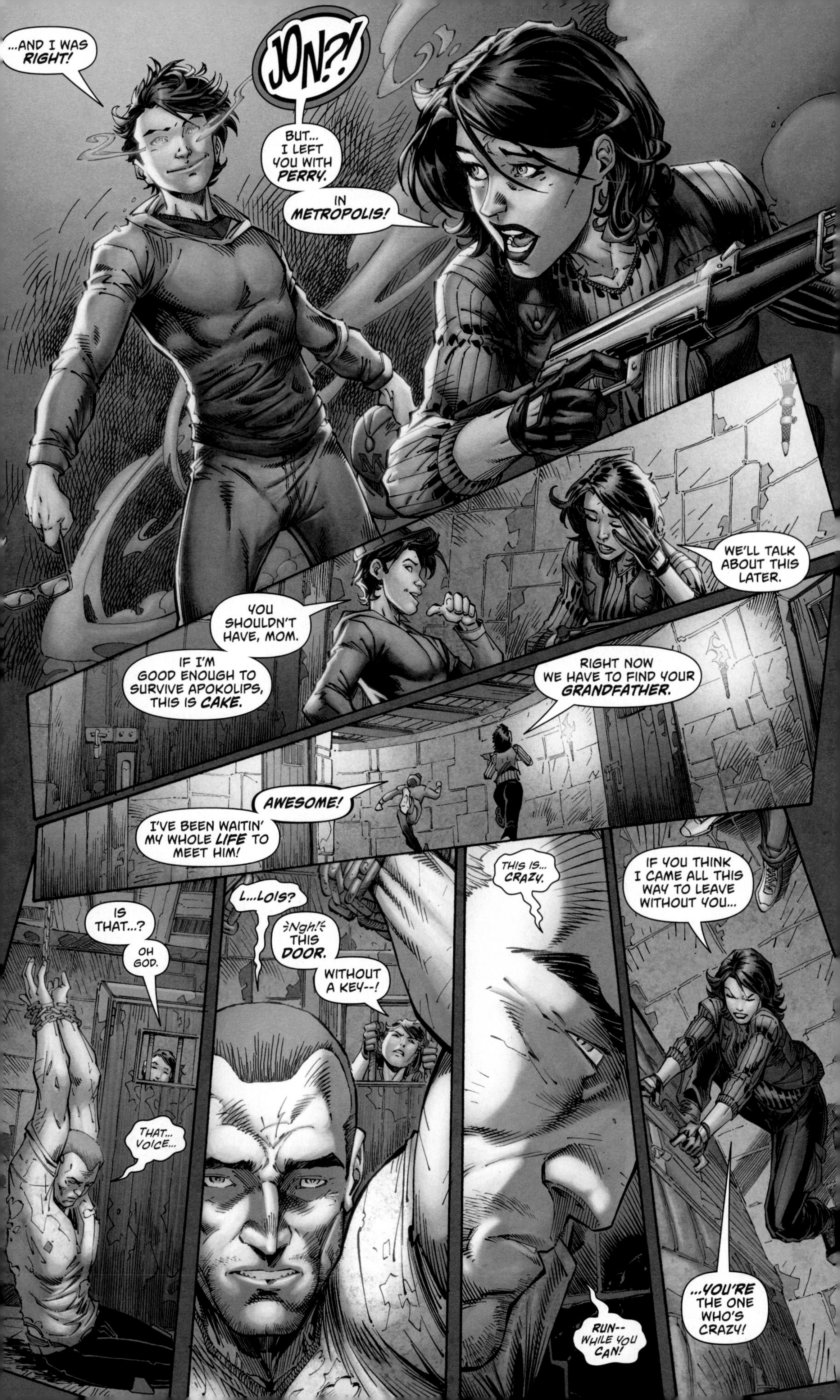
...AND I WAS RIGHT!
JON?!
BUT... I LEFT YOU WITH PERRY.
IN METROPOLIS!
WE'LL TALK ABOUT THIS LATER.
YOU SHOULDN'T HAVE, MOM.
IF I'M GOOD ENOUGH TO SURVIVE APOKOLIPS, THIS IS CAKE.
RIGHT NOW WE HAVE TO FIND YOUR GRANDFATHER.
AWESOME!
I'VE BEEN WAITIN' MY WHOLE LIFE TO MEET HIM!
IS THAT...?
OH GOD.
THAT... VOICE...
L...LOIS?
Ngh! THIS DOOR.
WITHOUT A KEY--!
THIS IS... CRAZY.
RUN-- WHILE YOU CAN!
IF YOU THINK I CAME ALL THIS WAY TO LEAVE WITHOUT YOU...
...YOU'RE THE ONE WHO'S CRAZY!

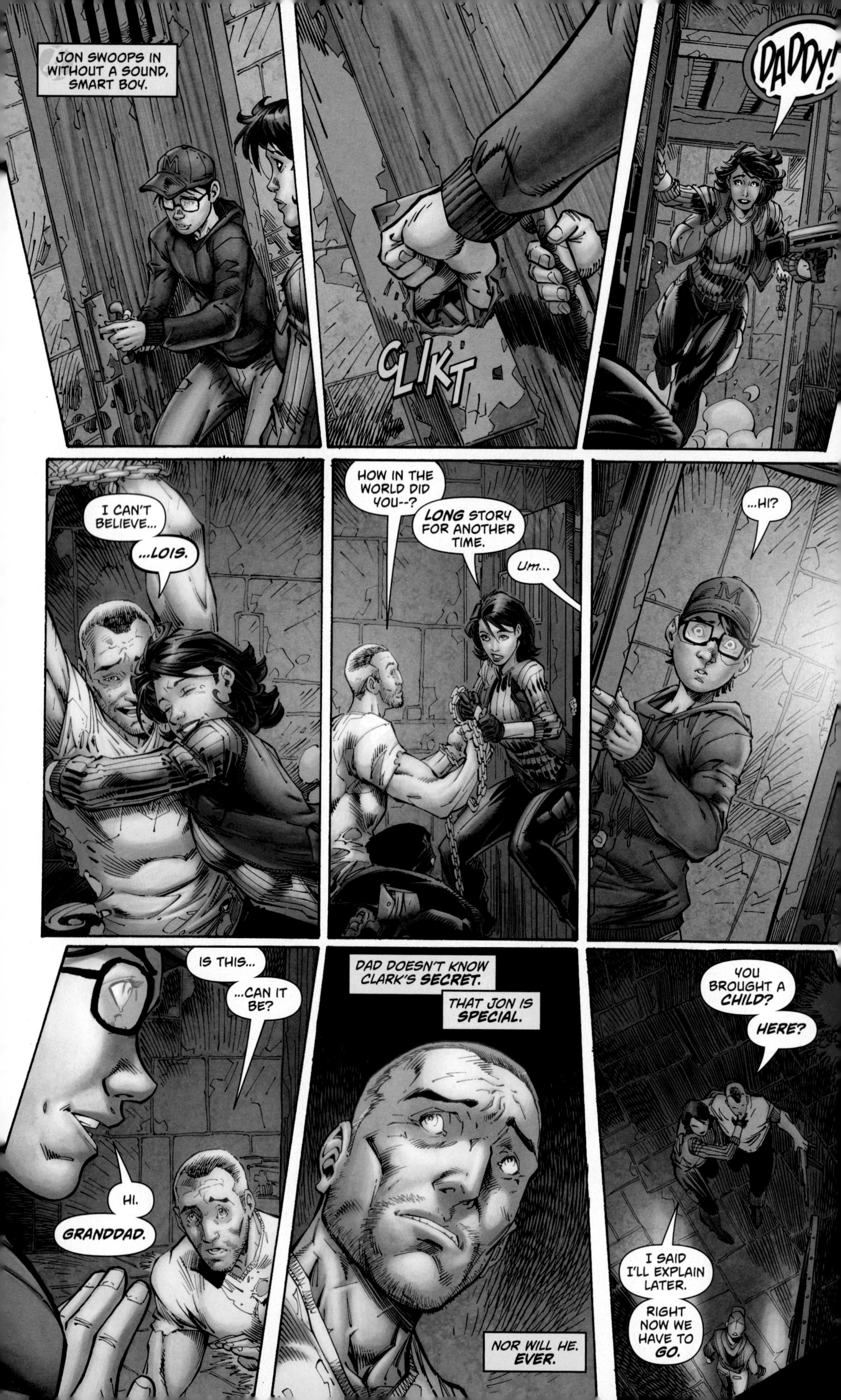
JON SWOOPS IN WITHOUT A SOUND, SMART BOY.
CLIKT
DADDY!
I CAN'T BELIEVE...
...LOIS.
HOW IN THE WORLD DID YOU--?
LONG STORY FOR ANOTHER TIME.
Um...
...HI?
IS THIS...
...CAN IT BE?
HI.
GRANDDAD.
DAD DOESN'T KNOW CLARK'S SECRET.
THAT JON IS SPECIAL.
NOR WILL HE. EVER.
YOU BROUGHT A CHILD?
HERE?
I SAID I'LL EXPLAIN LATER.
RIGHT NOW WE HAVE TO GO.

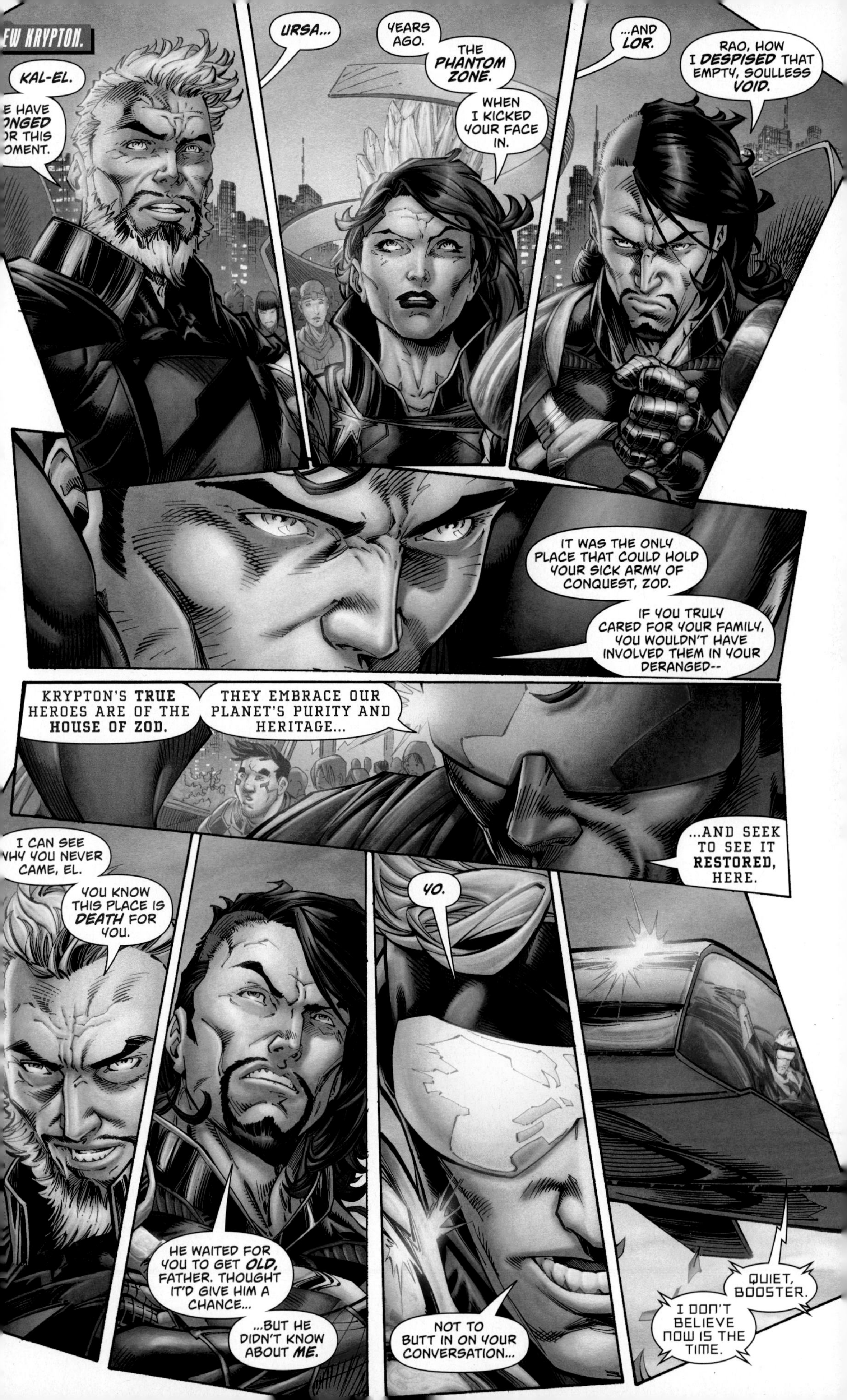

EW KRYPTON.
KAL-EL.
E HAVE ONGED OR THIS OMENT.
URSA...
YEARS AGO.
THE PHANTOM ZONE.
WHEN I KICKED YOUR FACE IN.
...AND LOR.
RAO, HOW I DESPISED THAT EMPTY, SOULLESS VOID.
IT WAS THE ONLY PLACE THAT COULD HOLD YOUR SICK ARMY OF CONQUEST, ZOD.
IF YOU TRULY CARED FOR YOUR FAMILY, YOU WOULDN'T HAVE INVOLVED THEM IN YOUR DERANGED--
KRYPTON'S TRUE HEROES ARE OF THE HOUSE OF ZOD.
THEY EMBRACE OUR PLANET'S PURITY AND HERITAGE...
...AND SEEK TO SEE IT RESTORED, HERE.
I CAN SEE VHY YOU NEVER CAME, EL.
YOU KNOW THIS PLACE IS DEATH FOR YOU.
HE WAITED FOR YOU TO GET OLD, FATHER. THOUGHT IT'D GIVE HIM A CHANCE...
...BUT HE DIDN'T KNOW ABOUT ME.
YO.
NOT TO BUTT IN ON YOUR CONVERSATION...
QUIET, BOOSTER.
I DON'T BELIEVE NOW IS THE TIME.

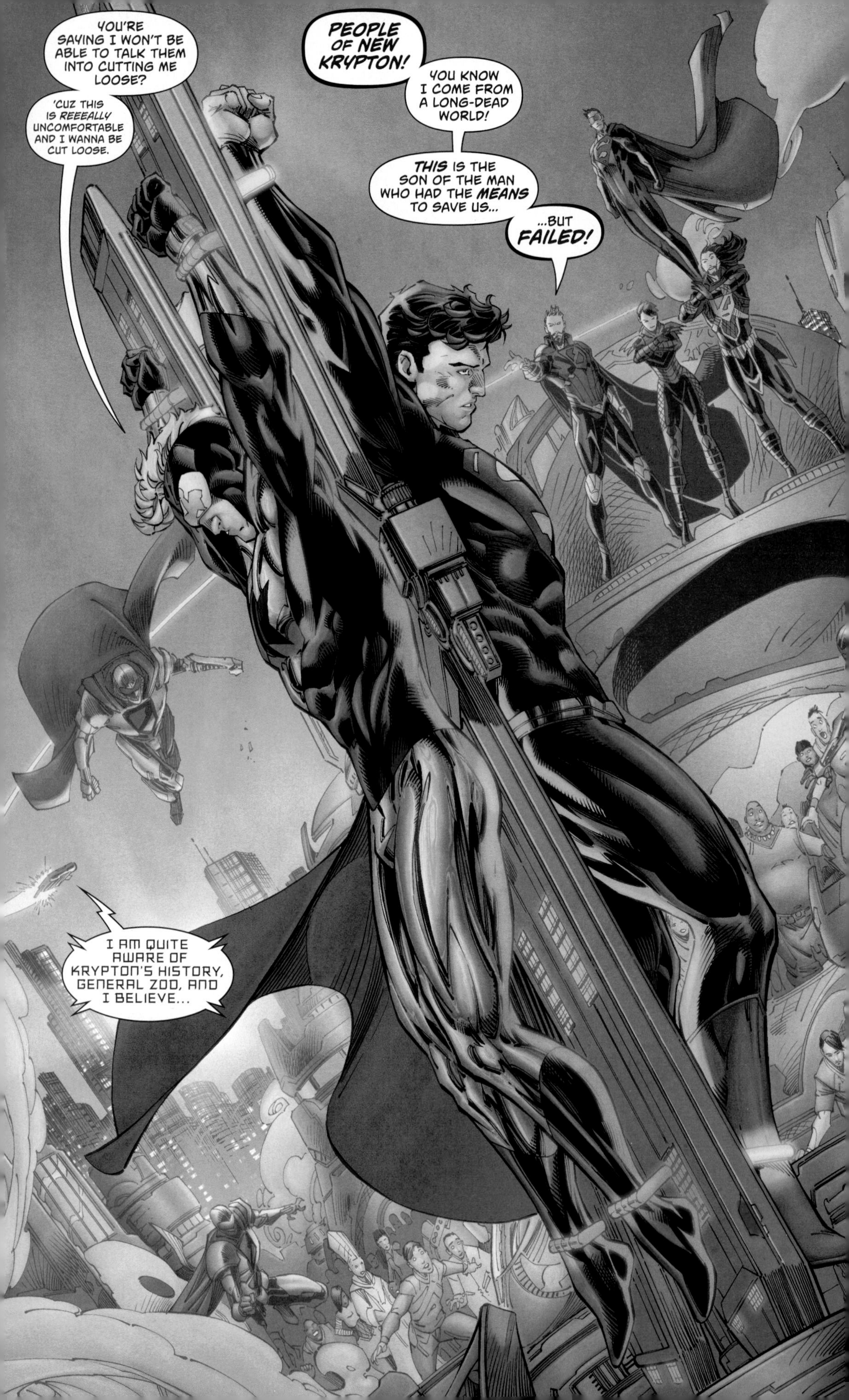
YOU'RE SAYING I WON'T BE ABLE TO TALK THEM INTO CUTTING ME LOOSE?
'CUZ THIS IS REEEALLY UNCOMFORTABLE AND I WANNA BE CUT LOOSE.
PEOPLE OF NEW KRYPTON!
YOU KNOW I COME FROM A LONG-DEAD WORLD!
THIS IS THE SON OF THE MAN WHO HAD THE MEANS TO SAVE US...
...BUT FAILED!
I AM QUITE AWARE OF KRYPTON'S HISTORY, GENERAL ZOD, AND I BELIEVE...

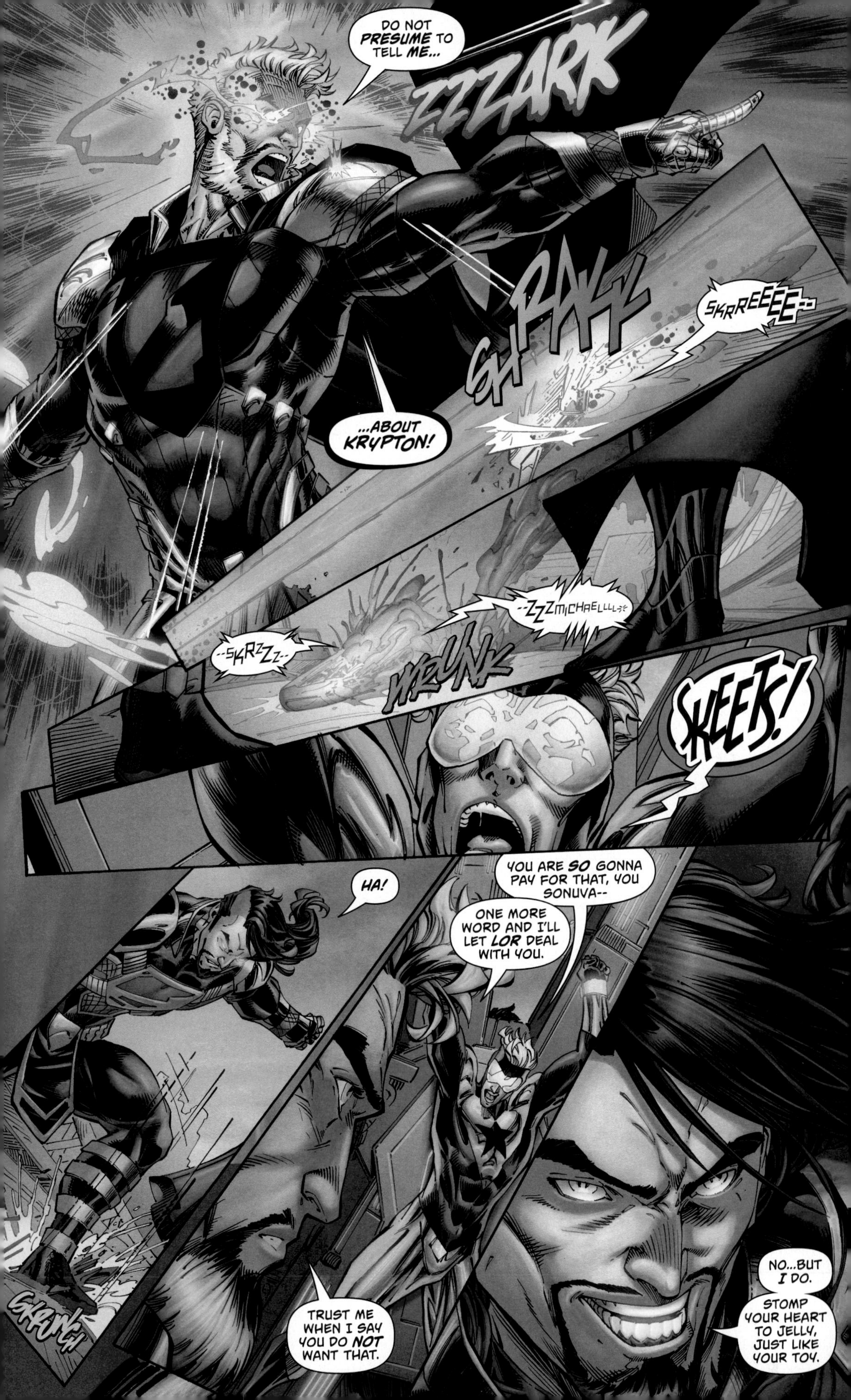
DO NOT PRESUME TO TELL ME...
ZZZARK
...ABOUT KRYPTON!
SHRAKK
SKRREEEE--
--ZZZMICHAELLLL--
--SKRZZZ--
WRUNK
SKEETS!
HA!
YOU ARE SO GONNA PAY FOR THAT, YOU SONUVA--
ONE MORE WORD AND I'LL LET LOR DEAL WITH YOU.
SKRUNCH
TRUST ME WHEN I SAY YOU DO NOT WANT THAT.
NO...BUT I DO.
STOMP YOUR HEART TO JELLY, JUST LIKE YOUR TOY.

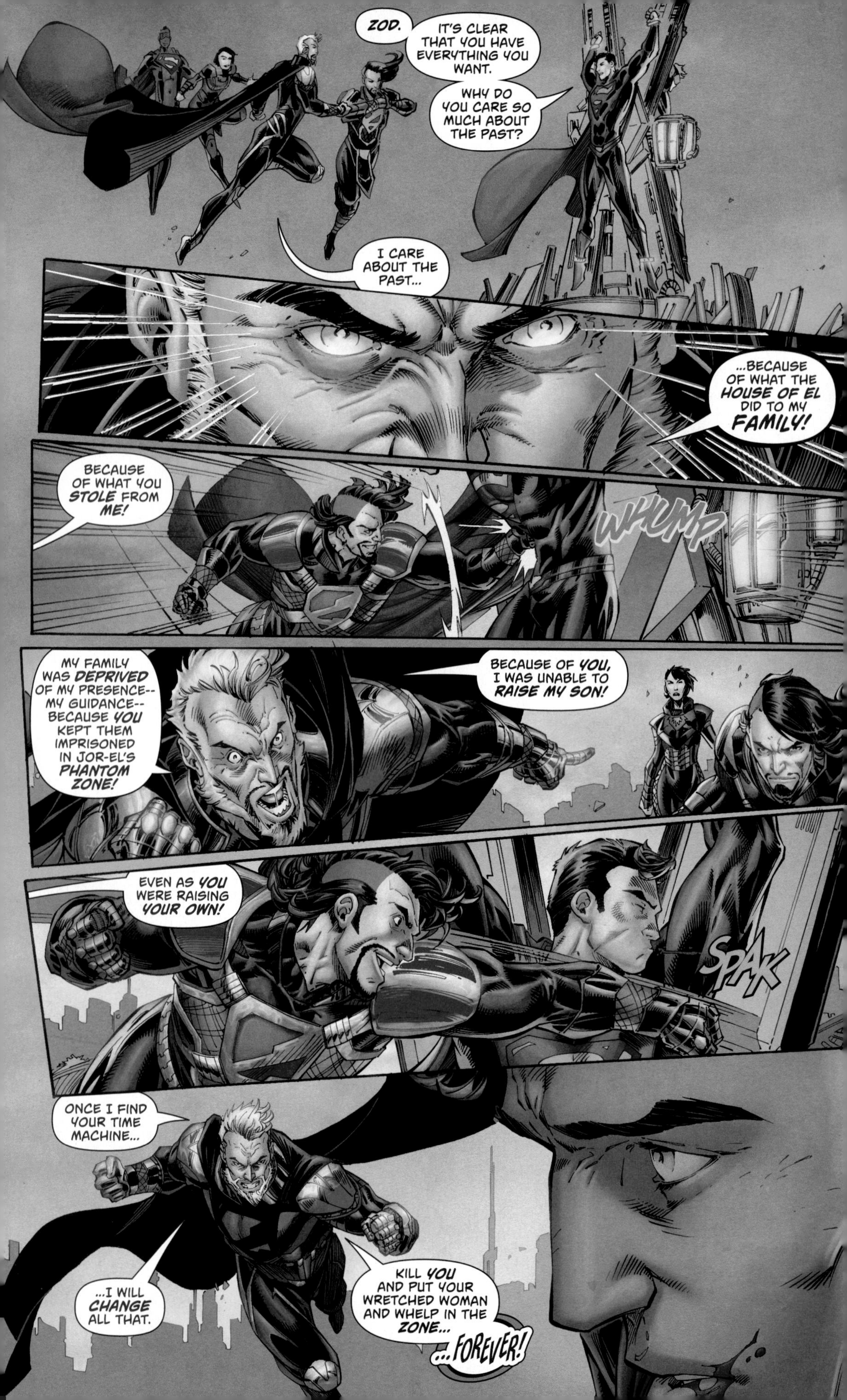
ZOD.
IT'S CLEAR THAT YOU HAVE EVERYTHING YOU WANT.
WHY DO YOU CARE SO MUCH ABOUT THE PAST?
I CARE ABOUT THE PAST...
...BECAUSE OF WHAT THE HOUSE OF EL DID TO MY FAMILY!
BECAUSE OF WHAT YOU STOLE FROM ME!
WHUMP
MY FAMILY WAS DEPRIVED OF MY PRESENCE-- MY GUIDANCE-- BECAUSE YOU KEPT THEM IMPRISONED IN JOR-EL'S PHANTOM ZONE!
BECAUSE OF YOU, I WAS UNABLE TO RAISE MY SON!
EVEN AS YOU WERE RAISING YOUR OWN!
SPAK
ONCE I FIND YOUR TIME MACHINE...
...I WILL CHANGE ALL THAT.
KILL YOU AND PUT YOUR WRETCHED WOMAN AND WHELP IN THE ZONE...
...FOREVER!

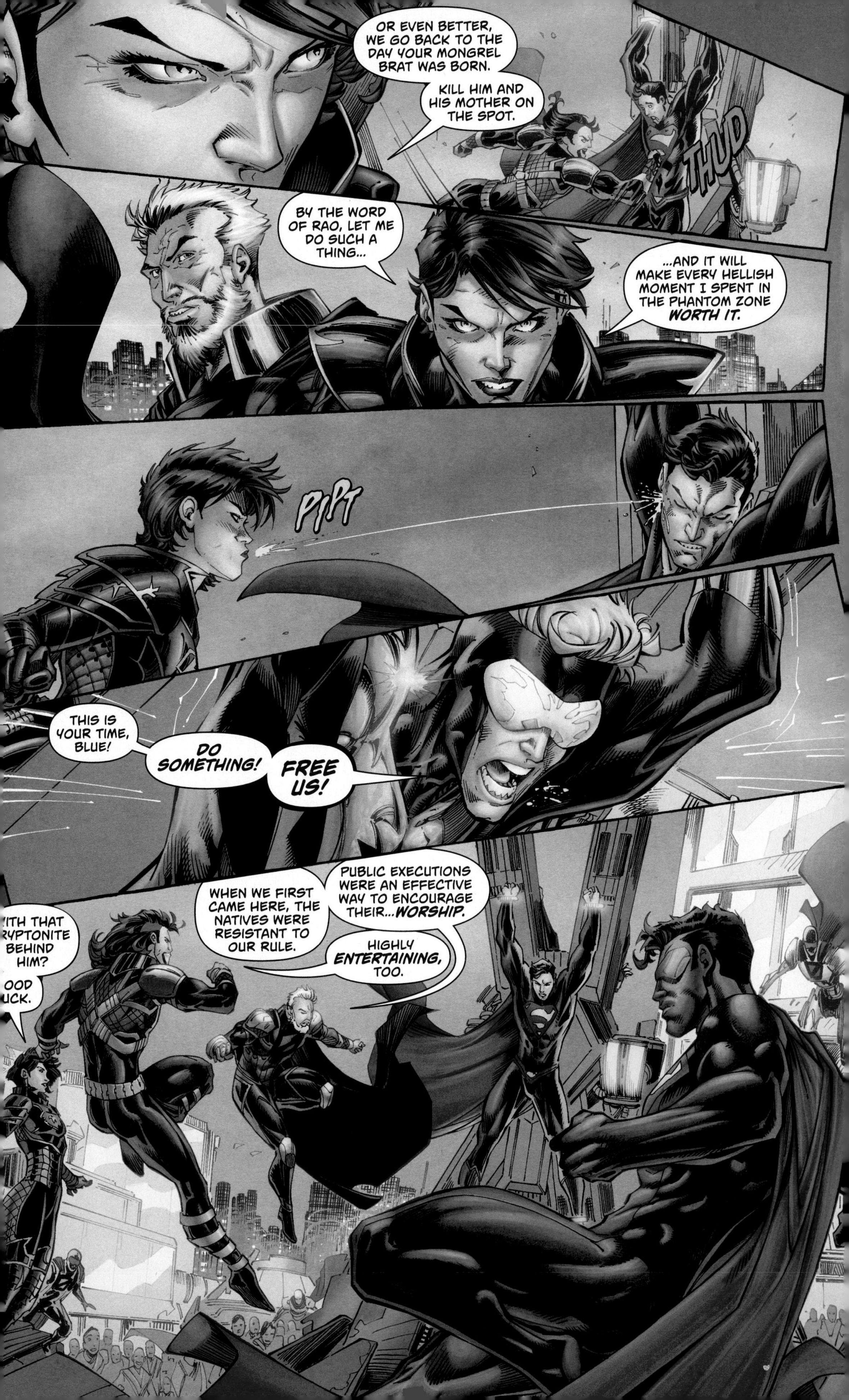

OR EVEN BETTER, WE GO BACK TO THE DAY YOUR MONGREL BRAT WAS BORN.
KILL HIM AND HIS MOTHER ON THE SPOT.
THUD
BY THE WORD OF RAO, LET ME DO SUCH A THING...
...AND IT WILL MAKE EVERY HELLISH MOMENT I SPENT IN THE PHANTOM ZONE WORTH IT.
PIPT
THIS IS YOUR TIME, BLUE!
DO SOMETHING!
FREE US!
WHEN WE FIRST CAME HERE, THE NATIVES WERE RESISTANT TO OUR RULE.
PUBLIC EXECUTIONS WERE AN EFFECTIVE WAY TO ENCOURAGE THEIR...WORSHIP.
HIGHLY ENTERTAINING, TOO.

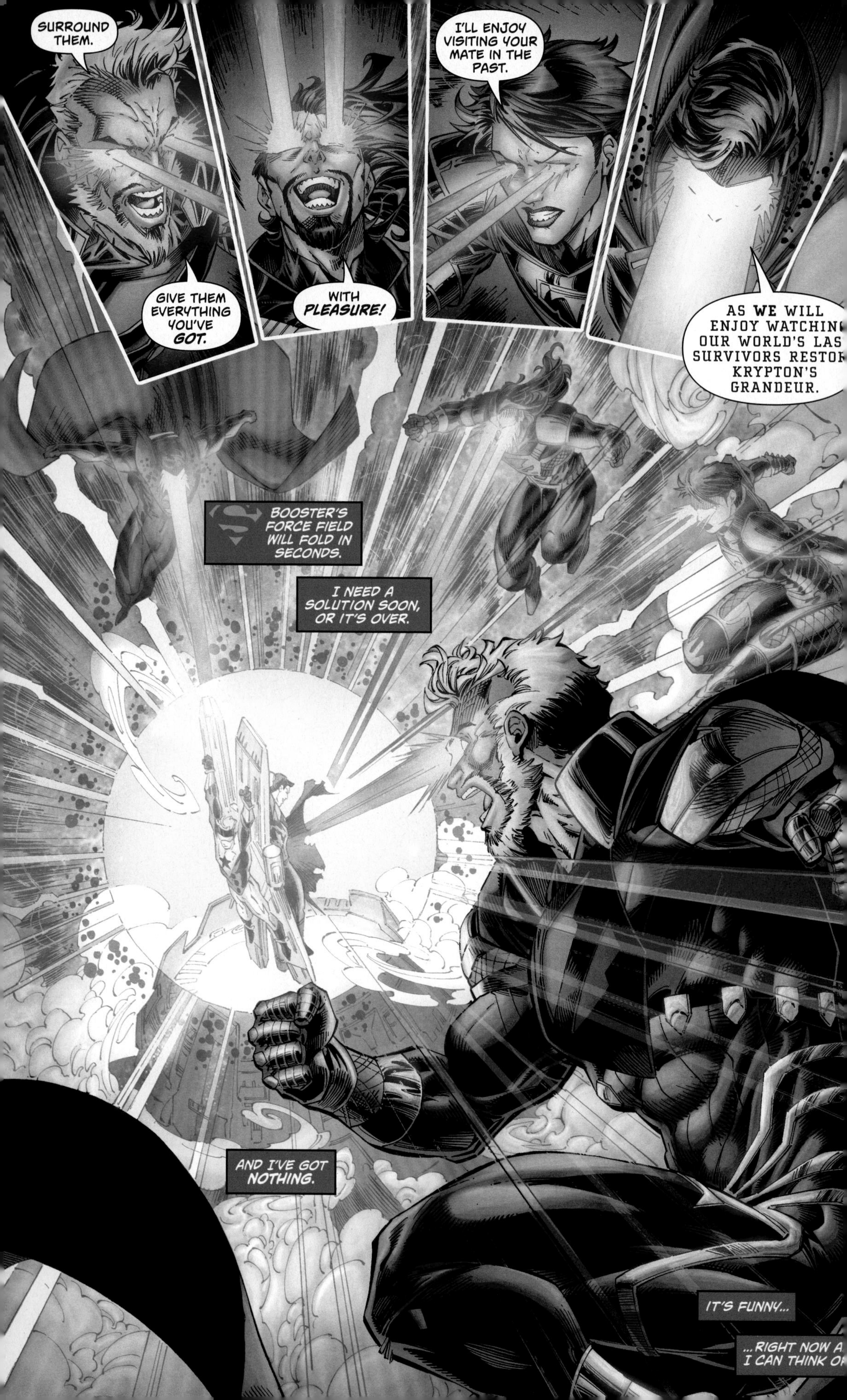
SURROUND THEM.
GIVE THEM EVERYTHING YOU'VE GOT.
WITH PLEASURE!
I'LL ENJOY VISITING YOUR MATE IN THE PAST.
AS WE WILL ENJOY WATCHING OUR WORLD'S LAS SURVIVORS RESTOR KRYPTON'S GRANDEUR.
BOOSTER'S FORCE FIELD WILL FOLD IN SECONDS.
I NEED A SOLUTION SOON, OR IT'S OVER.
AND I'VE GOT NOTHING.
IT'S FUNNY...
...RIGHT NOW A I CAN THINK O

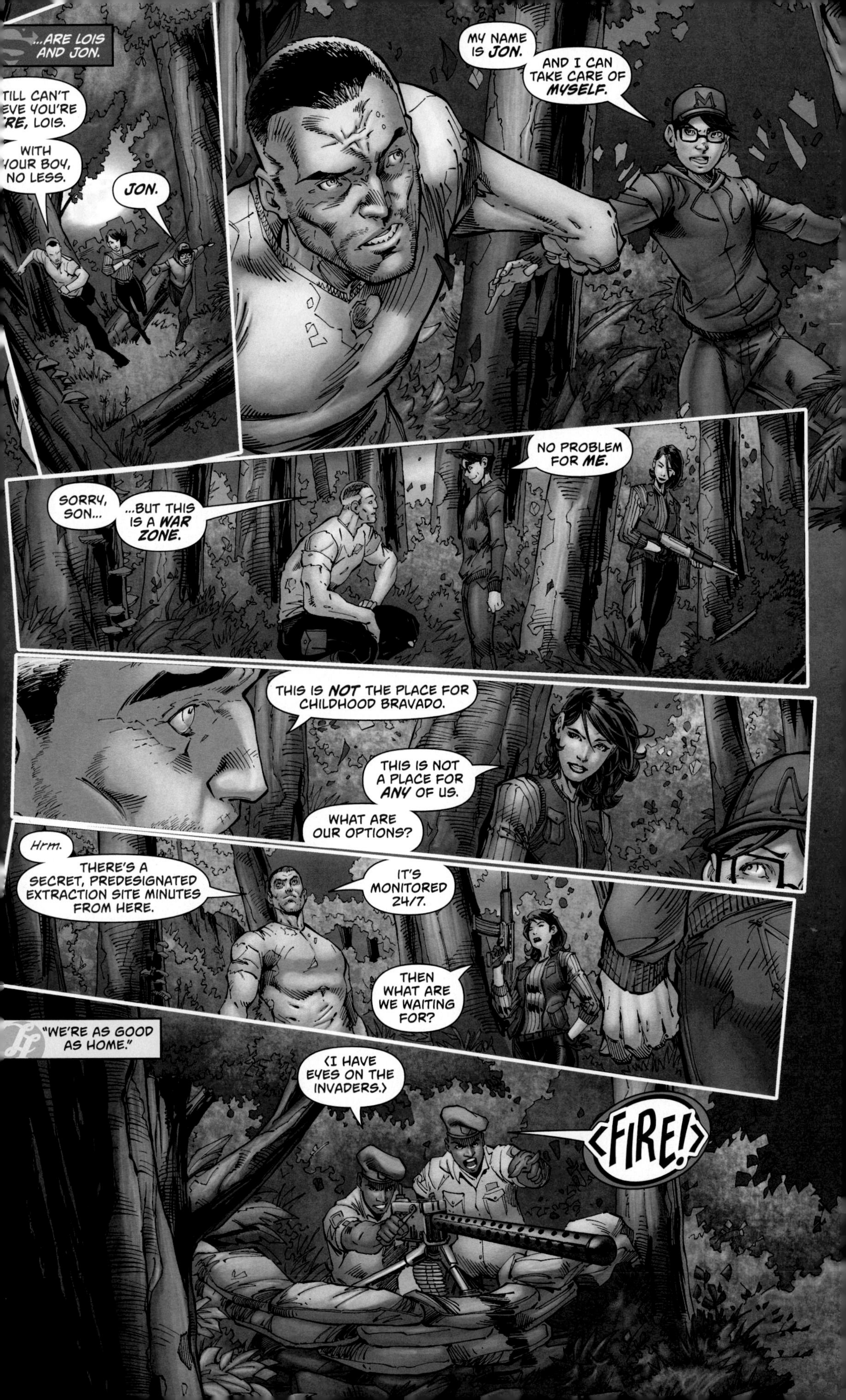
...ARE LOIS AND JON.
TILL CAN'T EVE YOU'RE RE, LOIS.
WITH YOUR BOY, NO LESS.
JON.
MY NAME IS JON.
AND I CAN TAKE CARE OF MYSELF.
SORRY, SON...
...BUT THIS IS A WAR ZONE.
NO PROBLEM FOR ME.
THIS IS NOT THE PLACE FOR CHILDHOOD BRAVADO.
THIS IS NOT A PLACE FOR ANY OF US.
WHAT ARE OUR OPTIONS?
Hrm.
THERE'S A SECRET, PREDESIGNATED EXTRACTION SITE MINUTES FROM HERE.
IT'S MONITORED 24/7.
THEN WHAT ARE WE WAITING FOR?
"WE'RE AS GOOD AS HOME."
<I HAVE EYES ON THE INVADERS.>
<FIRE!>

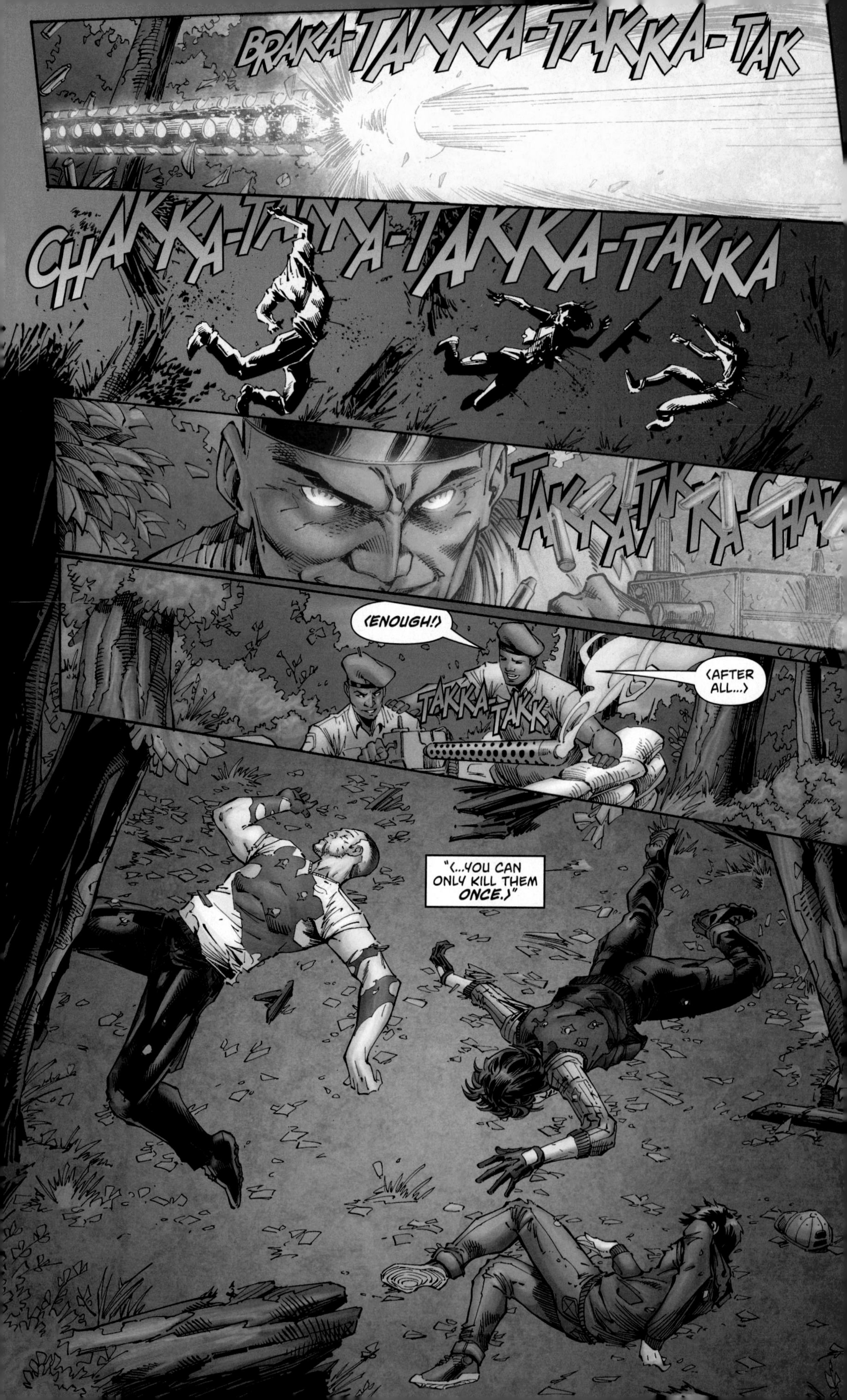
BRAKA-TAKKA-TAKKA-TAK
CHAKKA-TAKKA-TAKKA-TAKKA
TAKKA-TAKKA-CHA
‹ENOUGH!›
‹AFTER ALL...›
TAKKA-TAKK
"‹...YOU CAN ONLY KILL THEM ONCE.›"

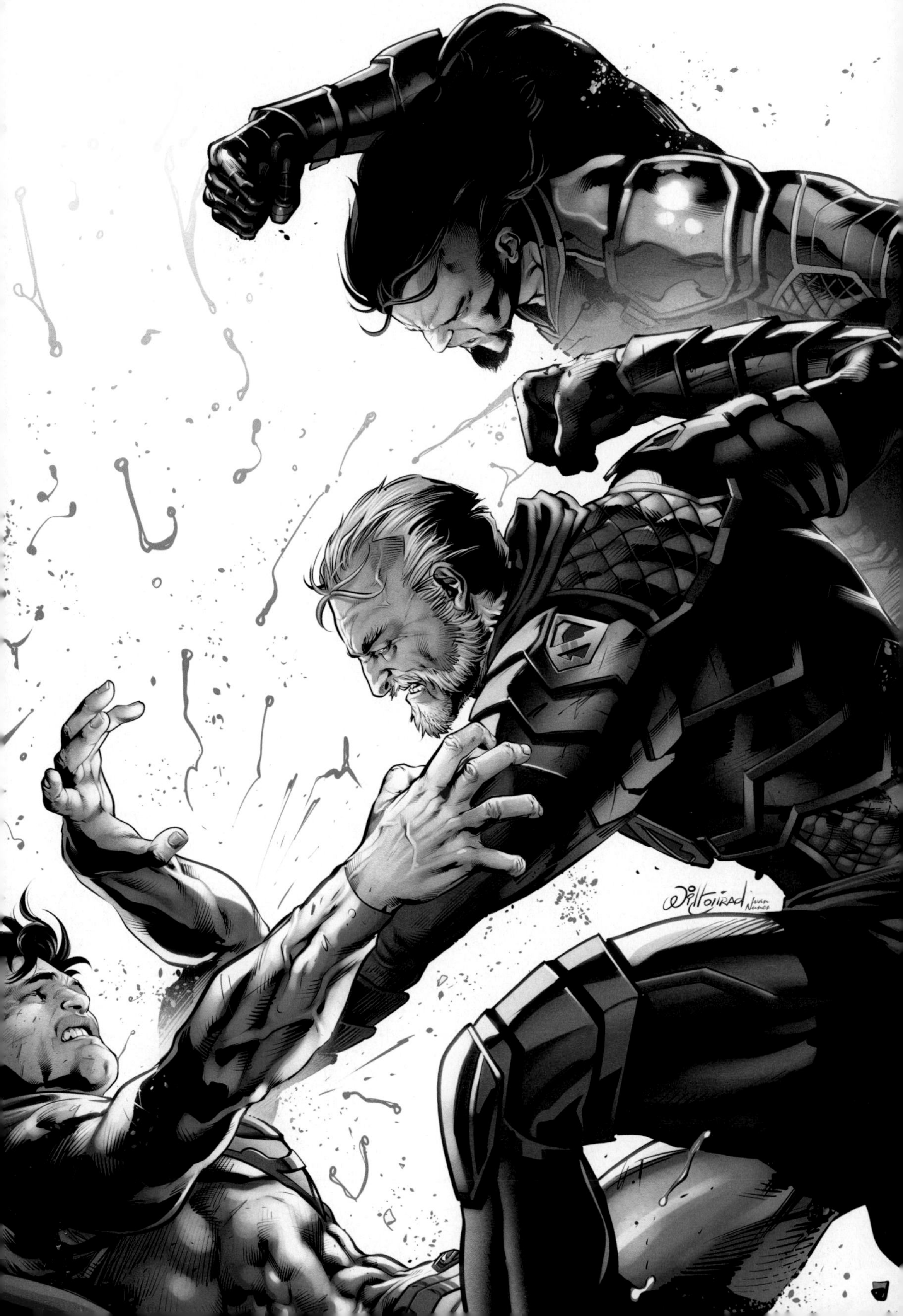

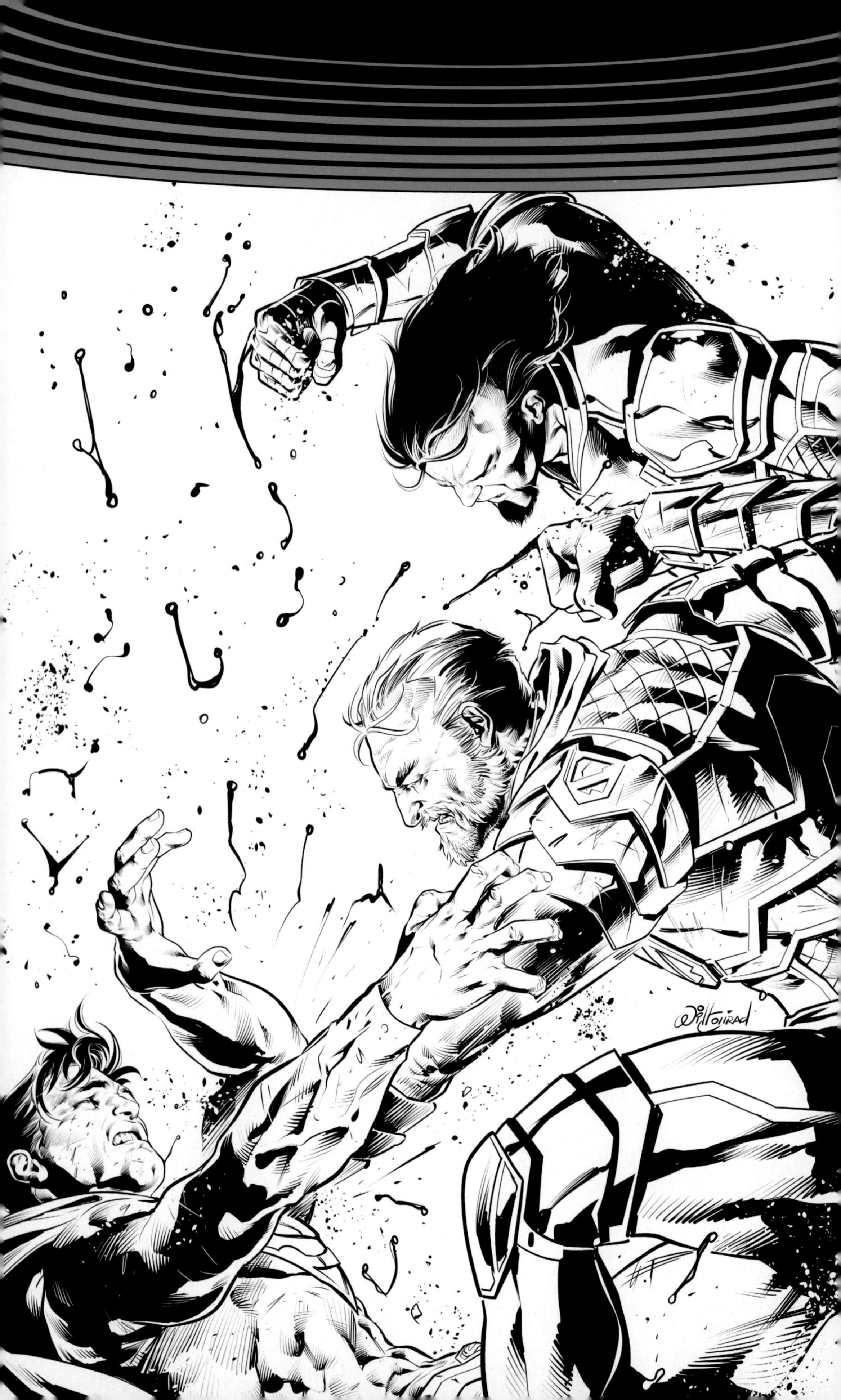

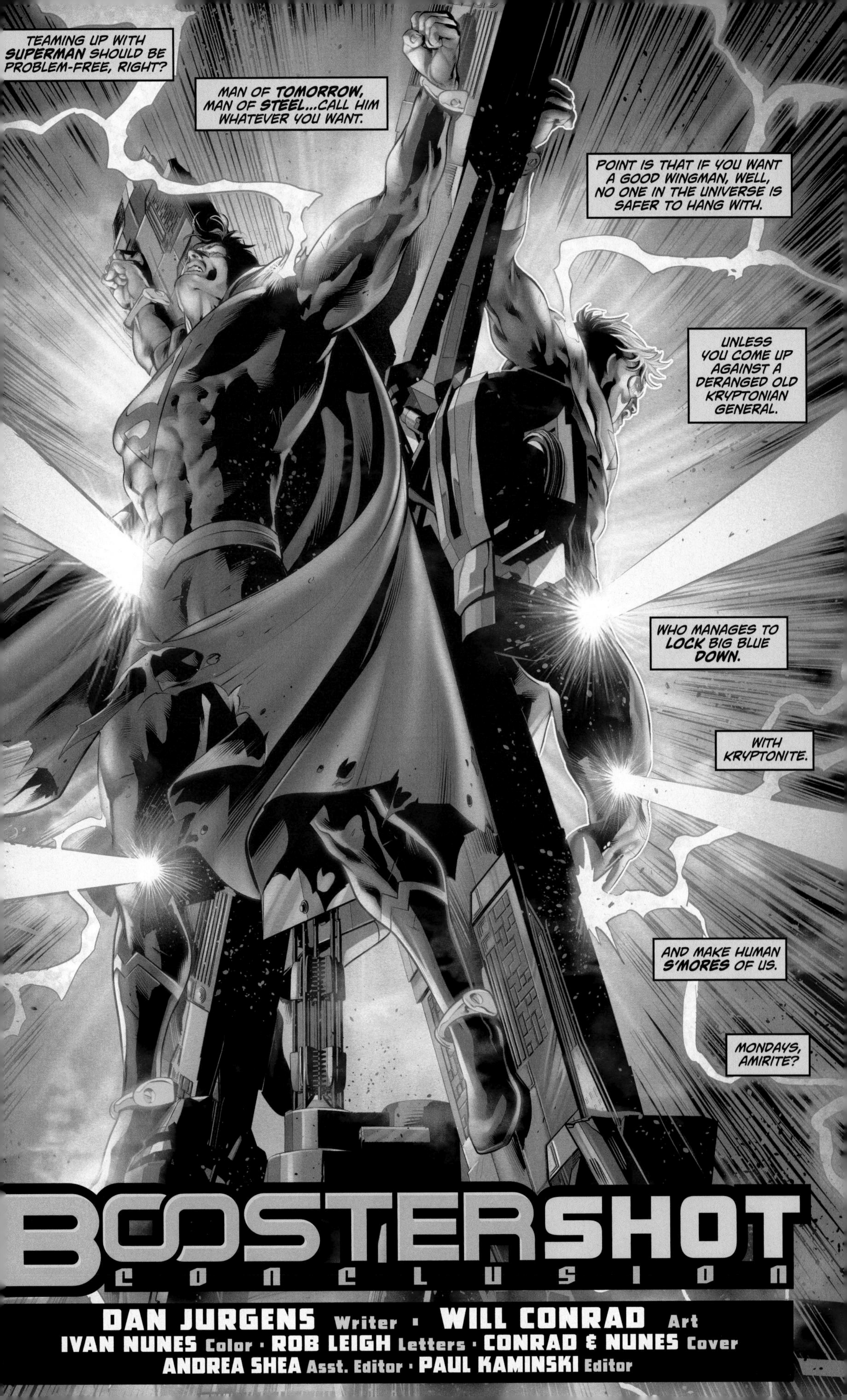
TEAMING UP WITH SUPERMAN SHOULD BE PROBLEM-FREE, RIGHT?
MAN OF TOMORROW, MAN OF STEEL...CALL HIM WHATEVER YOU WANT.
POINT IS THAT IF YOU WANT A GOOD WINGMAN, WELL, NO ONE IN THE UNIVERSE IS SAFER TO HANG WITH.
UNLESS YOU COME UP AGAINST A DERANGED OLD KRYPTONIAN GENERAL.
WHO MANAGES TO LOCK BIG BLUE DOWN.
WITH KRYPTONITE.
AND MAKE HUMAN S'MORES OF US.
MONDAYS, AMIRITE?
BOOSTERSHOT
CONCLUSION
DAN JURGENS Writer · WILL CONRAD Art
IVAN NUNES Color · ROB LEIGH Letters · CONRAD & NUNES Cover
ANDREA SHEA Asst. Editor · PAUL KAMINSKI Editor

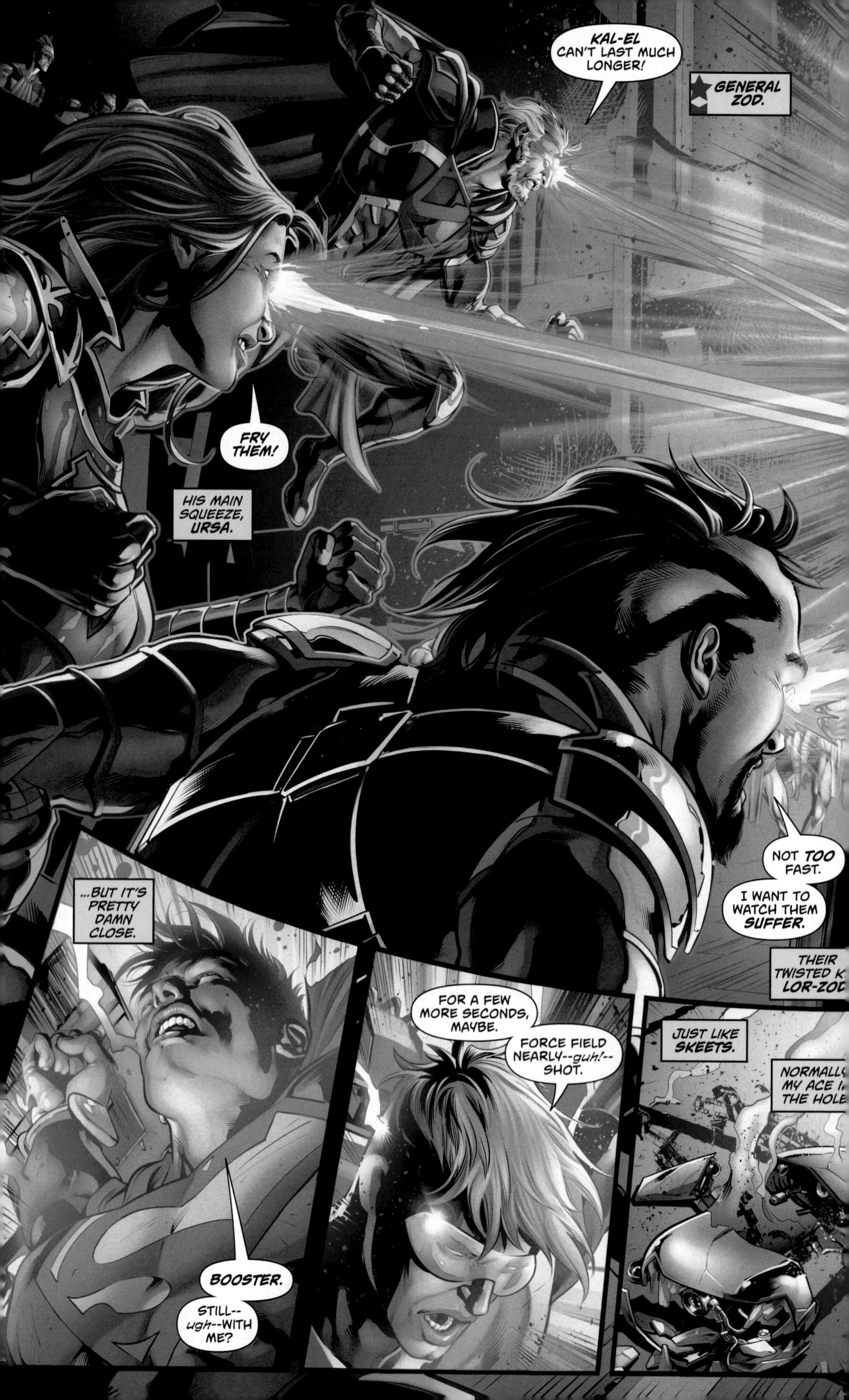
KAL-EL CAN'T LAST MUCH LONGER!
GENERAL ZOD.
FRY THEM!
HIS MAIN SQUEEZE, URSA.
NOT TOO FAST.
I WANT TO WATCH THEM SUFFER.
THEIR TWISTED K
LOR-ZOD
...BUT IT'S PRETTY DAMN CLOSE.
BOOSTER.
STILL-- ugh--WITH ME?
FOR A FEW MORE SECONDS, MAYBE.
FORCE FIELD NEARLY--guh!--SHOT.
JUST LIKE SKEETS.
NORMALL
MY ACE I
THE HOLE

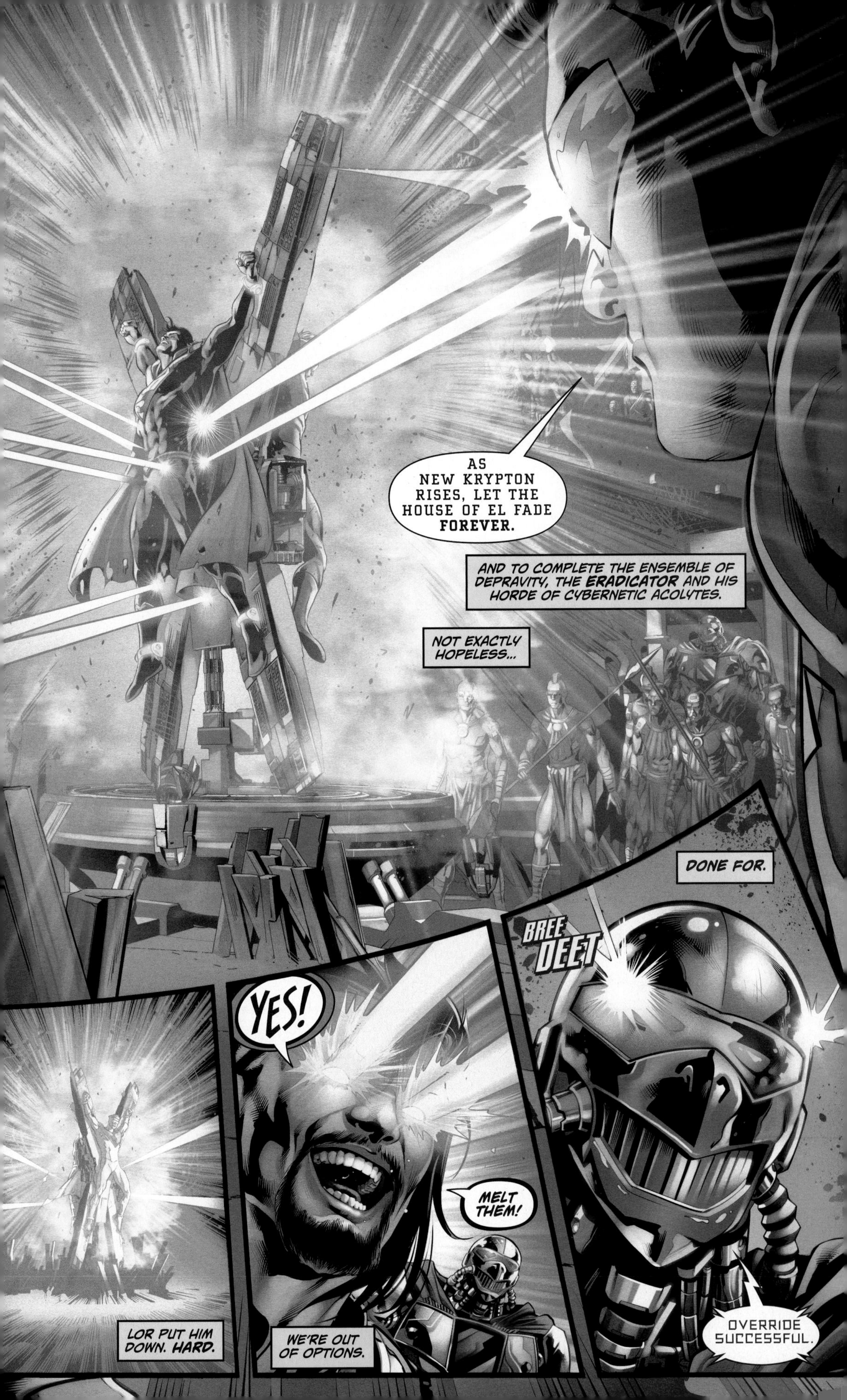
AS NEW KRYPTON RISES, LET THE HOUSE OF EL FADE FOREVER.
AND TO COMPLETE THE ENSEMBLE OF DEPRAVITY, THE ERADICATOR AND HIS HORDE OF CYBERNETIC ACOLYTES.
NOT EXACTLY HOPELESS...
DONE FOR.
LOR PUT HIM DOWN. HARD.
YES!
MELT THEM!
WE'RE OUT OF OPTIONS.
BREE DEET
OVERRIDE SUCCESSFUL.

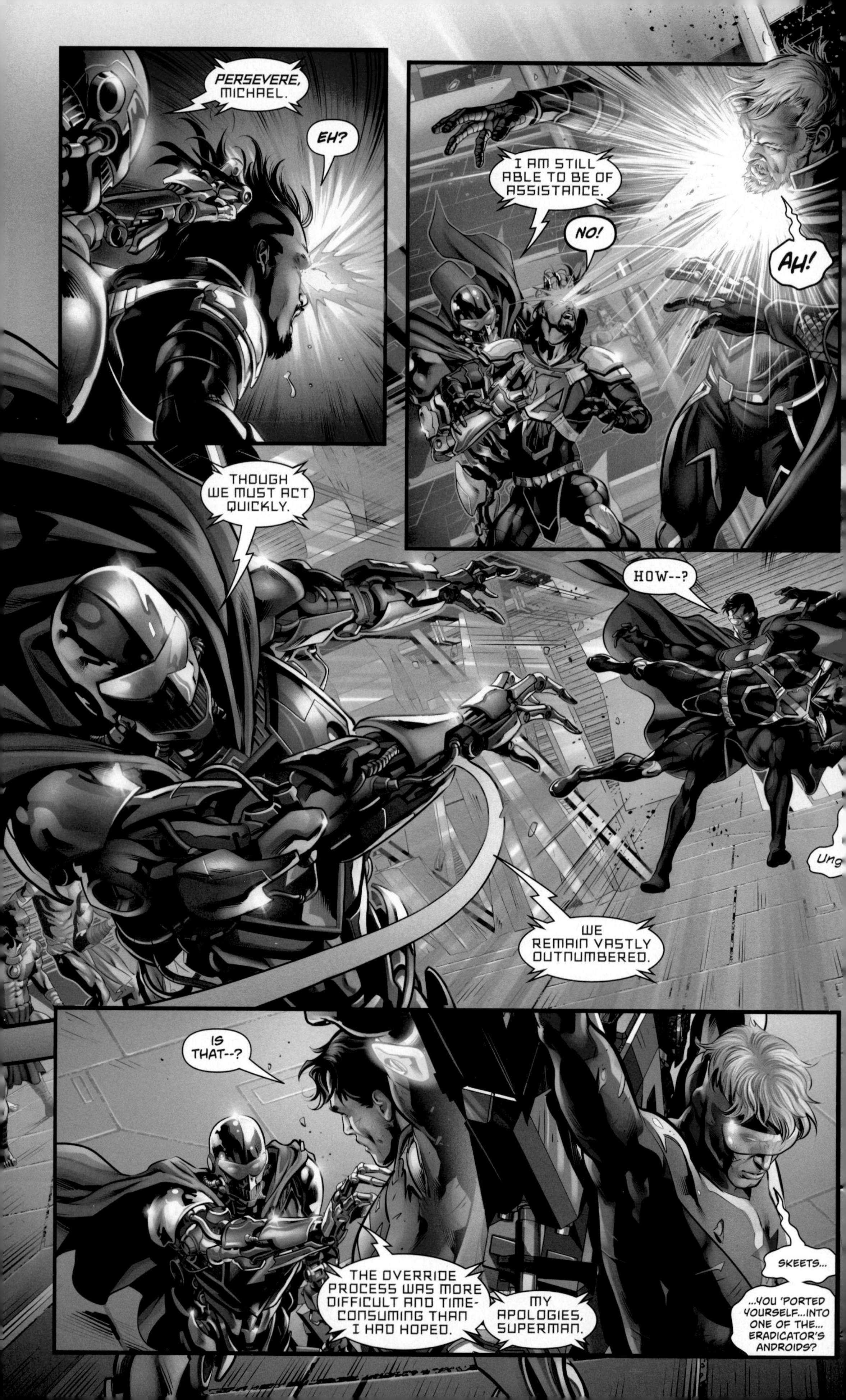
PERSEVERE, MICHAEL.
EH?
I AM STILL ABLE TO BE OF ASSISTANCE.
NO!
AH!
THOUGH WE MUST ACT QUICKLY.
HOW--?
WE REMAIN VASTLY OUTNUMBERED.
Ung
IS THAT--?
THE OVERRIDE PROCESS WAS MORE DIFFICULT AND TIME-CONSUMING THAN I HAD HOPED.
MY APOLOGIES, SUPERMAN.
SKEETS...
...YOU 'PORTED YOURSELF...INTO ONE OF THE... ERADICATOR'S ANDROIDS?

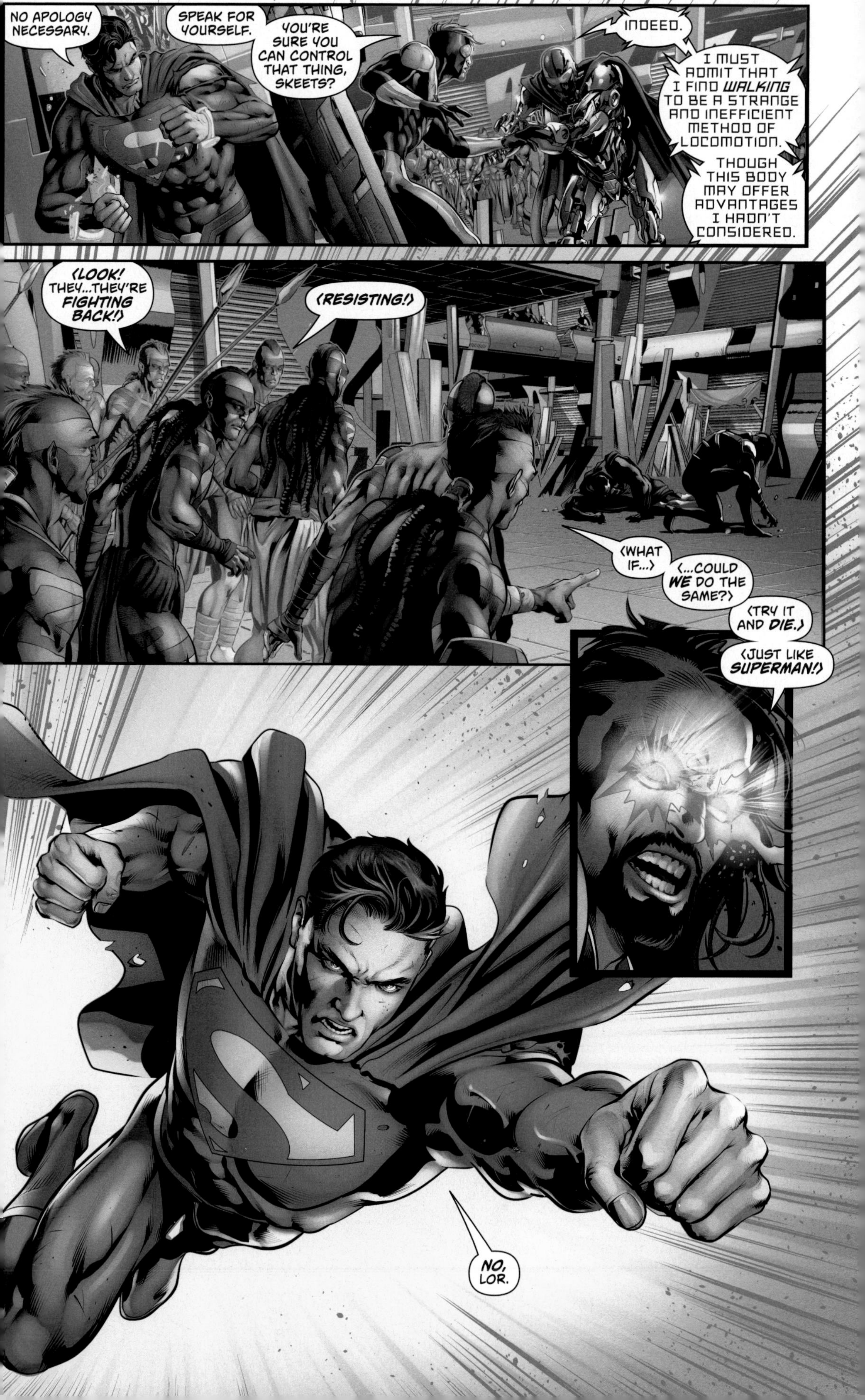

NO APOLOGY NECESSARY.
SPEAK FOR YOURSELF.
YOU'RE SURE YOU CAN CONTROL THAT THING, SKEETS?
INDEED.
I MUST ADMIT THAT I FIND WALKING TO BE A STRANGE AND INEFFICIENT METHOD OF LOCOMOTION.
THOUGH THIS BODY MAY OFFER ADVANTAGES I HADN'T CONSIDERED.
<LOOK! THEY...THEY'RE FIGHTING BACK!>
<RESISTING!>
<WHAT IF...>
<...COULD WE DO THE SAME?>
<TRY IT AND DIE.>
<JUST LIKE SUPERMAN!>
NO, LOR.

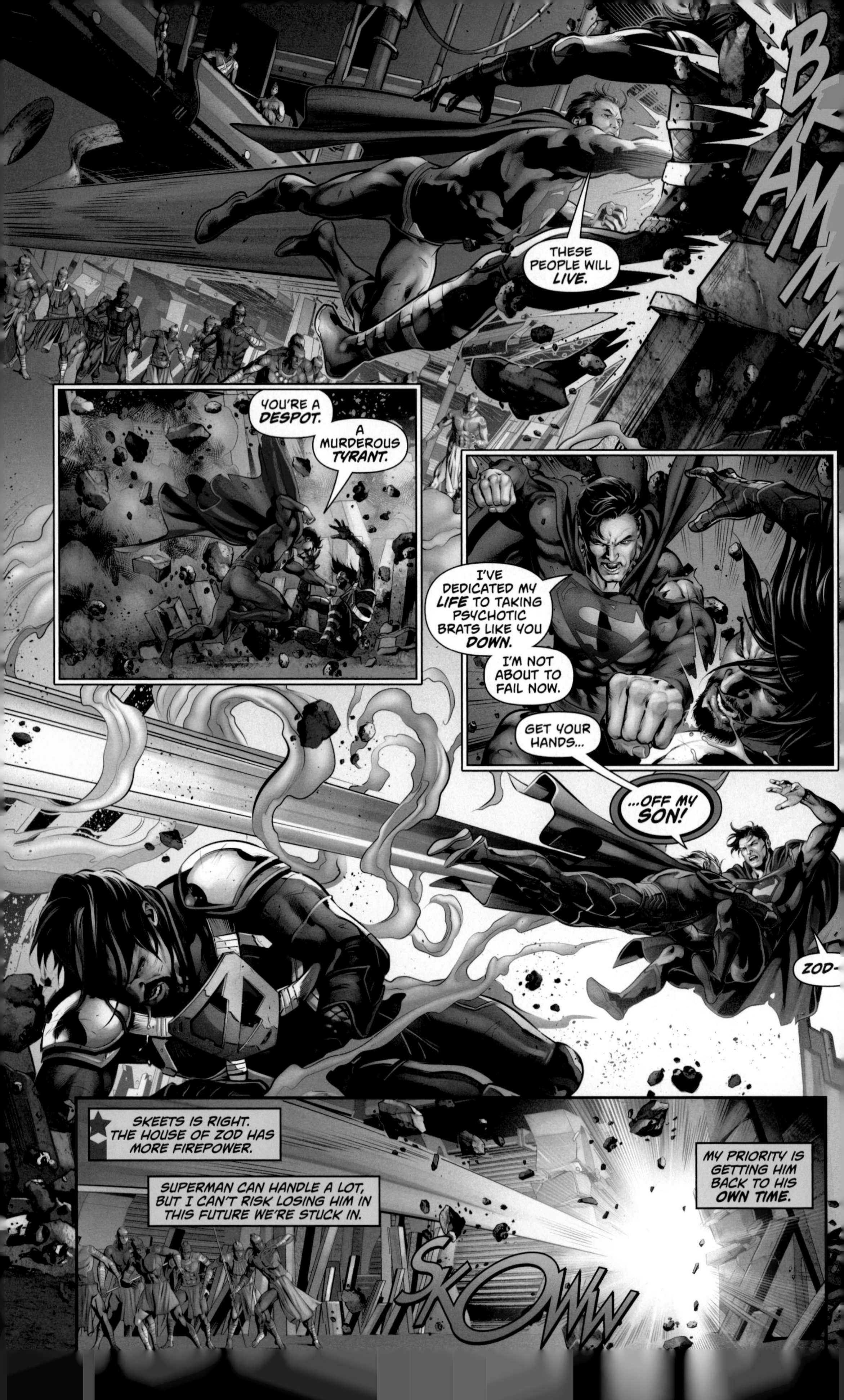
BRAMMM
THESE PEOPLE WILL LIVE.
YOU'RE A DESPOT.
A MURDEROUS TYRANT.
I'VE DEDICATED MY LIFE TO TAKING PSYCHOTIC BRATS LIKE YOU DOWN.
I'M NOT ABOUT TO FAIL NOW.
GET YOUR HANDS...
...OFF MY SON!
ZOD-
SKEETS IS RIGHT. THE HOUSE OF ZOD HAS MORE FIREPOWER.
SUPERMAN CAN HANDLE A LOT, BUT I CAN'T RISK LOSING HIM IN THIS FUTURE WE'RE STUCK IN.
MY PRIORITY IS GETTING HIM BACK TO HIS OWN TIME.
SKOWW

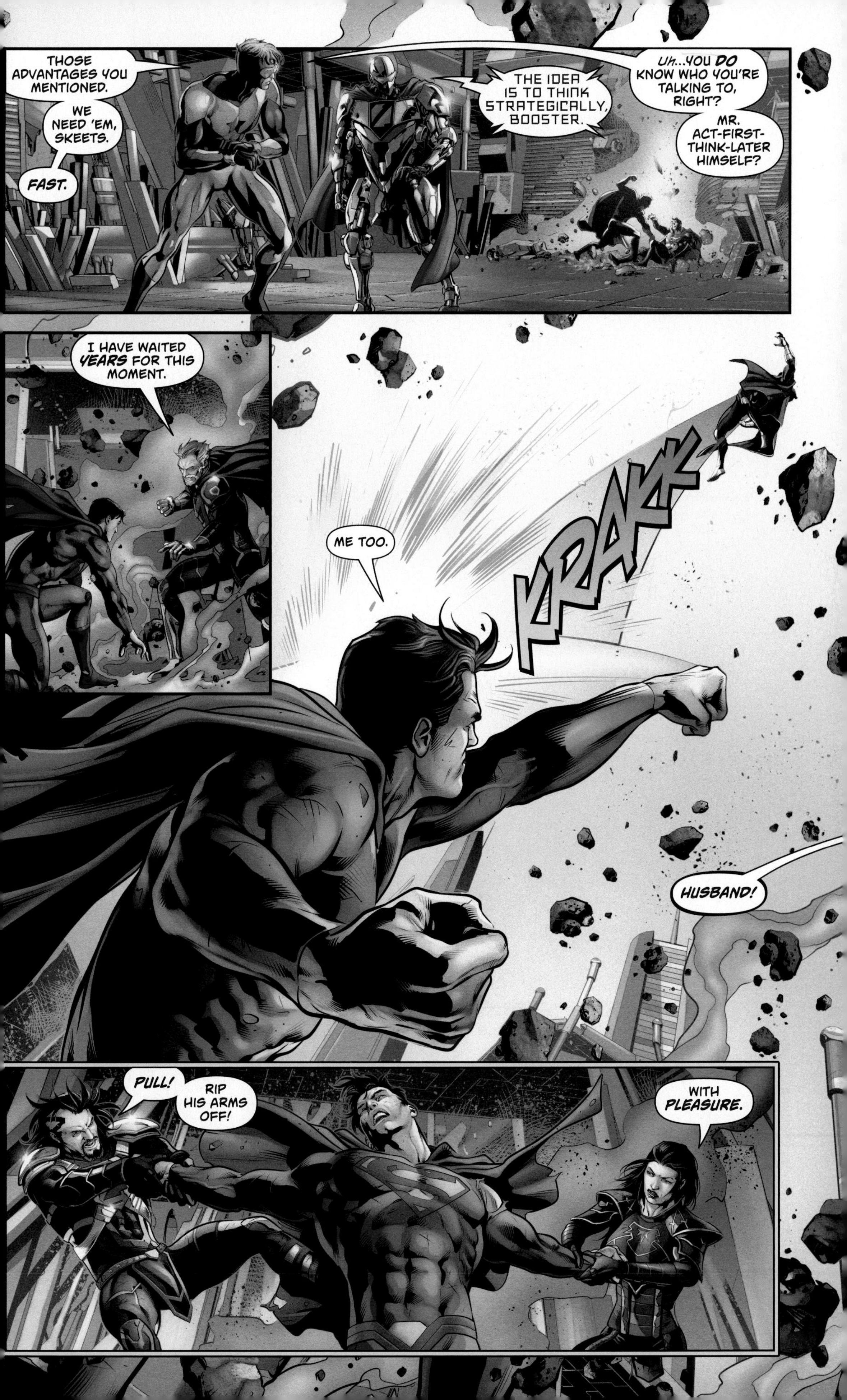

THOSE ADVANTAGES YOU MENTIONED.
WE NEED 'EM, SKEETS.
FAST.
THE IDEA IS TO THINK STRATEGICALLY, BOOSTER.
Uh...YOU DO KNOW WHO YOU'RE TALKING TO, RIGHT?
MR. ACT-FIRST-THINK-LATER HIMSELF?
I HAVE WAITED YEARS FOR THIS MOMENT.
ME TOO.
KRAKK
HUSBAND!
PULL!
RIP HIS ARMS OFF!
WITH PLEASURE.

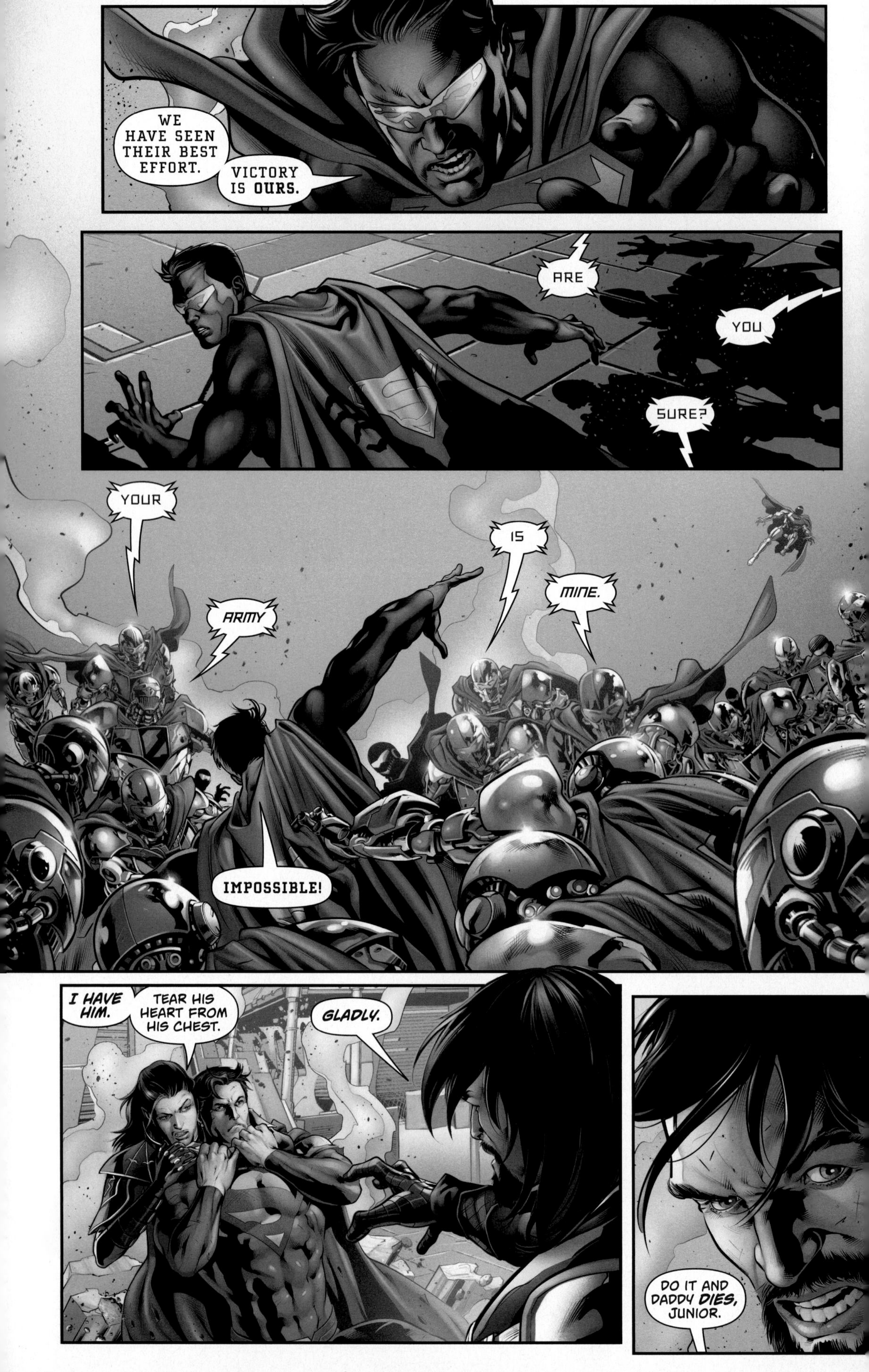
WE HAVE SEEN THEIR BEST EFFORT.
VICTORY IS OURS.
ARE
YOU
SURE?
YOUR
ARMY
IS
MINE.
IMPOSSIBLE!
I HAVE HIM.
TEAR HIS HEART FROM HIS CHEST.
GLADLY.
DO IT AND DADDY DIES, JUNIOR.

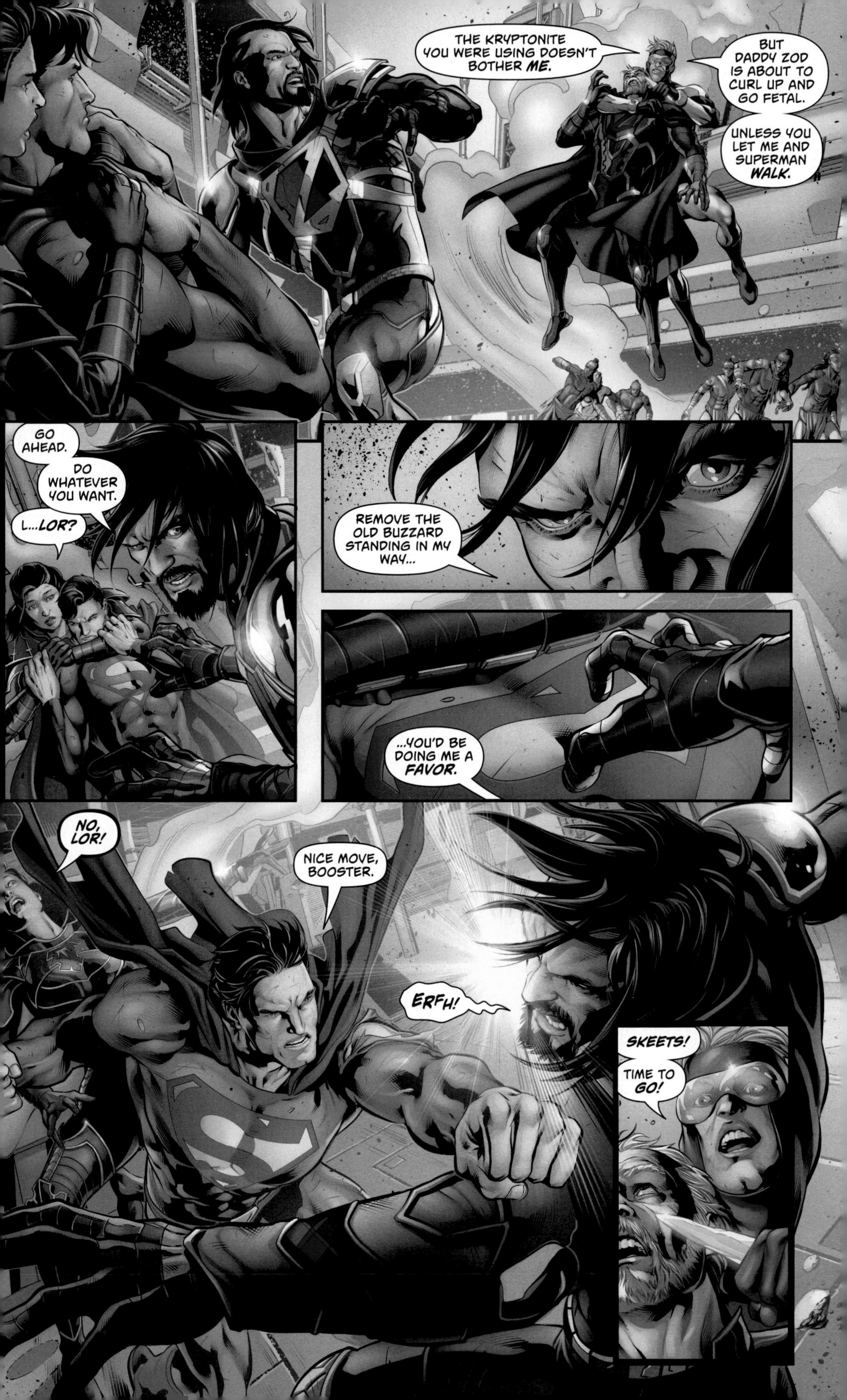
THE KRYPTONITE YOU WERE USING DOESN'T BOTHER ME.
BUT DADDY ZOD IS ABOUT TO CURL UP AND GO FETAL.
UNLESS YOU LET ME AND SUPERMAN WALK.
GO AHEAD.
DO WHATEVER YOU WANT.
L...LOR?
REMOVE THE OLD BUZZARD STANDING IN MY WAY...
...YOU'D BE DOING ME A FAVOR.
NO, LOR!
NICE MOVE, BOOSTER.
ERFH!
SKEETS!
TIME TO GO!

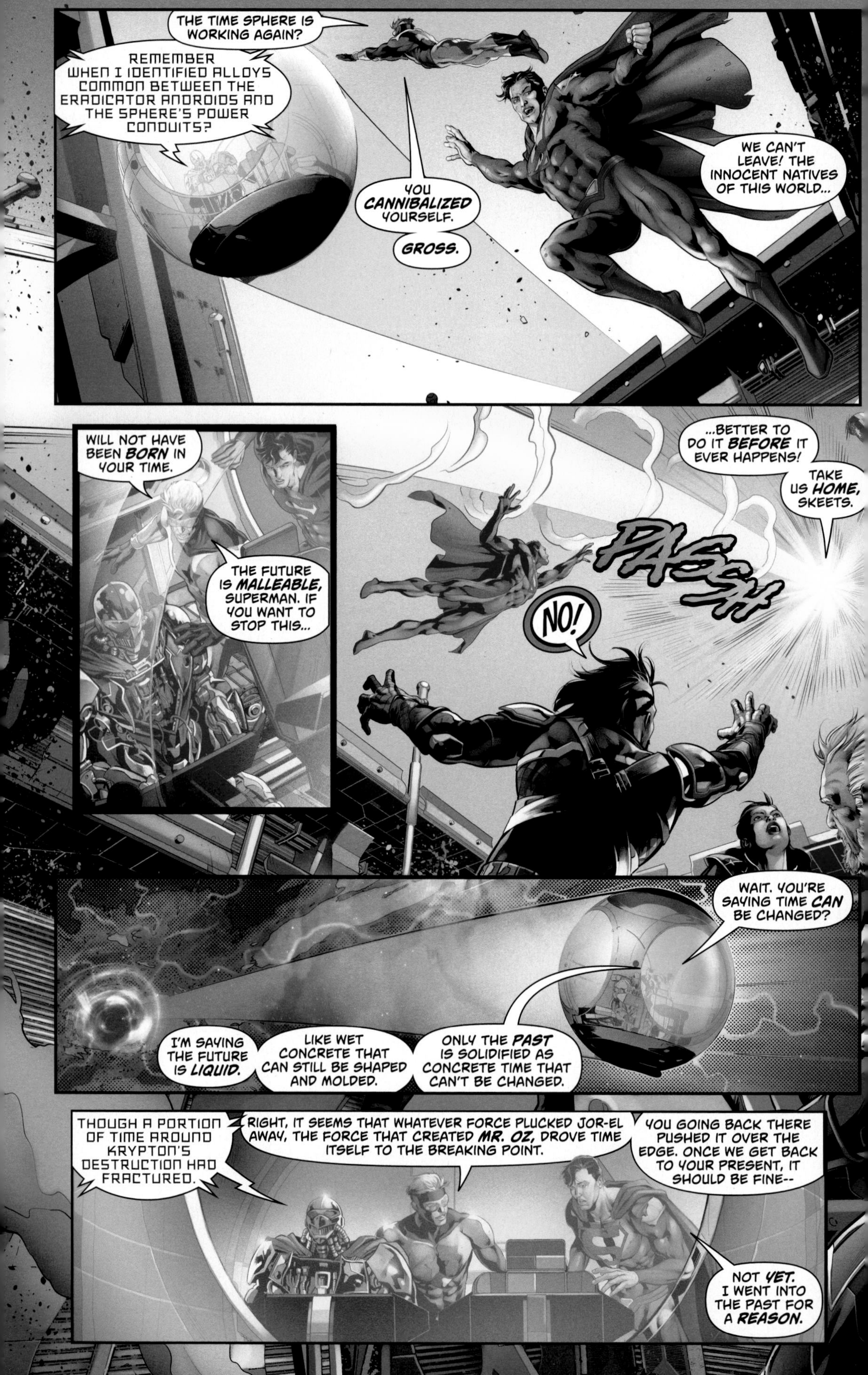
THE TIME SPHERE IS WORKING AGAIN?
REMEMBER WHEN I IDENTIFIED ALLOYS COMMON BETWEEN THE ERADICATOR ANDROIDS AND THE SPHERE'S POWER CONDUITS?
YOU CANNIBALIZED YOURSELF.
GROSS.
WE CAN'T LEAVE! THE INNOCENT NATIVES OF THIS WORLD...
WILL NOT HAVE BEEN BORN IN YOUR TIME.
THE FUTURE IS MALLEABLE, SUPERMAN. IF YOU WANT TO STOP THIS...
...BETTER TO DO IT BEFORE IT EVER HAPPENS!
TAKE US HOME, SKEETS.
PASSSH
NO!
WAIT. YOU'RE SAYING TIME CAN BE CHANGED?
I'M SAYING THE FUTURE IS LIQUID.
LIKE WET CONCRETE THAT CAN STILL BE SHAPED AND MOLDED.
ONLY THE PAST IS SOLIDIFIED AS CONCRETE TIME THAT CAN'T BE CHANGED.
THOUGH A PORTION OF TIME AROUND KRYPTON'S DESTRUCTION HAD FRACTURED.
RIGHT, IT SEEMS THAT WHATEVER FORCE PLUCKED JOR-EL AWAY, THE FORCE THAT CREATED MR. OZ, DROVE TIME ITSELF TO THE BREAKING POINT.
YOU GOING BACK THERE PUSHED IT OVER THE EDGE. ONCE WE GET BACK TO YOUR PRESENT, IT SHOULD BE FINE--
NOT YET. I WENT INTO THE PAST FOR A REASON.

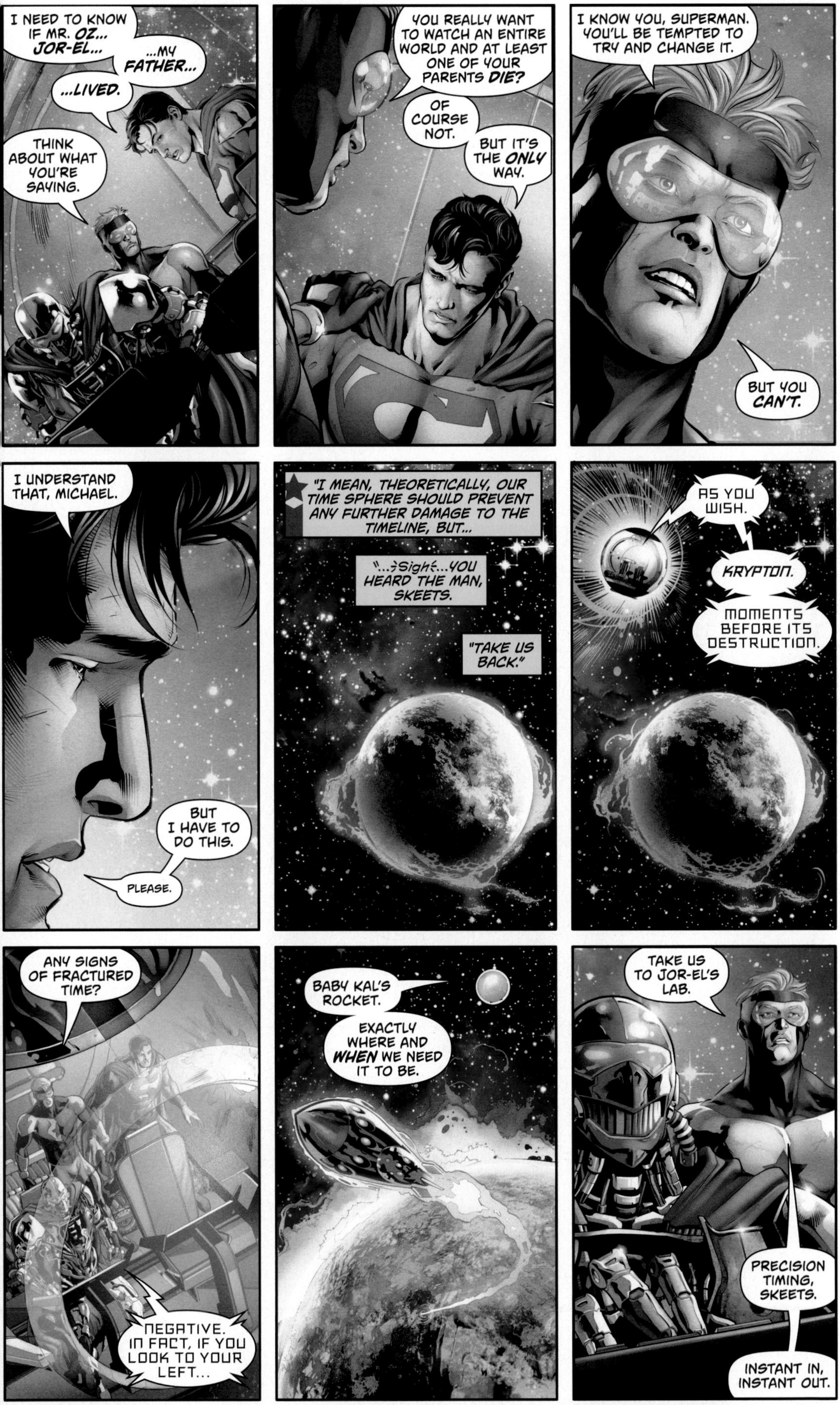
I NEED TO KNOW IF MR. OZ... JOR-EL...
...MY FATHER...
...LIVED.
THINK ABOUT WHAT YOU'RE SAYING.
YOU REALLY WANT TO WATCH AN ENTIRE WORLD AND AT LEAST ONE OF YOUR PARENTS DIE?
OF COURSE NOT.
BUT IT'S THE ONLY WAY.
I KNOW YOU, SUPERMAN. YOU'LL BE TEMPTED TO TRY AND CHANGE IT.
BUT YOU CAN'T.
I UNDERSTAND THAT, MICHAEL.
BUT I HAVE TO DO THIS.
PLEASE.
"I MEAN, THEORETICALLY, OUR TIME SPHERE SHOULD PREVENT ANY FURTHER DAMAGE TO THE TIMELINE, BUT...
"...{Sigh}...YOU HEARD THE MAN, SKEETS.
"TAKE US BACK."
AS YOU WISH.
KRYPTON.
MOMENTS BEFORE ITS DESTRUCTION.
ANY SIGNS OF FRACTURED TIME?
NEGATIVE. IN FACT, IF YOU LOOK TO YOUR LEFT...
BABY KAL'S ROCKET.
EXACTLY WHERE AND WHEN WE NEED IT TO BE.
TAKE US TO JOR-EL'S LAB.
PRECISION TIMING, SKEETS.
INSTANT IN, INSTANT OUT.

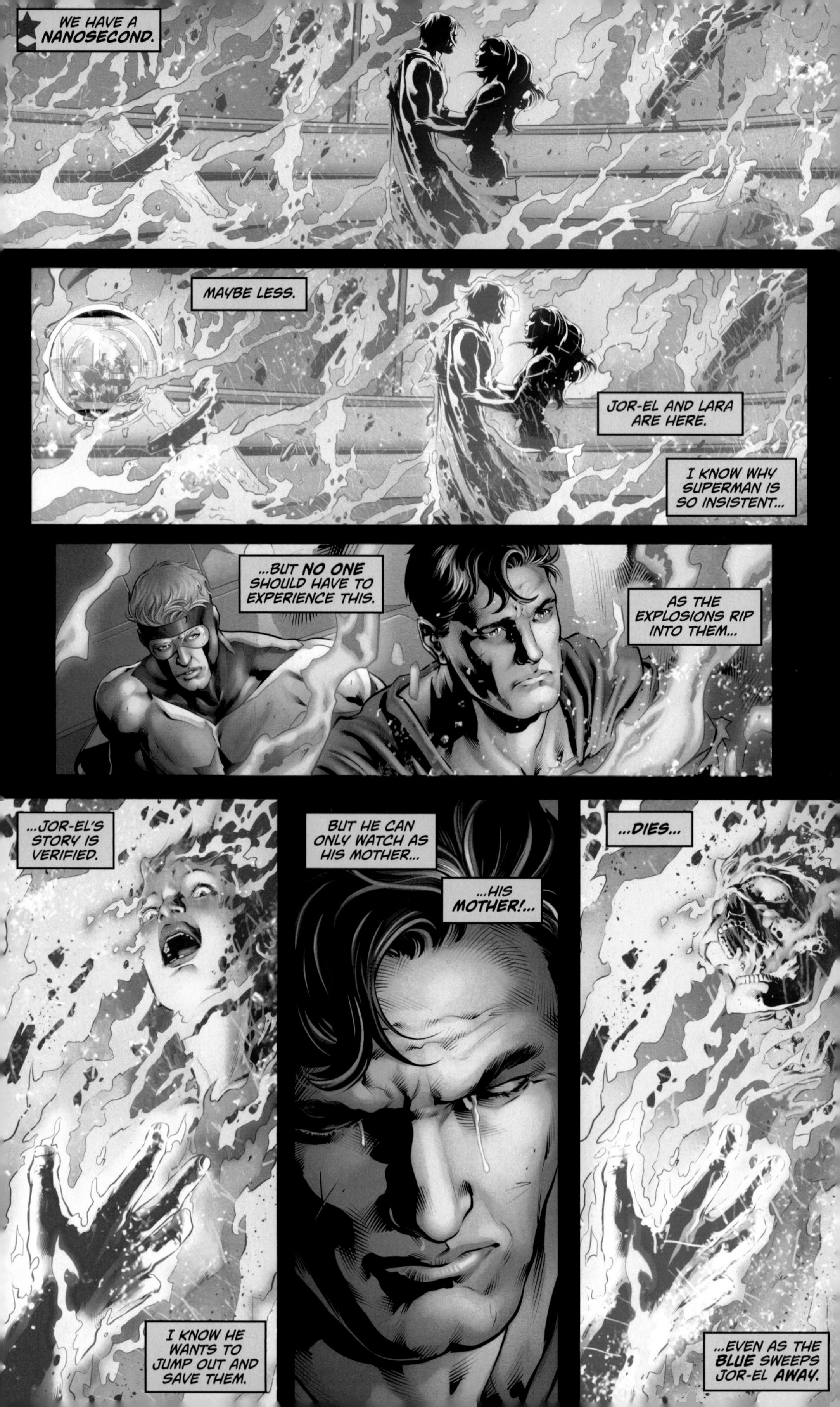

WE HAVE A NANOSECOND.
MAYBE LESS.
JOR-EL AND LARA ARE HERE.
I KNOW WHY SUPERMAN IS SO INSISTENT...
...BUT NO ONE SHOULD HAVE TO EXPERIENCE THIS.
AS THE EXPLOSIONS RIP INTO THEM...
...JOR-EL'S STORY IS VERIFIED.
I KNOW HE WANTS TO JUMP OUT AND SAVE THEM.
BUT HE CAN ONLY WATCH AS HIS MOTHER...
...HIS MOTHER!...
...DIES...
...EVEN AS THE BLUE SWEEPS JOR-EL AWAY.

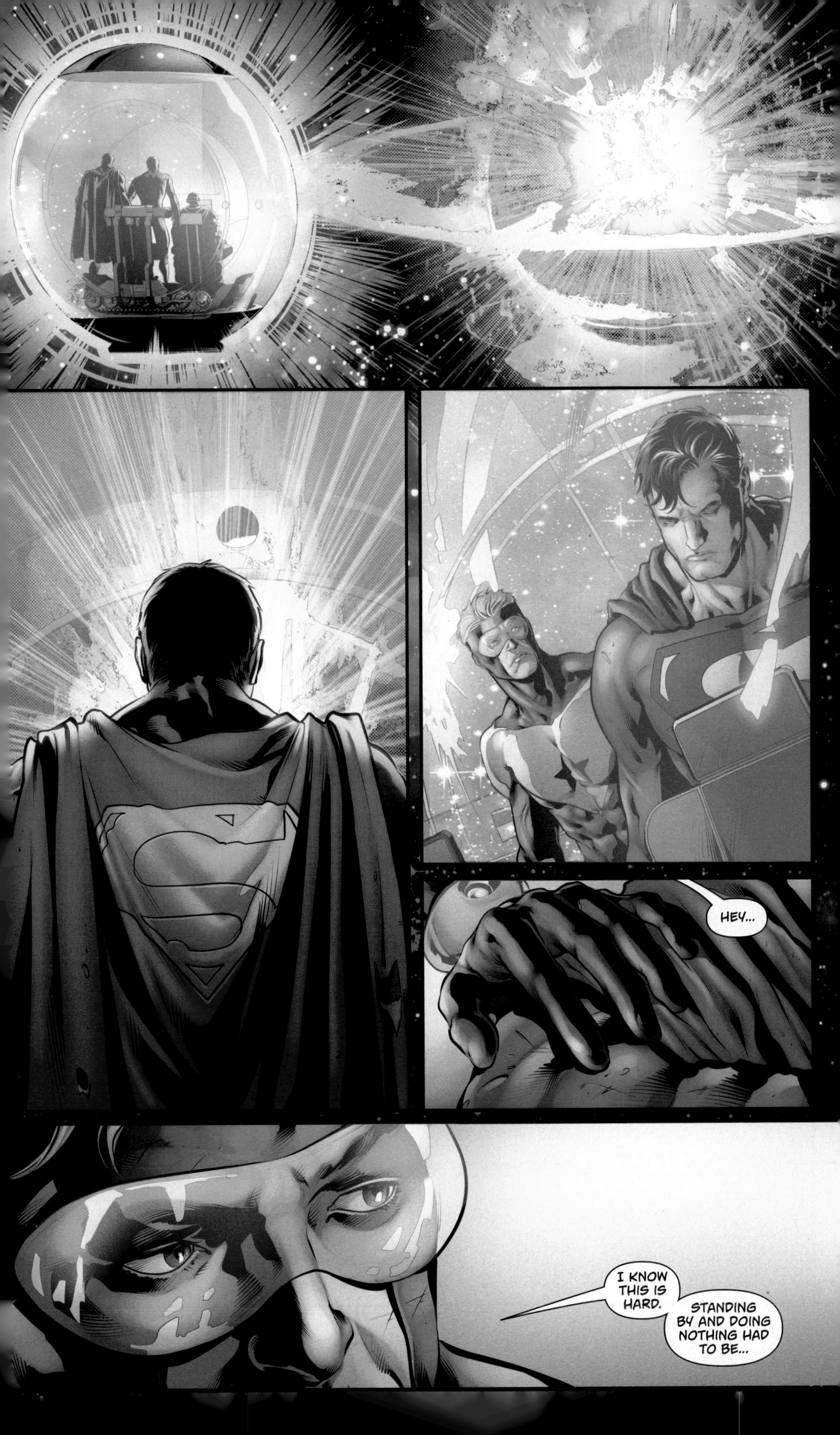
HEY...
I KNOW THIS IS HARD.
STANDING BY AND DOING NOTHING HAD TO BE...

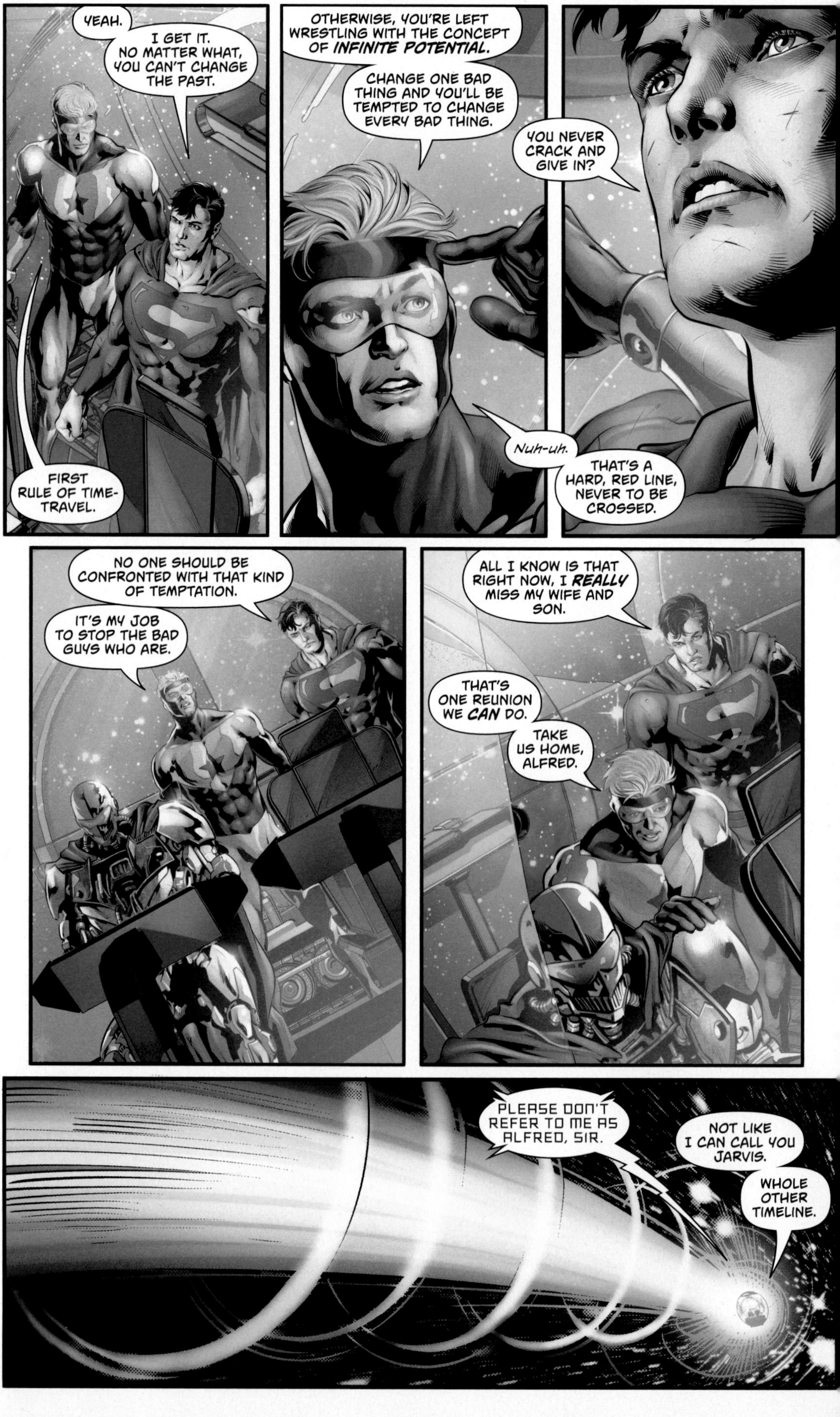
YEAH.
I GET IT. NO MATTER WHAT, YOU CAN'T CHANGE THE PAST.
FIRST RULE OF TIME-TRAVEL.
OTHERWISE, YOU'RE LEFT WRESTLING WITH THE CONCEPT OF INFINITE POTENTIAL.
CHANGE ONE BAD THING AND YOU'LL BE TEMPTED TO CHANGE EVERY BAD THING.
YOU NEVER CRACK AND GIVE IN?
Nuh-uh.
THAT'S A HARD, RED LINE, NEVER TO BE CROSSED.
NO ONE SHOULD BE CONFRONTED WITH THAT KIND OF TEMPTATION.
IT'S MY JOB TO STOP THE BAD GUYS WHO ARE.
ALL I KNOW IS THAT RIGHT NOW, I REALLY MISS MY WIFE AND SON.
THAT'S ONE REUNION WE CAN DO.
TAKE US HOME, ALFRED.
PLEASE DON'T REFER TO ME AS ALFRED, SIR.
NOT LIKE I CAN CALL YOU JARVIS.
WHOLE OTHER TIMELINE.

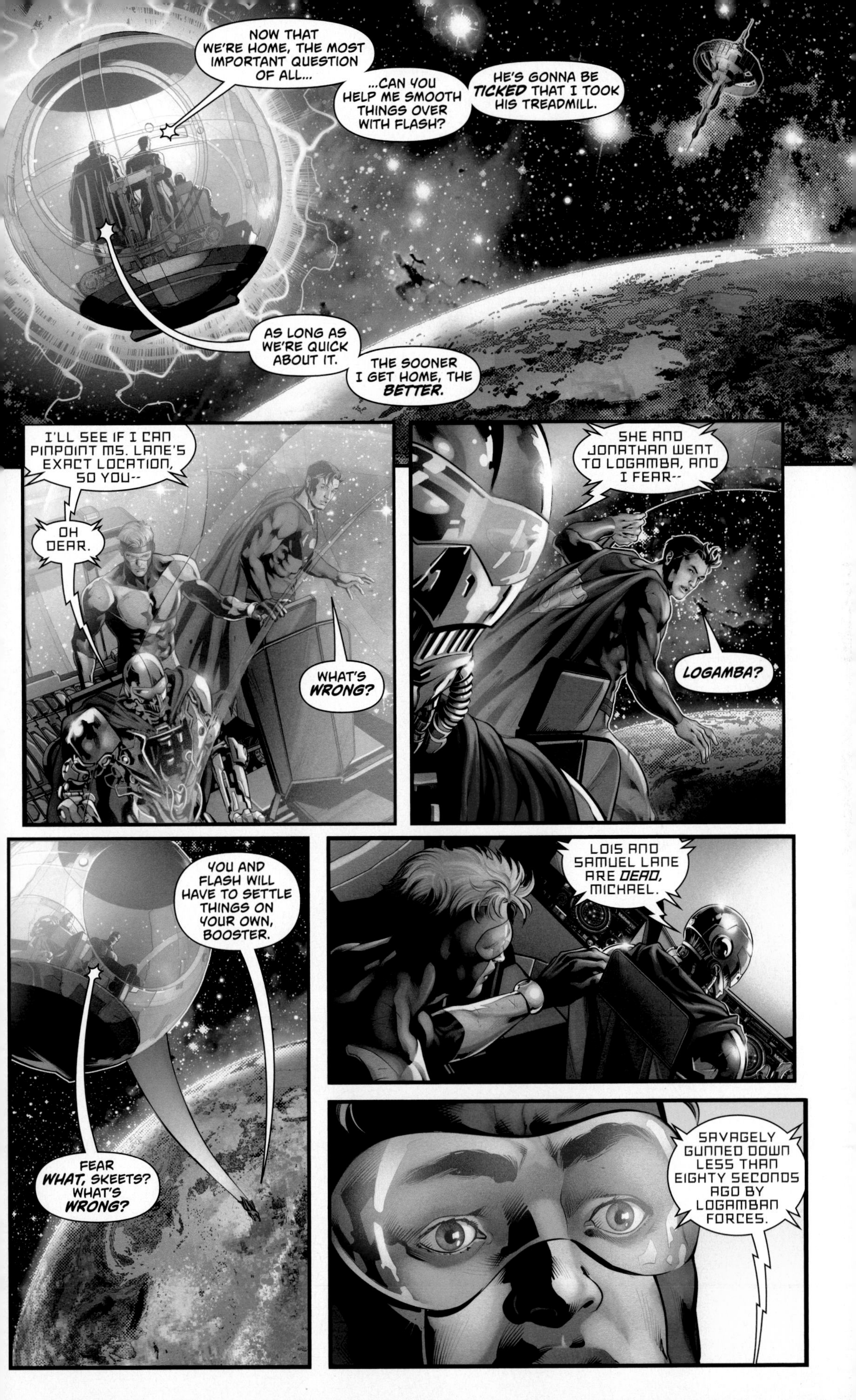
NOW THAT WE'RE HOME, THE MOST IMPORTANT QUESTION OF ALL...
...CAN YOU HELP ME SMOOTH THINGS OVER WITH FLASH?
HE'S GONNA BE *TICKED* THAT I TOOK HIS TREADMILL.
AS LONG AS WE'RE QUICK ABOUT IT.
THE SOONER I GET HOME, THE *BETTER.*
I'LL SEE IF I CAN PINPOINT MS. LANE'S EXACT LOCATION, SO YOU--
OH DEAR.
WHAT'S *WRONG?*
SHE AND JONATHAN WENT TO LOGAMBA, AND I FEAR--
LOGAMBA?
YOU AND FLASH WILL HAVE TO SETTLE THINGS ON YOUR OWN, BOOSTER.
FEAR *WHAT,* SKEETS? WHAT'S *WRONG?*
LOIS AND SAMUEL LANE ARE *DEAD,* MICHAEL.
SAVAGELY GUNNED DOWN LESS THAN EIGHTY SECONDS AGO BY LOGAMBAN FORCES.

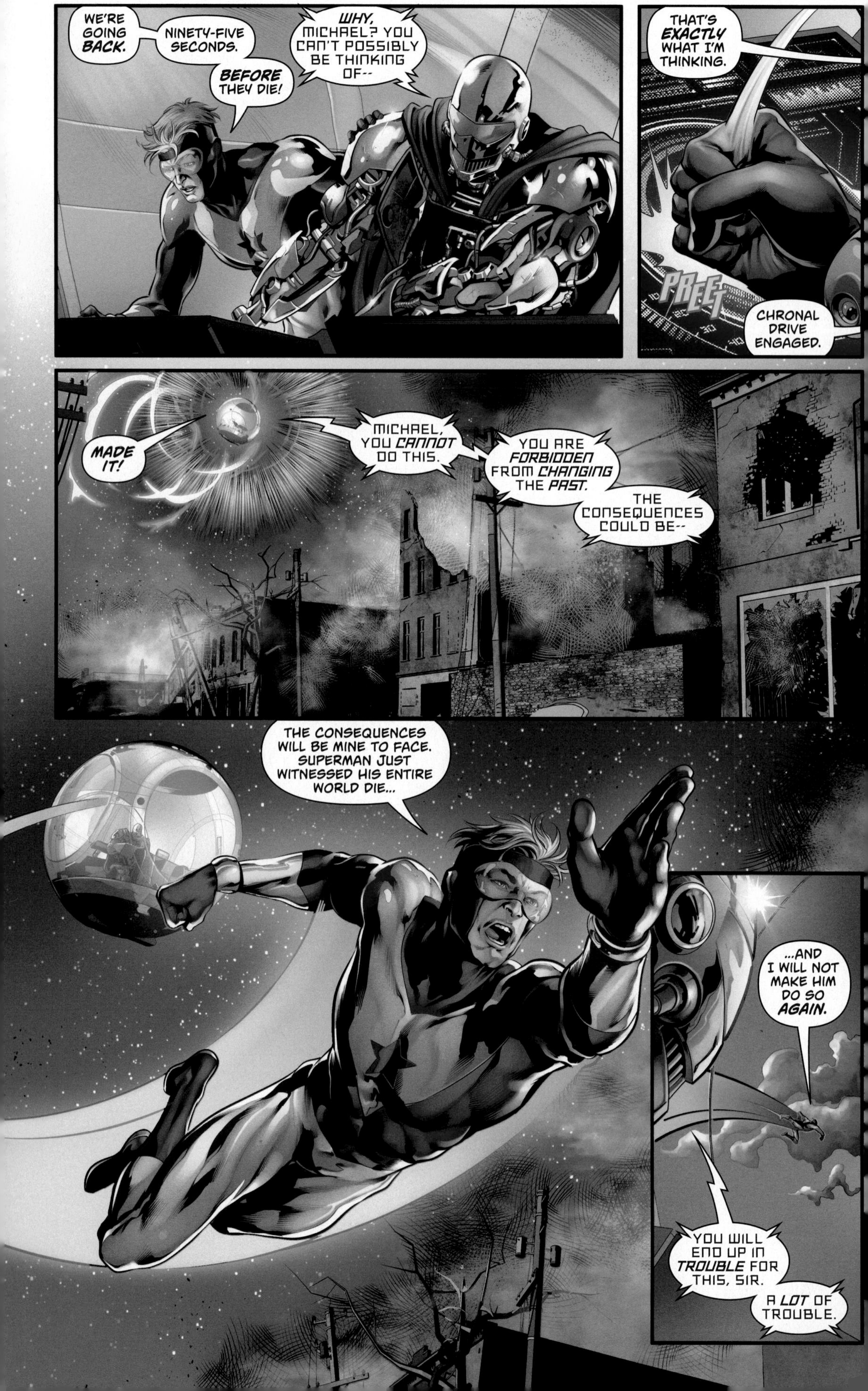
WE'RE GOING BACK.
NINETY-FIVE SECONDS.
BEFORE THEY DIE!
WHY, MICHAEL? YOU CAN'T POSSIBLY BE THINKING OF--
THAT'S EXACTLY WHAT I'M THINKING.
PREET
CHRONAL DRIVE ENGAGED.
MADE IT!
MICHAEL, YOU CANNOT DO THIS.
YOU ARE FORBIDDEN FROM CHANGING THE PAST.
THE CONSEQUENCES COULD BE--
THE CONSEQUENCES WILL BE MINE TO FACE. SUPERMAN JUST WITNESSED HIS ENTIRE WORLD DIE...
...AND I WILL NOT MAKE HIM DO SO AGAIN.
YOU WILL END UP IN TROUBLE FOR THIS, SIR.
A LOT OF TROUBLE.

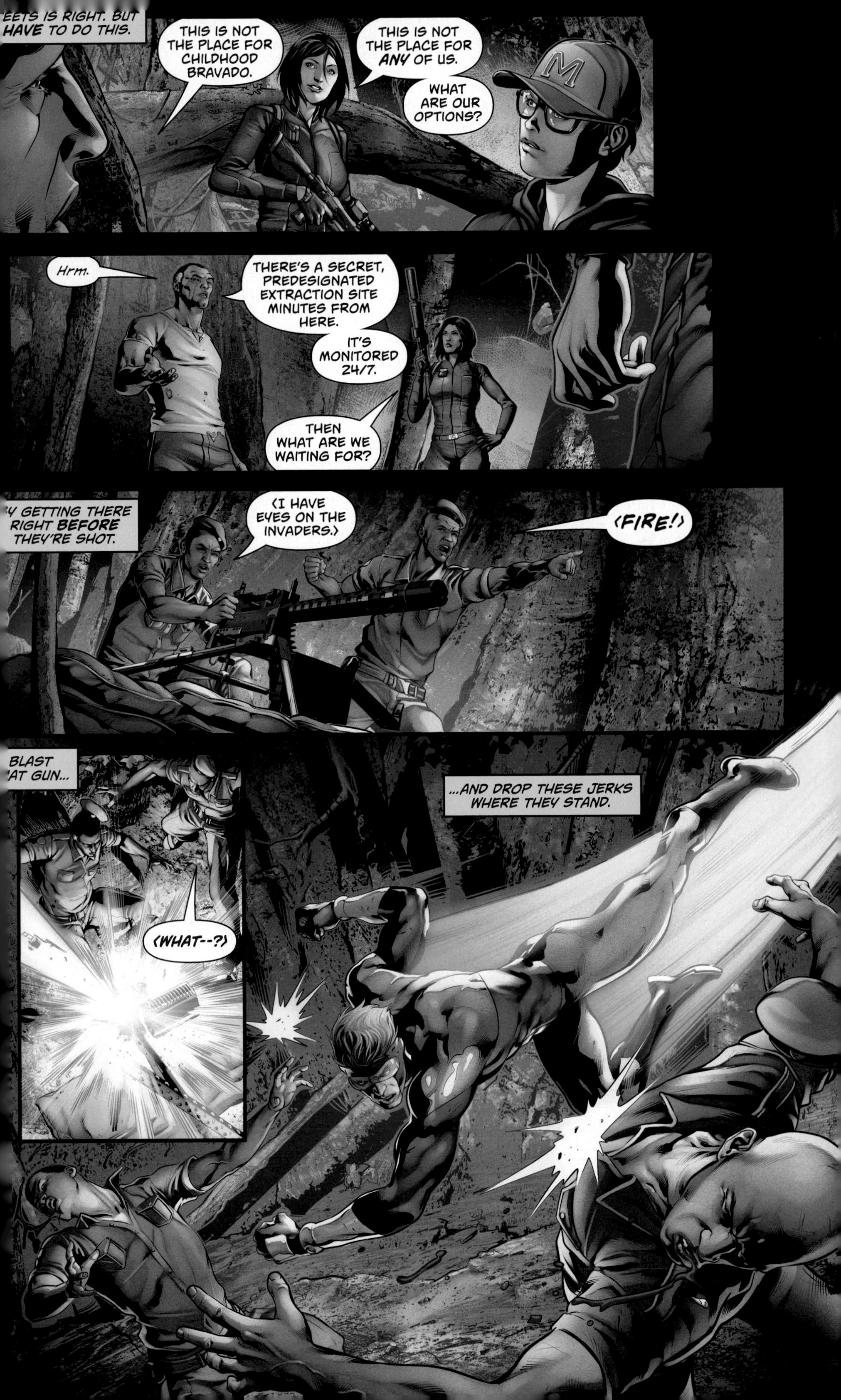
EETS IS RIGHT. BUT
HAVE TO DO THIS.
THIS IS NOT THE PLACE FOR CHILDHOOD BRAVADO.
THIS IS NOT THE PLACE FOR ANY OF US.
WHAT ARE OUR OPTIONS?
Hrm.
THERE'S A SECRET, PREDESIGNATED EXTRACTION SITE MINUTES FROM HERE.
IT'S MONITORED 24/7.
THEN WHAT ARE WE WAITING FOR?
Y GETTING THERE RIGHT BEFORE THEY'RE SHOT.
‹I HAVE EYES ON THE INVADERS.›
‹FIRE!›
BLAST
AT GUN...
‹WHAT--?›
...AND DROP THESE JERKS WHERE THEY STAND.

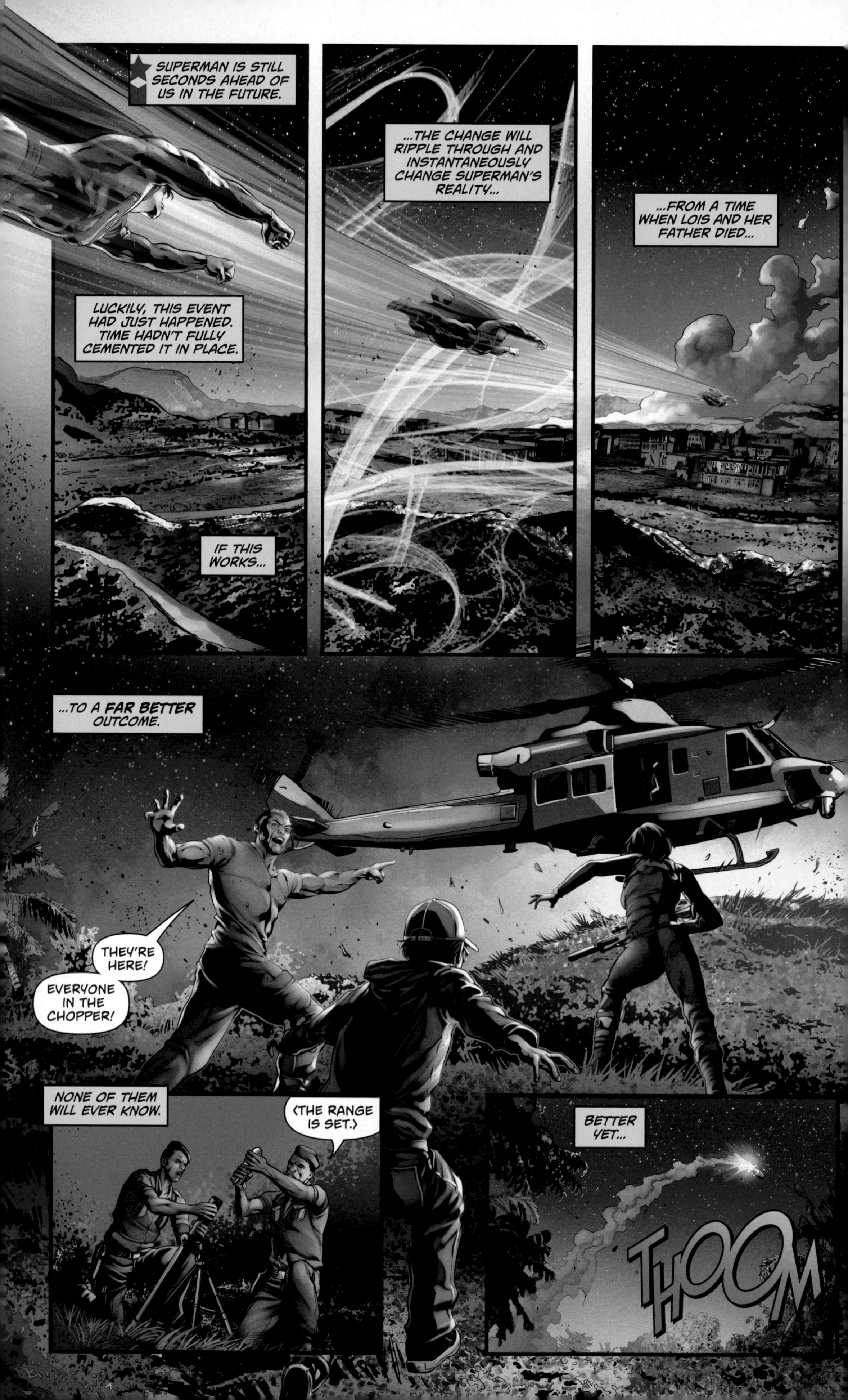
SUPERMAN IS STILL SECONDS AHEAD OF US IN THE FUTURE.
LUCKILY, THIS EVENT HAD JUST HAPPENED. TIME HADN'T FULLY CEMENTED IT IN PLACE.
IF THIS WORKS...
...THE CHANGE WILL RIPPLE THROUGH AND INSTANTANEOUSLY CHANGE SUPERMAN'S REALITY...
...FROM A TIME WHEN LOIS AND HER FATHER DIED...
...TO A FAR BETTER OUTCOME.
THEY'RE HERE!
EVERYONE IN THE CHOPPER!
NONE OF THEM WILL EVER KNOW.
⟨THE RANGE IS SET.⟩
BETTER YET...
THOOM

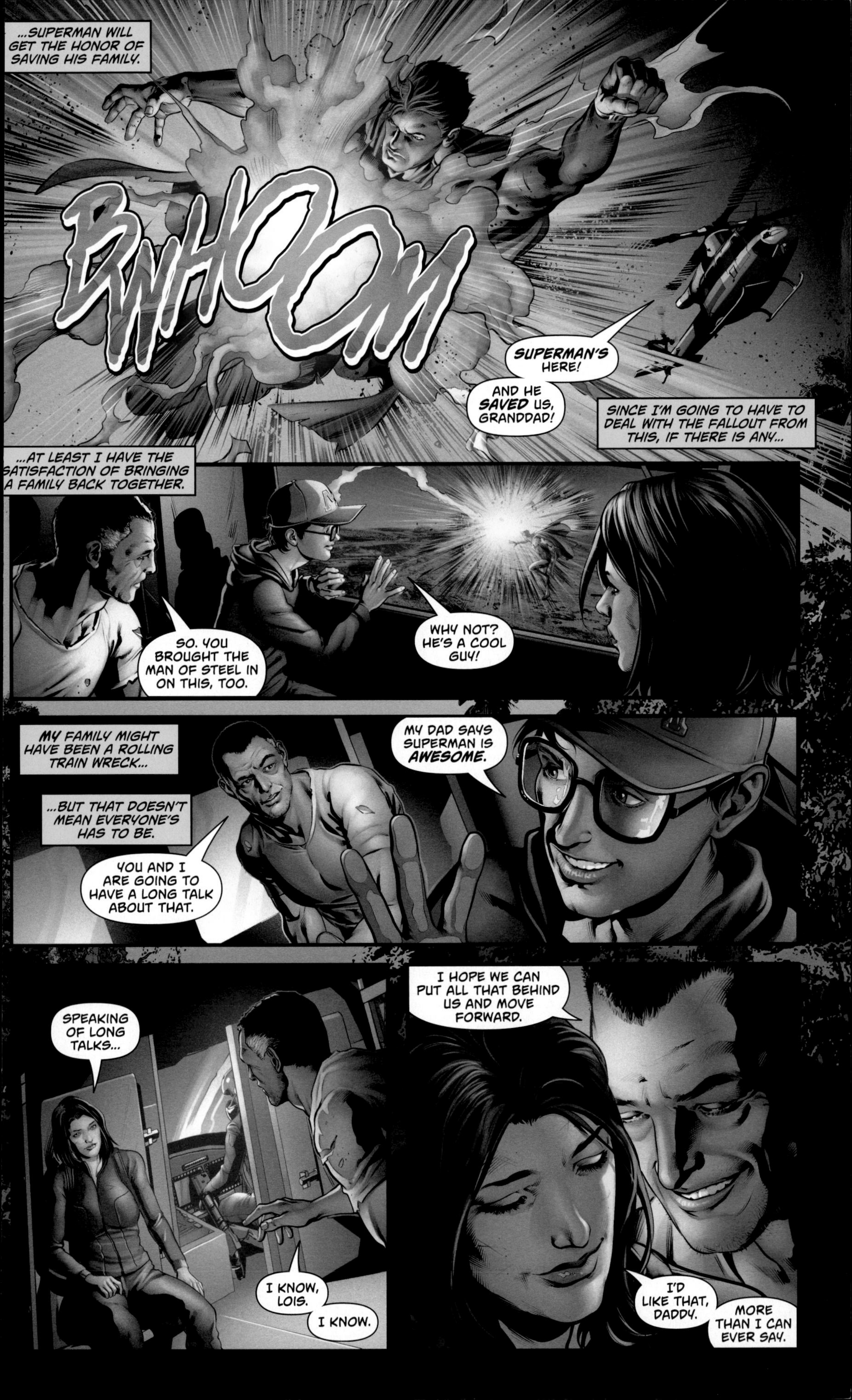
...SUPERMAN WILL GET THE HONOR OF SAVING HIS FAMILY.
BWHOOM
SUPERMAN'S HERE!
AND HE *SAVED* US, GRANDDAD!
SINCE I'M GOING TO HAVE TO DEAL WITH THE FALLOUT FROM THIS, IF THERE IS ANY...
...AT LEAST I HAVE THE SATISFACTION OF BRINGING A FAMILY BACK TOGETHER.
SO. YOU BROUGHT THE MAN OF STEEL IN ON THIS, TOO.
WHY NOT? HE'S A COOL GUY!
MY FAMILY MIGHT HAVE BEEN A ROLLING TRAIN WRECK...
...BUT THAT DOESN'T MEAN EVERYONE'S HAS TO BE.
MY DAD SAYS SUPERMAN IS *AWESOME*.
YOU AND I ARE GOING TO HAVE A LONG TALK ABOUT THAT.
SPEAKING OF LONG TALKS...
I KNOW, LOIS.
I KNOW.
I HOPE WE CAN PUT ALL THAT BEHIND US AND MOVE FORWARD.
I'D LIKE THAT, DADDY.
MORE THAN I CAN EVER SAY.

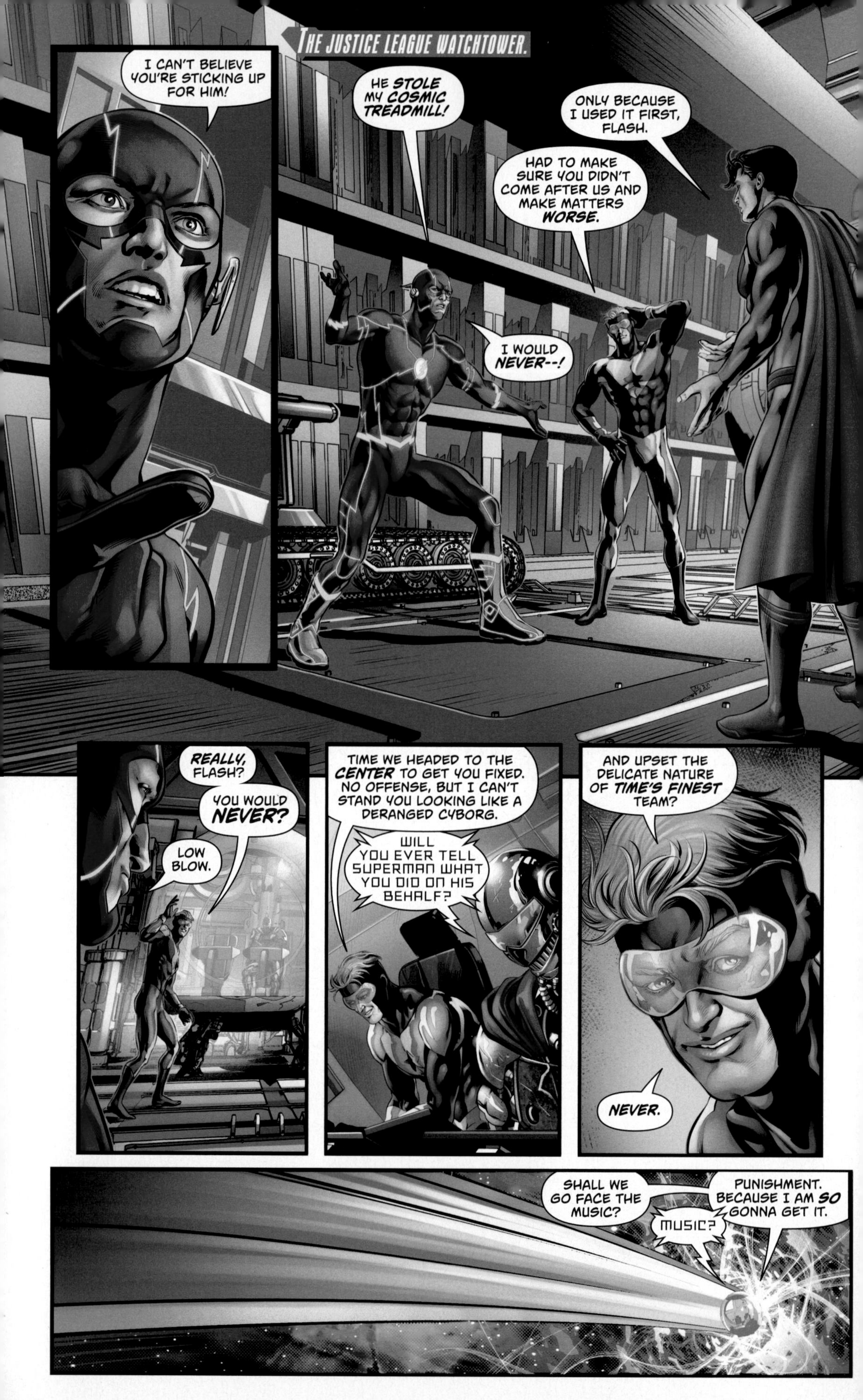
THE JUSTICE LEAGUE WATCHTOWER.
I CAN'T BELIEVE YOU'RE STICKING UP FOR HIM!
HE STOLE MY COSMIC TREADMILL!
ONLY BECAUSE I USED IT FIRST, FLASH.
HAD TO MAKE SURE YOU DIDN'T COME AFTER US AND MAKE MATTERS WORSE.
I WOULD NEVER--!
REALLY, FLASH?
YOU WOULD NEVER?
LOW BLOW.
TIME WE HEADED TO THE CENTER TO GET YOU FIXED. NO OFFENSE, BUT I CAN'T STAND YOU LOOKING LIKE A DERANGED CYBORG.
WILL YOU EVER TELL SUPERMAN WHAT YOU DID ON HIS BEHALF?
AND UPSET THE DELICATE NATURE OF TIME'S FINEST TEAM?
NEVER.
SHALL WE GO FACE THE MUSIC?
MUSIC?
PUNISHMENT. BECAUSE I AM SO GONNA GET IT.

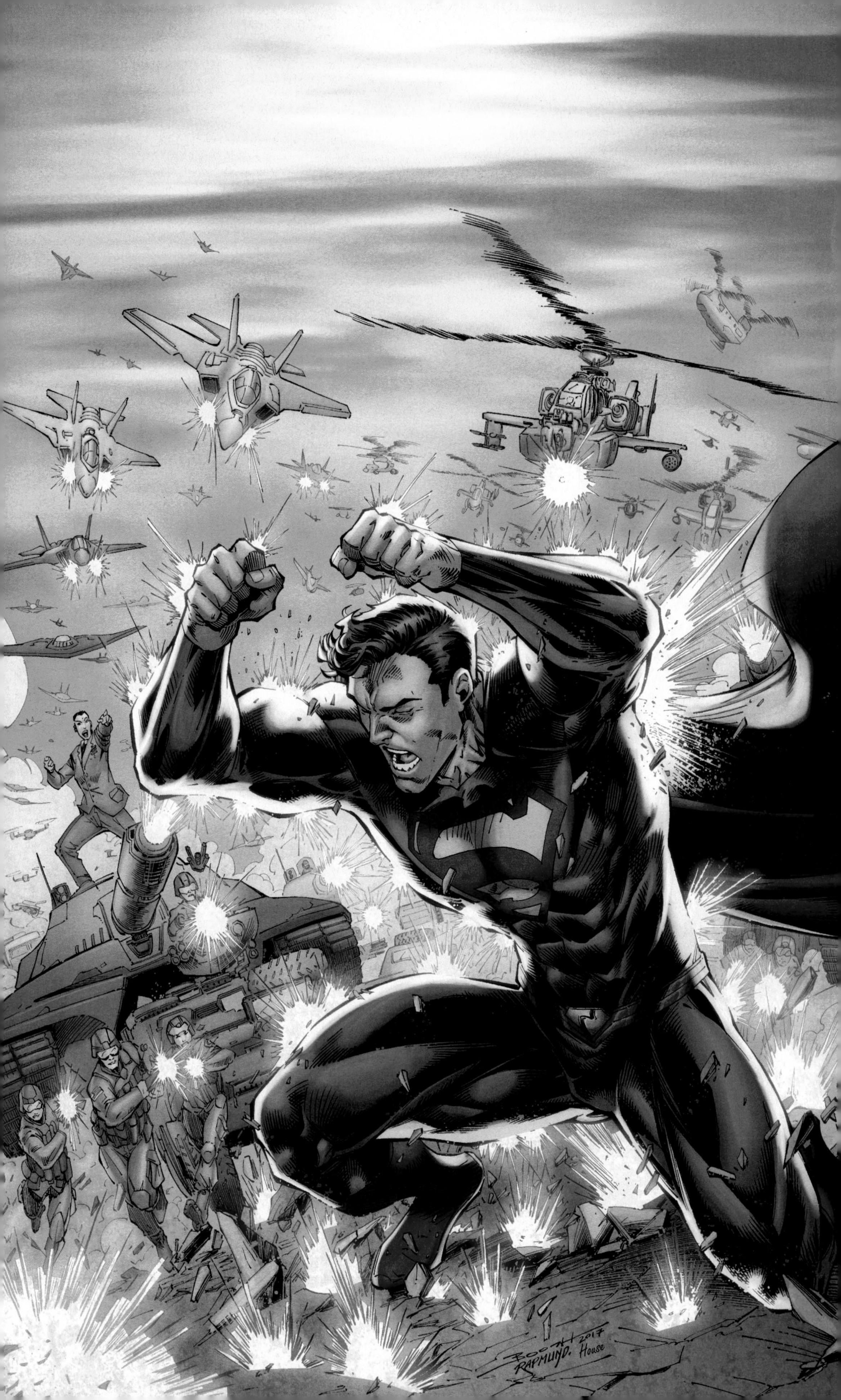
BOOTH 2017
RAPMUND. House

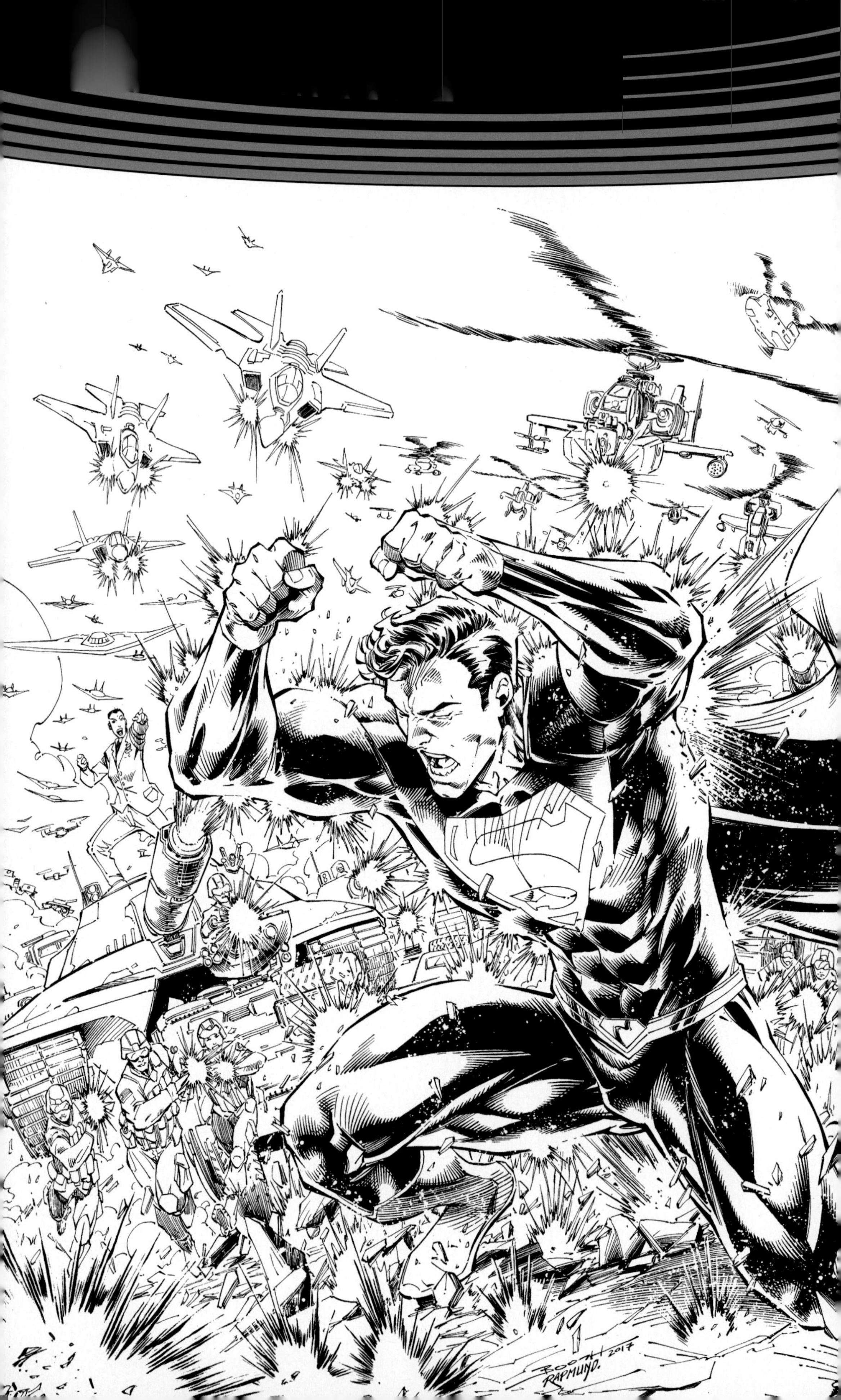
BOOTH 2017
RAPMUND.

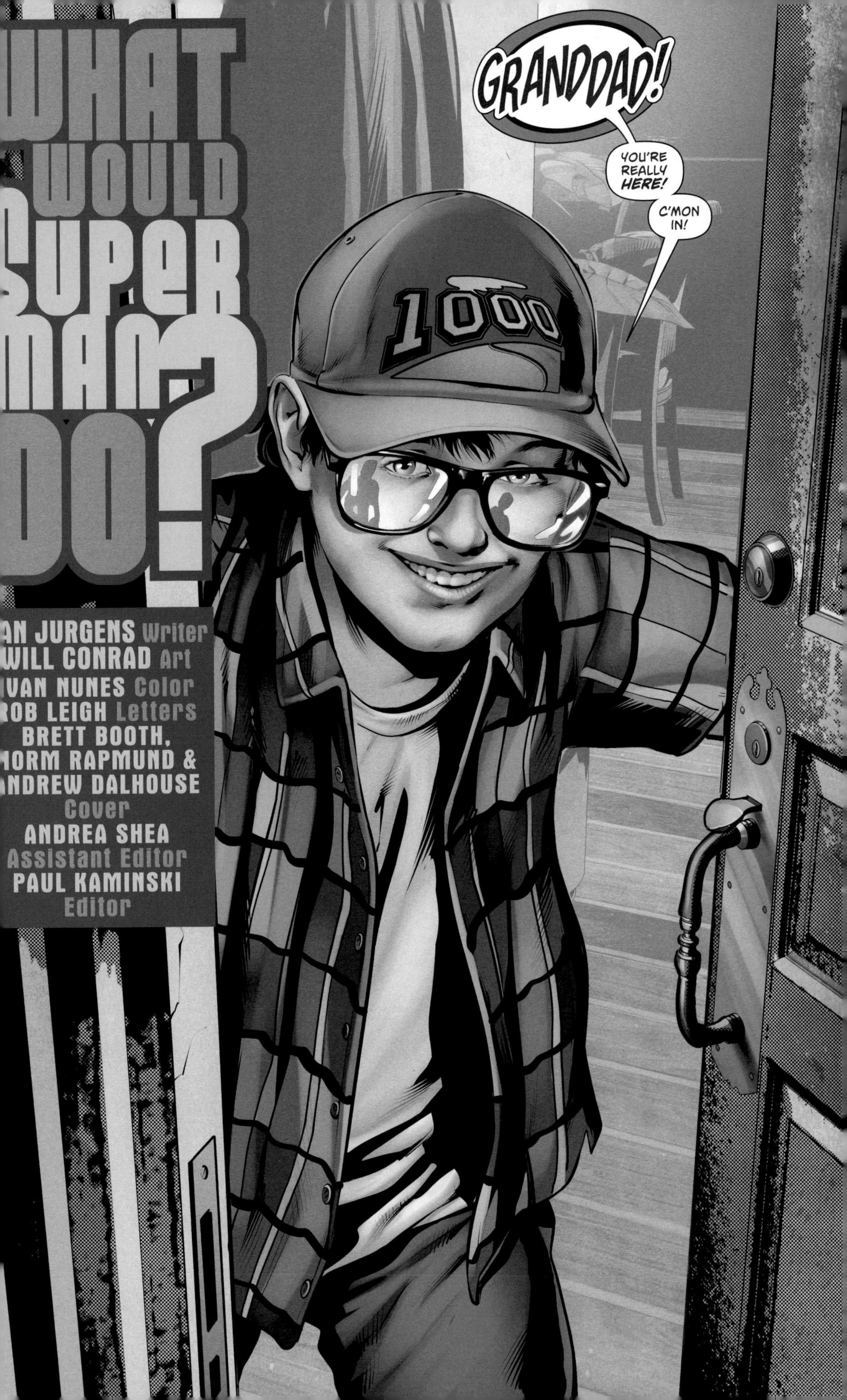
WHAT WOULD SUPER MAN DO?
AN JURGENS Writer
WILL CONRAD Art
VAN NUNES Color
OB LEIGH Letters
BRETT BOOTH,
ORM RAPMUND &
NDREW DALHOUSE
Cover
ANDREA SHEA
Assistant Editor
PAUL KAMINSKI
Editor
GRANDDAD!
YOU'RE REALLY HERE!
C'MON IN!
1000

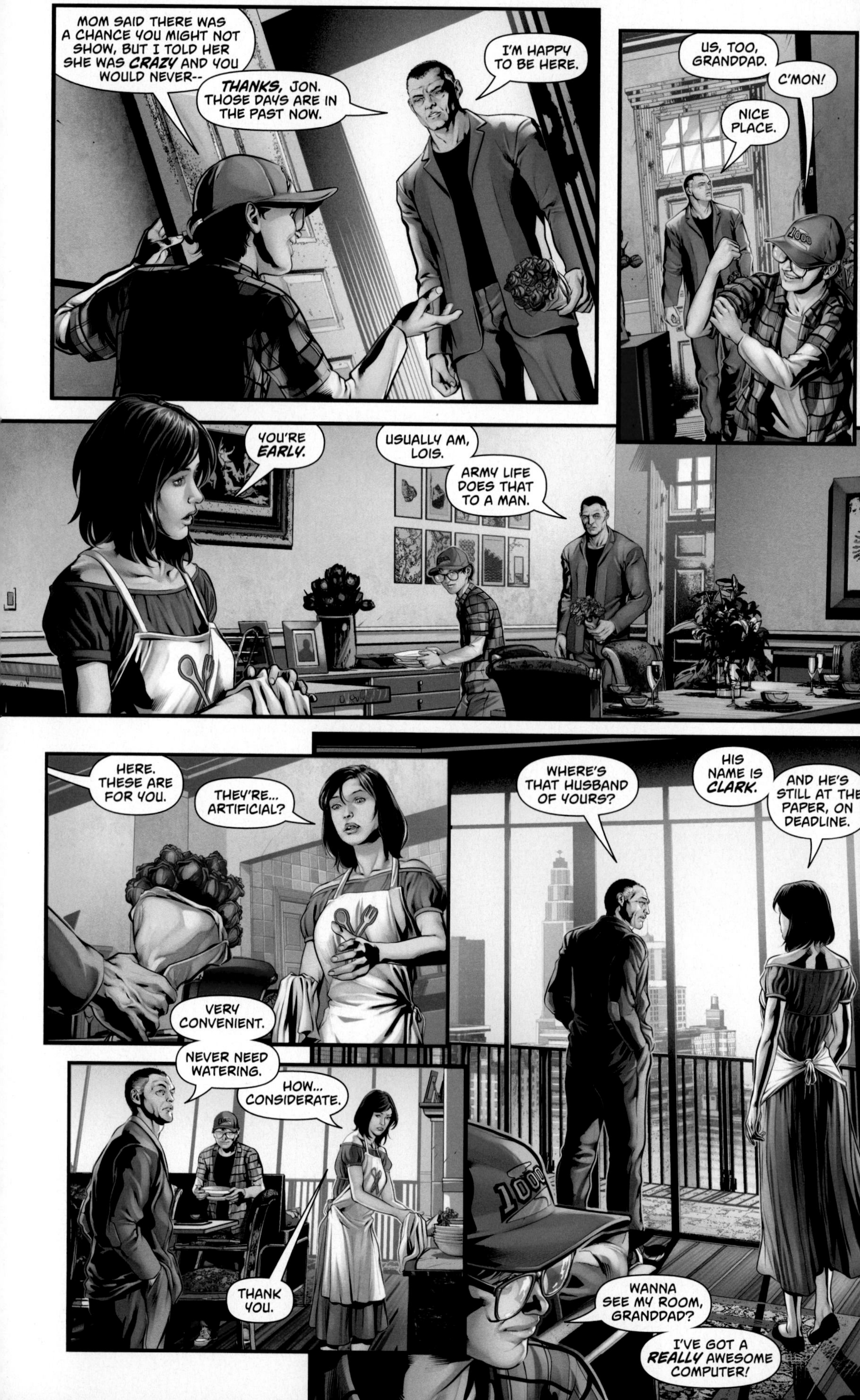
MOM SAID THERE WAS A CHANCE YOU MIGHT NOT SHOW, BUT I TOLD HER SHE WAS CRAZY AND YOU WOULD NEVER--
THANKS, JON. THOSE DAYS ARE IN THE PAST NOW.
I'M HAPPY TO BE HERE.
US, TOO, GRANDDAD.
C'MON!
NICE PLACE.
YOU'RE EARLY.
USUALLY AM, LOIS.
ARMY LIFE DOES THAT TO A MAN.
HERE. THESE ARE FOR YOU.
THEY'RE... ARTIFICIAL?
VERY CONVENIENT.
NEVER NEED WATERING.
HOW... CONSIDERATE.
THANK YOU.
WHERE'S THAT HUSBAND OF YOURS?
HIS NAME IS CLARK.
AND HE'S STILL AT THE PAPER, ON DEADLINE.
WANNA SEE MY ROOM, GRANDDAD?
I'VE GOT A REALLY AWESOME COMPUTER!

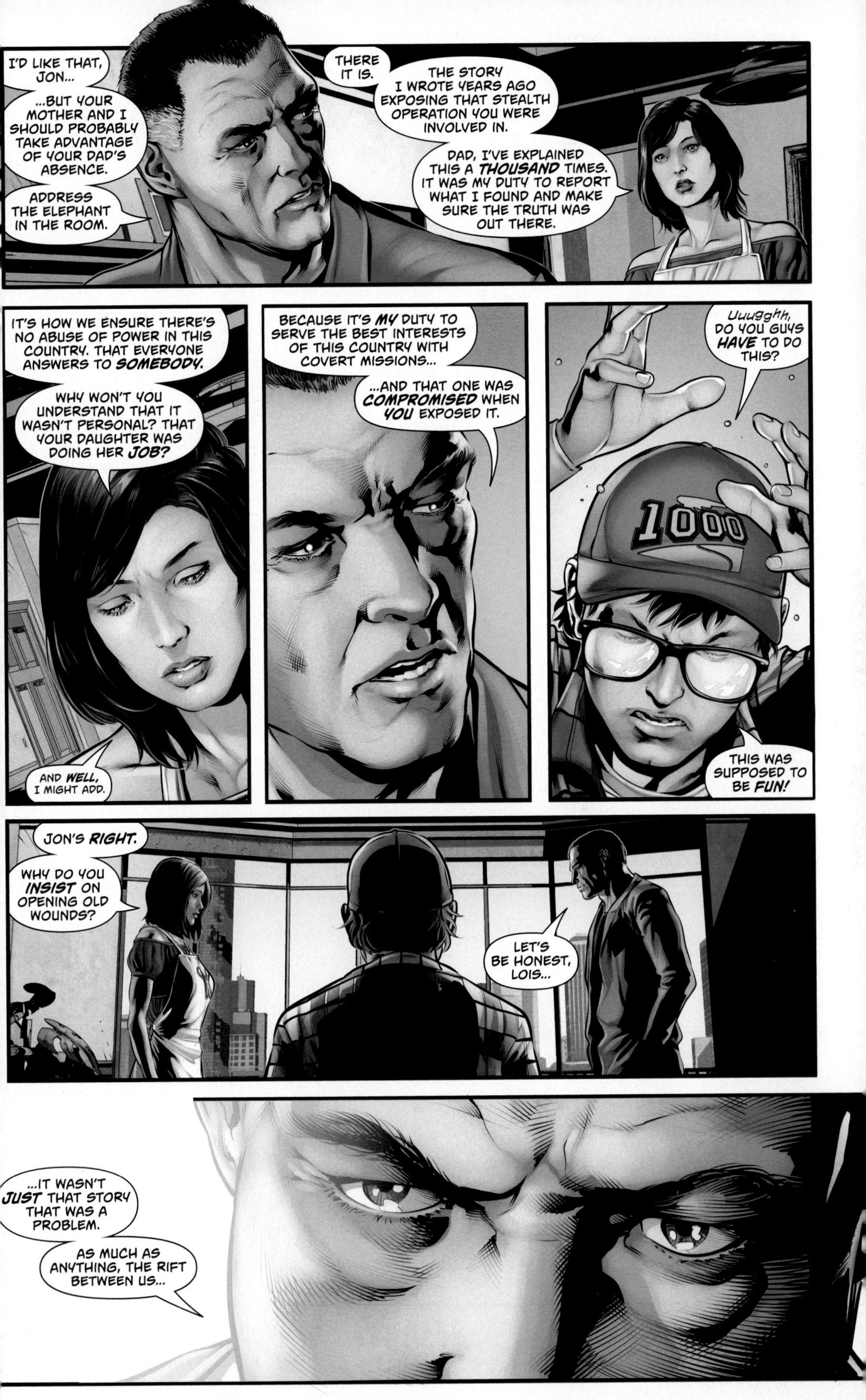

I'D LIKE THAT, JON...
...BUT YOUR MOTHER AND I SHOULD PROBABLY TAKE ADVANTAGE OF YOUR DAD'S ABSENCE.
ADDRESS THE ELEPHANT IN THE ROOM.
THERE IT IS.
THE STORY I WROTE YEARS AGO EXPOSING THAT STEALTH OPERATION YOU WERE INVOLVED IN.
DAD, I'VE EXPLAINED THIS A THOUSAND TIMES. IT WAS MY DUTY TO REPORT WHAT I FOUND AND MAKE SURE THE TRUTH WAS OUT THERE.
IT'S HOW WE ENSURE THERE'S NO ABUSE OF POWER IN THIS COUNTRY. THAT EVERYONE ANSWERS TO SOMEBODY.
WHY WON'T YOU UNDERSTAND THAT IT WASN'T PERSONAL? THAT YOUR DAUGHTER WAS DOING HER JOB?
AND WELL, I MIGHT ADD.
BECAUSE IT'S MY DUTY TO SERVE THE BEST INTERESTS OF THIS COUNTRY WITH COVERT MISSIONS...
...AND THAT ONE WAS COMPROMISED WHEN YOU EXPOSED IT.
Uuugghh, DO YOU GUYS HAVE TO DO THIS?
1000
THIS WAS SUPPOSED TO BE FUN!
JON'S RIGHT.
WHY DO YOU INSIST ON OPENING OLD WOUNDS?
LET'S BE HONEST, LOIS...
...IT WASN'T JUST THAT STORY THAT WAS A PROBLEM.
AS MUCH AS ANYTHING, THE RIFT BETWEEN US...

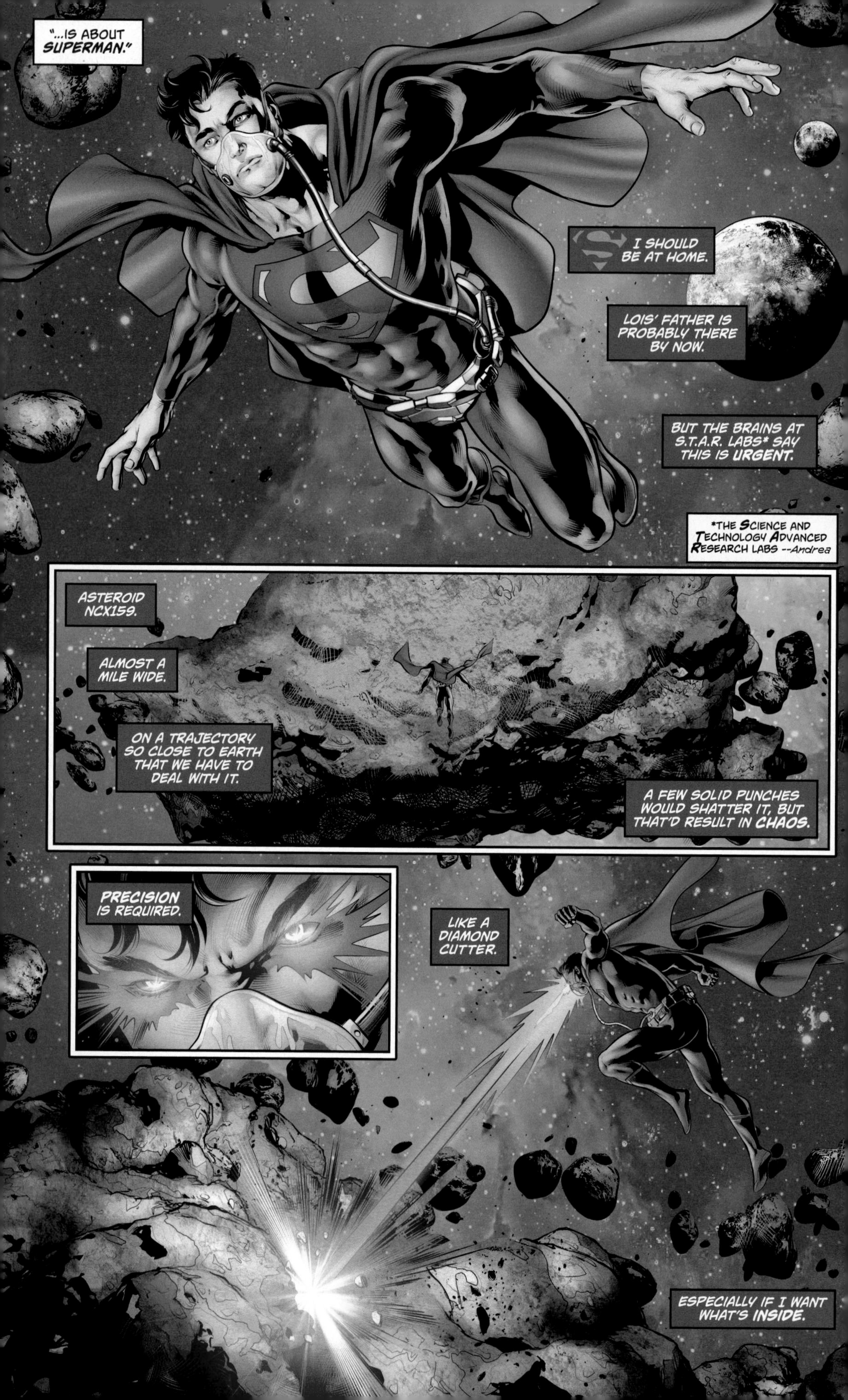
"...IS ABOUT SUPERMAN."
I SHOULD BE AT HOME.
LOIS' FATHER IS PROBABLY THERE BY NOW.
BUT THE BRAINS AT S.T.A.R. LABS* SAY THIS IS URGENT.
*THE SCIENCE AND TECHNOLOGY ADVANCED RESEARCH LABS --Andrea
ASTEROID NCX159.
ALMOST A MILE WIDE.
ON A TRAJECTORY SO CLOSE TO EARTH THAT WE HAVE TO DEAL WITH IT.
A FEW SOLID PUNCHES WOULD SHATTER IT, BUT THAT'D RESULT IN CHAOS.
PRECISION IS REQUIRED.
LIKE A DIAMOND CUTTER.
ESPECIALLY IF I WANT WHAT'S INSIDE.

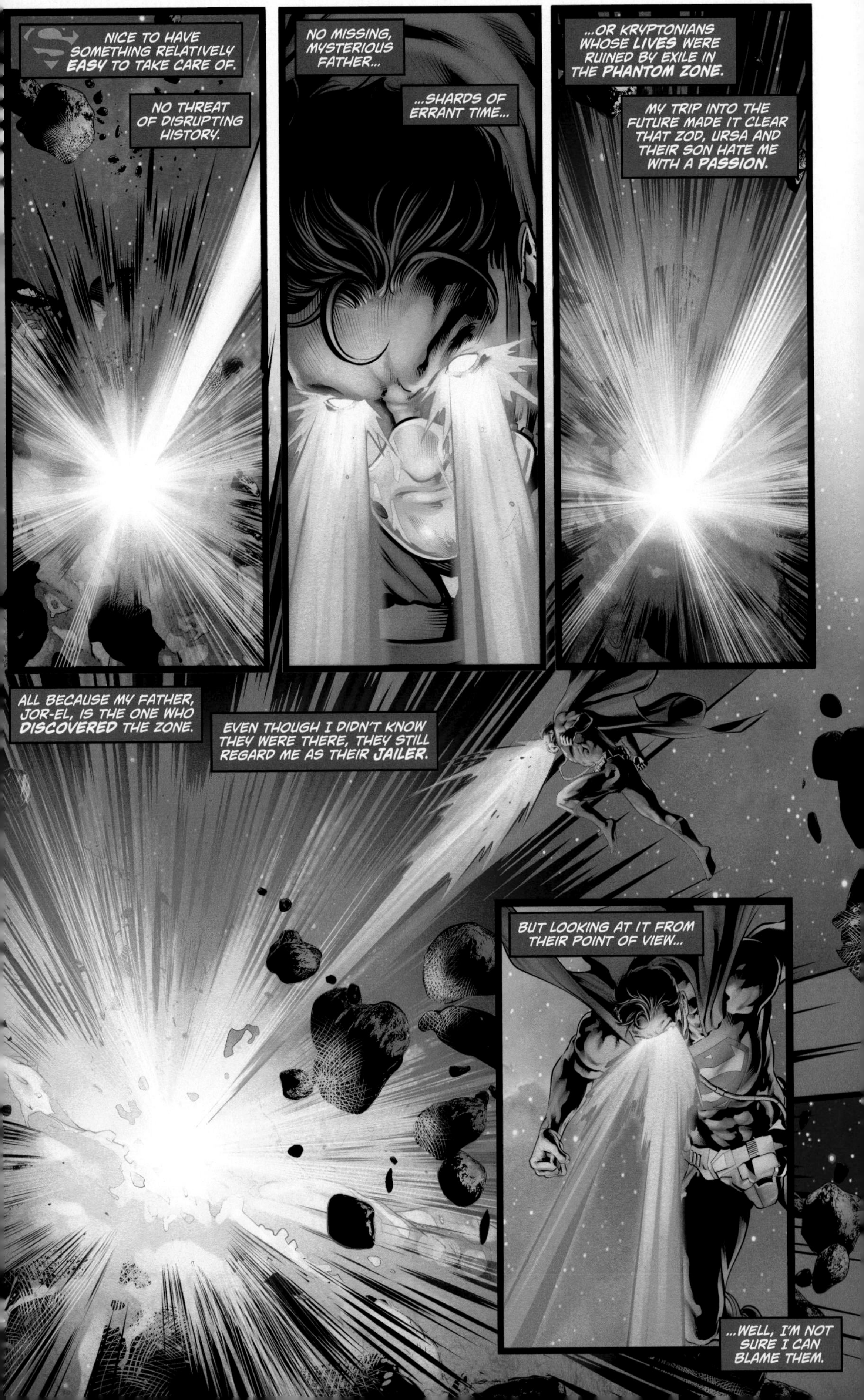
NICE TO HAVE SOMETHING RELATIVELY EASY TO TAKE CARE OF.
NO THREAT OF DISRUPTING HISTORY.
NO MISSING, MYSTERIOUS FATHER...
...SHARDS OF ERRANT TIME...
...OR KRYPTONIANS WHOSE LIVES WERE RUINED BY EXILE IN THE PHANTOM ZONE.
MY TRIP INTO THE FUTURE MADE IT CLEAR THAT ZOD, URSA AND THEIR SON HATE ME WITH A PASSION.
ALL BECAUSE MY FATHER, JOR-EL, IS THE ONE WHO DISCOVERED THE ZONE.
EVEN THOUGH I DIDN'T KNOW THEY WERE THERE, THEY STILL REGARD ME AS THEIR JAILER.
BUT LOOKING AT IT FROM THEIR POINT OF VIEW...
...WELL, I'M NOT SURE I CAN BLAME THEM.

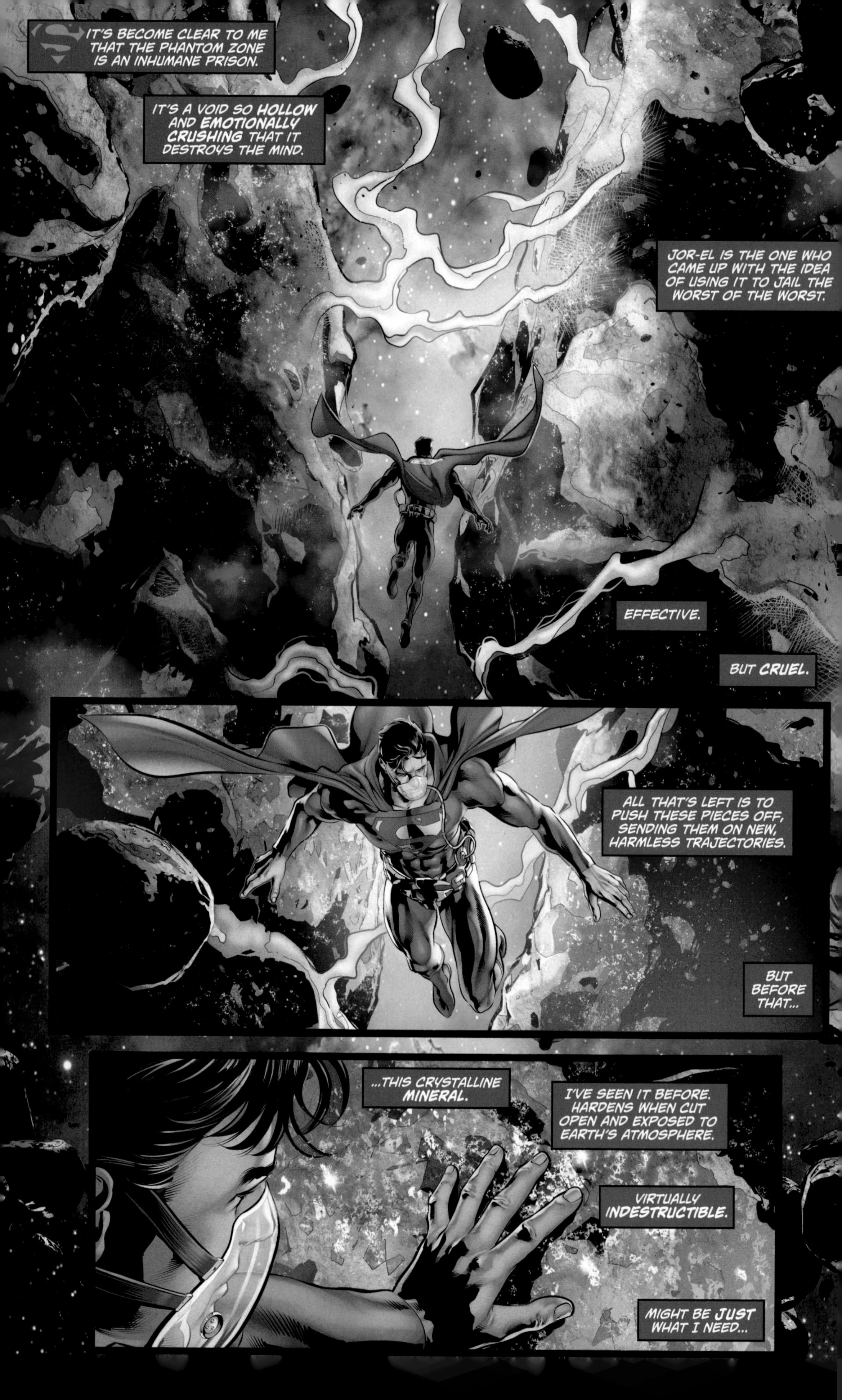
IT'S BECOME CLEAR TO ME THAT THE PHANTOM ZONE IS AN INHUMANE PRISON.
IT'S A VOID SO HOLLOW AND EMOTIONALLY CRUSHING THAT IT DESTROYS THE MIND.
JOR-EL IS THE ONE WHO CAME UP WITH THE IDEA OF USING IT TO JAIL THE WORST OF THE WORST.
EFFECTIVE.
BUT CRUEL.
ALL THAT'S LEFT IS TO PUSH THESE PIECES OFF, SENDING THEM ON NEW, HARMLESS TRAJECTORIES.
BUT BEFORE THAT...
...THIS CRYSTALLINE MINERAL.
I'VE SEEN IT BEFORE. HARDENS WHEN CUT OPEN AND EXPOSED TO EARTH'S ATMOSPHERE.
VIRTUALLY INDESTRUCTIBLE.
MIGHT BE JUST WHAT I NEED...

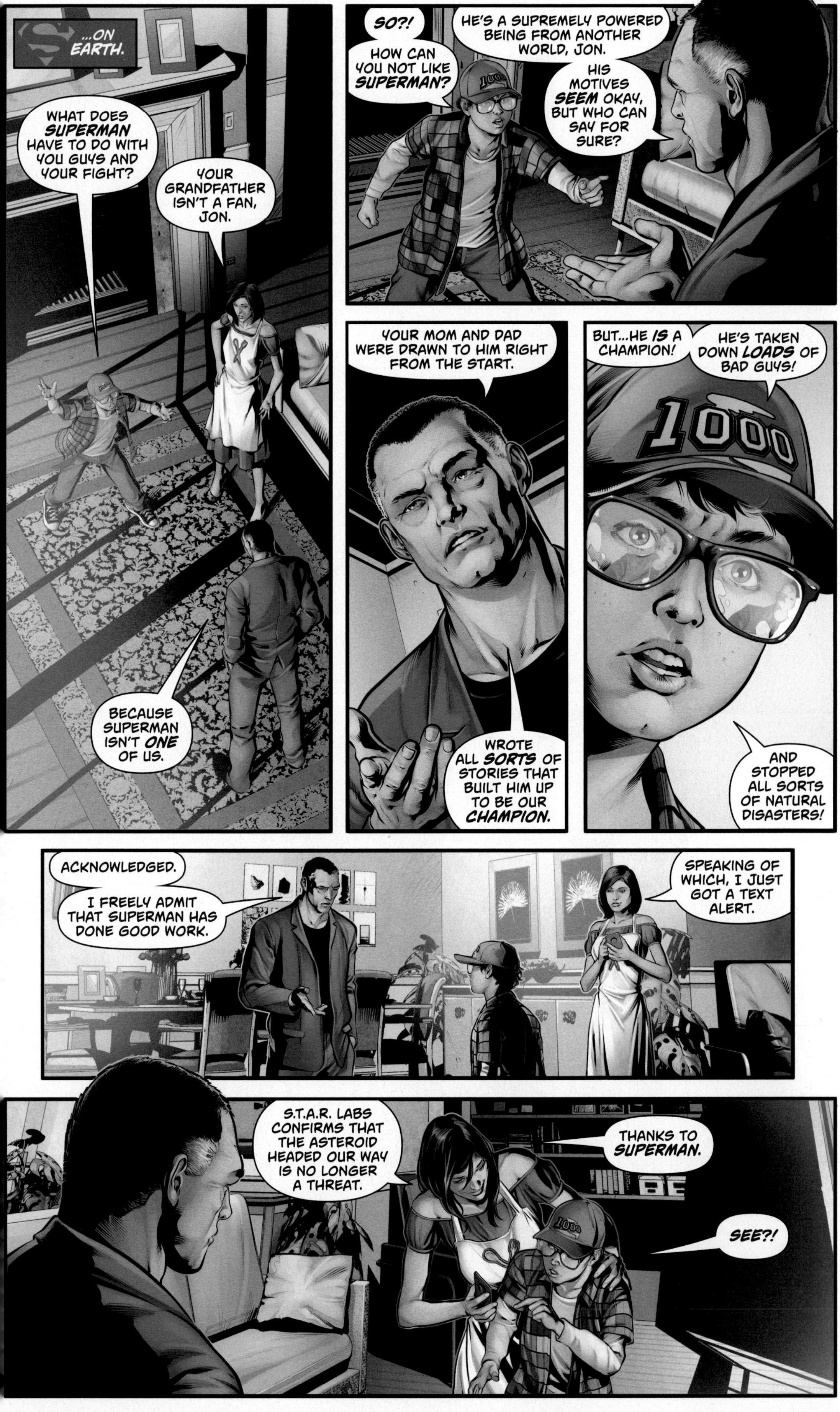
...ON EARTH.
WHAT DOES SUPERMAN HAVE TO DO WITH YOU GUYS AND YOUR FIGHT?
YOUR GRANDFATHER ISN'T A FAN, JON.
BECAUSE SUPERMAN ISN'T ONE OF US.
SO?!
HOW CAN YOU NOT LIKE SUPERMAN?
HE'S A SUPREMELY POWERED BEING FROM ANOTHER WORLD, JON.
HIS MOTIVES SEEM OKAY, BUT WHO CAN SAY FOR SURE?
YOUR MOM AND DAD WERE DRAWN TO HIM RIGHT FROM THE START.
WROTE ALL SORTS OF STORIES THAT BUILT HIM UP TO BE OUR CHAMPION.
BUT...HE IS A CHAMPION!
HE'S TAKEN DOWN LOADS OF BAD GUYS!
AND STOPPED ALL SORTS OF NATURAL DISASTERS!
ACKNOWLEDGED.
I FREELY ADMIT THAT SUPERMAN HAS DONE GOOD WORK.
SPEAKING OF WHICH, I JUST GOT A TEXT ALERT.
S.T.A.R. LABS CONFIRMS THAT THE ASTEROID HEADED OUR WAY IS NO LONGER A THREAT.
THANKS TO SUPERMAN.
SEE?!

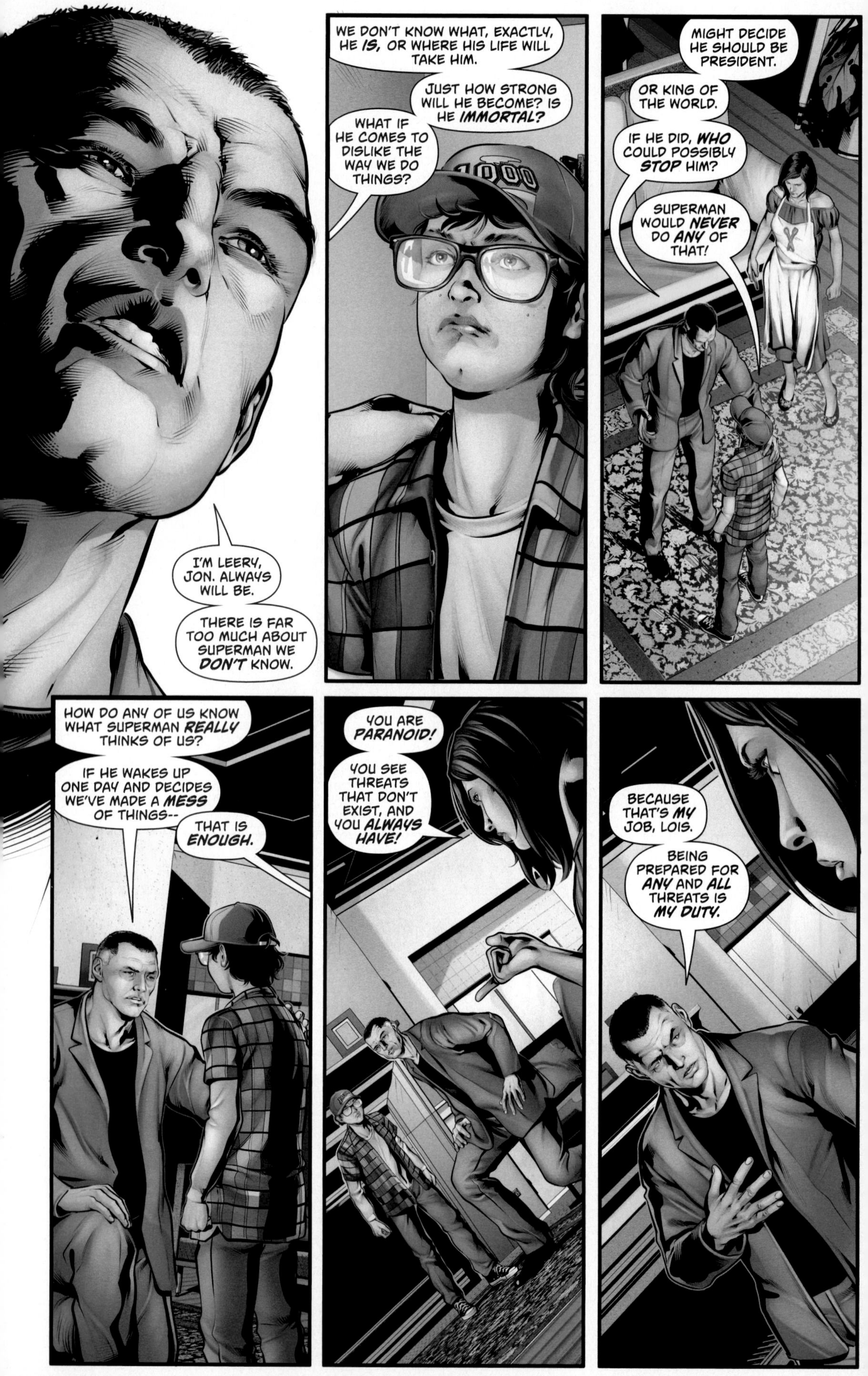
I'M LEERY, JON. ALWAYS WILL BE.
THERE IS FAR TOO MUCH ABOUT SUPERMAN WE DON'T KNOW.
WE DON'T KNOW WHAT, EXACTLY, HE IS, OR WHERE HIS LIFE WILL TAKE HIM.
JUST HOW STRONG WILL HE BECOME? IS HE IMMORTAL?
WHAT IF HE COMES TO DISLIKE THE WAY WE DO THINGS?
MIGHT DECIDE HE SHOULD BE PRESIDENT.
OR KING OF THE WORLD.
IF HE DID, WHO COULD POSSIBLY STOP HIM?
SUPERMAN WOULD NEVER DO ANY OF THAT!
HOW DO ANY OF US KNOW WHAT SUPERMAN REALLY THINKS OF US?
IF HE WAKES UP ONE DAY AND DECIDES WE'VE MADE A MESS OF THINGS--
THAT IS ENOUGH.
YOU ARE PARANOID!
YOU SEE THREATS THAT DON'T EXIST, AND YOU ALWAYS HAVE!
BECAUSE THAT'S MY JOB, LOIS.
BEING PREPARED FOR ANY AND ALL THREATS IS MY DUTY.

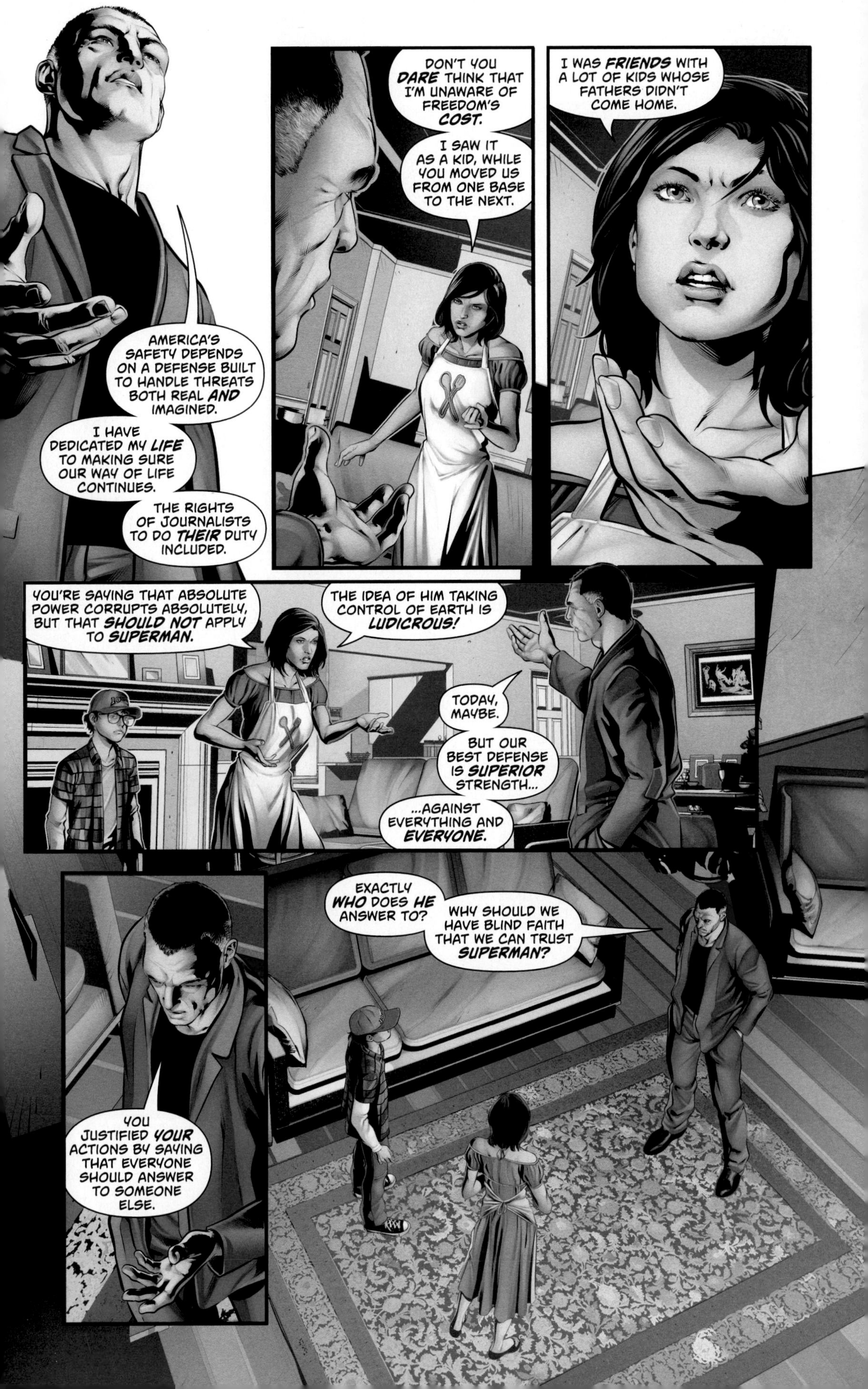
DON'T YOU DARE THINK THAT I'M UNAWARE OF FREEDOM'S COST.
I SAW IT AS A KID, WHILE YOU MOVED US FROM ONE BASE TO THE NEXT.
I WAS FRIENDS WITH A LOT OF KIDS WHOSE FATHERS DIDN'T COME HOME.
AMERICA'S SAFETY DEPENDS ON A DEFENSE BUILT TO HANDLE THREATS BOTH REAL AND IMAGINED.
I HAVE DEDICATED MY LIFE TO MAKING SURE OUR WAY OF LIFE CONTINUES.
THE RIGHTS OF JOURNALISTS TO DO THEIR DUTY INCLUDED.
YOU'RE SAYING THAT ABSOLUTE POWER CORRUPTS ABSOLUTELY, BUT THAT SHOULD NOT APPLY TO SUPERMAN.
THE IDEA OF HIM TAKING CONTROL OF EARTH IS LUDICROUS!
TODAY, MAYBE.
BUT OUR BEST DEFENSE IS SUPERIOR STRENGTH...
...AGAINST EVERYTHING AND EVERYONE.
YOU JUSTIFIED YOUR ACTIONS BY SAYING THAT EVERYONE SHOULD ANSWER TO SOMEONE ELSE.
EXACTLY WHO DOES HE ANSWER TO?
WHY SHOULD WE HAVE BLIND FAITH THAT WE CAN TRUST SUPERMAN?

I'M FORTUNATE TO HAVE **FEW** REGRETS IN LIFE.

I THANK THE KENTS FOR THAT.

RAISED ME RIGHT.

I'VE ALSO MANAGED TO AVOID A LOT OF TRAGEDY.

OTHERS HAVEN'T BEEN SO LUCKY.

LIKE HANK HENSHAW.

CYBORG SUPERMAN...

...DESTROYER OF **COAST CITY** AND KILLER OF THE MILLIONS LIVING THERE.

THEY WERE DOING THEIR DUTY FOR GOD AND COUNTRY...

HE AND HIS CREW WERE RETURNING HOME FROM SPACE WHEN THEY WERE HIT BY RADIATION THAT ALTERED THEIR BODIES ON A **CELLULAR** LEVEL.

...WHICH ENDED THE MINUTE THEIR BODIES BEGAN TO MUTATE...INTO SOMETHING **AWFUL**.

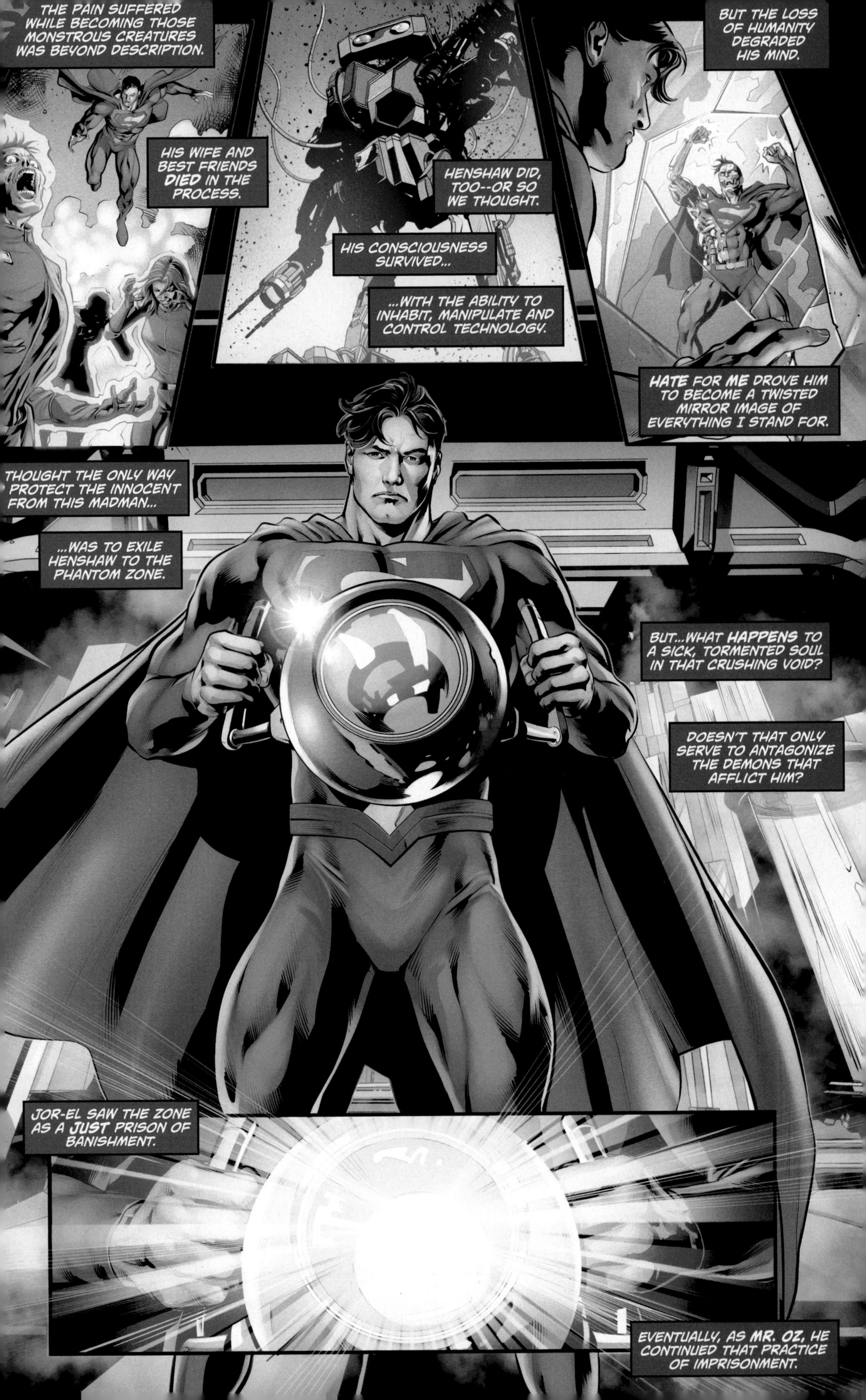
THE PAIN SUFFERED WHILE BECOMING THOSE MONSTROUS CREATURES WAS BEYOND DESCRIPTION.
HIS WIFE AND BEST FRIENDS DIED IN THE PROCESS.
HENSHAW DID, TOO--OR SO WE THOUGHT.
HIS CONSCIOUSNESS SURVIVED...
...WITH THE ABILITY TO INHABIT, MANIPULATE AND CONTROL TECHNOLOGY.
BUT THE LOSS OF HUMANITY DEGRADED HIS MIND.
HATE FOR ME DROVE HIM TO BECOME A TWISTED MIRROR IMAGE OF EVERYTHING I STAND FOR.
THOUGHT THE ONLY WAY PROTECT THE INNOCENT FROM THIS MADMAN...
...WAS TO EXILE HENSHAW TO THE PHANTOM ZONE.
BUT...WHAT HAPPENS TO A SICK, TORMENTED SOUL IN THAT CRUSHING VOID?
DOESN'T THAT ONLY SERVE TO ANTAGONIZE THE DEMONS THAT AFFLICT HIM?
JOR-EL SAW THE ZONE AS A JUST PRISON OF BANISHMENT.
EVENTUALLY, AS MR. OZ, HE CONTINUED THAT PRACTICE OF IMPRISONMENT.

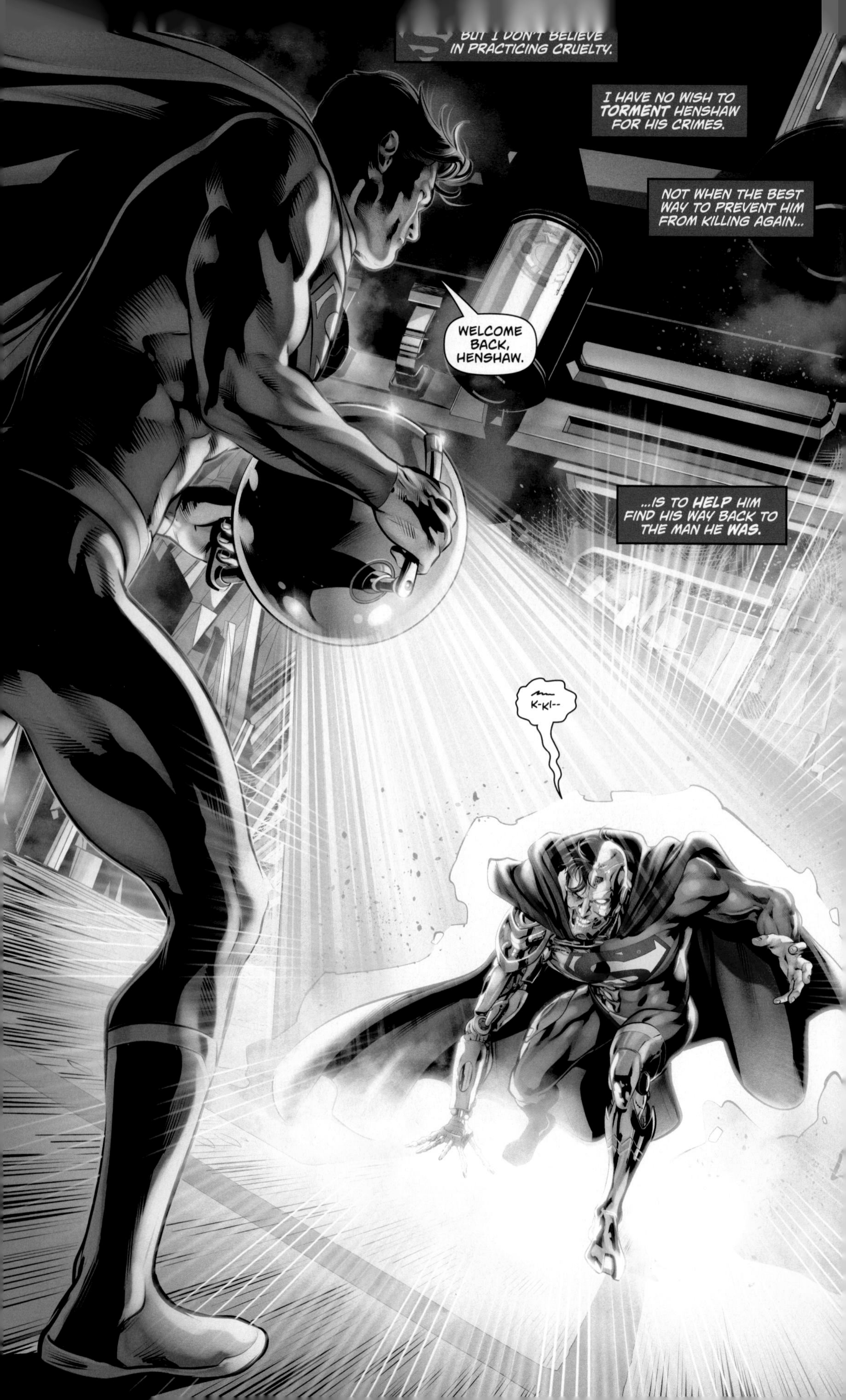
BUT I DON'T BELIEVE IN PRACTICING CRUELTY.
I HAVE NO WISH TO TORMENT HENSHAW FOR HIS CRIMES.
NOT WHEN THE BEST WAY TO PREVENT HIM FROM KILLING AGAIN...
WELCOME BACK, HENSHAW.
...IS TO HELP HIM FIND HIS WAY BACK TO THE MAN HE WAS.
K-KI--

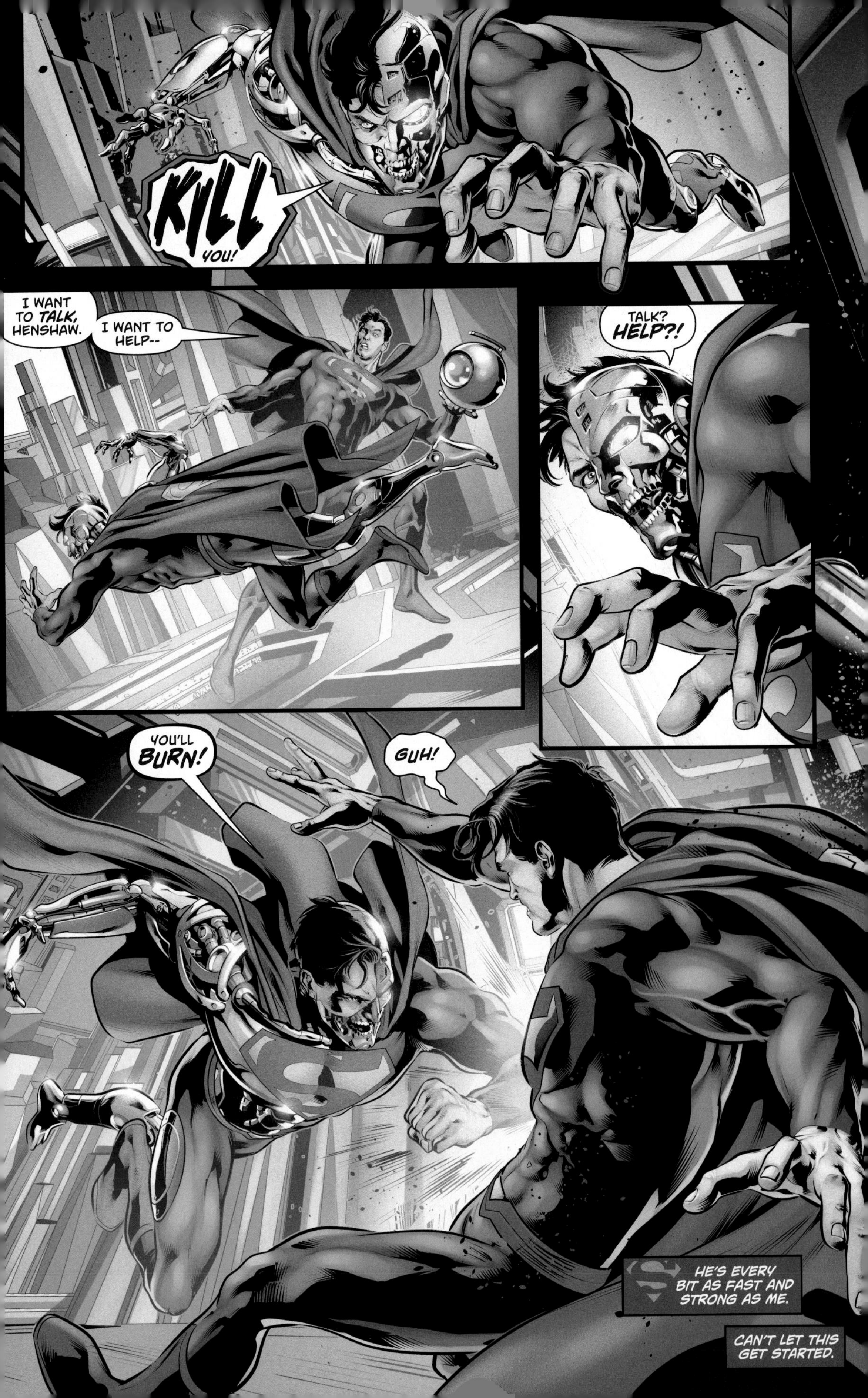
KILL YOU!
I WANT TO TALK, HENSHAW.
I WANT TO HELP--
TALK? HELP?!
YOU'LL BURN!
GUH!
HE'S EVERY BIT AS FAST AND STRONG AS ME.
CAN'T LET THIS GET STARTED.

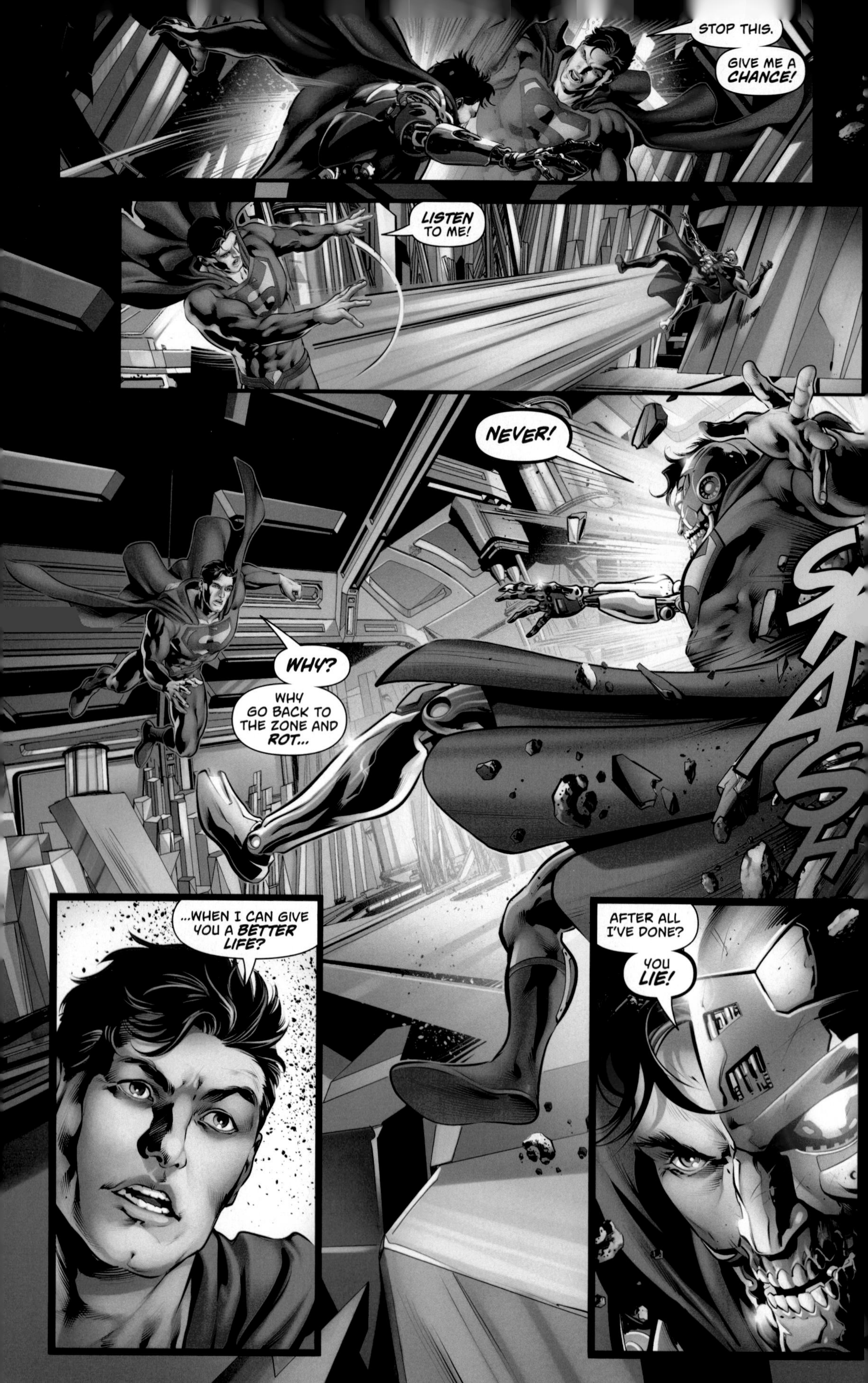
STOP THIS.
GIVE ME A CHANCE!
LISTEN TO ME!
NEVER!
WHY?
WHY GO BACK TO THE ZONE AND ROT...
...WHEN I CAN GIVE YOU A BETTER LIFE?
AFTER ALL I'VE DONE?
YOU LIE!

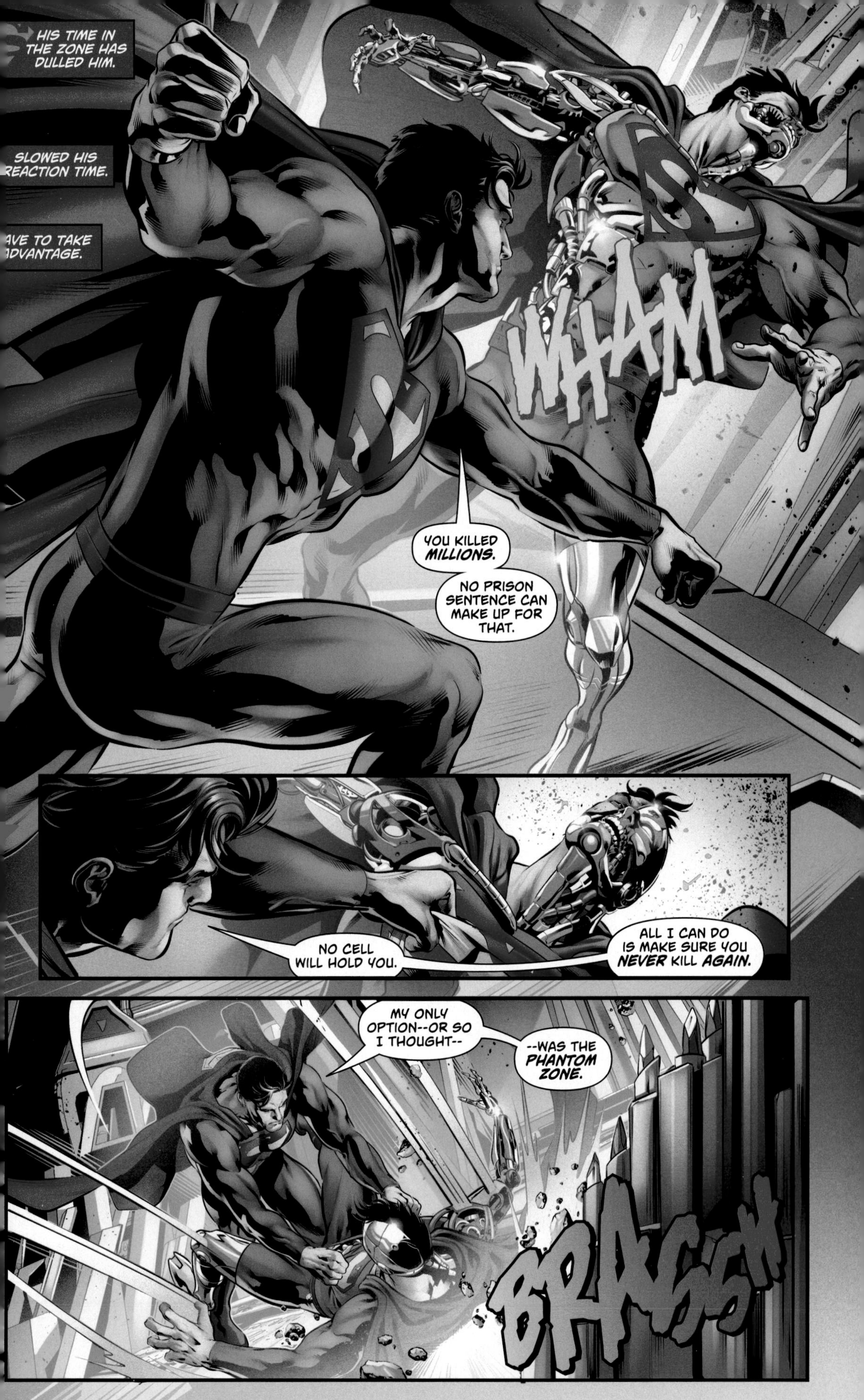

HIS TIME IN THE ZONE HAS DULLED HIM.
SLOWED HIS REACTION TIME.
AVE TO TAKE ADVANTAGE.
WHAM
YOU KILLED *MILLIONS.*
NO PRISON SENTENCE CAN MAKE UP FOR THAT.
NO CELL WILL HOLD YOU.
ALL I CAN DO IS MAKE SURE YOU *NEVER* KILL *AGAIN.*
MY ONLY OPTION--OR SO I THOUGHT--
--WAS THE *PHANTOM ZONE.*
BRASSH

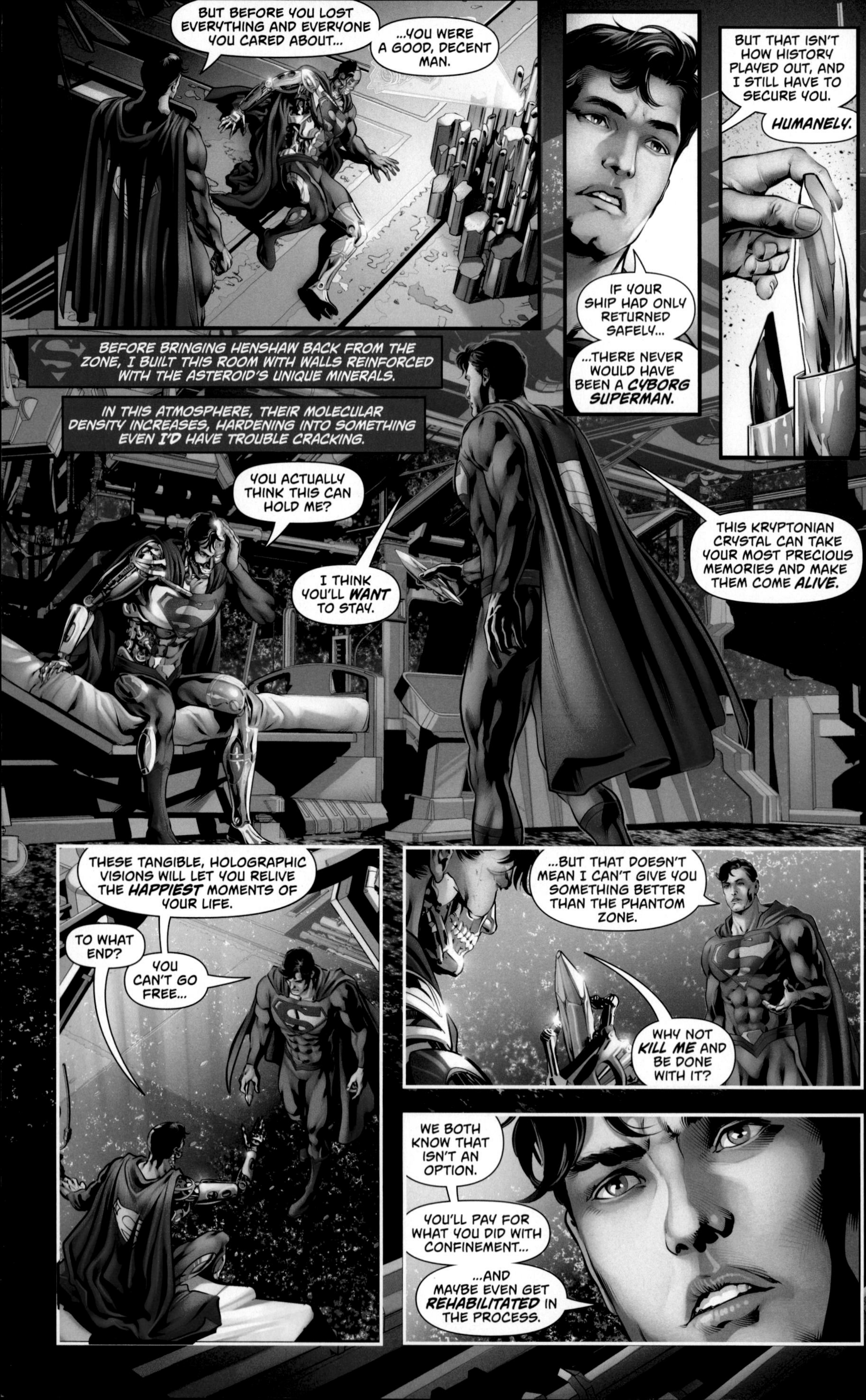

BUT BEFORE YOU LOST EVERYTHING AND EVERYONE YOU CARED ABOUT...
...YOU WERE A GOOD, DECENT MAN.
IF YOUR SHIP HAD ONLY RETURNED SAFELY...
...THERE NEVER WOULD HAVE BEEN A CYBORG SUPERMAN.
BUT THAT ISN'T HOW HISTORY PLAYED OUT, AND I STILL HAVE TO SECURE YOU.
HUMANELY.
BEFORE BRINGING HENSHAW BACK FROM THE ZONE, I BUILT THIS ROOM WITH WALLS REINFORCED WITH THE ASTEROID'S UNIQUE MINERALS.
IN THIS ATMOSPHERE, THEIR MOLECULAR DENSITY INCREASES, HARDENING INTO SOMETHING EVEN I'D HAVE TROUBLE CRACKING.
YOU ACTUALLY THINK THIS CAN HOLD ME?
I THINK YOU'LL WANT TO STAY.
THIS KRYPTONIAN CRYSTAL CAN TAKE YOUR MOST PRECIOUS MEMORIES AND MAKE THEM COME ALIVE.
THESE TANGIBLE, HOLOGRAPHIC VISIONS WILL LET YOU RELIVE THE HAPPIEST MOMENTS OF YOUR LIFE.
TO WHAT END?
YOU CAN'T GO FREE...
...BUT THAT DOESN'T MEAN I CAN'T GIVE YOU SOMETHING BETTER THAN THE PHANTOM ZONE.
WHY NOT KILL ME AND BE DONE WITH IT?
WE BOTH KNOW THAT ISN'T AN OPTION.
YOU'LL PAY FOR WHAT YOU DID WITH CONFINEMENT...
...AND MAYBE EVEN GET REHABILITATED IN THE PROCESS.

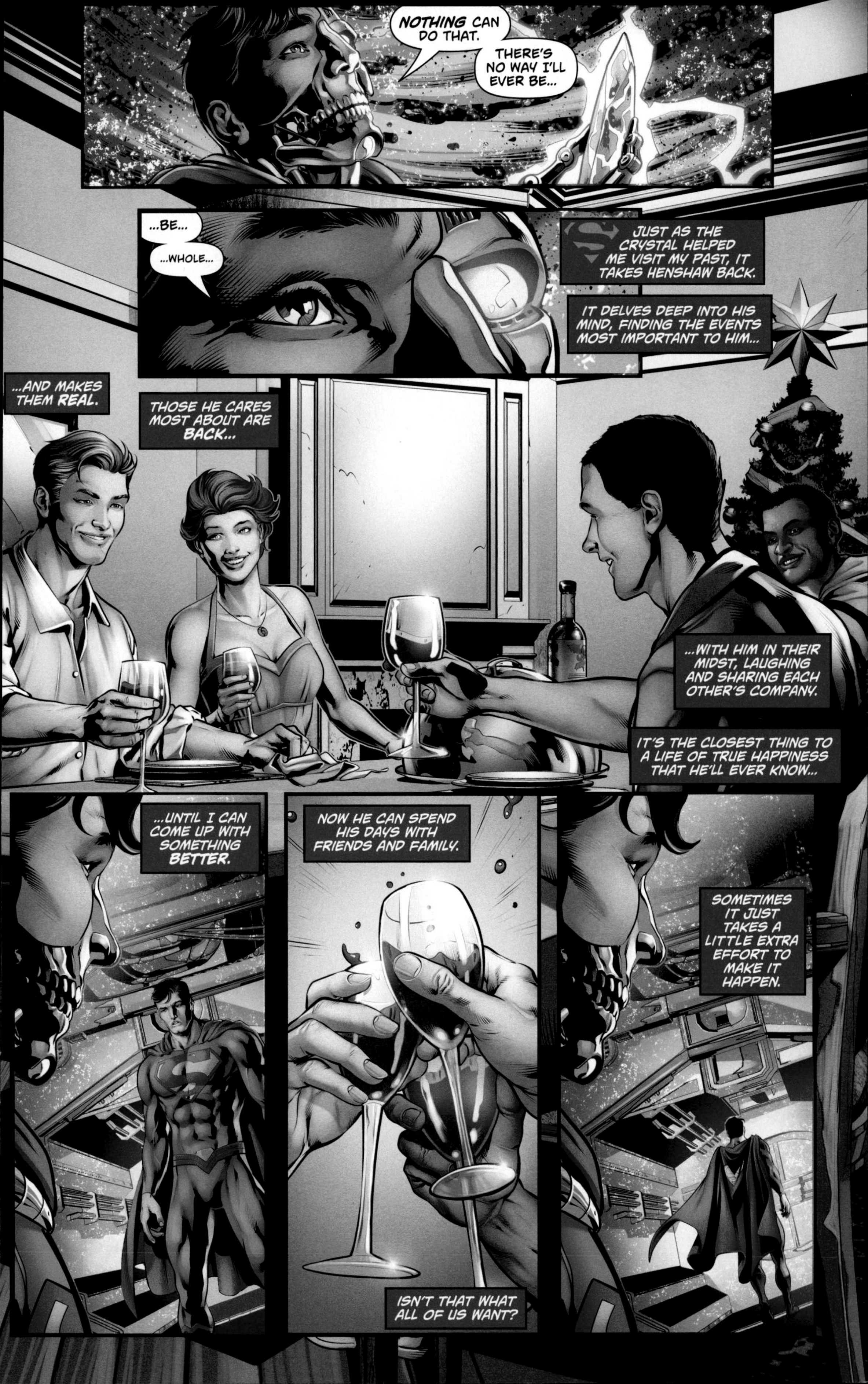
NOTHING CAN DO THAT.
THERE'S NO WAY I'LL EVER BE...
...BE...
...WHOLE...
JUST AS THE CRYSTAL HELPED ME VISIT MY PAST, IT TAKES HENSHAW BACK.
IT DELVES DEEP INTO HIS MIND, FINDING THE EVENTS MOST IMPORTANT TO HIM...
...AND MAKES THEM REAL.
THOSE HE CARES MOST ABOUT ARE BACK...
...WITH HIM IN THEIR MIDST, LAUGHING AND SHARING EACH OTHER'S COMPANY.
IT'S THE CLOSEST THING TO A LIFE OF TRUE HAPPINESS THAT HE'LL EVER KNOW...
...UNTIL I CAN COME UP WITH SOMETHING BETTER.
NOW HE CAN SPEND HIS DAYS WITH FRIENDS AND FAMILY.
ISN'T THAT WHAT ALL OF US WANT?
SOMETIMES IT JUST TAKES A LITTLE EXTRA EFFORT TO MAKE IT HAPPEN.

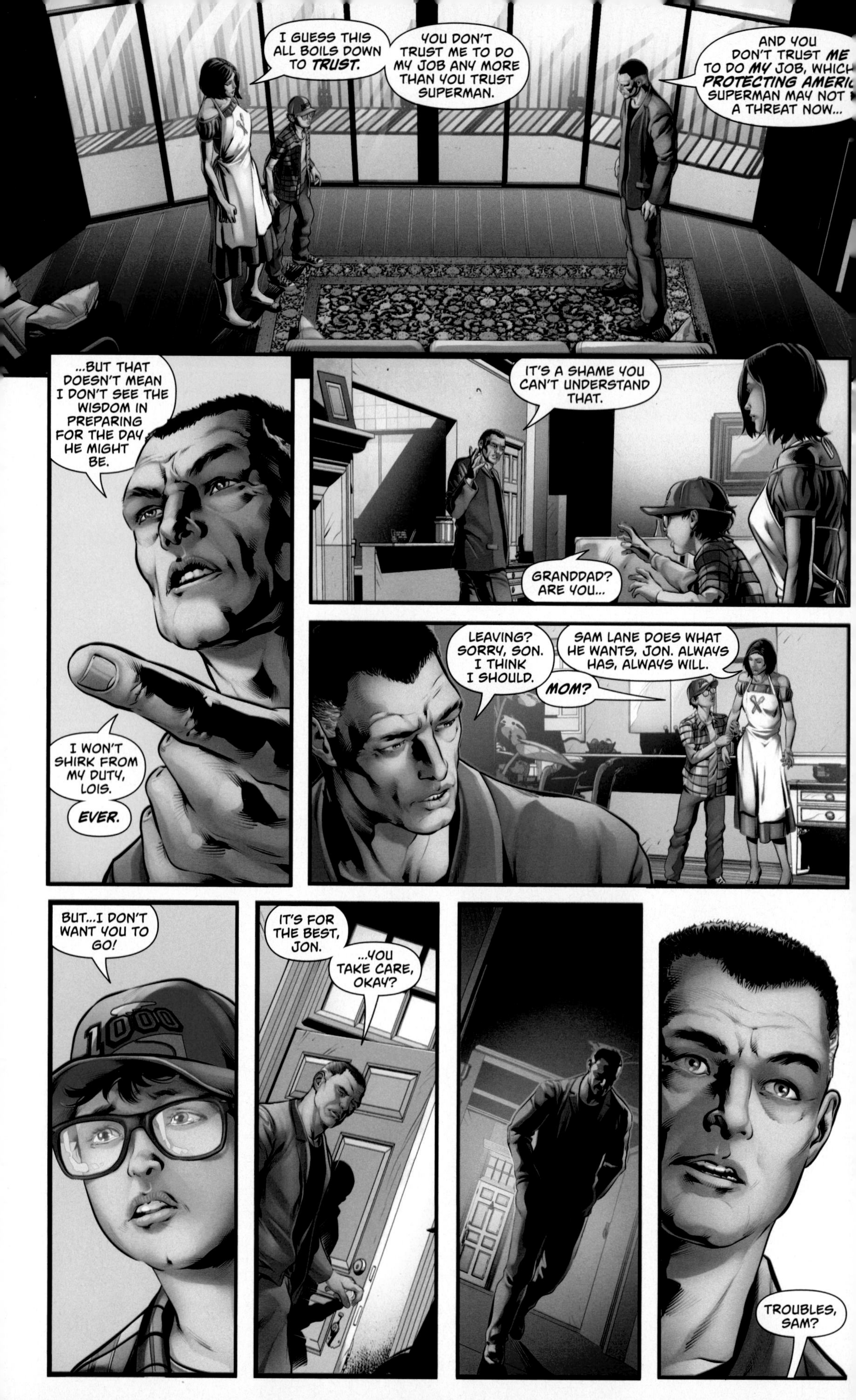
I GUESS THIS ALL BOILS DOWN TO TRUST.
YOU DON'T TRUST ME TO DO MY JOB ANY MORE THAN YOU TRUST SUPERMAN.
AND YOU DON'T TRUST ME TO DO MY JOB, WHICH PROTECTING AMERIC SUPERMAN MAY NOT A THREAT NOW...
...BUT THAT DOESN'T MEAN I DON'T SEE THE WISDOM IN PREPARING FOR THE DAY HE MIGHT BE.
I WON'T SHIRK FROM MY DUTY, LOIS.
EVER.
IT'S A SHAME YOU CAN'T UNDERSTAND THAT.
GRANDDAD? ARE YOU...
LEAVING? SORRY, SON. I THINK I SHOULD.
SAM LANE DOES WHAT HE WANTS, JON. ALWAYS HAS, ALWAYS WILL.
MOM?
BUT...I DON'T WANT YOU TO GO!
IT'S FOR THE BEST, JON.
...YOU TAKE CARE, OKAY?
TROUBLES, SAM?

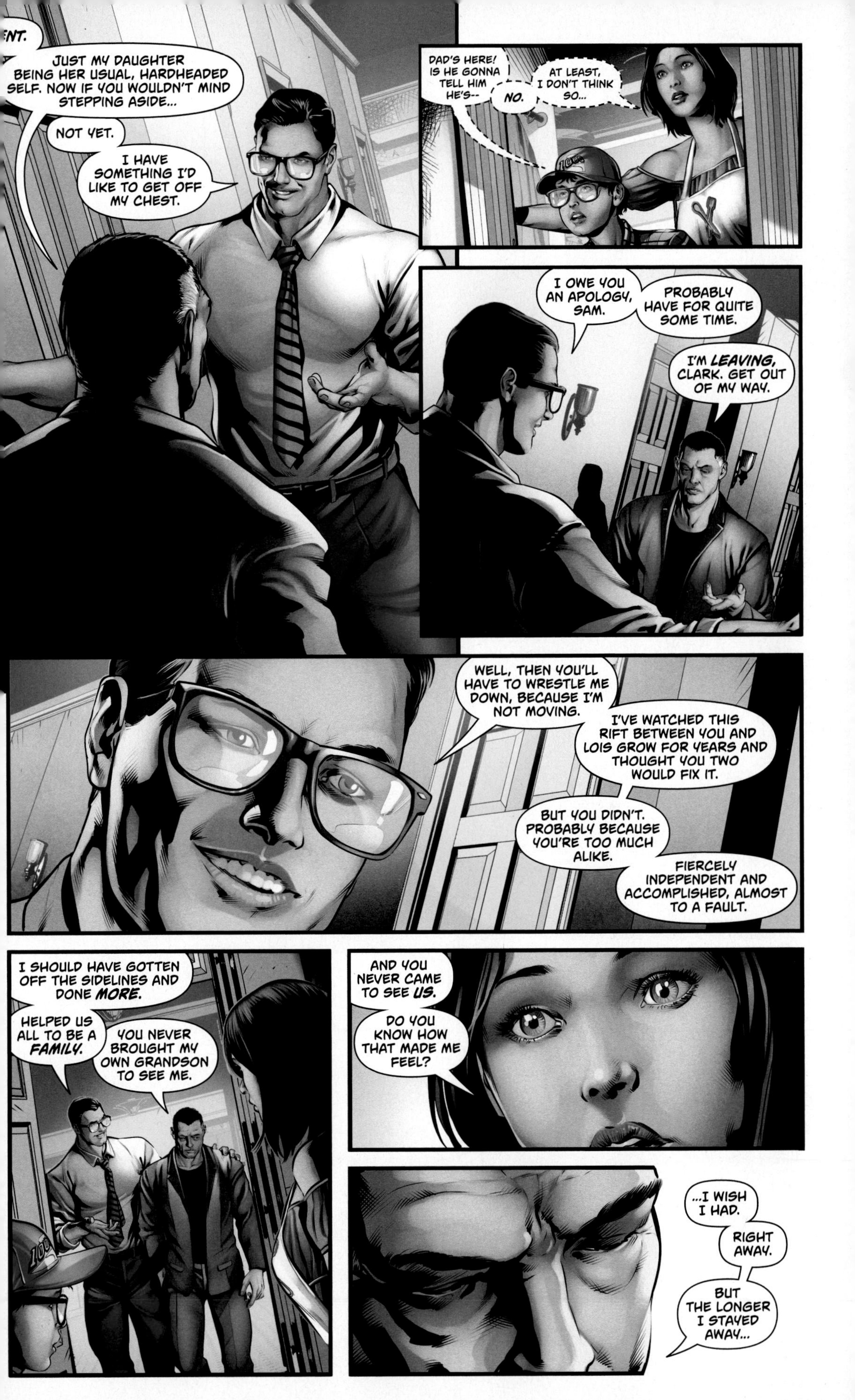
ENT.
JUST MY DAUGHTER BEING HER USUAL, HARDHEADED SELF. NOW IF YOU WOULDN'T MIND STEPPING ASIDE...
NOT YET.
I HAVE SOMETHING I'D LIKE TO GET OFF MY CHEST.
DAD'S HERE! IS HE GONNA TELL HIM HE'S--
NO.
AT LEAST, I DON'T THINK SO...
I OWE YOU AN APOLOGY, SAM.
PROBABLY HAVE FOR QUITE SOME TIME.
I'M LEAVING, CLARK. GET OUT OF MY WAY.
WELL, THEN YOU'LL HAVE TO WRESTLE ME DOWN, BECAUSE I'M NOT MOVING.
I'VE WATCHED THIS RIFT BETWEEN YOU AND LOIS GROW FOR YEARS AND THOUGHT YOU TWO WOULD FIX IT.
BUT YOU DIDN'T. PROBABLY BECAUSE YOU'RE TOO MUCH ALIKE.
FIERCELY INDEPENDENT AND ACCOMPLISHED, ALMOST TO A FAULT.
I SHOULD HAVE GOTTEN OFF THE SIDELINES AND DONE MORE.
HELPED US ALL TO BE A FAMILY.
YOU NEVER BROUGHT MY OWN GRANDSON TO SEE ME.
AND YOU NEVER CAME TO SEE US.
DO YOU KNOW HOW THAT MADE ME FEEL?
...I WISH I HAD.
RIGHT AWAY.
BUT THE LONGER I STAYED AWAY...

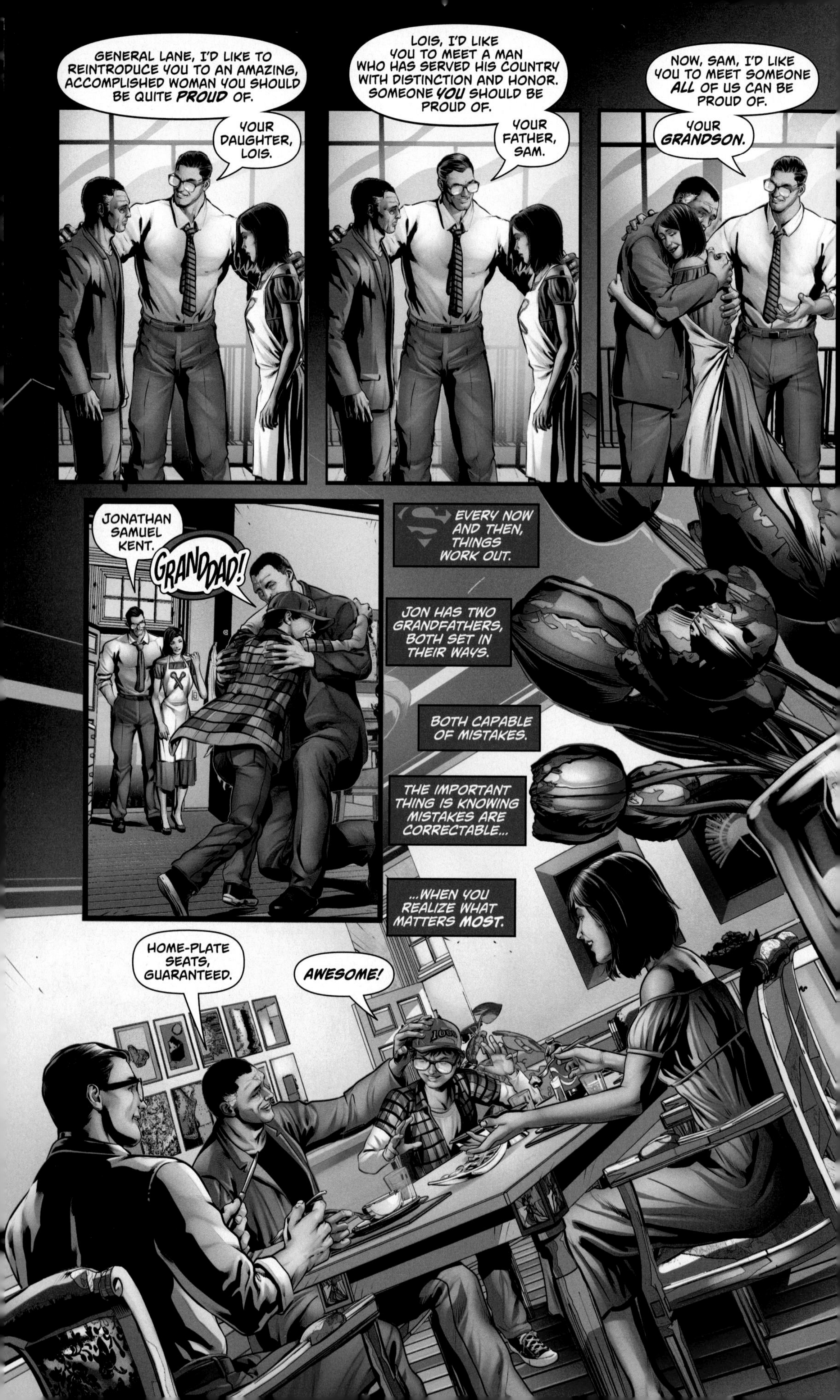
GENERAL LANE, I'D LIKE TO REINTRODUCE YOU TO AN AMAZING, ACCOMPLISHED WOMAN YOU SHOULD BE QUITE PROUD OF.
YOUR DAUGHTER, LOIS.
LOIS, I'D LIKE YOU TO MEET A MAN WHO HAS SERVED HIS COUNTRY WITH DISTINCTION AND HONOR. SOMEONE YOU SHOULD BE PROUD OF.
YOUR FATHER, SAM.
NOW, SAM, I'D LIKE YOU TO MEET SOMEONE ALL OF US CAN BE PROUD OF.
YOUR GRANDSON.
JONATHAN SAMUEL KENT.
GRANDDAD!
EVERY NOW AND THEN, THINGS WORK OUT.
JON HAS TWO GRANDFATHERS, BOTH SET IN THEIR WAYS.
BOTH CAPABLE OF MISTAKES.
THE IMPORTANT THING IS KNOWING MISTAKES ARE CORRECTABLE...
...WHEN YOU REALIZE WHAT MATTERS MOST.
HOME-PLATE SEATS, GUARANTEED.
AWESOME!

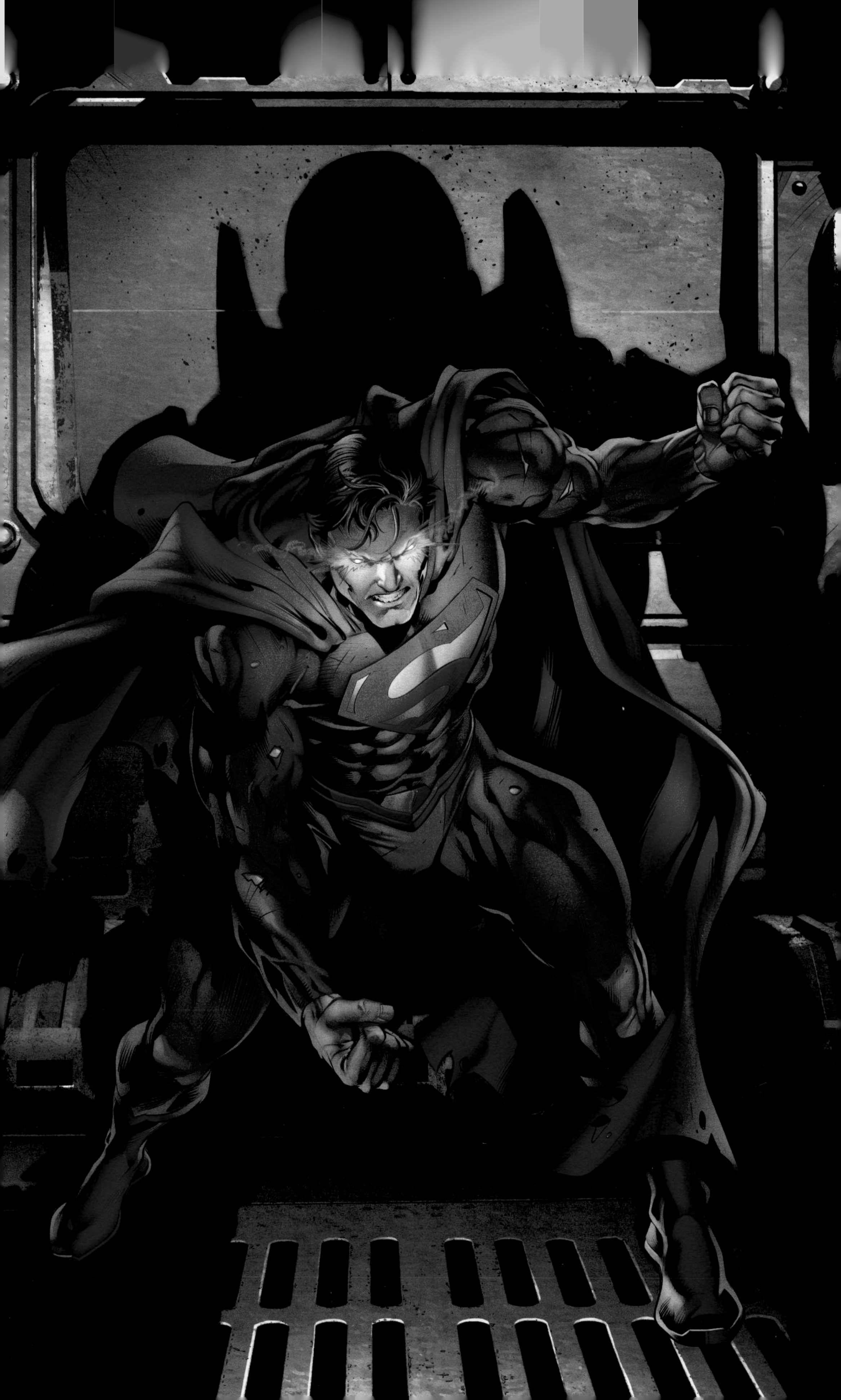

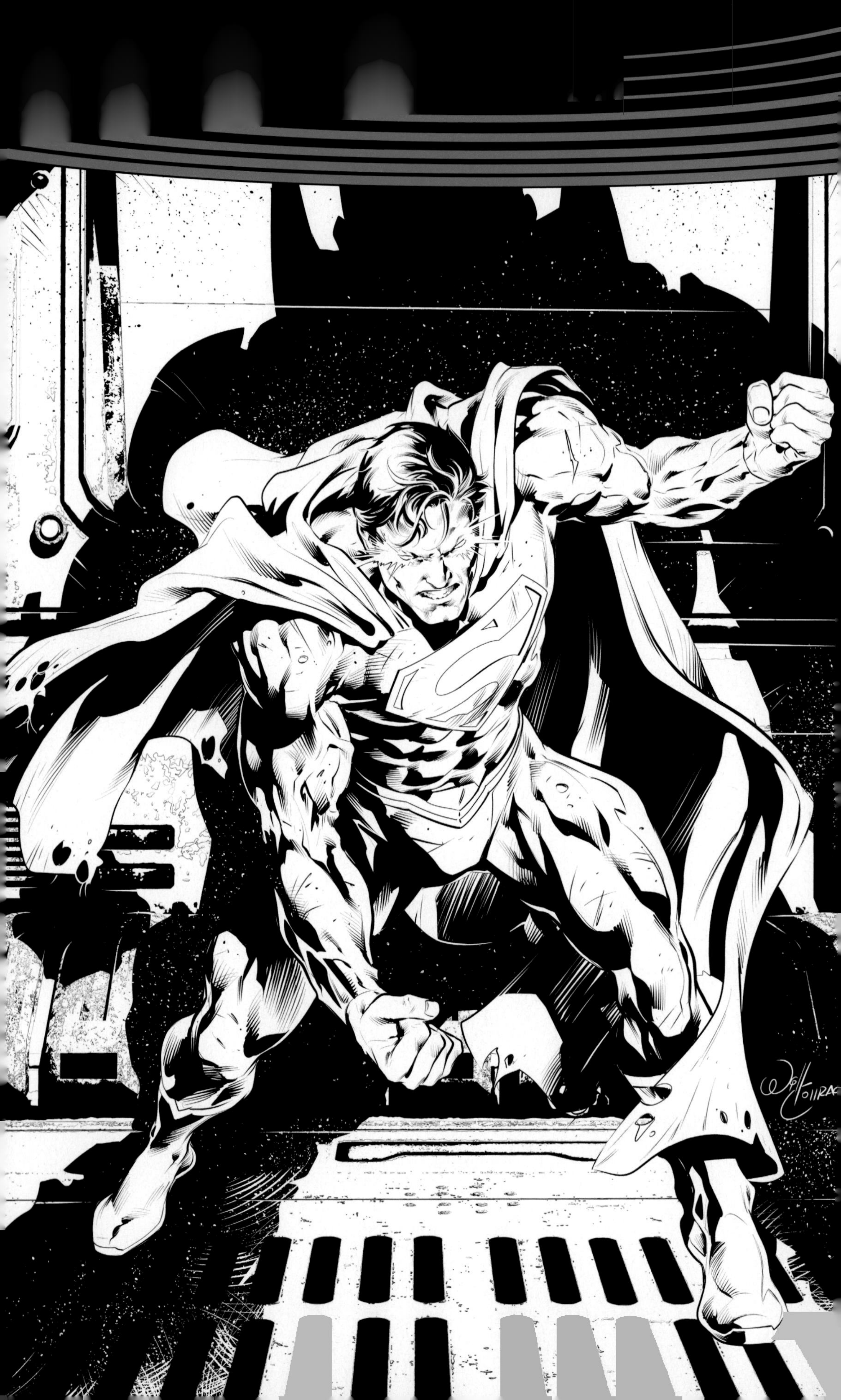

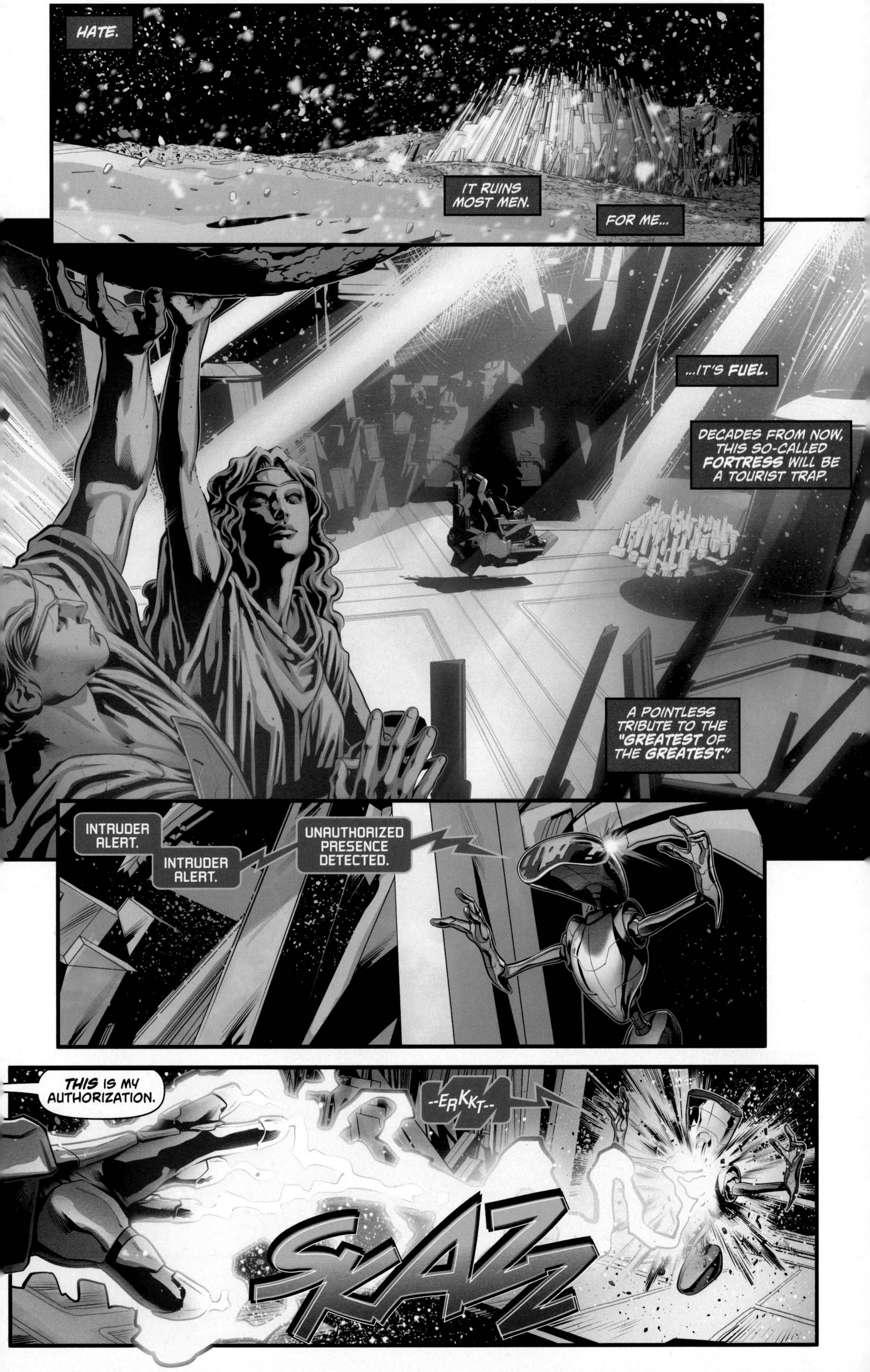
HATE.
IT RUINS MOST MEN.
FOR ME...
...IT'S **FUEL.**
DECADES FROM NOW, THIS SO-CALLED **FORTRESS** WILL BE A TOURIST TRAP.
A POINTLESS TRIBUTE TO THE **"GREATEST** OF THE **GREATEST."**
INTRUDER ALERT.
INTRUDER ALERT.
UNAUTHORIZED PRESENCE DETECTED.
THIS IS MY AUTHORIZATION.
--ERKKT--
SKAZZ

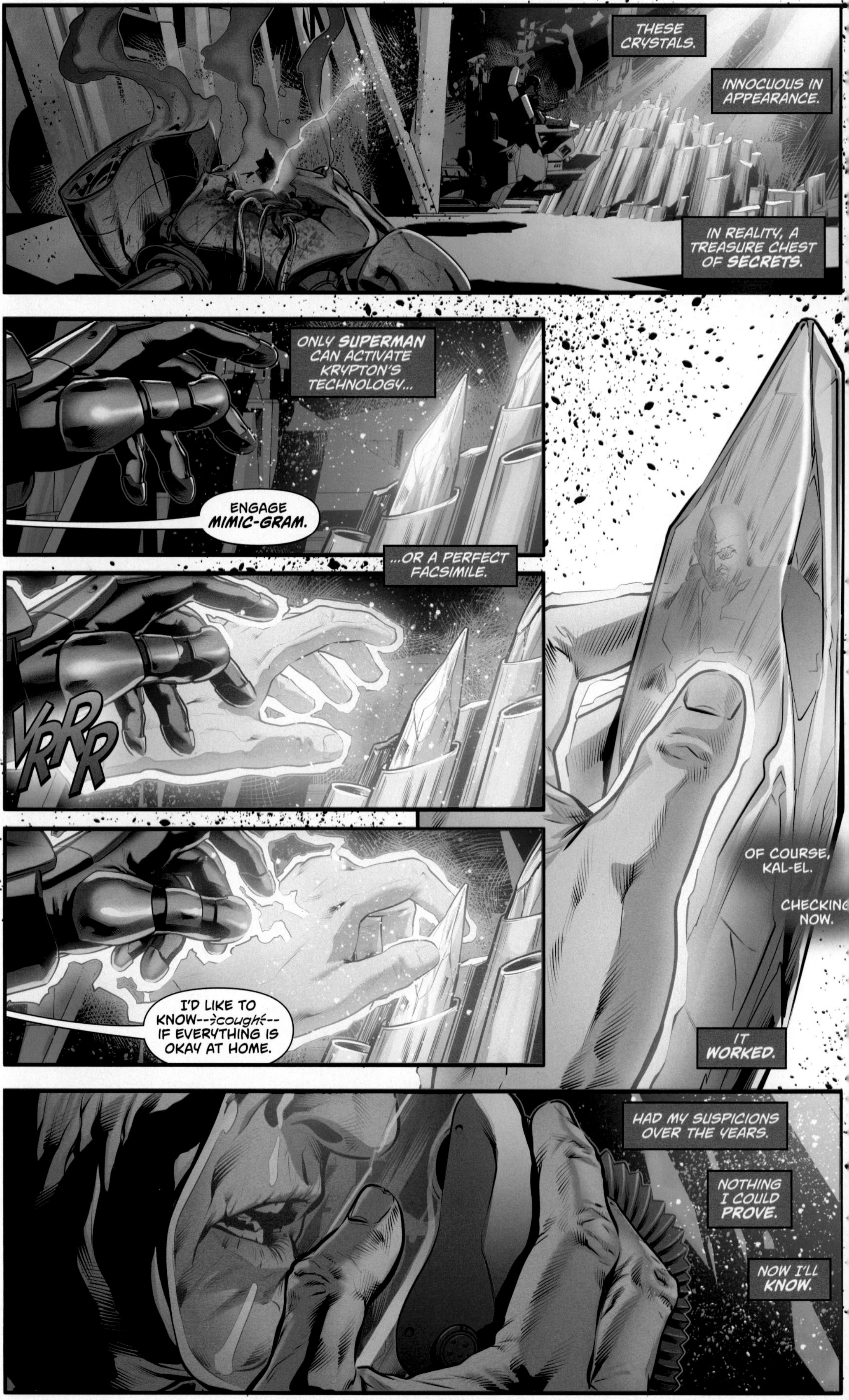
THESE CRYSTALS.
INNOCUOUS IN APPEARANCE.
IN REALITY, A TREASURE CHEST OF SECRETS.
ONLY SUPERMAN CAN ACTIVATE KRYPTON'S TECHNOLOGY...
ENGAGE MIMIC-GRAM.
...OR A PERFECT FACSIMILE.
VRRR
I'D LIKE TO KNOW--*cough*--IF EVERYTHING IS OKAY AT HOME.
OF COURSE, KAL-EL.
CHECKING NOW.
IT WORKED.
HAD MY SUSPICIONS OVER THE YEARS.
NOTHING I COULD PROVE.
NOW I'LL KNOW.

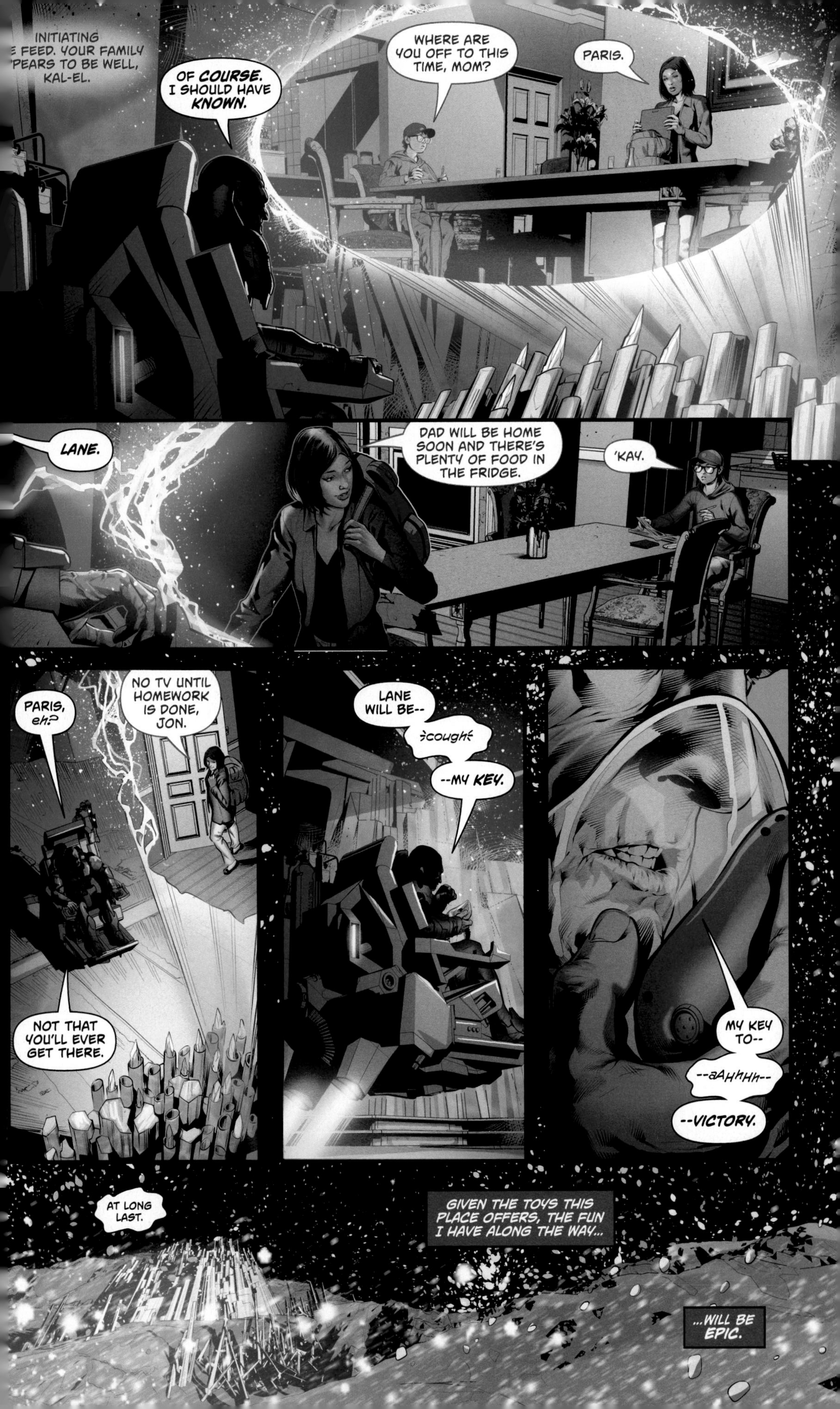

INITIATING
E FEED. YOUR FAMILY
PPEARS TO BE WELL,
KAL-EL.
OF COURSE. I SHOULD HAVE KNOWN.
WHERE ARE YOU OFF TO THIS TIME, MOM?
PARIS.
LANE.
DAD WILL BE HOME SOON AND THERE'S PLENTY OF FOOD IN THE FRIDGE.
'KAY.
PARIS, eh?
NO TV UNTIL HOMEWORK IS DONE, JON.
NOT THAT YOU'LL EVER GET THERE.
LANE WILL BE--
cough
--MY KEY.
MY KEY TO--
--aAhhhh--
--VICTORY.
AT LONG LAST.
GIVEN THE TOYS THIS PLACE OFFERS, THE FUN I HAVE ALONG THE WAY...
...WILL BE EPIC.

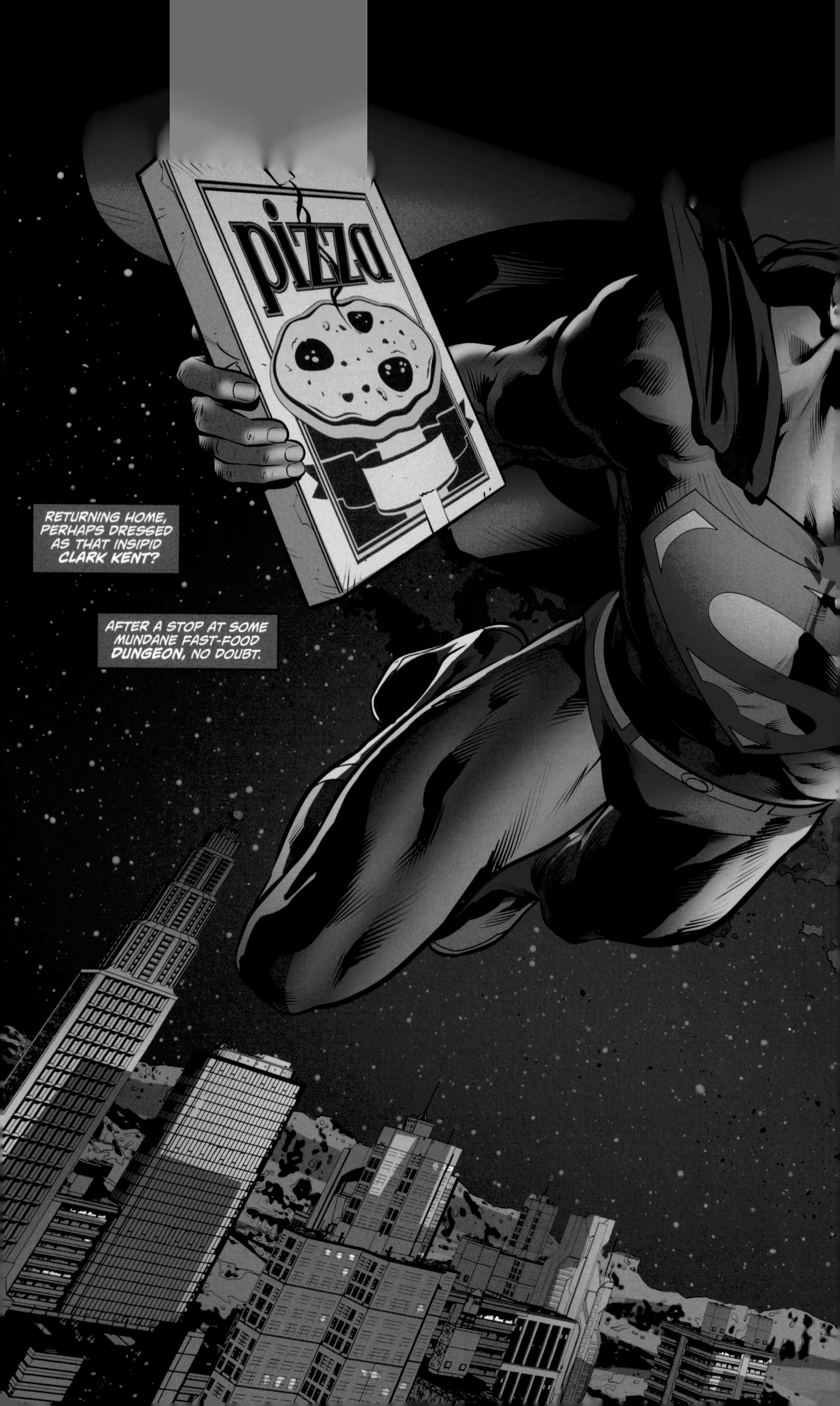

pizza
RETURNING HOME, PERHAPS DRESSED AS THAT INSIPID CLARK KENT?
AFTER A STOP AT SOME MUNDANE FAST-FOOD DUNGEON, NO DOUBT.

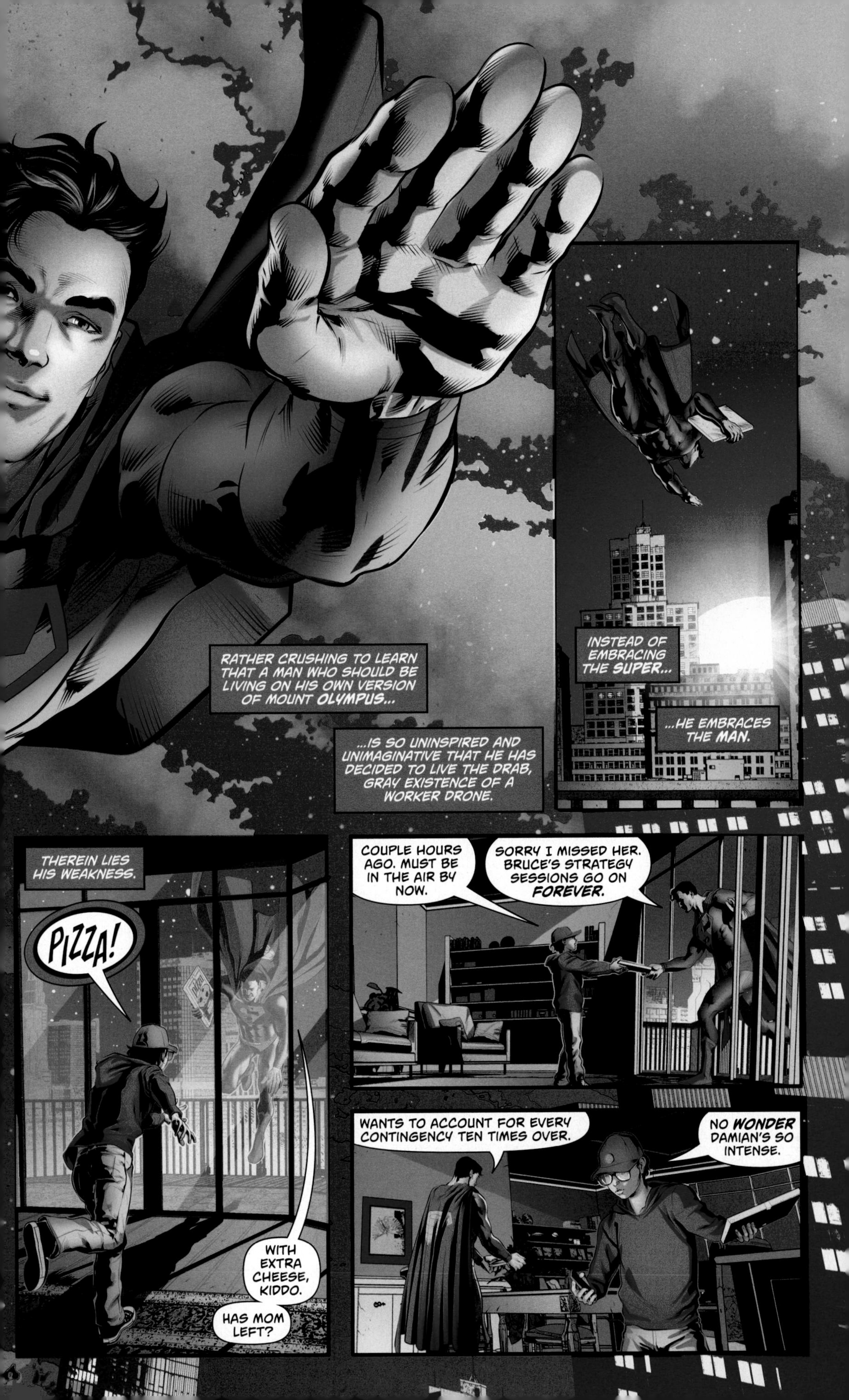
RATHER CRUSHING TO LEARN THAT A MAN WHO SHOULD BE LIVING ON HIS OWN VERSION OF MOUNT OLYMPUS...
...IS SO UNINSPIRED AND UNIMAGINATIVE THAT HE HAS DECIDED TO LIVE THE DRAB, GRAY EXISTENCE OF A WORKER DRONE.
INSTEAD OF EMBRACING THE SUPER...
...HE EMBRACES THE MAN.
THEREIN LIES HIS WEAKNESS.
PIZZA!
WITH EXTRA CHEESE, KIDDO.
HAS MOM LEFT?
COUPLE HOURS AGO. MUST BE IN THE AIR BY NOW.
SORRY I MISSED HER. BRUCE'S STRATEGY SESSIONS GO ON FOREVER.
WANTS TO ACCOUNT FOR EVERY CONTINGENCY TEN TIMES OVER.
NO WONDER DAMIAN'S SO INTENSE.

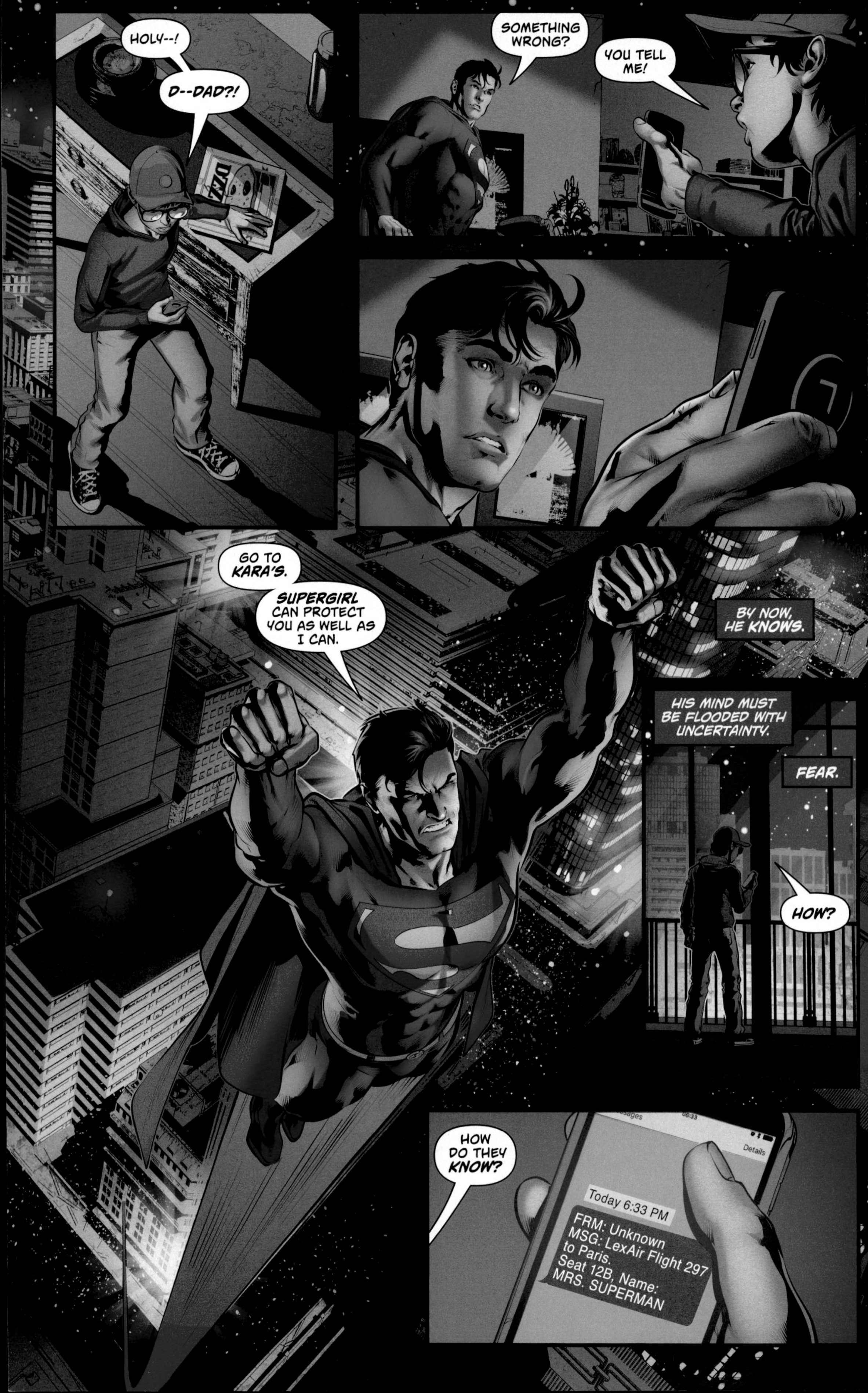

HOLY--!
D--DAD?!
SOMETHING WRONG?
YOU TELL ME!
GO TO KARA'S.
SUPERGIRL CAN PROTECT YOU AS WELL AS I CAN.
BY NOW, HE KNOWS.
HIS MIND MUST BE FLOODED WITH UNCERTAINTY.
FEAR.
HOW?
HOW DO THEY KNOW?
Details
Today 6:33 PM
FRM: Unknown
MSG: LexAir Flight 297 to Paris.
Seat 12B, Name: MRS. SUPERMAN

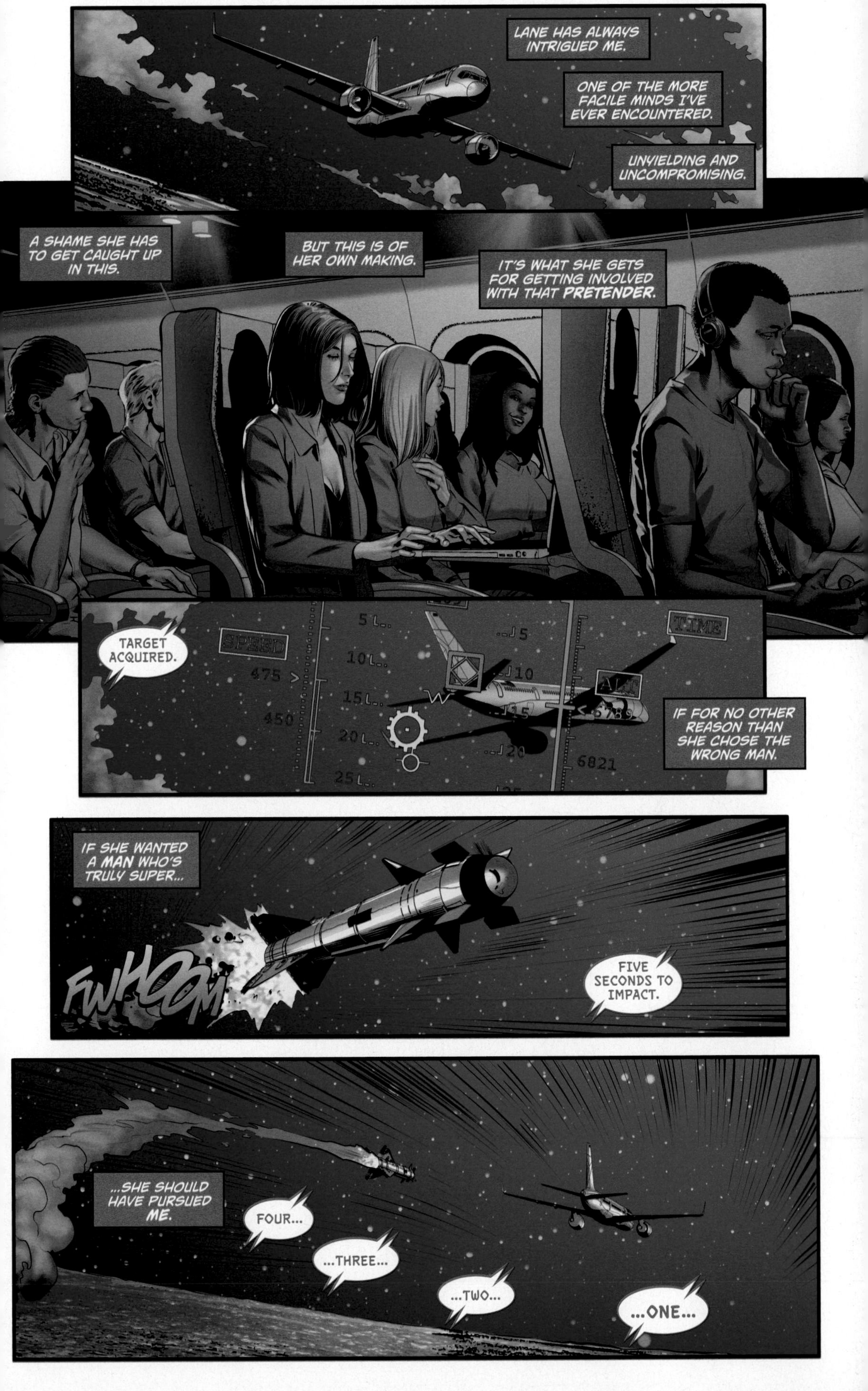
LANE HAS ALWAYS INTRIGUED ME.
ONE OF THE MORE FACILE MINDS I'VE EVER ENCOUNTERED.
UNYIELDING AND UNCOMPROMISING.
A SHAME SHE HAS TO GET CAUGHT UP IN THIS.
BUT THIS IS OF HER OWN MAKING.
IT'S WHAT SHE GETS FOR GETTING INVOLVED WITH THAT PRETENDER.
TARGET ACQUIRED.
SPEED
TIME
ALT
IF FOR NO OTHER REASON THAN SHE CHOSE THE WRONG MAN.
IF SHE WANTED A MAN WHO'S TRULY SUPER...
FWHOOM
FIVE SECONDS TO IMPACT.
...SHE SHOULD HAVE PURSUED ME.
FOUR...
...THREE...
...TWO...
...ONE...

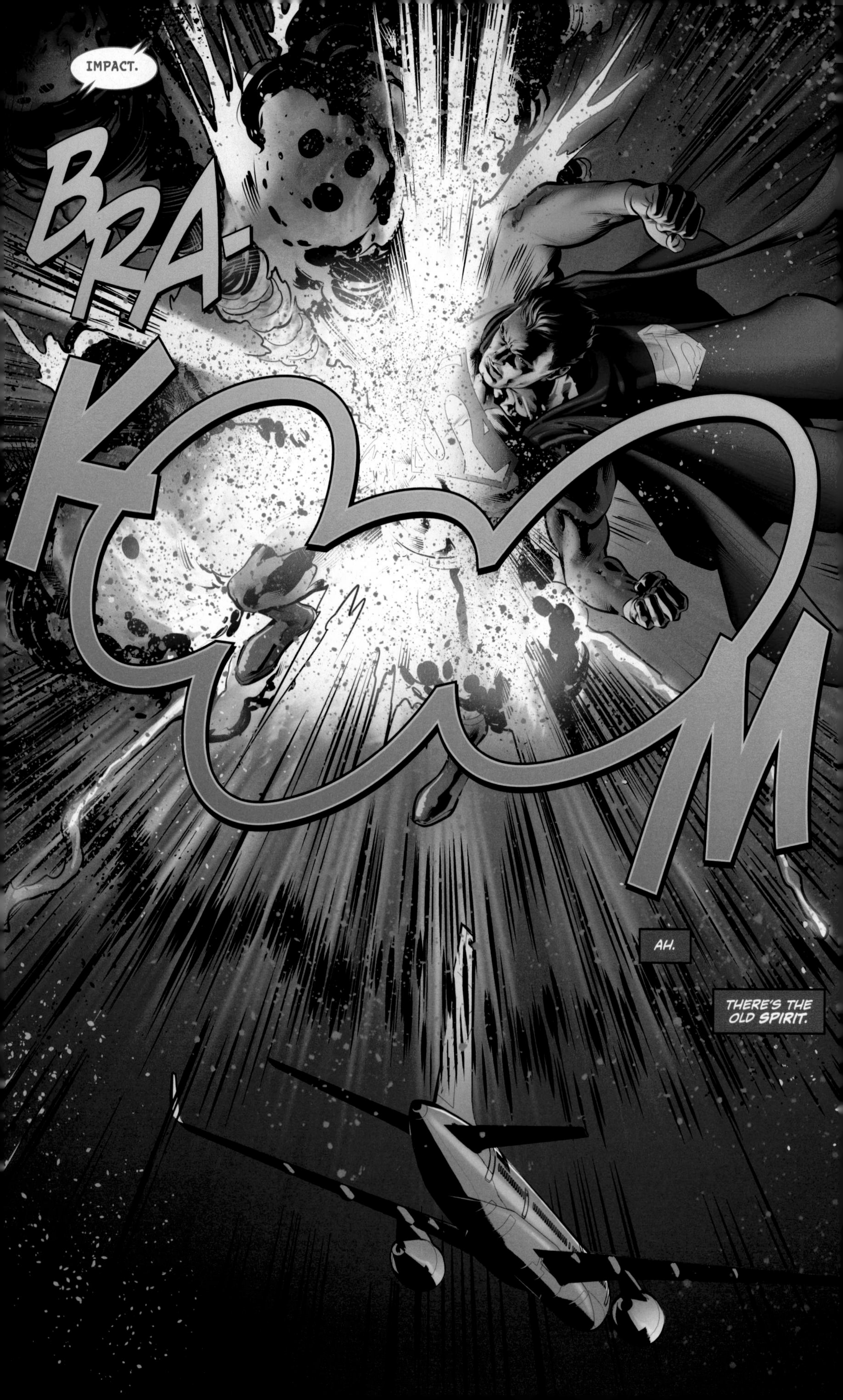
IMPACT.
BRA-
KOOOM
AH.
THERE'S THE OLD SPIRIT.

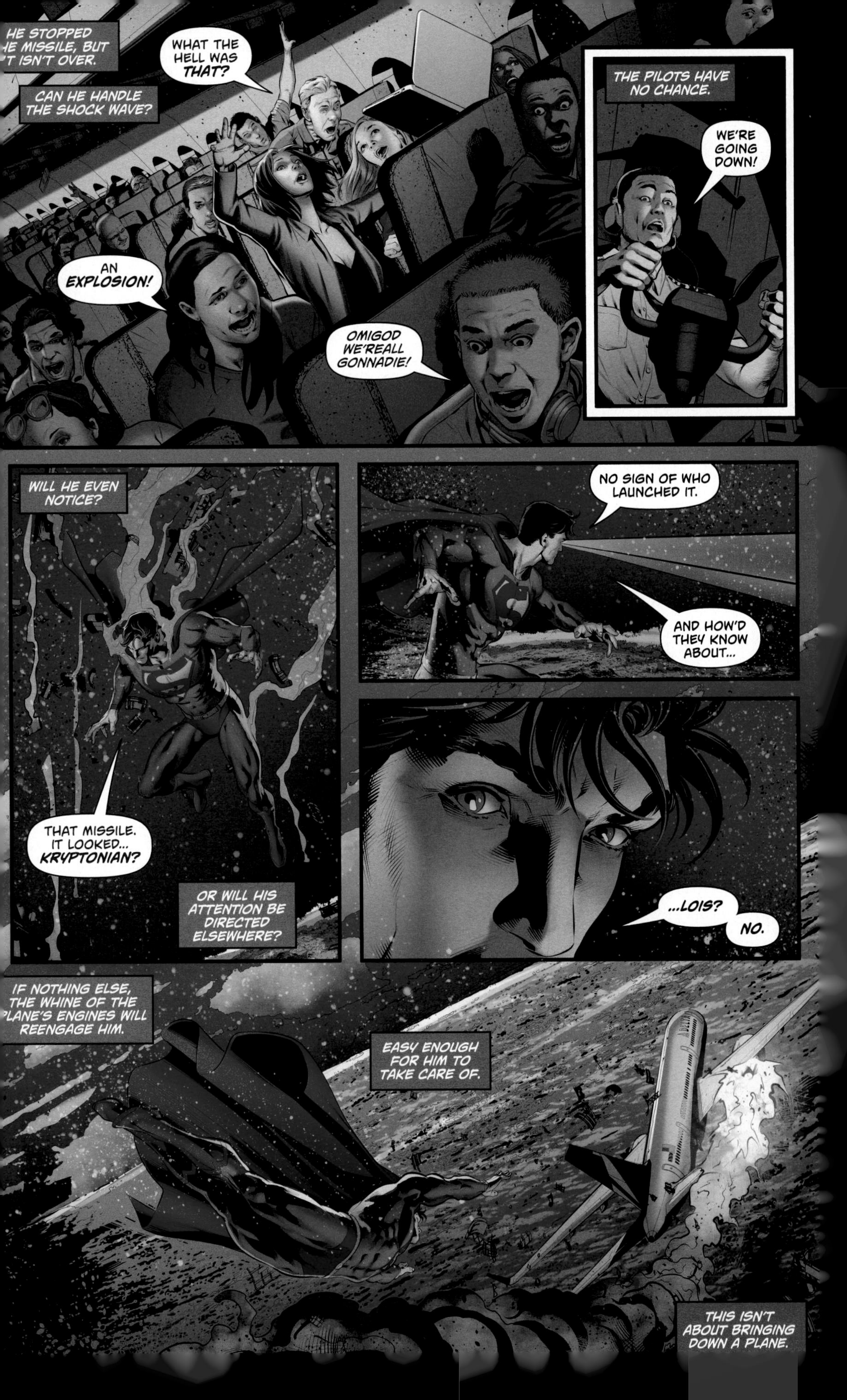
HE STOPPED
HE MISSILE, BUT
T ISN'T OVER.
CAN HE HANDLE THE SHOCK WAVE?
WHAT THE HELL WAS THAT?
AN EXPLOSION!
OMIGOD WE'REALL GONNADIE!
THE PILOTS HAVE NO CHANCE.
WE'RE GOING DOWN!
WILL HE EVEN NOTICE?
THAT MISSILE. IT LOOKED... KRYPTONIAN?
OR WILL HIS ATTENTION BE DIRECTED ELSEWHERE?
NO SIGN OF WHO LAUNCHED IT.
AND HOW'D THEY KNOW ABOUT...
...LOIS?
NO.
IF NOTHING ELSE, THE WHINE OF THE
LANE'S ENGINES WILL REENGAGE HIM.
EASY ENOUGH FOR HIM TO TAKE CARE OF.
THIS ISN'T ABOUT BRINGING DOWN A PLANE.

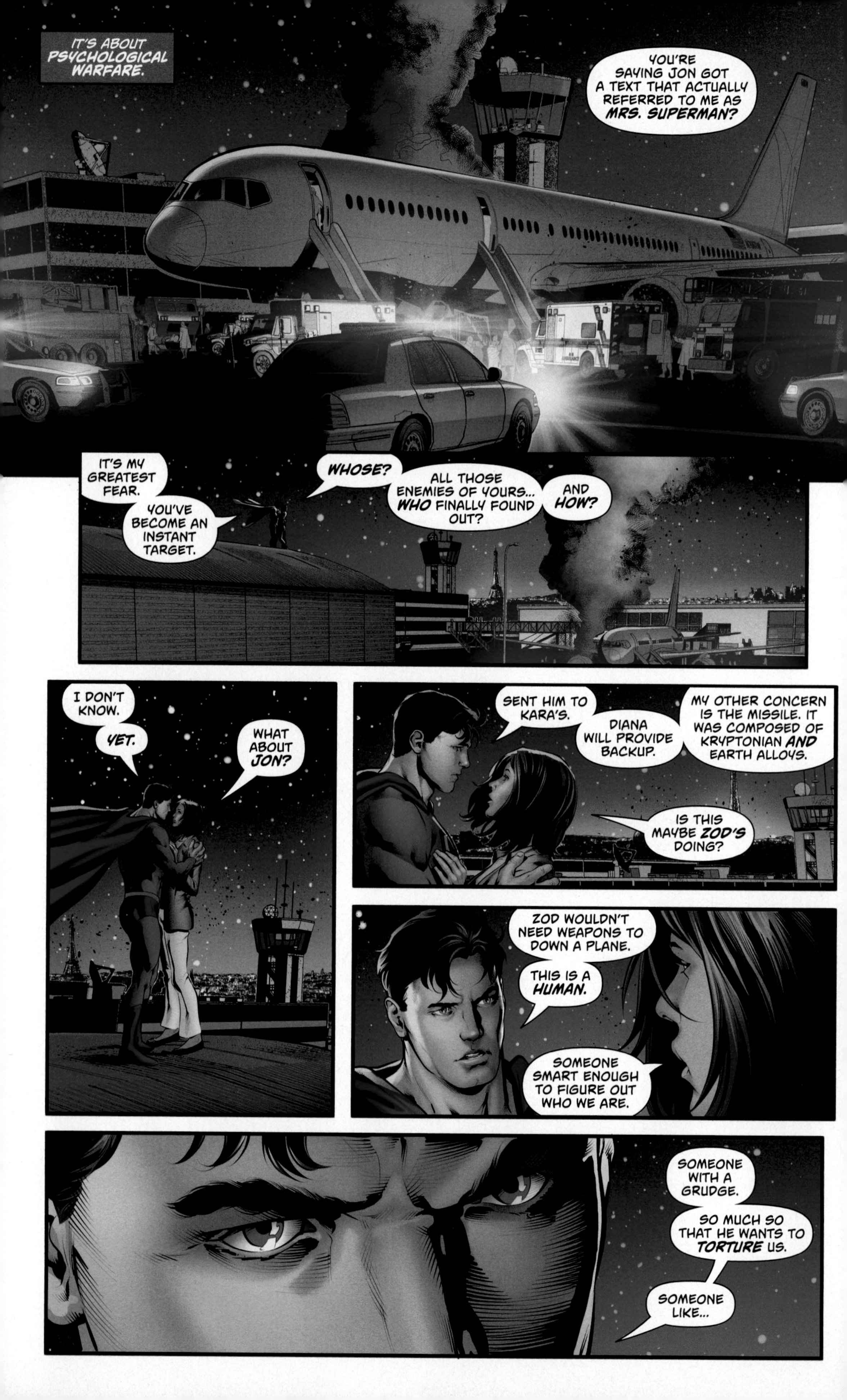
IT'S ABOUT PSYCHOLOGICAL WARFARE.
YOU'RE SAYING JON GOT A TEXT THAT ACTUALLY REFERRED TO ME AS MRS. SUPERMAN?
IT'S MY GREATEST FEAR.
YOU'VE BECOME AN INSTANT TARGET.
WHOSE?
ALL THOSE ENEMIES OF YOURS... WHO FINALLY FOUND OUT?
AND HOW?
I DON'T KNOW.
YET.
WHAT ABOUT JON?
SENT HIM TO KARA'S.
DIANA WILL PROVIDE BACKUP.
MY OTHER CONCERN IS THE MISSILE. IT WAS COMPOSED OF KRYPTONIAN AND EARTH ALLOYS.
IS THIS MAYBE ZOD'S DOING?
ZOD WOULDN'T NEED WEAPONS TO DOWN A PLANE.
THIS IS A HUMAN.
SOMEONE SMART ENOUGH TO FIGURE OUT WHO WE ARE.
SOMEONE WITH A GRUDGE.
SO MUCH SO THAT HE WANTS TO TORTURE US.
SOMEONE LIKE...

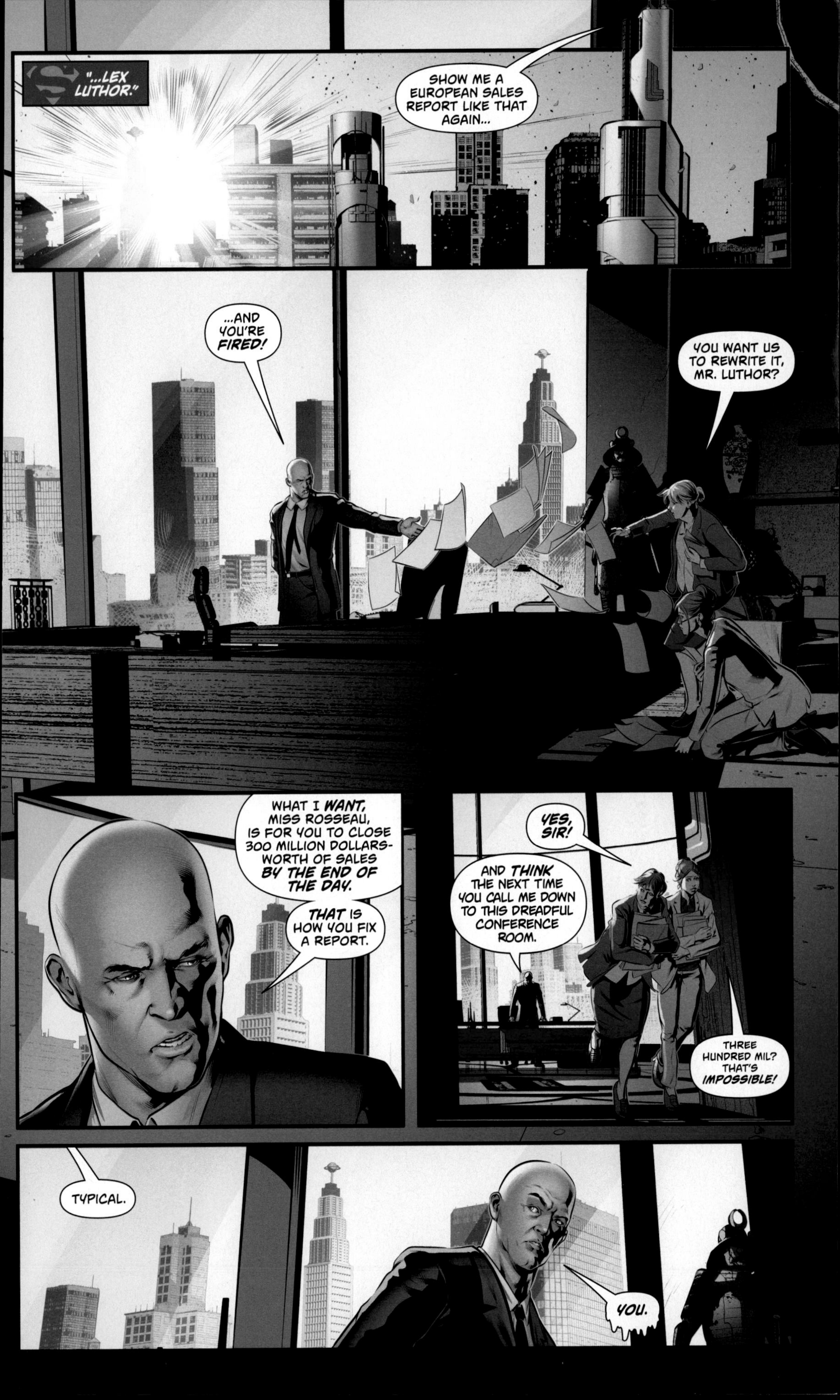
"...LEX LUTHOR."
SHOW ME A EUROPEAN SALES REPORT LIKE THAT AGAIN...
...AND YOU'RE FIRED!
YOU WANT US TO REWRITE IT, MR. LUTHOR?
WHAT I WANT, MISS ROSSEAU, IS FOR YOU TO CLOSE 300 MILLION DOLLARS-WORTH OF SALES BY THE END OF THE DAY.
THAT IS HOW YOU FIX A REPORT.
YES, SIR!
AND THINK THE NEXT TIME YOU CALL ME DOWN TO THIS DREADFUL CONFERENCE ROOM.
THREE HUNDRED MIL? THAT'S IMPOSSIBLE!
TYPICAL.
YOU.

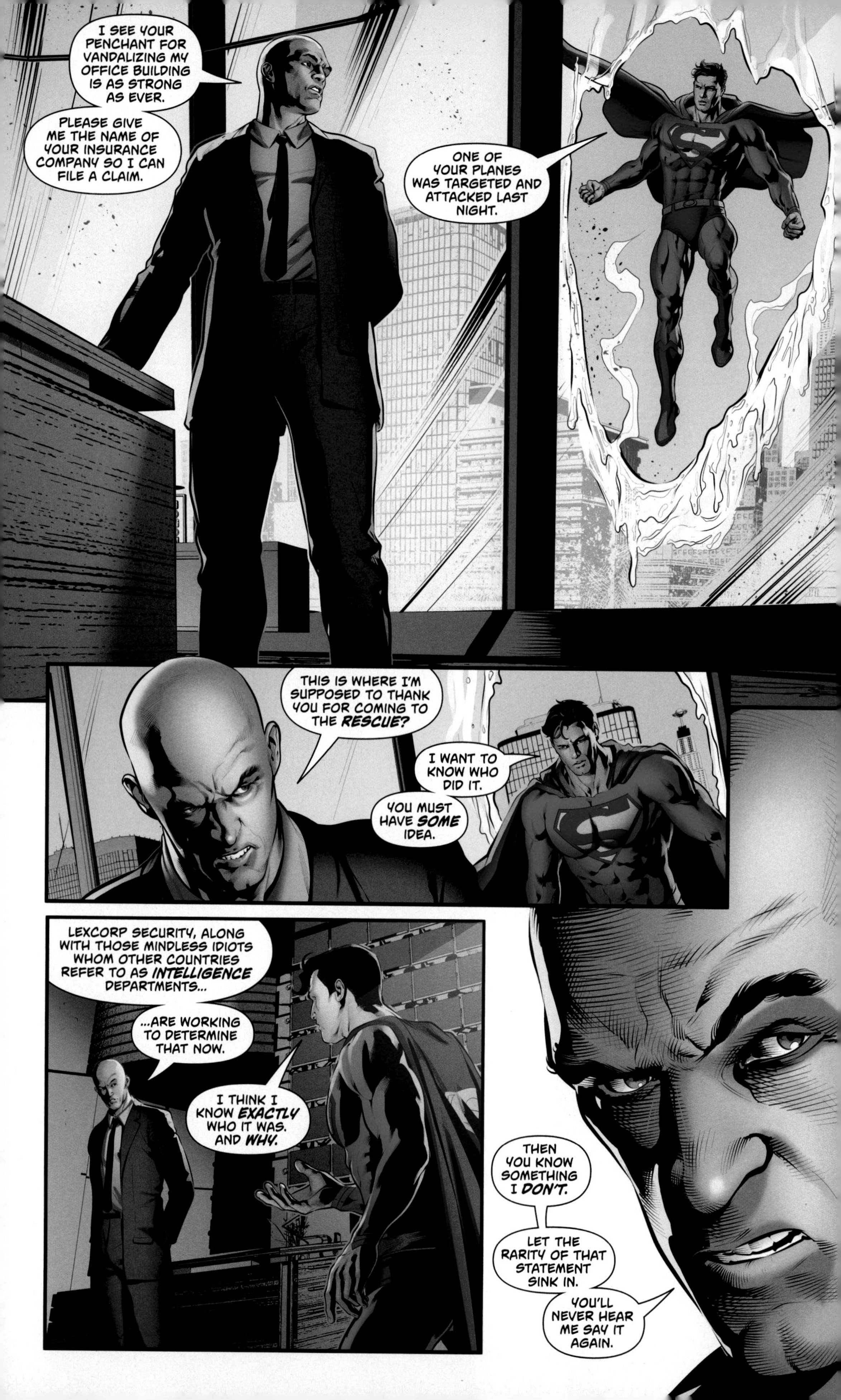
I SEE YOUR PENCHANT FOR VANDALIZING MY OFFICE BUILDING IS AS STRONG AS EVER.
PLEASE GIVE ME THE NAME OF YOUR INSURANCE COMPANY SO I CAN FILE A CLAIM.
ONE OF YOUR PLANES WAS TARGETED AND ATTACKED LAST NIGHT.
THIS IS WHERE I'M SUPPOSED TO THANK YOU FOR COMING TO THE *RESCUE?*
I WANT TO KNOW WHO DID IT.
YOU MUST HAVE *SOME* IDEA.
LEXCORP SECURITY, ALONG WITH THOSE MINDLESS IDIOTS WHOM OTHER COUNTRIES REFER TO AS *INTELLIGENCE* DEPARTMENTS...
...ARE WORKING TO DETERMINE THAT NOW.
I THINK I KNOW *EXACTLY* WHO IT WAS. AND *WHY.*
THEN YOU KNOW SOMETHING I *DON'T.*
LET THE RARITY OF THAT STATEMENT SINK IN.
YOU'LL NEVER HEAR ME SAY IT AGAIN.

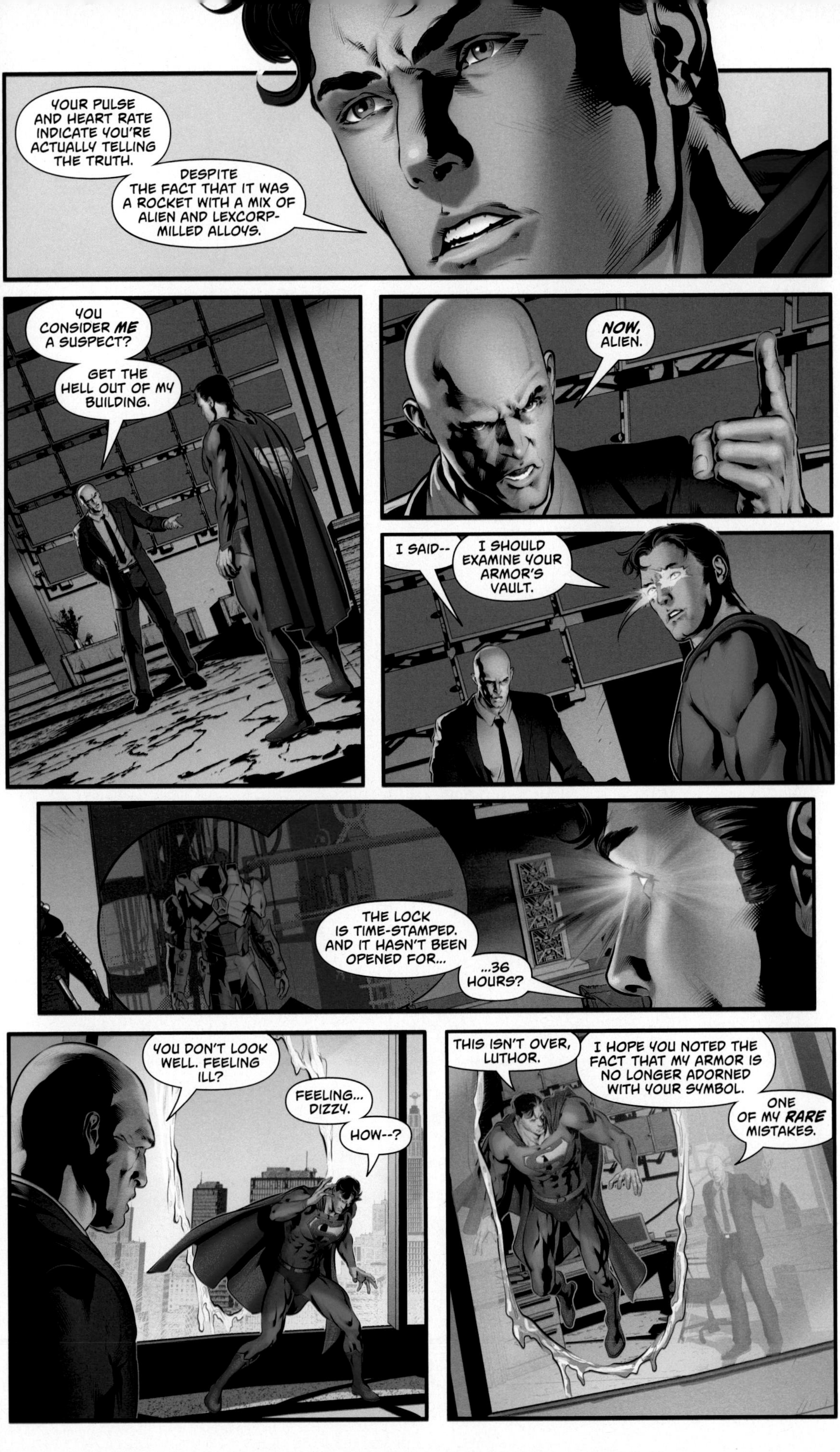
YOUR PULSE AND HEART RATE INDICATE YOU'RE ACTUALLY TELLING THE TRUTH.
DESPITE THE FACT THAT IT WAS A ROCKET WITH A MIX OF ALIEN AND LEXCORP-MILLED ALLOYS.
YOU CONSIDER ME A SUSPECT?
GET THE HELL OUT OF MY BUILDING.
NOW, ALIEN.
I SAID--
I SHOULD EXAMINE YOUR ARMOR'S VAULT.
THE LOCK IS TIME-STAMPED. AND IT HASN'T BEEN OPENED FOR...
...36 HOURS?
YOU DON'T LOOK WELL. FEELING ILL?
FEELING... DIZZY.
HOW--?
THIS ISN'T OVER, LUTHOR.
I HOPE YOU NOTED THE FACT THAT MY ARMOR IS NO LONGER ADORNED WITH YOUR SYMBOL.
ONE OF MY RARE MISTAKES.

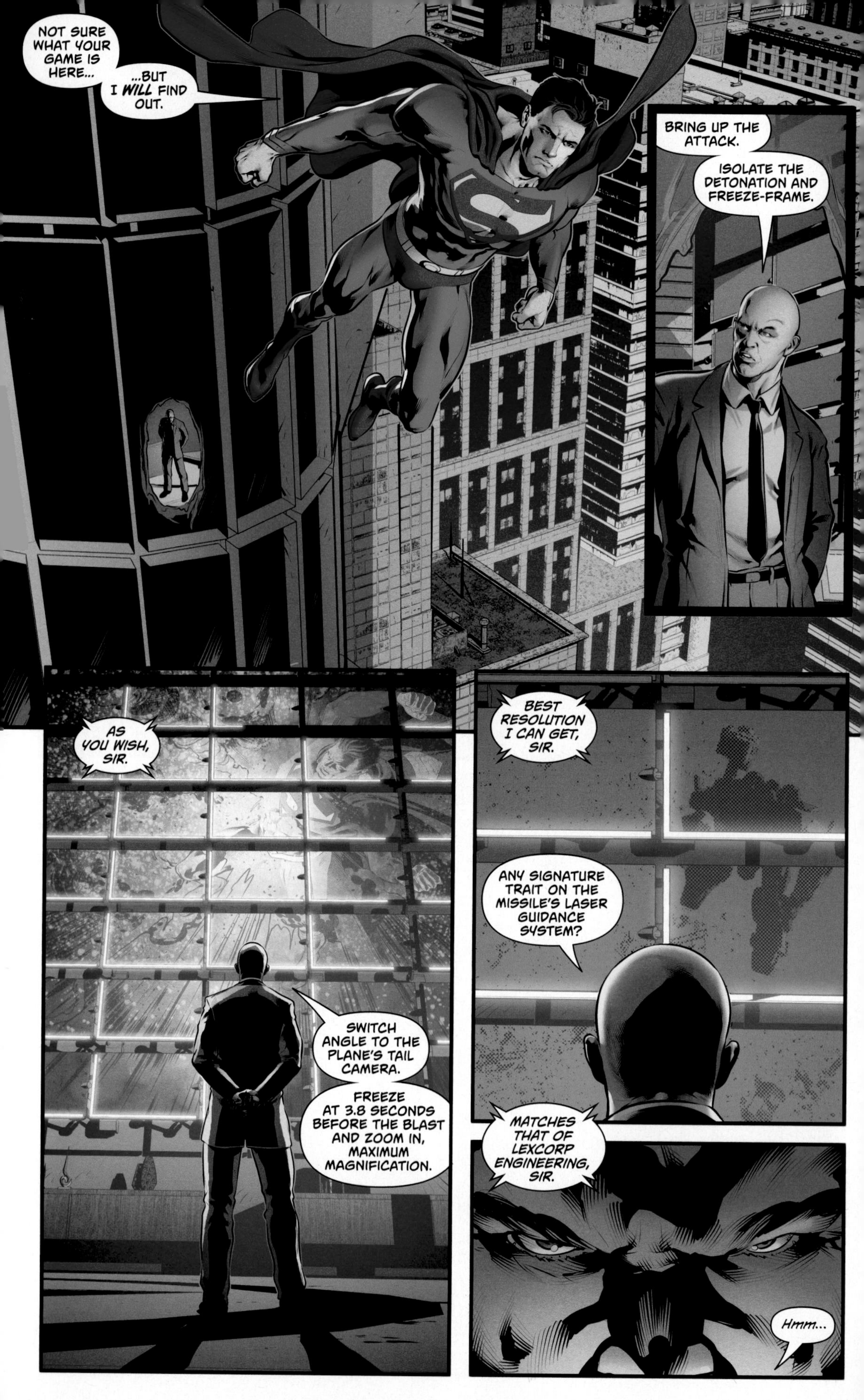
NOT SURE WHAT YOUR GAME IS HERE...
...BUT I WILL FIND OUT.
BRING UP THE ATTACK.
ISOLATE THE DETONATION AND FREEZE-FRAME.
AS YOU WISH, SIR.
SWITCH ANGLE TO THE PLANE'S TAIL CAMERA.
FREEZE AT 3.8 SECONDS BEFORE THE BLAST AND ZOOM IN, MAXIMUM MAGNIFICATION.
BEST RESOLUTION I CAN GET, SIR.
ANY SIGNATURE TRAIT ON THE MISSILE'S LASER GUIDANCE SYSTEM?
MATCHES THAT OF LEXCORP ENGINEERING, SIR.
Hmm...

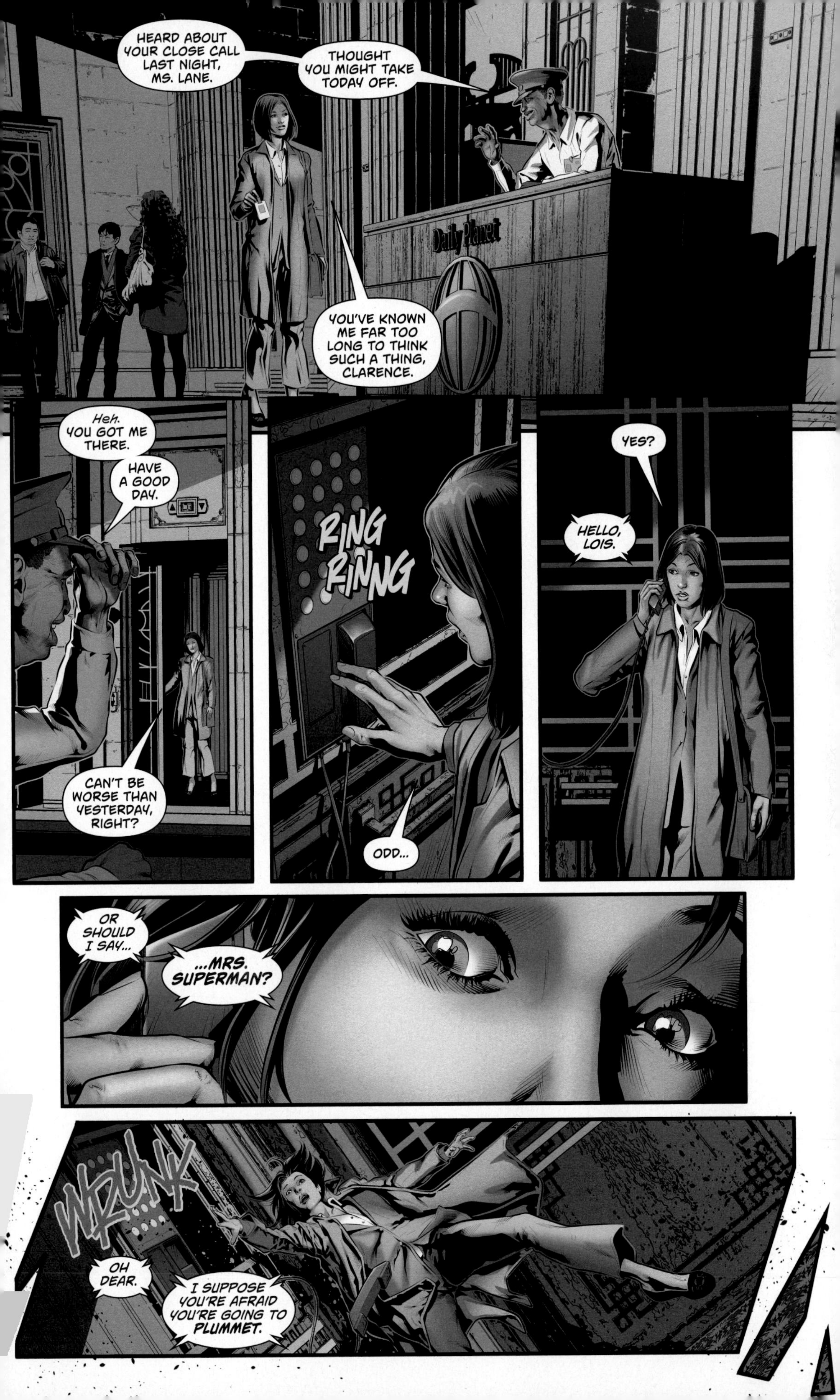
HEARD ABOUT YOUR CLOSE CALL LAST NIGHT, MS. LANE.
THOUGHT YOU MIGHT TAKE TODAY OFF.
Daily Planet
YOU'VE KNOWN ME FAR TOO LONG TO THINK SUCH A THING, CLARENCE.
Heh. YOU GOT ME THERE.
HAVE A GOOD DAY.
CAN'T BE WORSE THAN YESTERDAY, RIGHT?
RING RING
ODD...
YES?
HELLO, LOIS.
OR SHOULD I SAY...
...MRS. SUPERMAN?
WRUNK
OH DEAR.
I SUPPOSE YOU'RE AFRAID YOU'RE GOING TO PLUMMET.

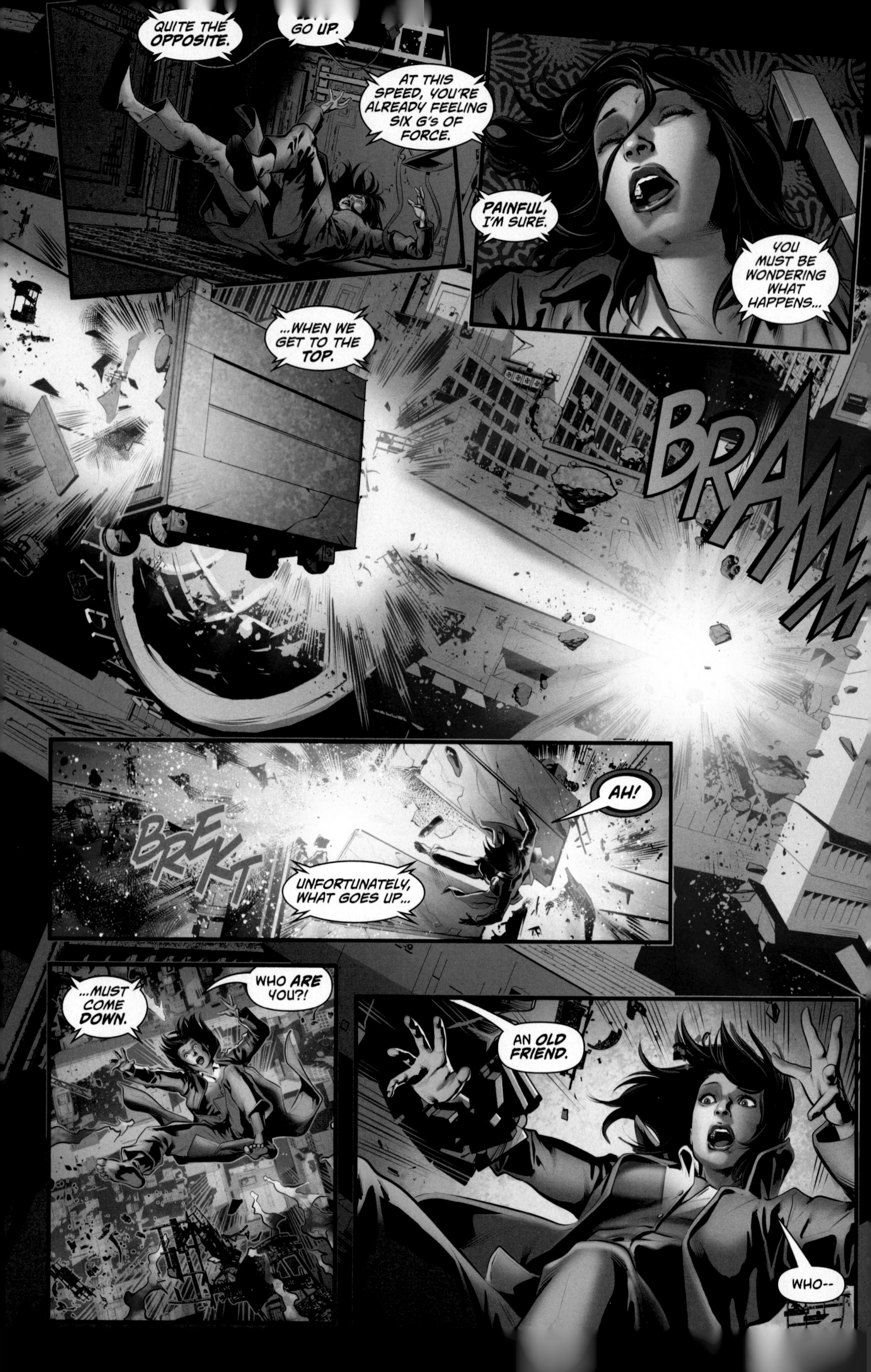
QUITE THE OPPOSITE.
GO UP.
AT THIS SPEED, YOU'RE ALREADY FEELING SIX G's OF FORCE.
PAINFUL, I'M SURE.
YOU MUST BE WONDERING WHAT HAPPENS...
...WHEN WE GET TO THE TOP.
BRAMM
BREKT
AH!
UNFORTUNATELY, WHAT GOES UP...
...MUST COME DOWN.
WHO ARE YOU?!
AN OLD FRIEND.
WHO--

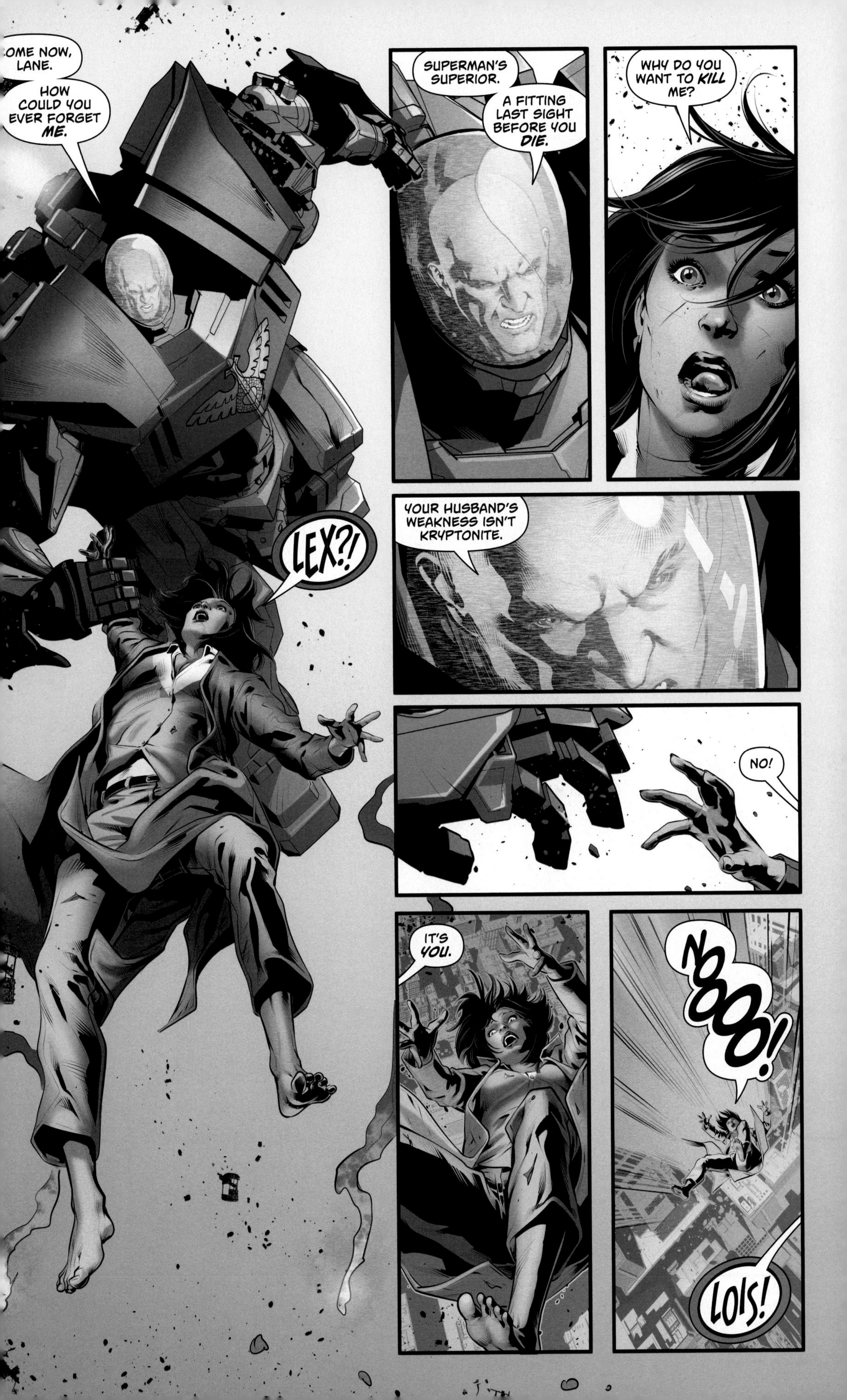
OME NOW, LANE.
HOW COULD YOU EVER FORGET ME.
LEX?!
SUPERMAN'S SUPERIOR.
A FITTING LAST SIGHT BEFORE YOU DIE.
WHY DO YOU WANT TO KILL ME?
YOUR HUSBAND'S WEAKNESS ISN'T KRYPTONITE.
NO!
IT'S YOU.
NOOOO!
LOIS!

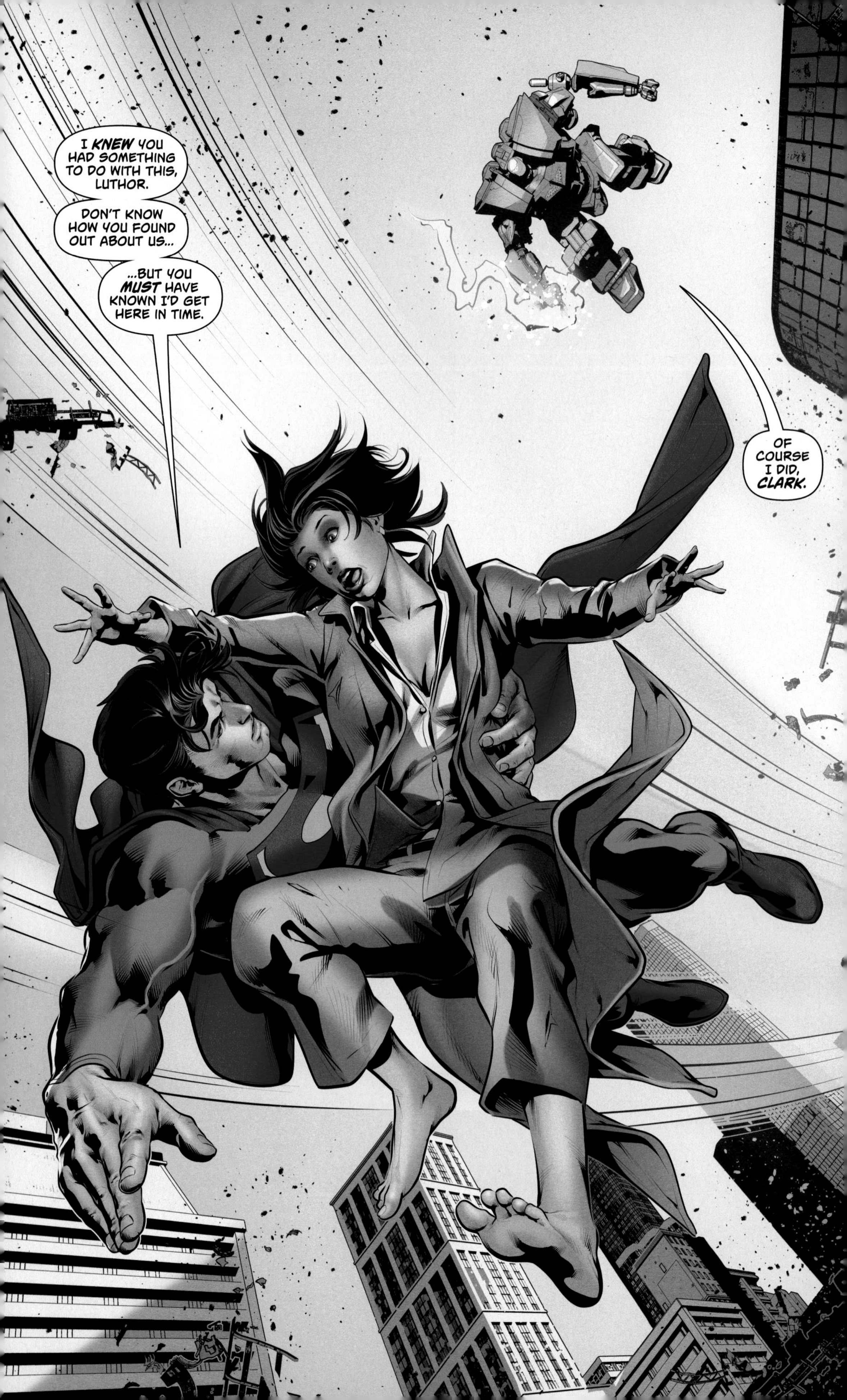
I KNEW YOU HAD SOMETHING TO DO WITH THIS, LUTHOR.
DON'T KNOW HOW YOU FOUND OUT ABOUT US...
...BUT YOU MUST HAVE KNOWN I'D GET HERE IN TIME.
OF COURSE I DID, CLARK.

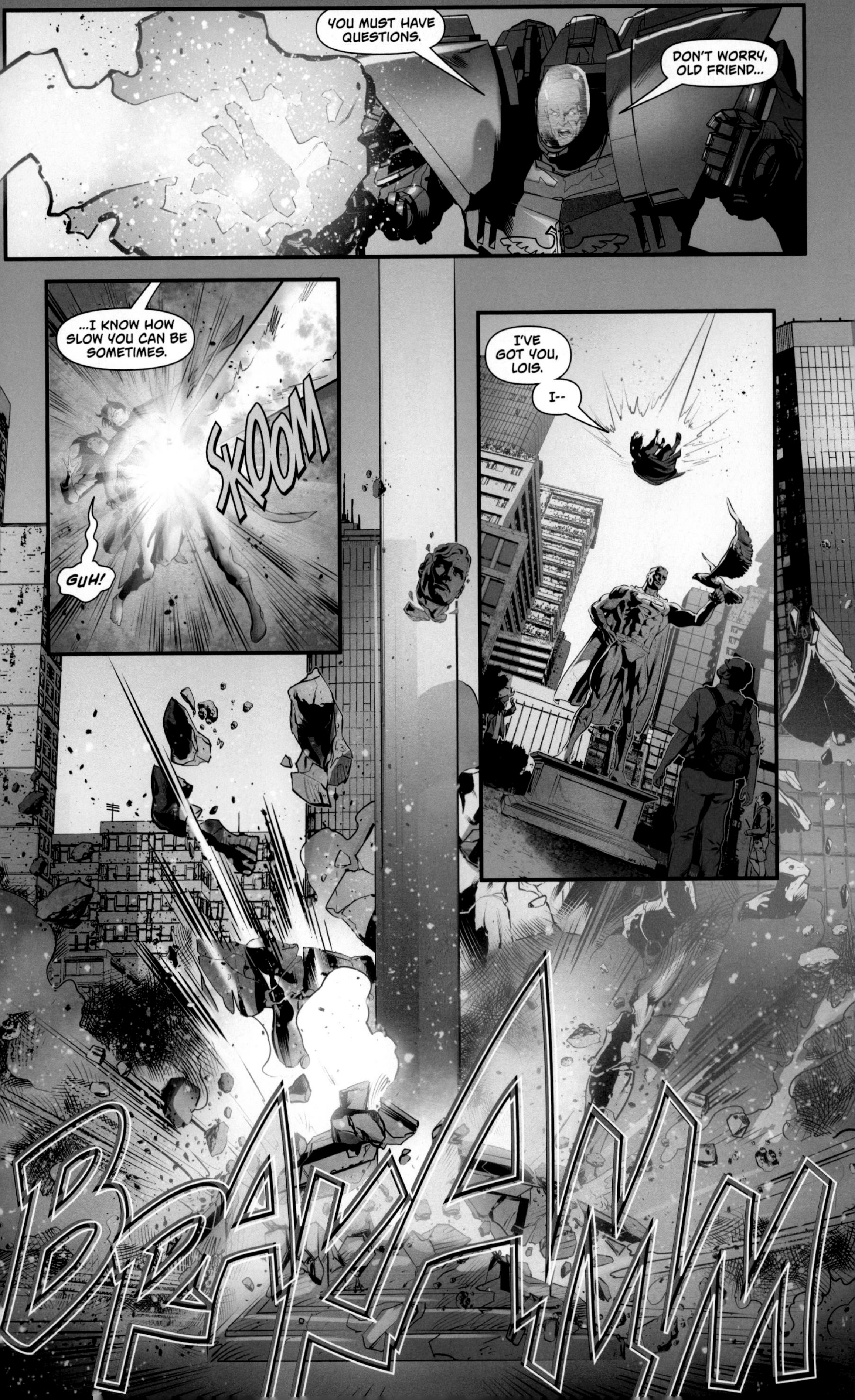
YOU MUST HAVE QUESTIONS.
DON'T WORRY, OLD FRIEND...
...I KNOW HOW SLOW YOU CAN BE SOMETIMES.
SKOOM
GUH!
I'VE GOT YOU, LOIS.
I--
BRAKAMM

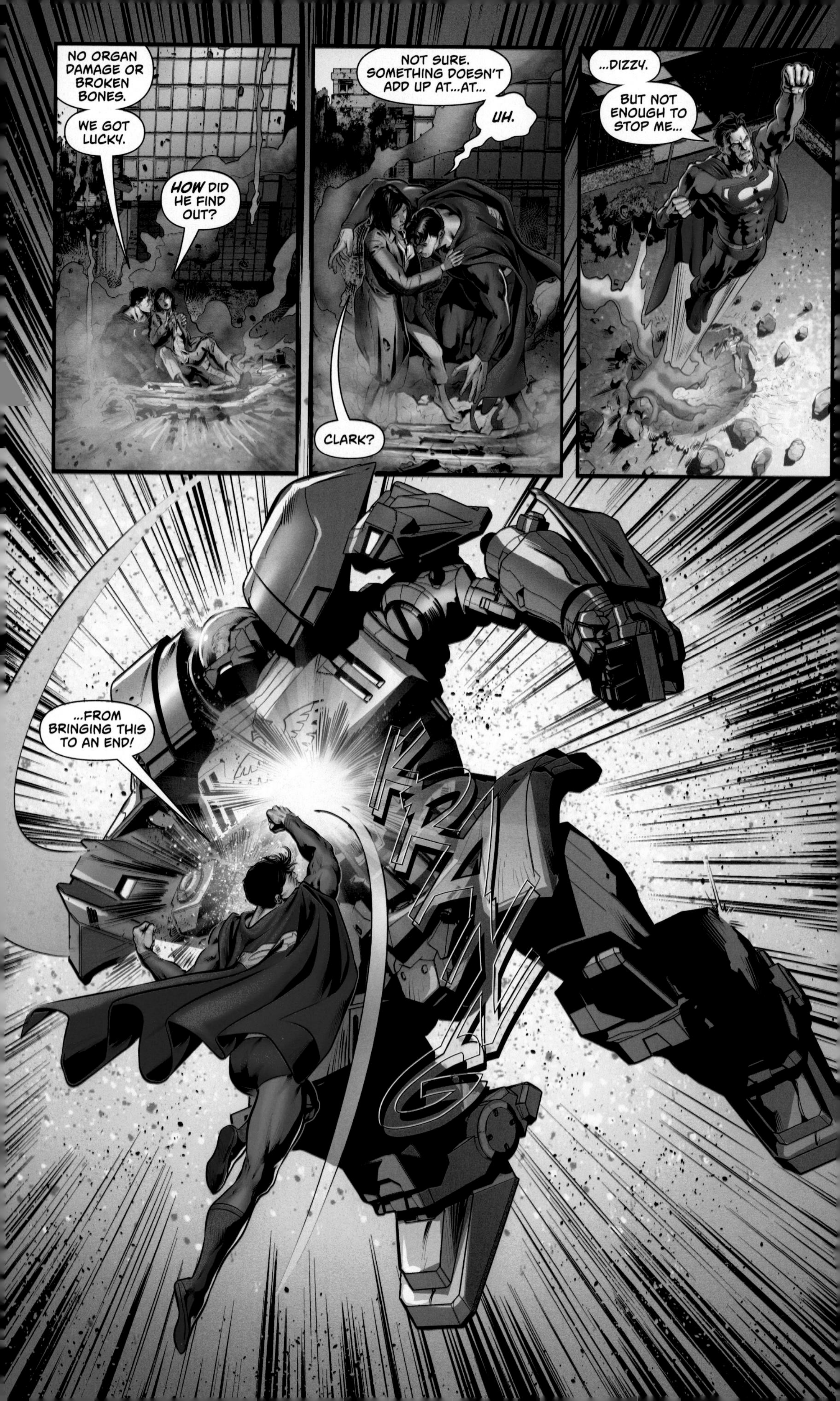
NO ORGAN DAMAGE OR BROKEN BONES.
WE GOT LUCKY.
HOW DID HE FIND OUT?
NOT SURE. SOMETHING DOESN'T ADD UP AT...AT...
UH.
CLARK?
...DIZZY.
BUT NOT ENOUGH TO STOP ME...
...FROM BRINGING THIS TO AN END!
KRANG

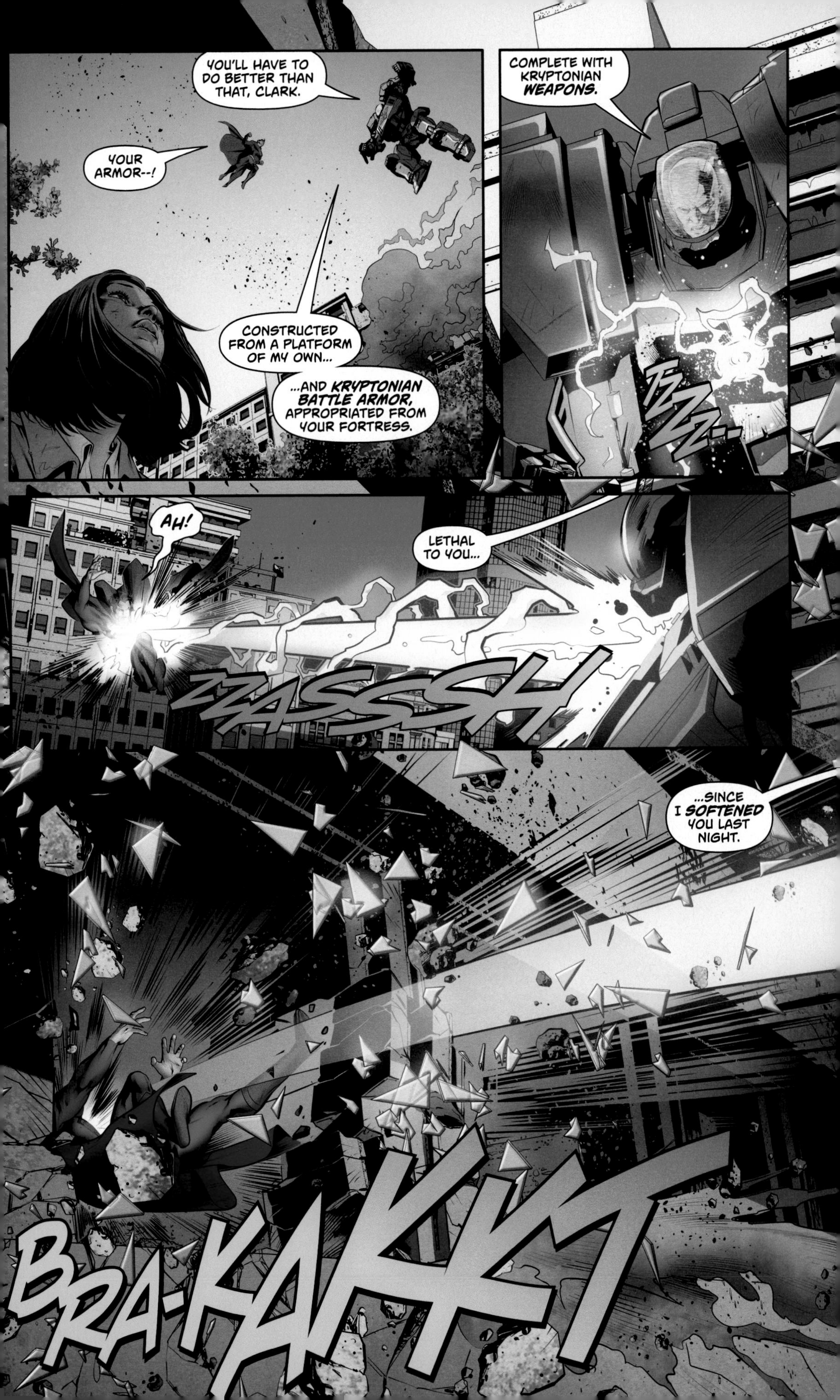
YOU'LL HAVE TO DO BETTER THAN THAT, CLARK.
YOUR ARMOR--!
CONSTRUCTED FROM A PLATFORM OF MY OWN...
...AND KRYPTONIAN BATTLE ARMOR, APPROPRIATED FROM YOUR FORTRESS.
COMPLETE WITH KRYPTONIAN WEAPONS.
ZZZZ...
AH!
LETHAL TO YOU...
ZZASSSH
...SINCE I SOFTENED YOU LAST NIGHT.
BRA-KAKKT

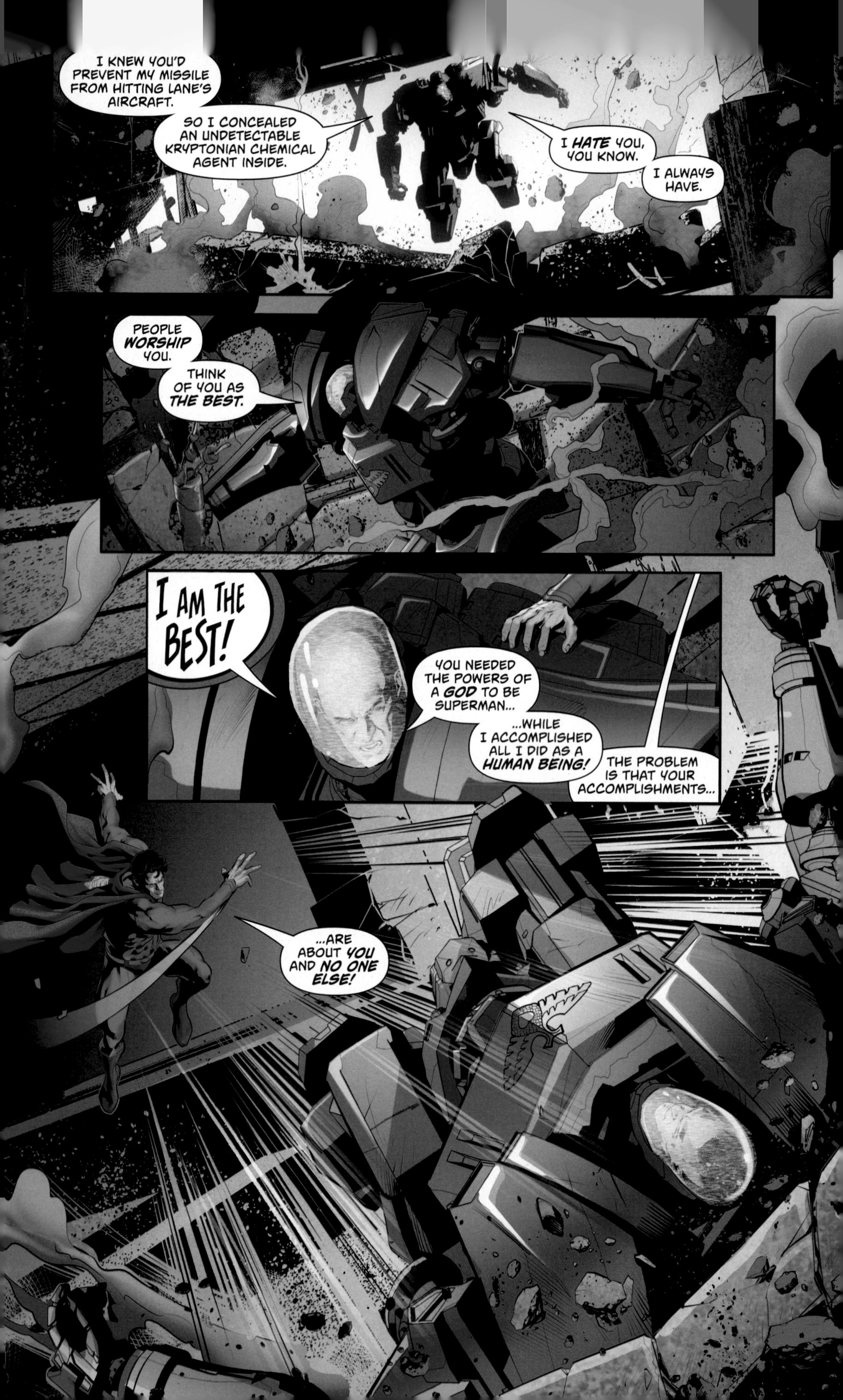
I KNEW YOU'D PREVENT MY MISSILE FROM HITTING LANE'S AIRCRAFT.
SO I CONCEALED AN UNDETECTABLE KRYPTONIAN CHEMICAL AGENT INSIDE.
I HATE YOU, YOU KNOW.
I ALWAYS HAVE.
PEOPLE WORSHIP YOU.
THINK OF YOU AS THE BEST.
I AM THE BEST!
YOU NEEDED THE POWERS OF A GOD TO BE SUPERMAN...
...WHILE I ACCOMPLISHED ALL I DID AS A HUMAN BEING!
THE PROBLEM IS THAT YOUR ACCOMPLISHMENTS...
...ARE ABOUT YOU AND NO ONE ELSE!

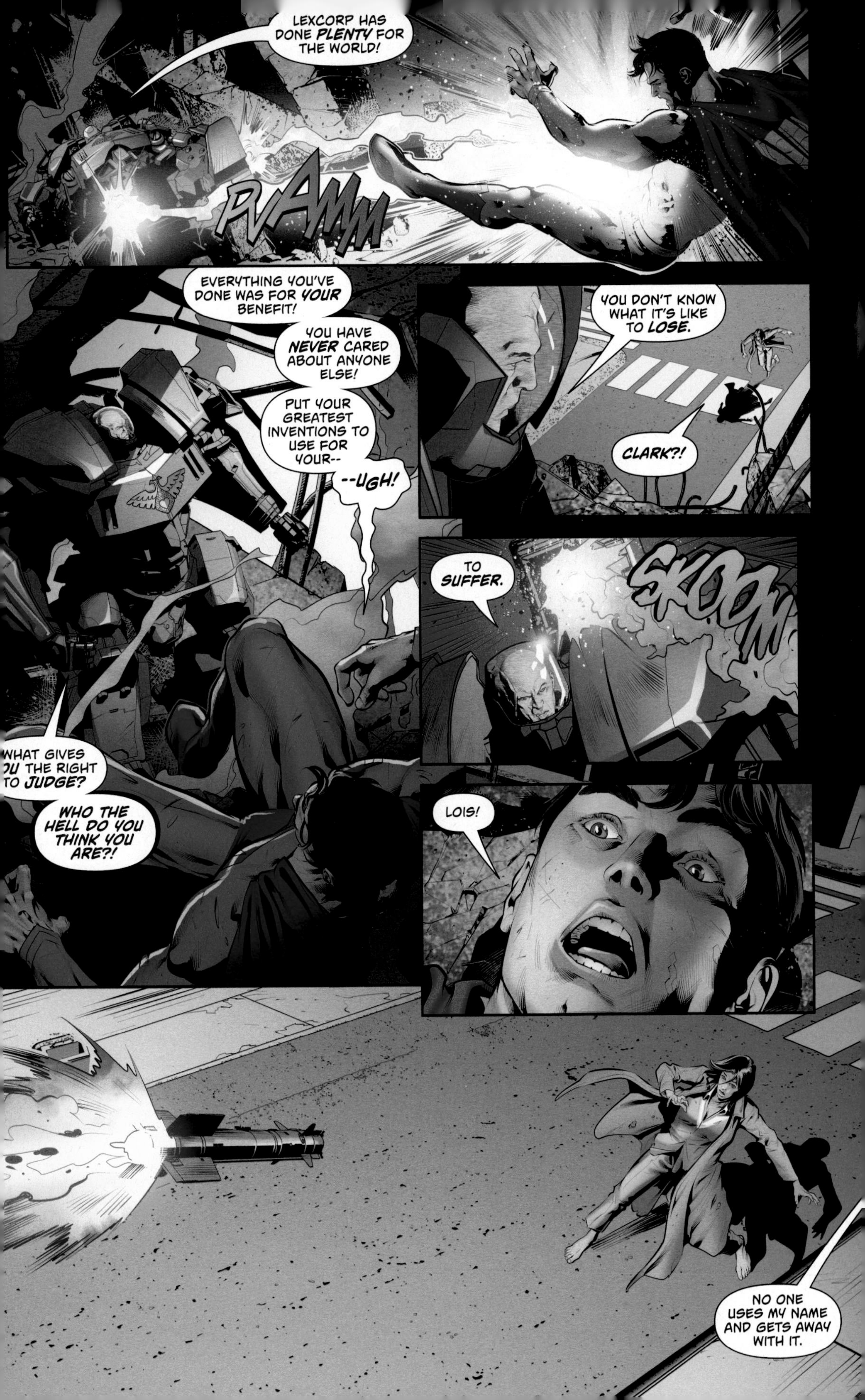
LEXCORP HAS DONE PLENTY FOR THE WORLD!
PVAMM
EVERYTHING YOU'VE DONE WAS FOR YOUR BENEFIT!
YOU HAVE NEVER CARED ABOUT ANYONE ELSE!
PUT YOUR GREATEST INVENTIONS TO USE FOR YOUR--
--UGH!
YOU DON'T KNOW WHAT IT'S LIKE TO LOSE.
CLARK?!
TO SUFFER.
SKOOM
WHAT GIVES YOU THE RIGHT TO JUDGE?
WHO THE HELL DO YOU THINK YOU ARE?!
LOIS!
NO ONE USES MY NAME AND GETS AWAY WITH IT.

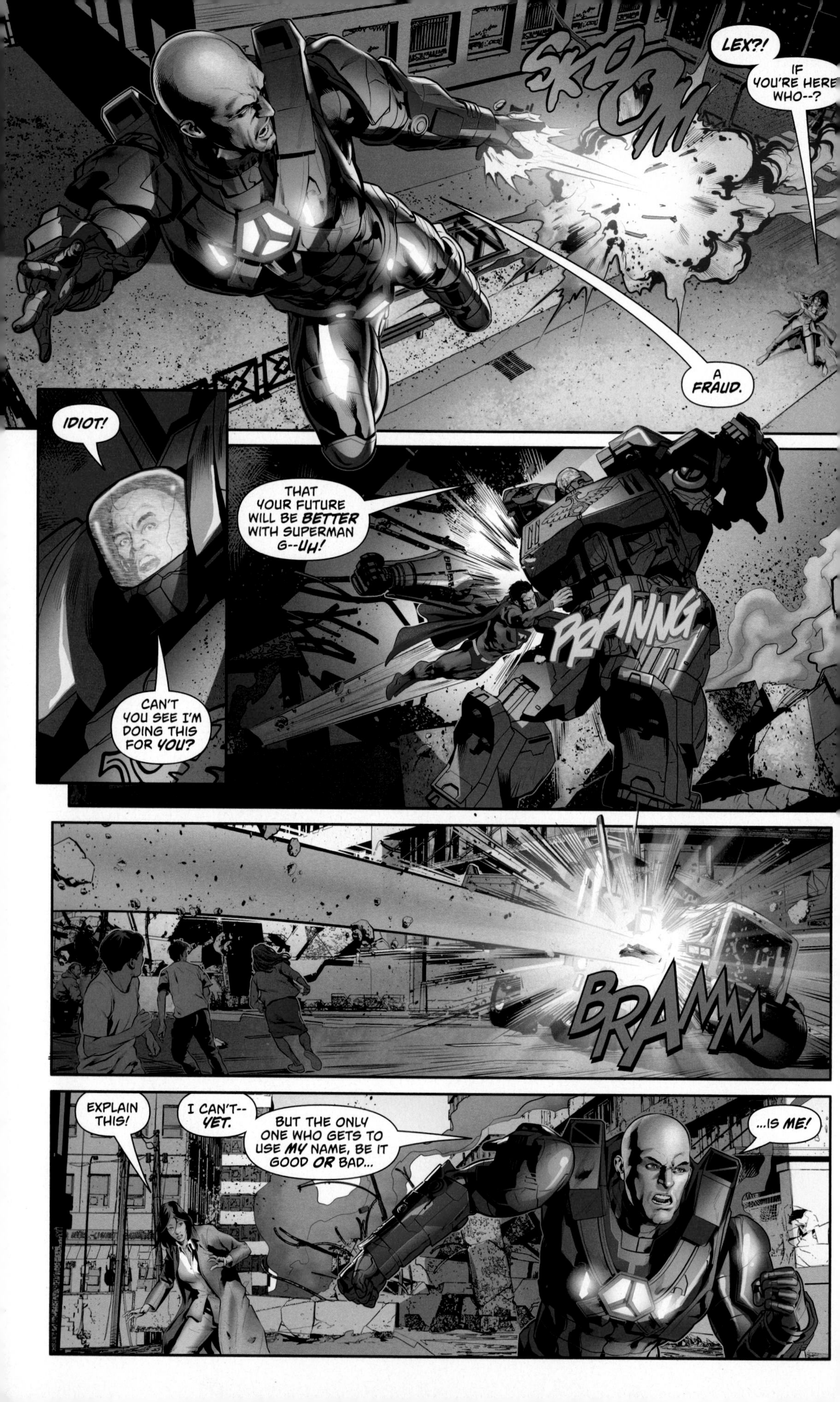

SKOOM
LEX?!
IF YOU'RE HERE WHO--?
A FRAUD.
IDIOT!
CAN'T YOU SEE I'M DOING THIS FOR YOU?
THAT YOUR FUTURE WILL BE BETTER WITH SUPERMAN G--UH!
PRANNG
BRAMM
EXPLAIN THIS!
I CAN'T-- YET.
BUT THE ONLY ONE WHO GETS TO USE MY NAME, BE IT GOOD OR BAD...
...IS ME!

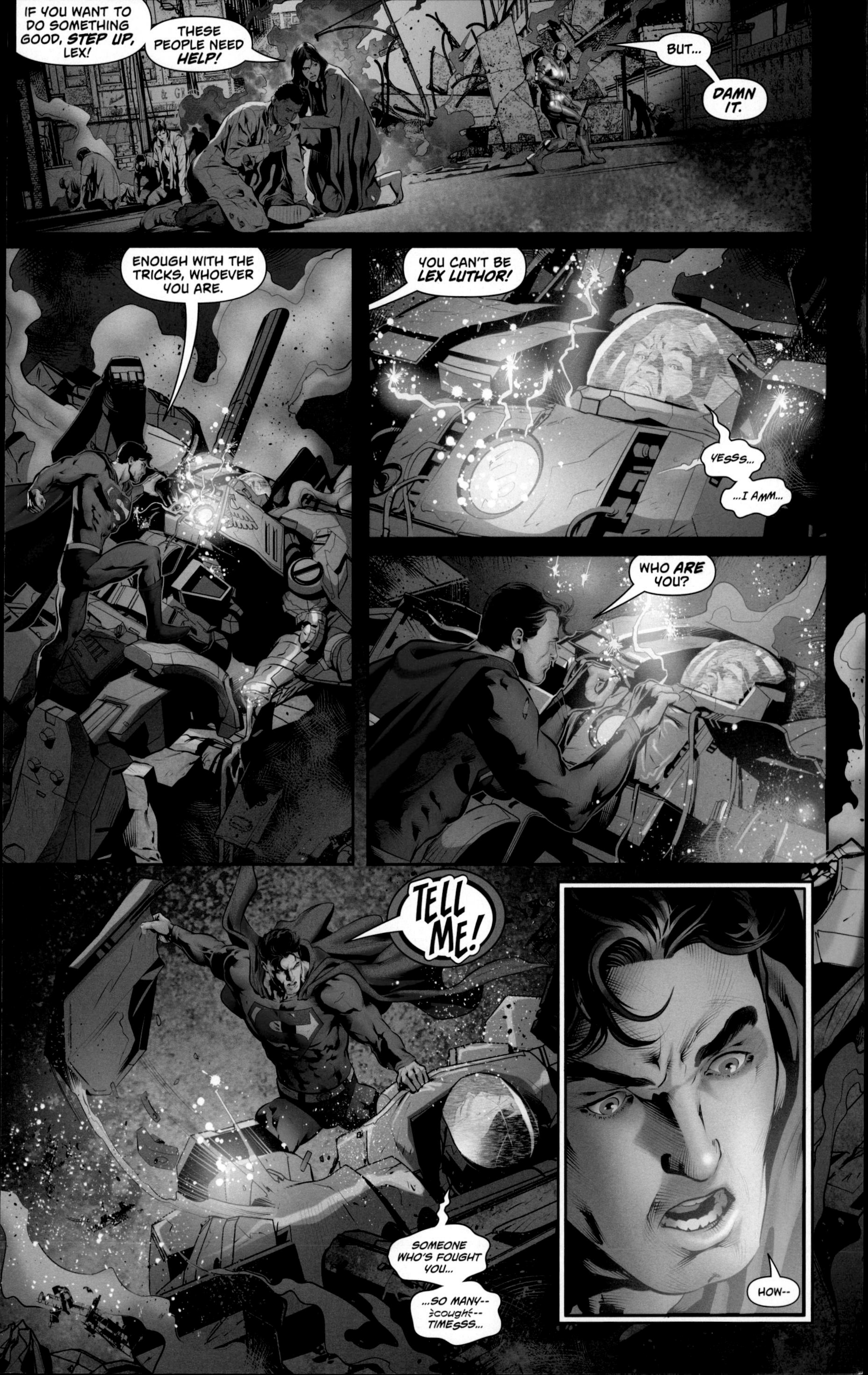
IF YOU WANT TO DO SOMETHING GOOD, STEP UP, LEX!
THESE PEOPLE NEED HELP!
BUT...
DAMN IT.
ENOUGH WITH THE TRICKS, WHOEVER YOU ARE.
YOU CAN'T BE LEX LUTHOR!
YESSS...
...I AMM...
WHO ARE YOU?
TELL ME!
SOMEONE WHO'S FOUGHT YOU...
...SO MANY-- *cough*-- TIMESSS...
HOW--

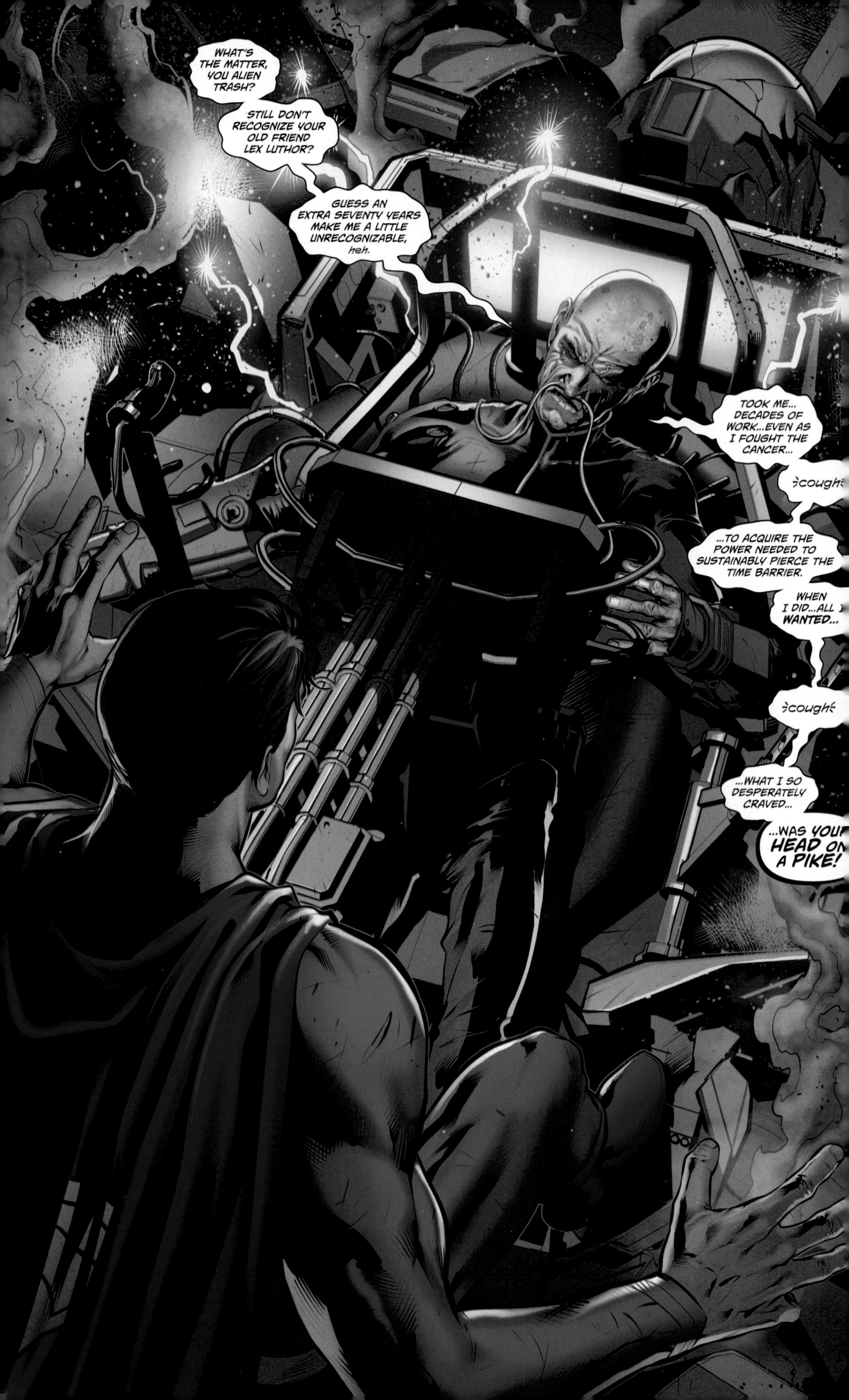
WHAT'S THE MATTER, YOU ALIEN TRASH?
STILL DON'T RECOGNIZE YOUR OLD FRIEND LEX LUTHOR?
GUESS AN EXTRA SEVENTY YEARS MAKE ME A LITTLE UNRECOGNIZABLE, heh.
TOOK ME... DECADES OF WORK...EVEN AS I FOUGHT THE CANCER...
cough
...TO ACQUIRE THE POWER NEEDED TO SUSTAINABLY PIERCE THE TIME BARRIER.
WHEN I DID...ALL I WANTED...
cough
...WHAT I SO DESPERATELY CRAVED...
...WAS YOUR HEAD ON A PIKE!

YOUR HATE RUNS SO DEEP THAT ALL YOU COULD THINK OF, GIVEN THE POWER OF TIME-TRAVEL, WAS *REVENGE?*

I--≶COUGH≶--ACHIEVED EVERYTHING IN LIFE.

BUT *YOU!* YOUR VERY EXISTENCE AND THAT STUPID *GRIN* UNDERMINED EVERYTHING.

I BUILT MYSELF UP FROM *NOTHING* TO SHAPE THIS WORLD IN MY IMAGE. A *HUMAN* IMAGE.

YET YOU--≶COUGH≶--ALWAYS *WON.*

OVER AND OVER AND *OVER!*

YOU--≶*COUGH*≶

--ALWAYS BEA...

...BUH...

BRRTZ

...k.kt...

HEART ATTACK.

BRRTZ

MAYBE I CAN--

THAT SPARK--!

BRRTZ

FWOOSH

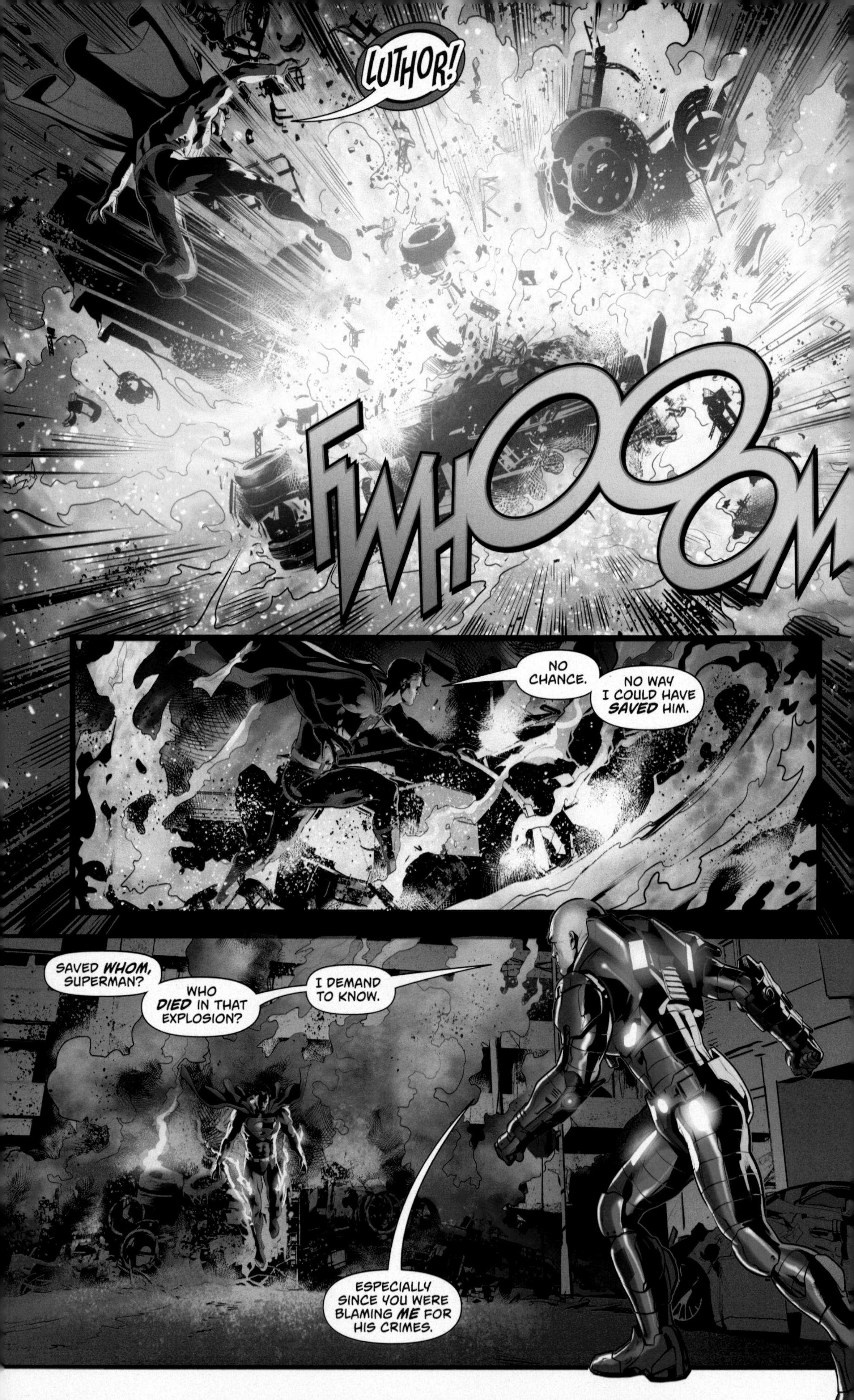
LUTHOR!
FWHOOOM
NO CHANCE.
NO WAY I COULD HAVE SAVED HIM.
SAVED WHOM, SUPERMAN?
WHO DIED IN THAT EXPLOSION?
I DEMAND TO KNOW.
ESPECIALLY SINCE YOU WERE BLAMING ME FOR HIS CRIMES.

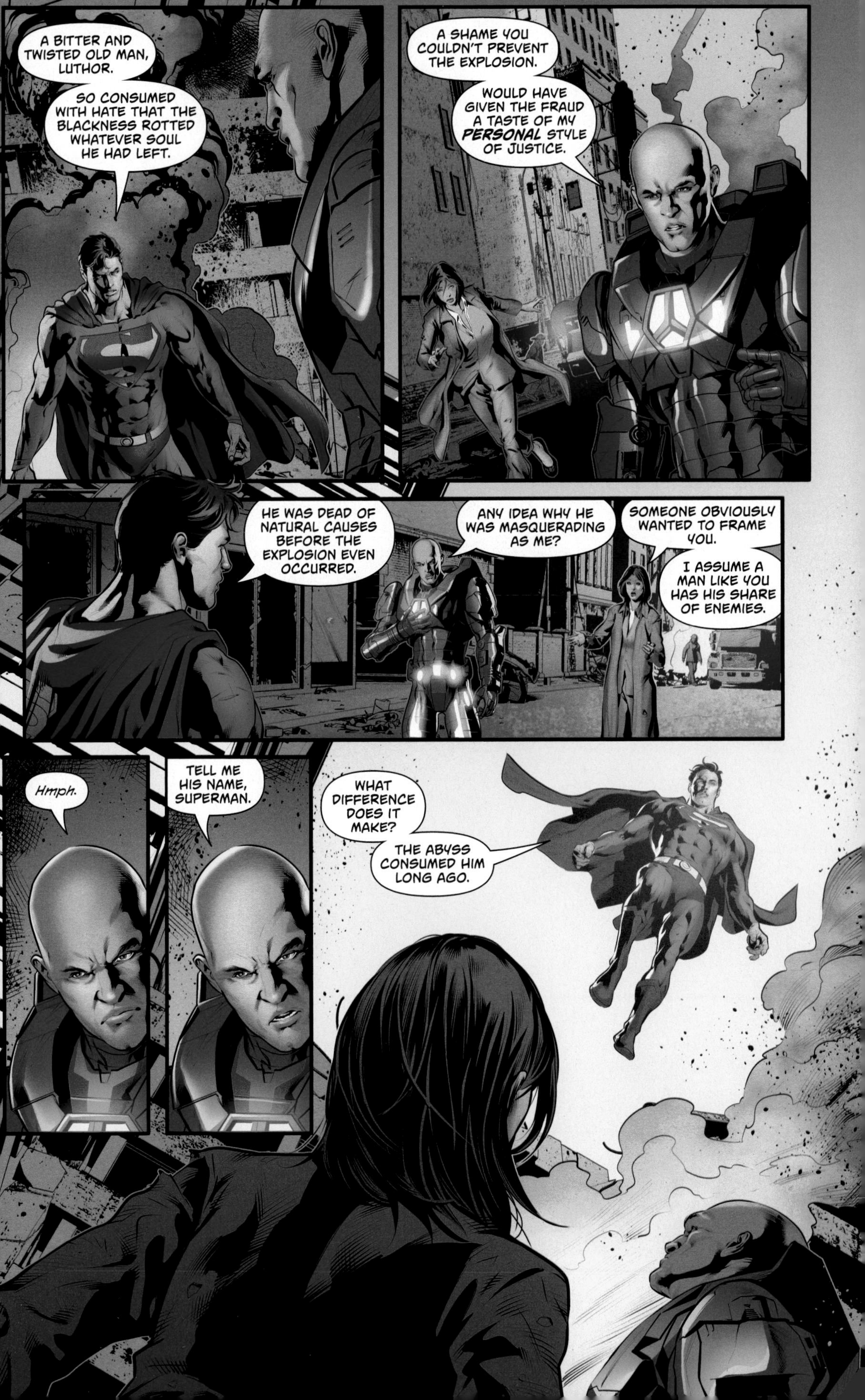

A BITTER AND TWISTED OLD MAN, LUTHOR.
SO CONSUMED WITH HATE THAT THE BLACKNESS ROTTED WHATEVER SOUL HE HAD LEFT.
A SHAME YOU COULDN'T PREVENT THE EXPLOSION.
WOULD HAVE GIVEN THE FRAUD A TASTE OF MY ***PERSONAL*** STYLE OF JUSTICE.
HE WAS DEAD OF NATURAL CAUSES BEFORE THE EXPLOSION EVEN OCCURRED.
ANY IDEA WHY HE WAS MASQUERADING AS ME?
SOMEONE OBVIOUSLY WANTED TO FRAME YOU.
I ASSUME A MAN LIKE YOU HAS HIS SHARE OF ENEMIES.
Hmph.
TELL ME HIS NAME, SUPERMAN.
WHAT DIFFERENCE DOES IT MAKE?
THE ABYSS CONSUMED HIM LONG AGO.

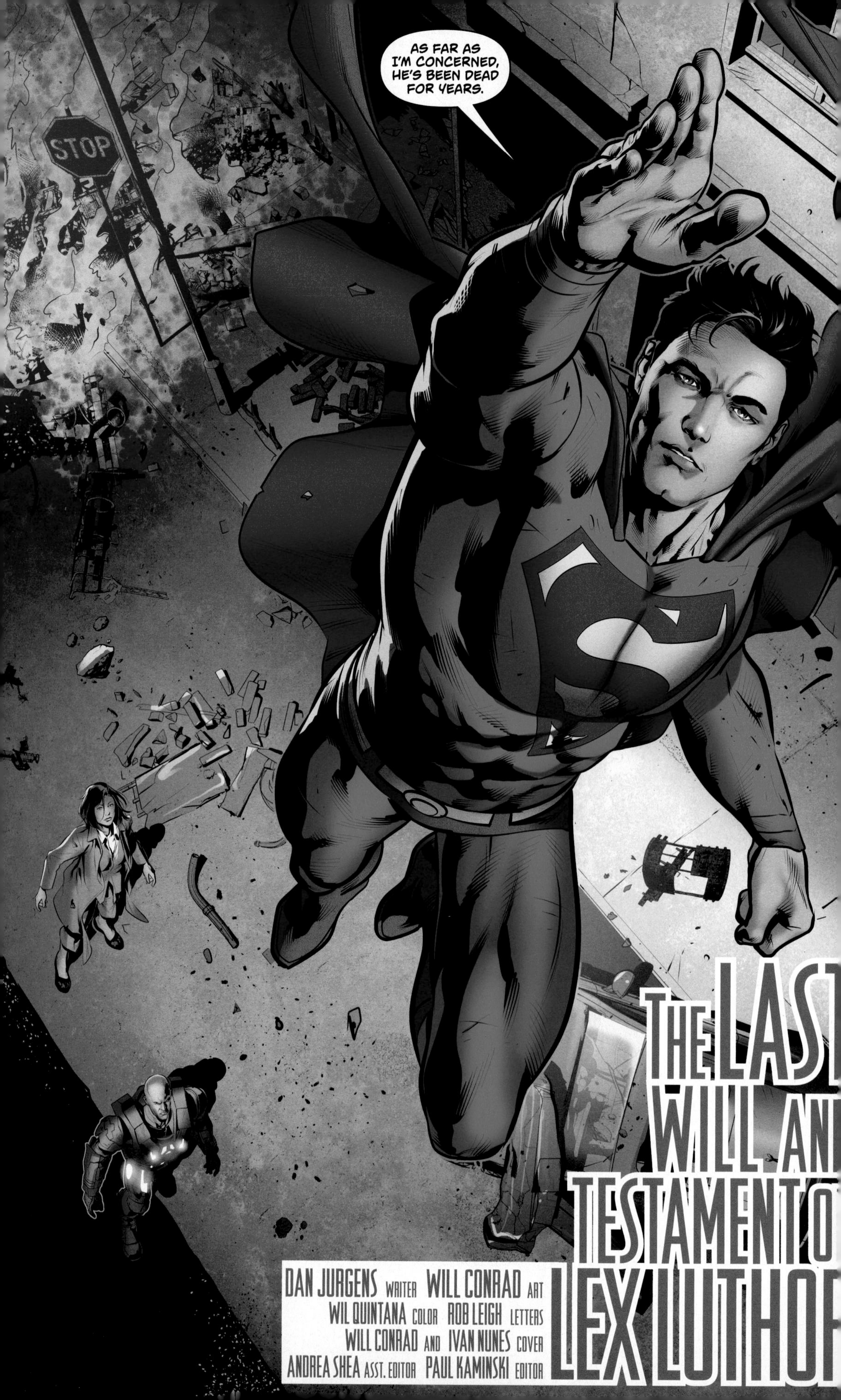
AS FAR AS I'M CONCERNED, HE'S BEEN DEAD FOR YEARS.
STOP
THE LAST WILL AND TESTAMENT OF LEX LUTHOR
DAN JURGENS WRITER WILL CONRAD ART
WIL QUINTANA COLOR ROB LEIGH LETTERS
WILL CONRAD AND IVAN NUNES COVER
ANDREA SHEA ASST. EDITOR PAUL KAMINSKI EDITOR

Variant cover art for ACTION COMICS #993 by FRANCIS MANAPUL

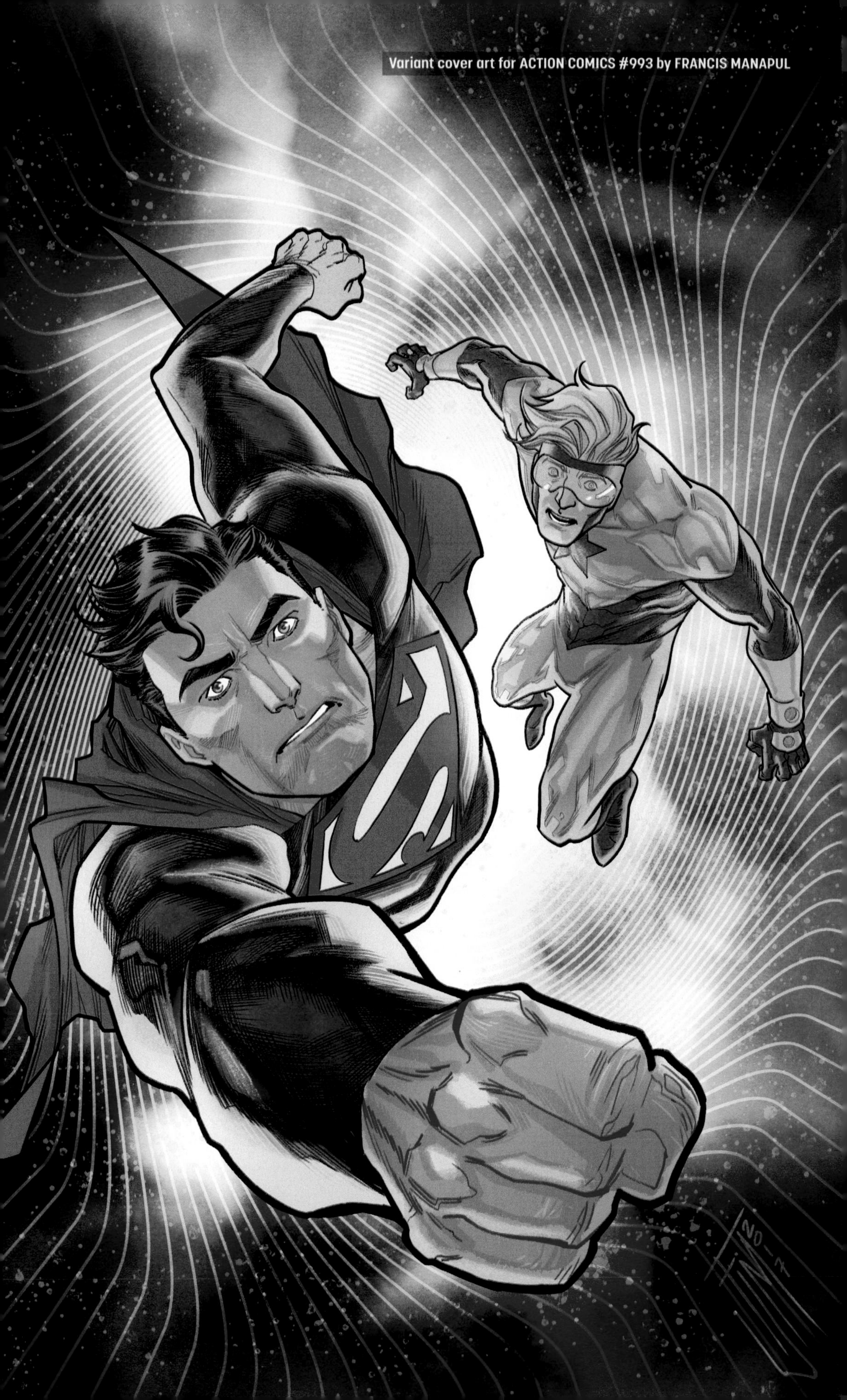

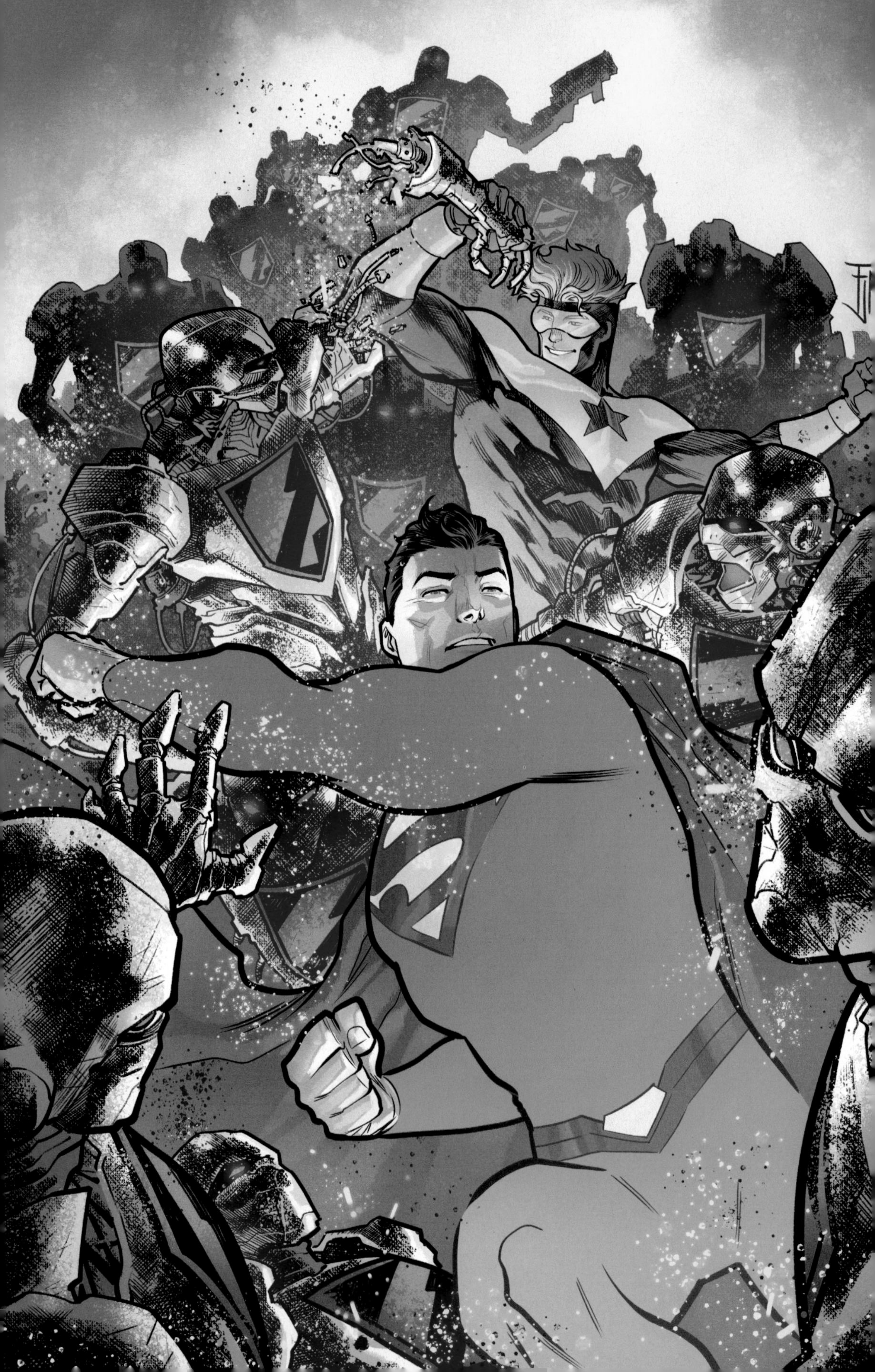

Variant cover art for ACTION COMICS #994 by FRANCIS MANAPUL

Variant cover art for ACTION COMICS #995 by DUSTIN NGUYEN

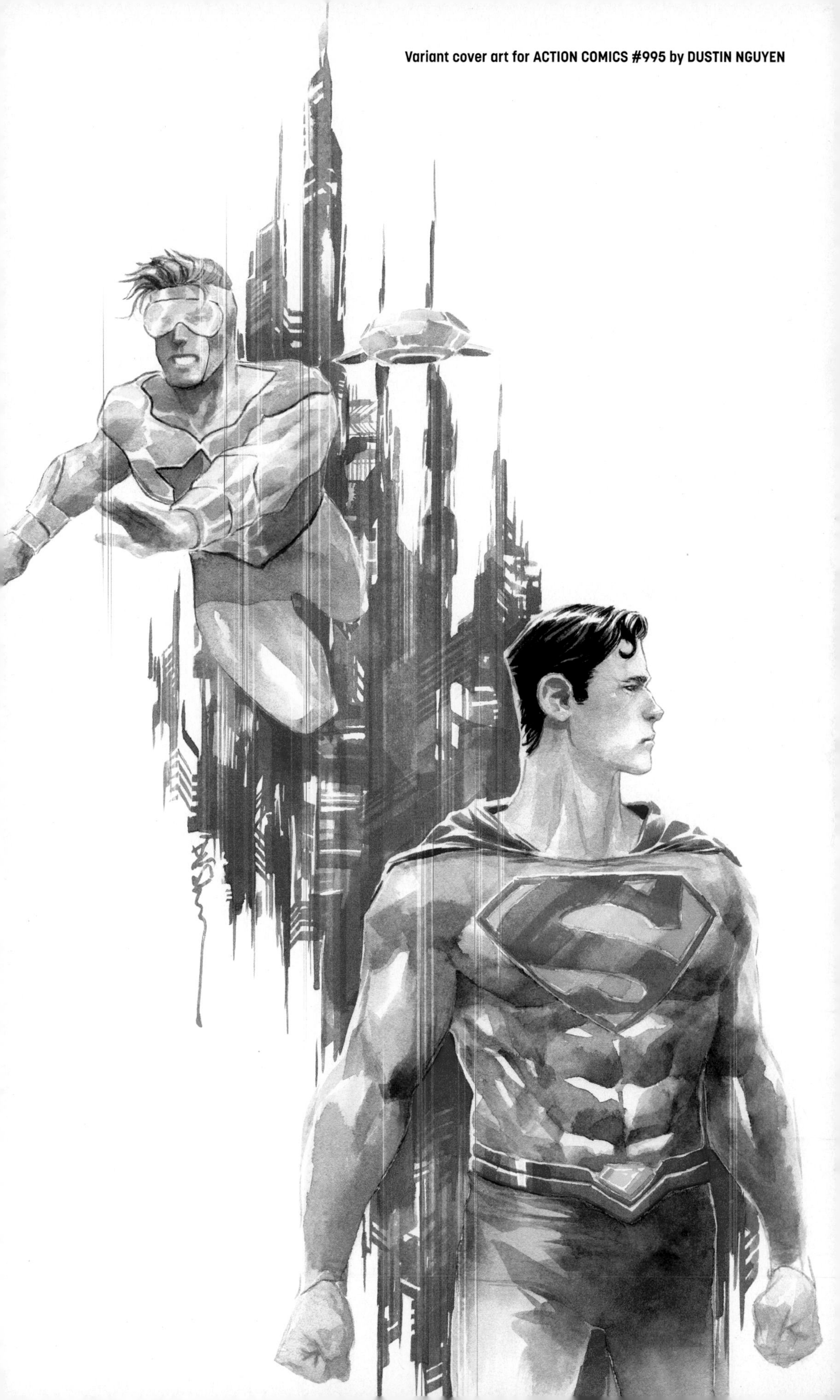

Variant cover art for ACTION COMICS #996 by DUSTIN NGUYEN

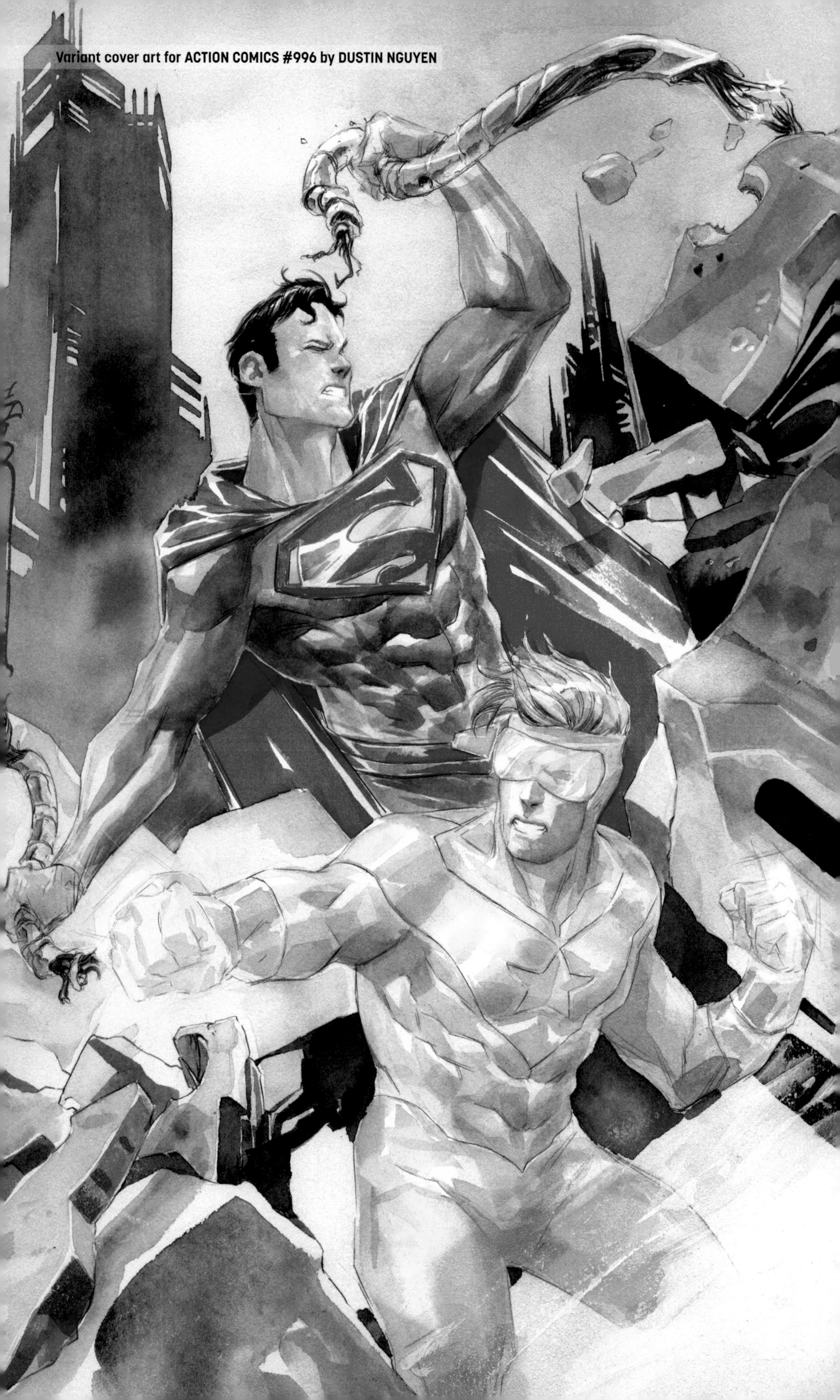

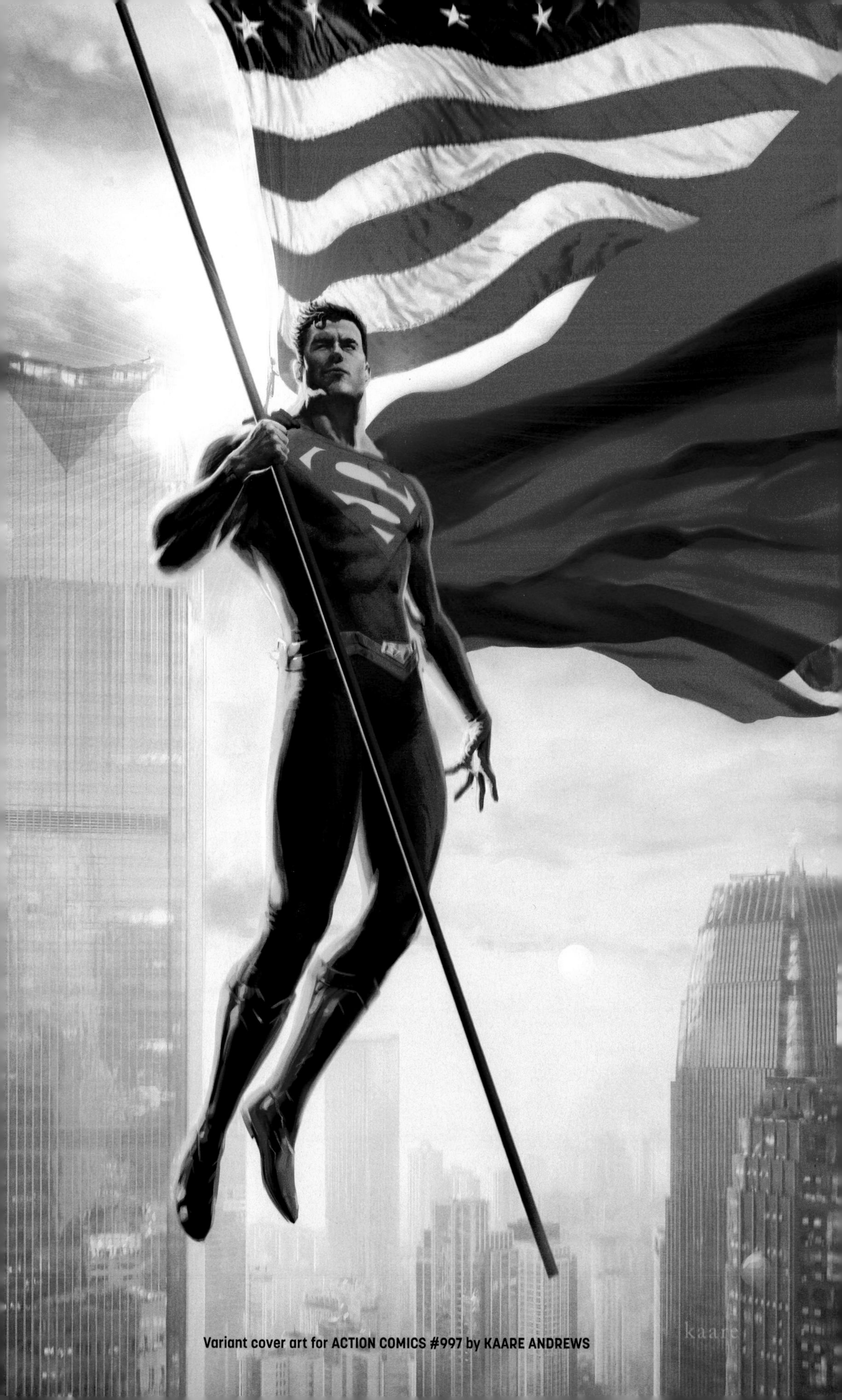
kaare

Variant cover art for ACTION COMICS #997 by KAARE ANDREWS

Variant cover art for ACTION COMICS #998 by KAARE ANDREWS

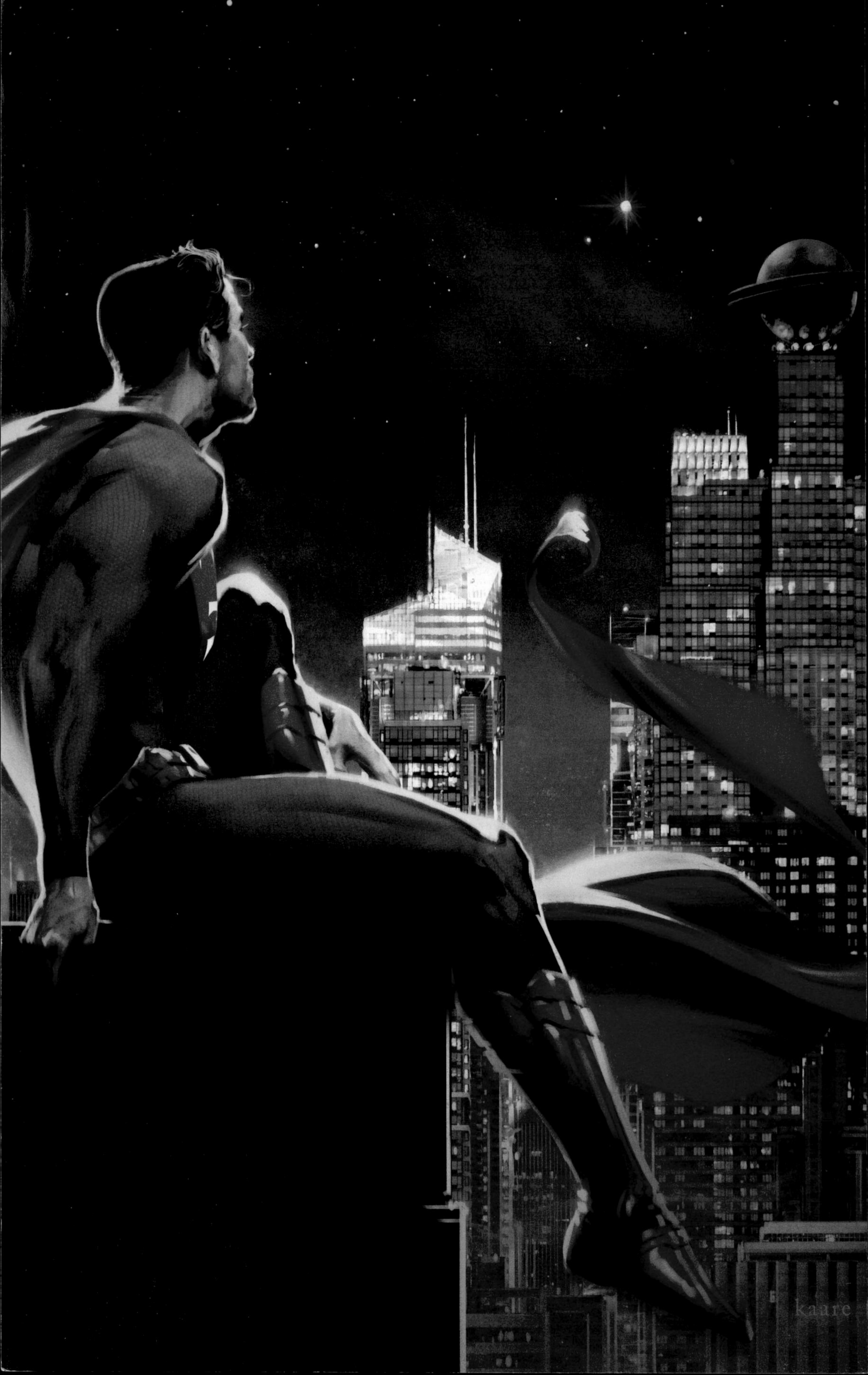

Variant cover art for ACTION COMICS #999 by KAARE ANDREWS

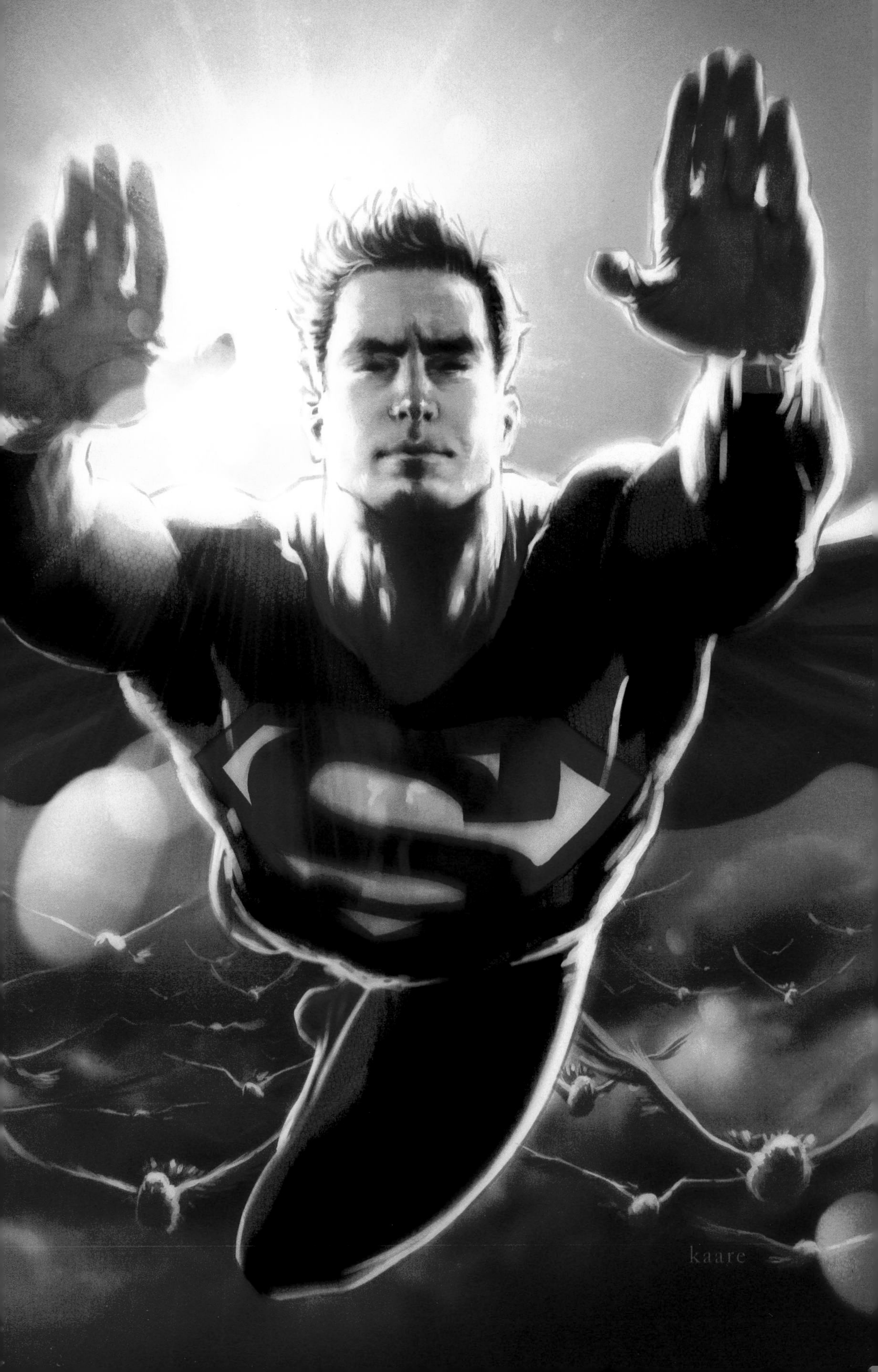
kaare

ACTION COMICS #993 cover sketches and pencils by DAN JURGENS

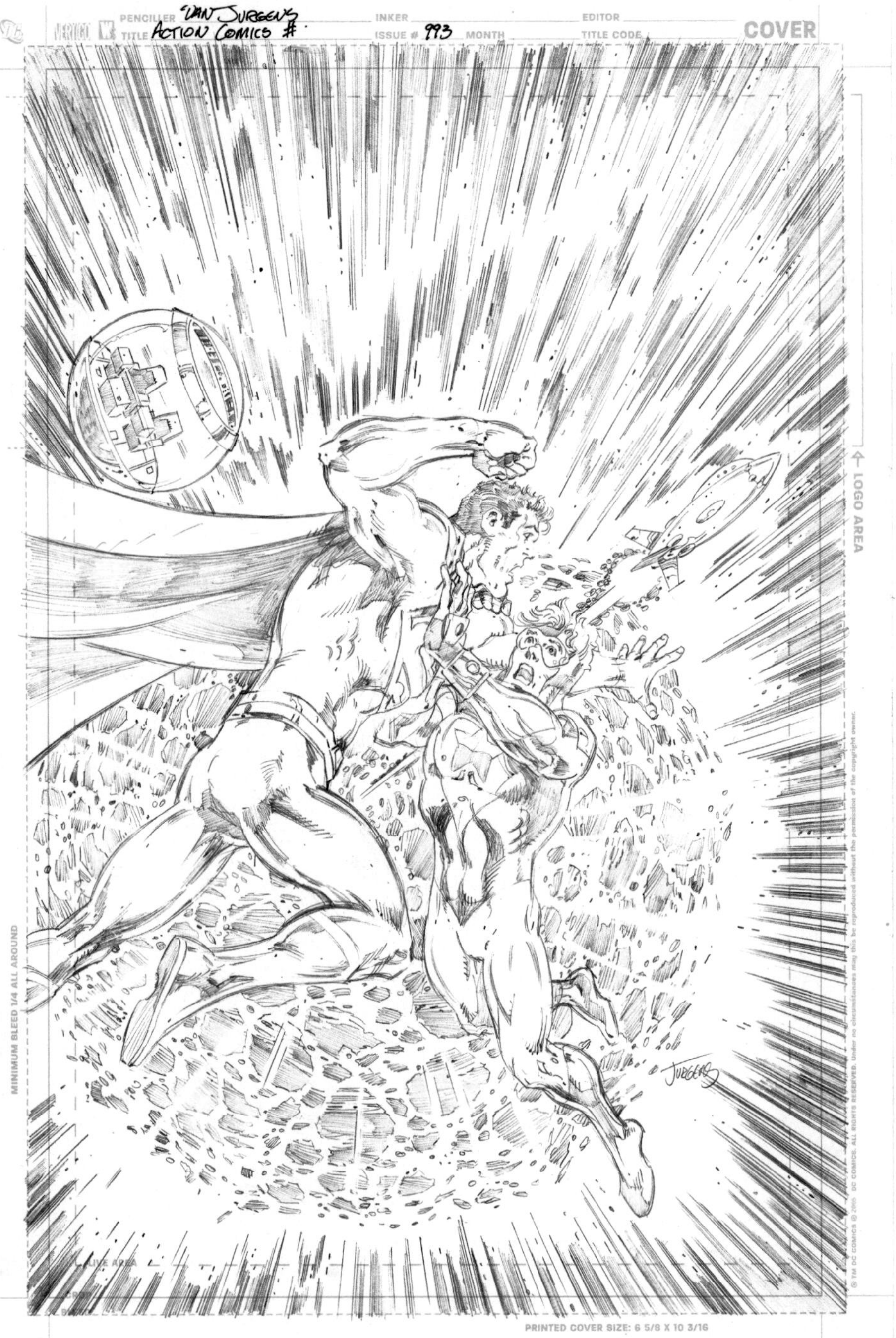
PENCILLER Dan Jurgens
TITLE Action Comics #
INKER
ISSUE # 993
MONTH
EDITOR
TITLE CODE
COVER
LOGO AREA
MINIMUM BLEED 1/4 ALL AROUND
JURGENS
PRINTED COVER SIZE: 6 5/8 X 10 3/16

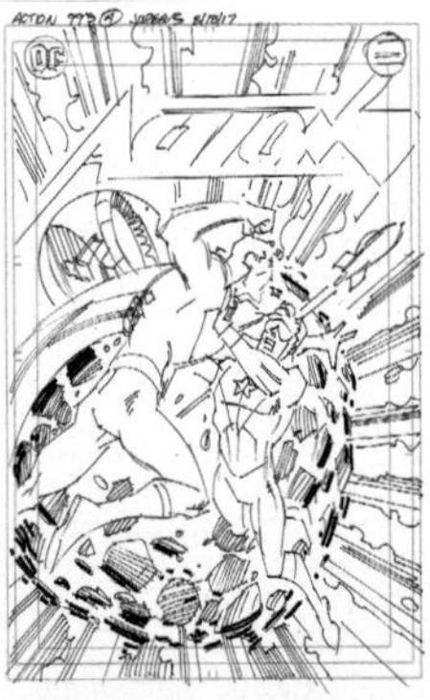

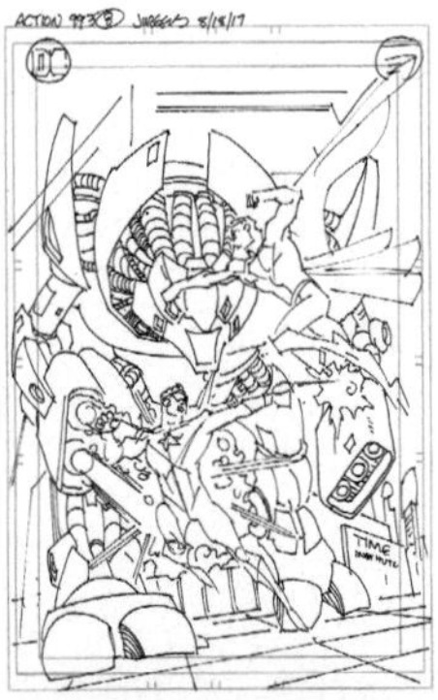

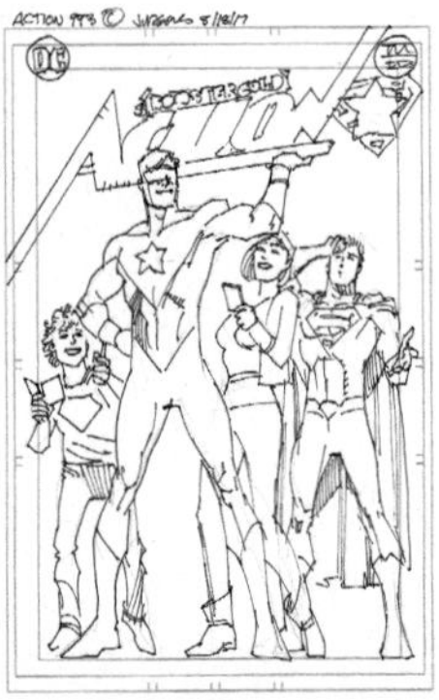

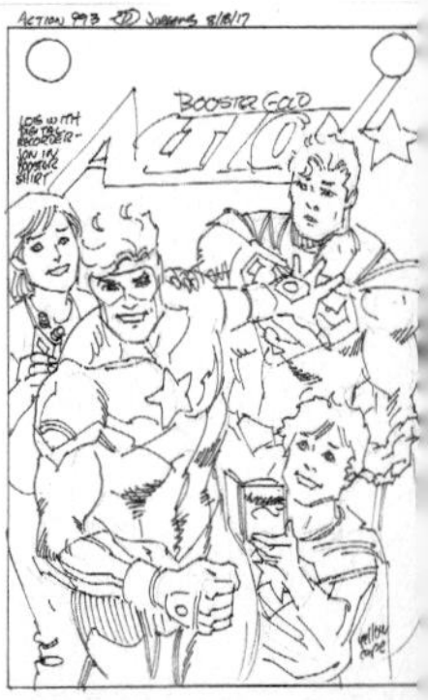

ACTION COMICS #994 cover sketches and pencils by DAN JURGENS

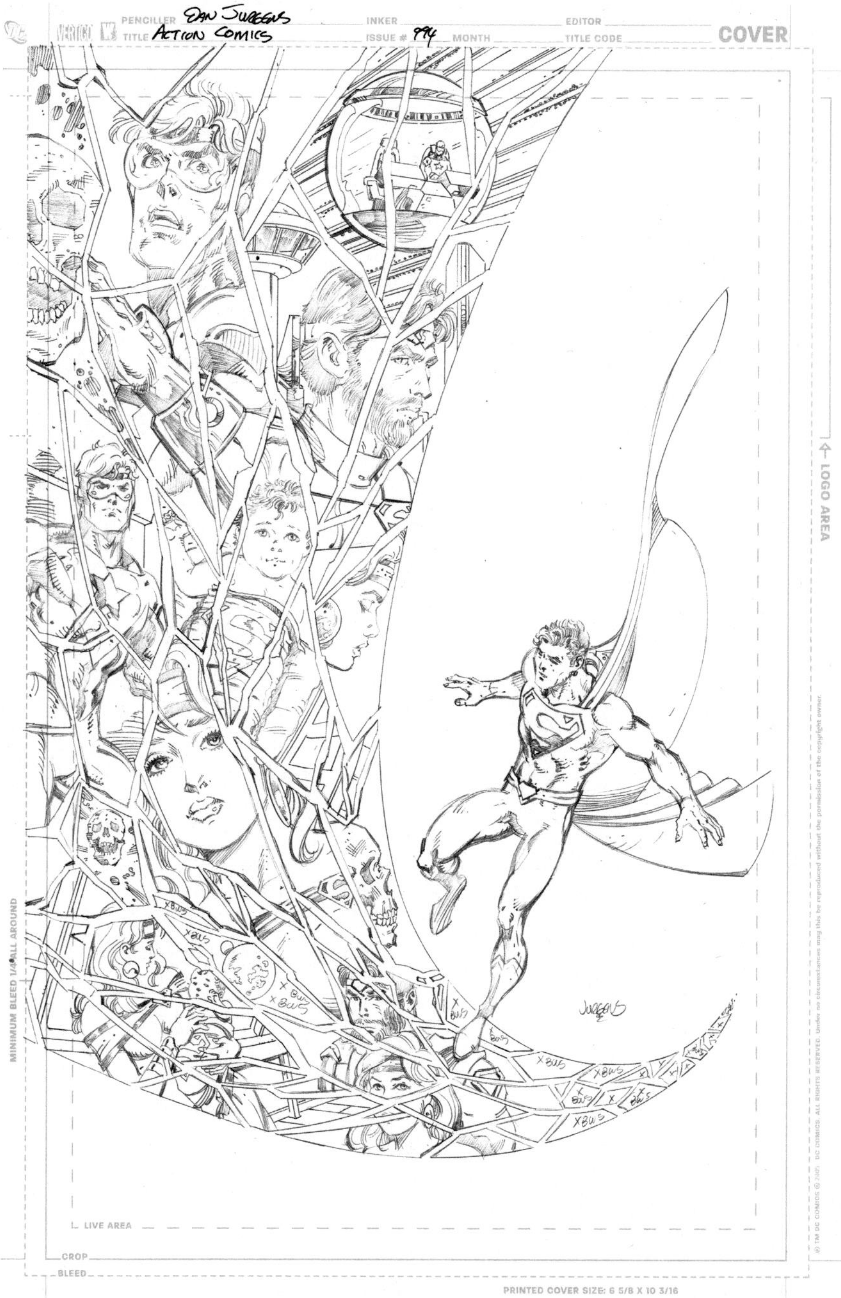
PENCILLER DAN JURGENS
TITLE ACTION COMICS
INKER
ISSUE # 994
MONTH
EDITOR
TITLE CODE
COVER
LOGO AREA
MINIMUM BLEED 1/4 ALL AROUND
JURGENS
LIVE AREA
CROP
BLEED
PRINTED COVER SIZE: 6 5/8 X 10 3/16

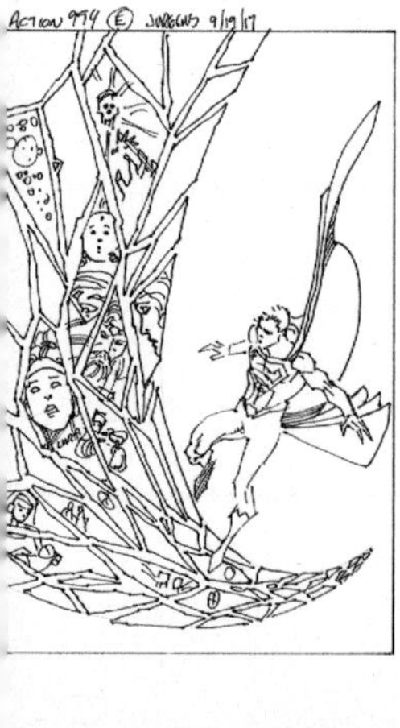
ACTION 994 (E) JURGENS 9/19/17

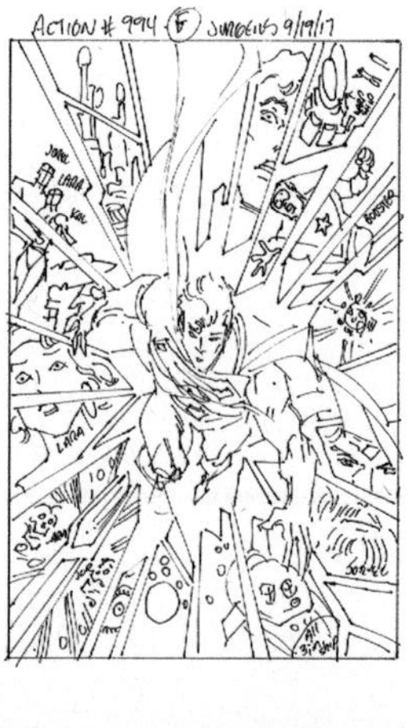
ACTION # 994 (F) JURGENS 9/19/17

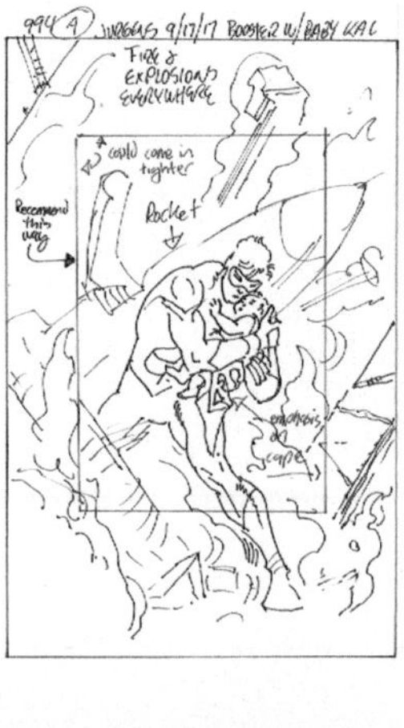
994 (A) JURGENS 9/17/17 BOOSTER W/ BABY KAL
Fire & EXPLOSIONS EVERYWHERE
could come in tighter
Recommend this way
Rocket

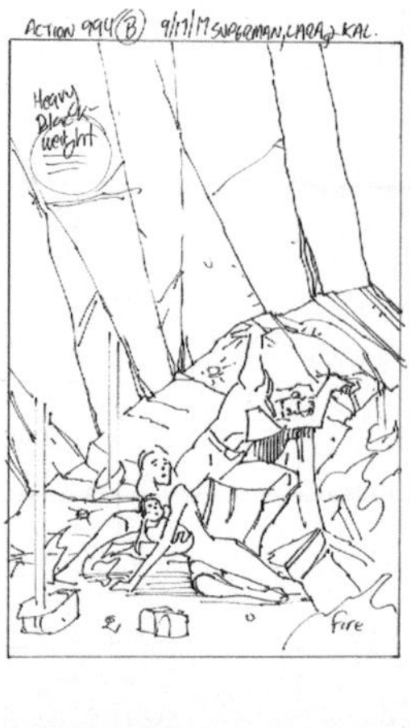
ACTION 994 (B) 9/17/17 SUPERMAN, LARA & KAL.
Heavy Black weight
Fire

ACTION COMICS #995 cover sketches and pencils by DAN JURGENS

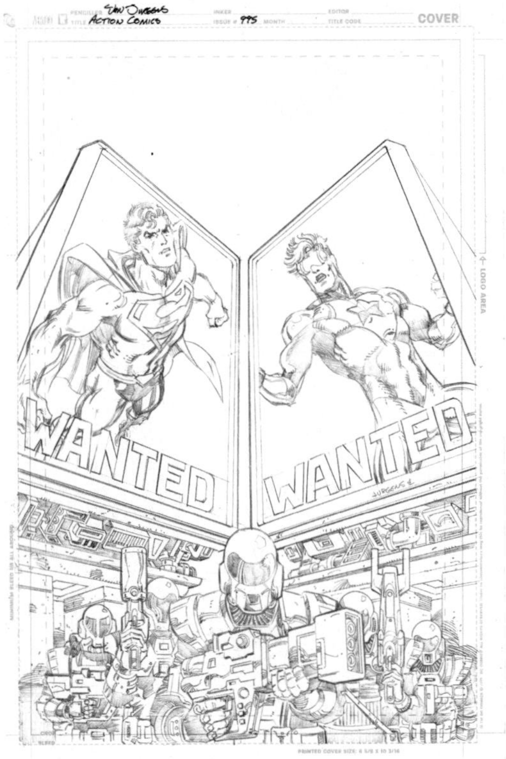
DAN JURGENS
ACTION COMICS
995
COVER
LOGO AREA
WANTED
WANTED
JURGENS

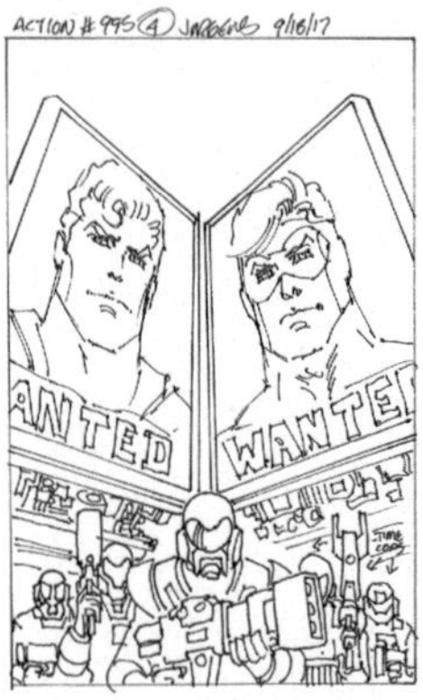
ACTION #995 (A) JURGENS 9/16/17
WANTED
WANTED

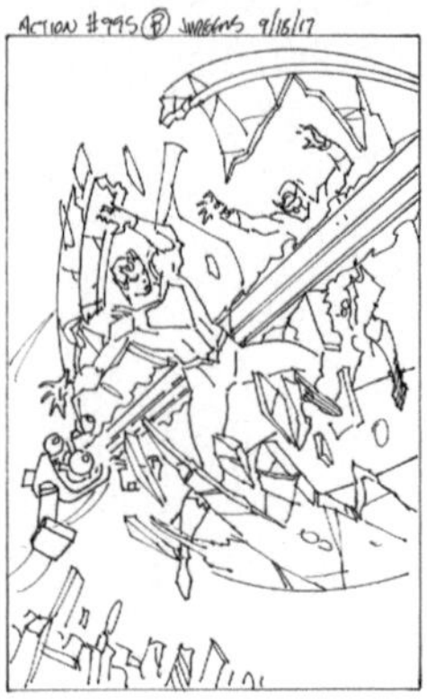
ACTION #995 (B) JURGENS 9/16/17

ACTION COMICS #996 cover sketches by DAN JURGENS

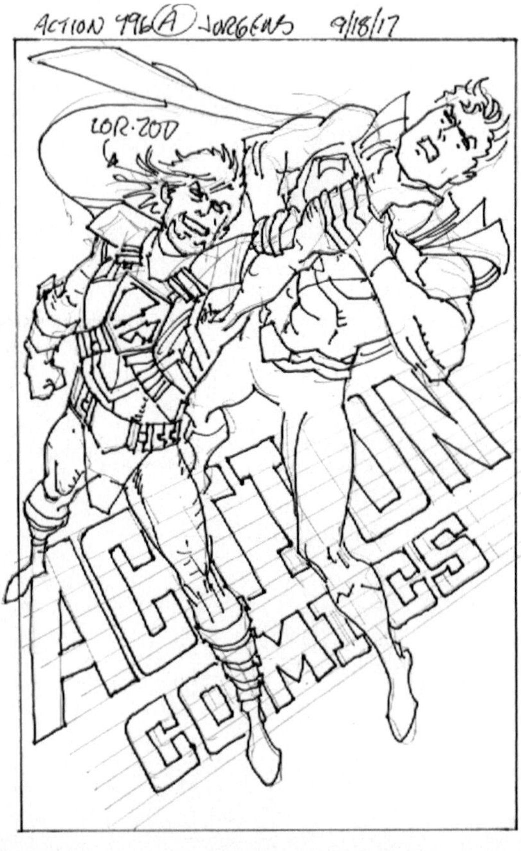
ACTION 996 (A) JURGENS 9/18/17
LOR-ZOD
ACTION
COMICS

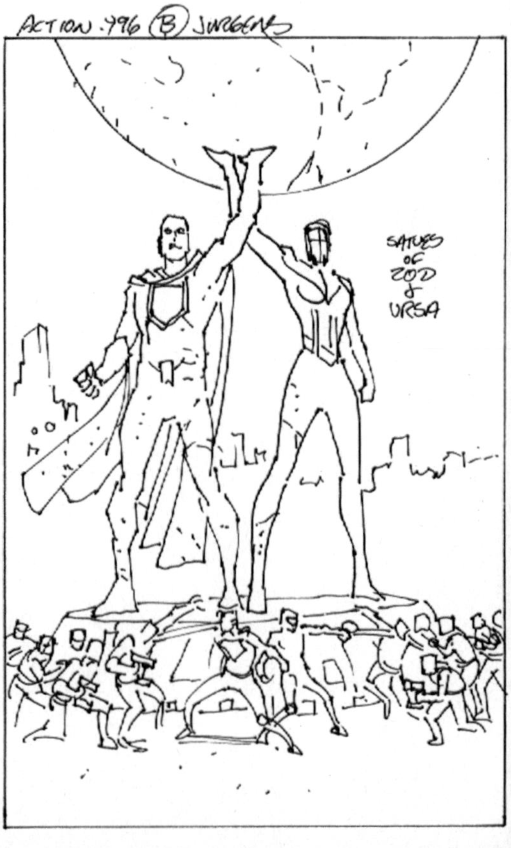
ACTION 996 (B) JURGENS
SATUES
OF
ZOD
&
URSA